Ned's Girl

BRYAN FORBES

Ned's Girl

The authorised biography of
Dame Edith Evans

Illustrated

ELM TREE BOOKS

HAMISH HAMILTON · LONDON

First published in Great Britain 1977
by Elm Tree Books / Hamish Hamilton Ltd
90 Great Russell Street London WC1B 3PT

Copyright © 1977 by Bryan Forbes Ltd
Shaw texts © 1977 The Trustees of the British Museum,
The Governors and Guardians of the National Gallery of Ireland
and Royal Academy of Dramatic Art

SBN 241 89600 2

Printed litho in Great Britain
by W & J Mackay Ltd, Chatham

To
R.V.M.
in gratitude
for so many things

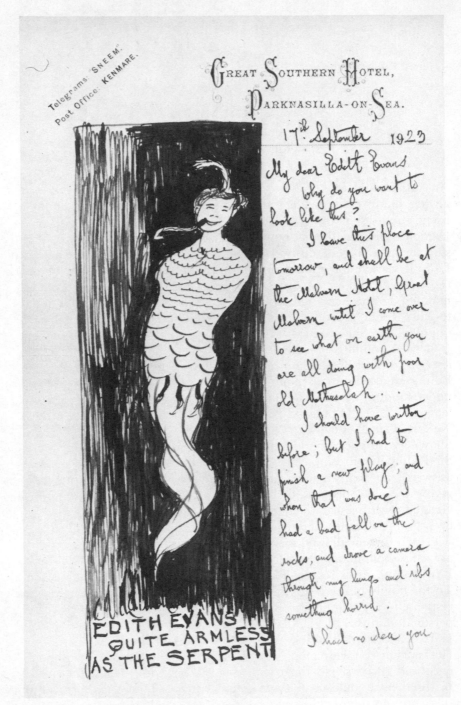

GREAT SOUTHERN HOTEL,
PARKNASILLA-ON-SEA.

17th September 1923

My dear Edith Evans
        Why do you want to
look like this?
        I leave this place
tomorrow, and shall be at
the Malvern Hotel, Great
Malvern until I come over
to see what on earth you
are all doing with poor
old Methuselah . .
        I should have written
before; but I had to
finish a new play; and
when that was done I
had a bad fall on the
rocks, and drove a camera
through my lungs and ribs
something horrid.
        I had no idea you

EDITH EVANS
QUITE ARMLESS
AS THE SERPENT

Letter from Bernard Shaw to Edith Evans
17th September 1923 (see page 70)

Acknowledgements

An author, and especially a biographer, never works alone: there are always many debts beyond the evidence, some to memory, some to friends and others to complete strangers. Obviously my first debt is to Dame Edith herself and I hope that I have repaid the trust and friendship she gave so generously. I also must pay tribute to Sir Michael and Lady Redgrave for granting me permission to quote from private correspondence and for giving of their time and help in the most unselfish manner. To the Academic Committee of the Bernard Shaw Estate, and to Miss Roma Woodnutt of the Society of Authors, in allowing me to quote all the Shaw letters intact, I am especially grateful. Likewise to J. C. Medley and K. G. Medley for permission to use the George Moore letters. To Enid Bagnold for not only allowing me to quote her letters to Edith, but also for many hours of pleasurable co-operation so vital to my understanding of Edith's character. To many of Edith's closest colleagues,—Gwen Frangcon-Davies, Dame Peggy Ashcroft, Cathleen Nesbitt, Cole Lesley, Patrick Garland, Michael Elliot, Maisie Knox-Shaw, Christopher Fry, J. B. Priestley, Julie Harris, Michael Parkinson, Sir Ralph Richardson, Margery Sharp, Robert Eddison, who patiently answered my many queries and took the time to write to me at length giving their recollections of Edith, I am more than grateful. Sir John Gielgud with his usual generosity allowed me to quote his letters and even granted permission for a somewhat unflattering reference to himself. John Casson allowed me to quote from his biography of his parents, as well as from many letters from his mother, Dame Sybil Thorndike, to Edith; and in this respect I am also grateful to his publisher, Collins. To the family of the late H. R. Barbor, I pay tribute to their generous response to my request for permission to use correspondence of a highly personal nature. Nigel Nicolson also allowed me to quote from Sir Harold Nicolson's Diaries, and the Executors of the late Eleanor and Herbert Farjeon were most helpful in granting me access to correspondence and reviews. No theatrical biographer of the twentieth century British theatre could survive without reference to James Agate, and I am therefore enormously grateful to George Mathew, his Executor, for many favours. Other critics, notably J. C. Trewin, Richard Findlater and Kenneth Tynan extended every courtesy, as indeed did the Executors of the late St. John Ervine and Charles Morgan. To my dear friend Alan 'Jock' Dent I am, as always, conscious that his vast knowledge of the theatre is as keen as ever. My thanks, also, to Miss Lilian Ross and *The New Yorker Magazine* for allowing me to quote from a profile of Sir Michael Redgrave, and to Messrs Heinemann for quotations from J. B. Priestley. Many strangers, lifelong fans of Edith, took the trouble to write to me when this biography was announced and although space does not allow me to list them all by name, I give thanks for their kindness. I am equally most appreciative of the help given to me by Mrs. Avis Merton, Mr. and Mrs. William Houghton, Peter Dixon, and especially John Booth. To Mrs. Margaret Reeves who patiently scanned my manuscript with her usual dedication, and to my dear wife, Nanette, who suffered the disorder of my writing habits with her customary loving fortitude. And finally to my two editors, Roger Donald of Little, Brown and Company, and Roger Machell of Hamish Hamilton, the latter being my prime mentor in this undertaking and to whom, with much affection, this book is dedicated.

Any sins of omission are mine alone, and I hope no lasting offence has or will be given, for even if my memory has served me ill, it was not prompted by malice aforethought.

Bryan Forbes
June 1977

Illustrations

In *The Old Ladies*, with Jean Cadell and Mary Jerrold, New Theatre, 1935 (*Mander & Mitchenson Collection*)

As Madame Arcadina, with John Gielgud, in *The Seagull*, New Theatre, 1936 (*Photo Houston Rogers*)

The Country Wife, Old Vic, 1936
   (a) among the cast
   (b) with Michael Redgrave (*Photos by courtesy Theatre Museum, London*)

The famous Rosalind—in *As You Like It*, with Michael Redgrave, Old Vic, 1936 and New Theatre, 1937 (*Theatre Museum, London*)

In *The Taming of the Shrew*, with Leslie Banks, New Theatre, 1937 (*Photo Houston Rogers*)

With Owen Nares in *Robert's Wife*, Globe Theatre, 1937 (*Photo Houston Rogers*)

The Importance of Being Earnest: Edith's first appearance as Lady Bracknell, with Gwen Ffrangcon-Davies and John Gielgud, Globe Theatre, 1939 (*Angus McBean Photograph Harvard Theatre Collection*)

Antony and Cleopatra, with Godfrey Tearle, Piccadilly Theatre, 1946 (*Photo Houston Rogers*)

In Bridie's *Daphne Laureola*, Wyndham's Theatre, 1949 (*Angus McBean Photograph Harvard Theatre Collection*)

With Sybil Thorndike in *Waters of the Moon*, Haymarket, 1951 (*Angus McBean Photograph Harvard Theatre Collection*)

Rehearsing *The Dark is Light Enough*, Aldwych Theatre, 1954 (*Photo Norman Parkinson*)

between pages 238 and 239

Mrs. St. Maugham in Enid Bagnold's *The Chalk Garden*, Haymarket, 1956 (*Photograph/Snowdon*)

In *All's Well That Ends Well*, Stratford-upon-Avon, 1959 (*Photo Daily Express*)

In Noël Coward's *Hay Fever*, National Theatre at the Old Vic, 1964 (*Angus McBean Photograph Harvard Theatre Collection*)

With Audrey Hepburn and Fred Zinnerman, *The Nun's Story*

With her friend Judith Wilson (*Photo P.I.C. Ltd.*)

On location in Nice for *The Madwoman of Chaillot*, with Giulietta Masani, Katharine Hepburn and Margaret Leighton, 1968 (*Photo Bryan Forbes*)

Mrs. Ross in *The Whisperers*, 1966 (*Photo Brian Duff, Daily Express*)

At Gatehouse during the making of the television documentary of her life (*Photo Bryan Forbes*)

Leading Edith on to the set for *The Slipper and the Rose*, Pinewood, 1975 (*Photo George Courteney Ward*)

The last photograph, Gatehouse, 5th October, 1976 (*Photo Bryan Forbes*)

Foreword

'An actress is not a lady,' wrote George Bernard Shaw at a time when, in the opinion of some contemporaries, he was scarcely acting as a gentleman. Having relieved himself of this generalisation he then went on to qualify it: 'at least when she is she is not an actress.'

Perhaps Shaw was never wholly at ease with women even when he invented them and despite his heroic efforts to be the supreme exponent of contradiction he sometimes fell into the trap of contradicting in life that which he strove to propagate in print. A paper seducer, a closet Frank Harris, 'inadequately equipped for love' by his own admission, he remained fascinated, not to say enslaved, by the romantic and all-too-frequently inaccurate popular conception of actresses, but was pedantically loath to sample that romanticism in the flesh. He cut his way into nineteenth century theatre at the point of a pen and attacked the bedroom door with the same easily blunted weapon.

His confident assertion that 'an actress is not a lady' was made in the Preface to the collected correspondence between Ellen Terry and himself (and according to Edward Gordon Craig he was already at work on the Preface two years before publication whilst at the same time declaring in the Press that the letters should never be published). It is possible that the master of paradox was determined to have his actress and the lady as well. Certainly he was at some pains over a period of three decades to treat Ellen Terry, whom he extolled as an actress, as a lady who could not be sullied. Yet he proved incapable of acting out a real-life Pygmalion. He placed several women on pedestals, but the final chisel blow was beyond him. This was a perhaps a major flaw, even *the* major flaw, in his extraordinarily complex character. His innate cleverness, his courage when defending unpopular causes, his undoubted charm and private kindnesses—all these attributes should, by rights, have pushed him into one great, consummated love affair which, in turn, might have led to the creation of a complete flesh and blood heroine to stand alongside the other female immortals of literature (and I am not forgetting St. Joan who remains resolutely hermaphrodite in every performance I have ever witnessed).

Contrary to popular contemporary belief, he was a religious man, curiously old-fashioned in some of his attitudes and there were sacred and profane remains of a prude lurking within his tweed suits.

His celebrated wooing of Ellen Terry from the safety of his desk reveals more than perhaps he realised. He found satisfaction in being a 'Sunday husband' as he put it, and he lied in saying that his marriage ended the old gallantries and flirtations. For a man who placed so much importance on sexual experience 'because of its power of producing a celestial flood of emotion and exaltation' he remained for the most part a professional virgin. True lovers seldom write for posterity, the average love letter is banal, and the man who commits adultery on paper only can be likened to a charlatan who solicits alms from the comfort of a Rolls Royce.

Shaw intrudes into this Foreword and into sections of the story that follows because no history of the theatre of this period can ignore his spiky presence and because he played a not inconspicuous role in the professional development of Edith Evans. Just as some of his Prefaces were longer and more fascinating than the plays they introduced, he could not resist explaining his every motive in advance. I have been fortunate enough to unearth a considerable number of hitherto unpublished letters and postcards which he wrote to Edith and whilst I must immediately admit that these bear no resemblance to the letters he exchanged with Ellen Terry, they not only provide further clues for the puzzle of his secret life but also give us additional insight into the relationships Shaw the dramatist sought to impose upon his leading ladies. They must make their appearances in the proper context of this story and will, I hope, speak for themselves.

Ellen Terry dovetails into the same story, for she played a vital role in Edith's early career and was undoubtedly a commanding influence on Edith. Her professional example determined many of the standards by which Edith lived her long life in the service of the theatre. She inscribed a copy of her autobiography to Edith with the perceptive words 'To a girl after my own heart' and sixty years after the inscription Edith still prized the comparison, referring to it only a week before her death.

So here we have three extraordinary lives, three separate theatrical legends. And those three lives touched—three ships ablaze with their own unique illuminations passing in the night, their wakes mingling briefly to ruffle the surface of the closed society they steamed through with such splendour. Ellen Terry and Shaw have been charted, Shaw exhaustively so, but until now there have been comparatively few map references for Edith. She sailed, for the most part, alone.

Having resisted all requests to write her autobiography and having previously refused to grant permission for an authorised biography, Edith in making me her literary executor and entrusting me with the telling of her story was at some pains to urge me to depart from the accepted form of theatrical history. It has been my aim to present her life as she demanded of me in all its reality and romance, 'not by soft touches of a picture, but in hard mosaic or tessellated pavement.'

I have been fortunate in the abundance of the materials Edith bequeathed to me. Actors are transients, frequently living their lives from suitcases and the sadness is that all too frequently the substance of their lives is scattered and lost. The shadows remain, gathering dust in yellowing newspaper files, to be taken out and examined, deciphered and translated like some Dead Sea Scrolls: well-intentioned interpretations, no doubt, but of necessity always the work of strangers to the original language. It is difficult, if not impossible, fully to understand the workings of an actor's mind unless you have some first-hand knowledge of the theatre. A spectator, however gifted, eats of the white bread of experience: the germ has been removed before it reaches him.

My association with Edith dated back thirty years, but it was a spasmodic relationship for eighteen of those years. I can only claim an intimate friendship during the last twelve years of her life and during that time I had the great good fortune to direct her four times. On one of those four occasions I instigated an hour-long television documentary. The idea for this film came to me shortly after she had suffered her first major illness—a near-fatal heart attack which she was reluctant to acknowledge—and my instincts and my understanding of her character convinced me that it was vital for her to believe that she could work again, that people wanted her to work again. The film was shot over a period of months, a few days every three weeks and it was fascinating, humbling to watch her utter determination to survive. At the beginning she had to be supported when she took a few faltering steps; by the end of the shooting period she was playing table tennis with my children. In the film I touched upon certain aspects of her life and beliefs, and revealed a side of her personality that few suspected and fewer still had ever seen. The revelations were not confined to the television audience; Edith herself became more and more fascinated by the unfolding of her own story; it was as if she had been suddenly confronted by a partial stranger—somebody who had worked so hard all her life that she had left little time for living. She talked about herself in the third person: looking at my images on the screen she would say, 'Isn't she funny? I never knew she did that.' There was nothing calculated in these remarks, she genuinely believed she was being confronted by a person she had never got to know. She was amazed by some of my research: 'I'd forgotten she did that,' she would say, 'what a lark.' And it was from this that she reversed all previous convictions and invited me to undertake the writing of her biography. It was a voyage of discovery that we undertook together, a journey we made together in the closest and happiest association until six days before her death.

She had always guarded her private life and was by nature a private person, taking care to preserve intact the public illusions. By that I do not wish to give the impression that she courted a Garbo-like existence, which to me has always smacked of a publicity man's gimmick. It is just that she always separated the two halves of her life into watertight compartments. In the theatre she never cheated her audiences and in her private life she never cheated herself. Despite the fact that in the twilight of her years she symbolised the very quintessence of theatricality to the general public, she was one of the least theatrical members of our profession I have ever met. Returning to Shaw's arrogant dictum about the impossibility of an actress ever being a lady, I can only state that Edith was living proof that he was talking through his hand-woven hat.

Curiously enough the word lady is not found outside the English language. One of the earliest definitions given is that of 'a woman who rules over subjects, or to whom obedience or feudal homage is due.' Shaw, for all his knowledge of the theatre, somehow failed to comprehend that a great leading actress commands such feudal homage within her own chosen territory and certainly makes devoted subjects of her audiences. In tracing Edith's life I have come to the conclusion that her particular and peculiar genius would not have flowered as it did without her being imbued by upbringing and inclination with those qualities commonly used to describe a lady.

She came from a background devoid of theatricality, from a simple family that set great store by moral values and 'ladylike' behaviour. She could not claim that 'acting was in my blood.' Nothing could have been further from the truth and her eventual transformation from milliner to actress was one of life's inventions that novelists scorn to employ. The wonder of it is that her parents apparently took such a traumatic change of direction in their stride. It was not so with certain other members of her family who seem to have adopted a more jaundiced view, anticipating Shaw's prejudices. Indeed Edith told me that one of her mother's sisters put the case more explicitly than Shaw. 'When she heard that I'd finally gone on the stage, she said, "Oh, poor Nell." I'd gone on the streets, you see. Shocking.' The scene has a distinct Dickensian flavour to it, even though enacted during the first World War.

In 1888, the year of Edith's birth and forty years after the birth of Ellen Terry, actors were still a 'despicable race apart' to many commentators—a self-segregated community who often preferred to live in artistic ghettos than to mingle freely with the outside world. Irving, whom Shaw condescended to, saw to it that a measure of respectability was laid like a wreath on his tomb in Westminster Abbey. He died as a prince of the theatre, more royal in some eyes, than the royals themselves, but even he had misgivings about the price to be paid for respectability (Gladstone offered him the knighthood as early as 1883, but Irving declined it until 1895). The burial in the Abbey proclaimed an uneasy truce, yet the ghettos remained inhabited until the advent of television when respectability finally became more important than talent.

Few books can ever give back an actor or actress who has gone from us; fame cannot be handed on to succeeding generations like the baton in a relay race, but at least our children will have the benefit of certain visual and audio records of the giants we worshipped.

It is rare for the actor of genius to get the critic he deserves at the time he deserves it, for a ream of praise will not of itself recapture the essence of any performer. We can get a heady whiff of Kean from Hazlitt who put him 'far beyond the touch of time' and said that Kean's voice was like 'the sound of years of departed happiness.' I think that is an admirable description of something, but I confess it does not give me Kean. Even at the exhalted level of Hazlitt, Coleridge or the poet Tom Moore we are denied a glimpse of those prime attributes which divide the truly great actor from his inferiors—namely his very presence before us, the fire in his eyes, the actual sound of his voice, the wrinkle in his tights. Unless we were actually present at the performance being described, praised or annihilated by the critic we have little or no conception of what took place and imagination is a poor substitute. Perhaps it is always easier to describe failure than to picture triumph. Certainly the average theatre or film critic is more adept at destroying a performance than he is at explaining the reasons for its imperfections. Mass circulation newspapers are not averse to success, but cynically they are conditioned to the belief that a fall from grace sells more copies.

In my own lifetime, though mindful of the fact that the critic is the natural enemy of the artist, I have been impressed by Agate and Tynan. The unholy Laurel and Hardy of criticism, both shared a passion for their craft and were equally possessed of the all-too-rare facility of being able to communicate that passion to their readers. A little knowledge in the theatre is often more lethal than a little knowledge in the operating room for when the killing knife slips into the back of an actor or dramatist there is no anaesthetist at hand to ease the descent into oblivion. Agate, who courted immortality, polished his own ego to the brightness of a guardsman's buttons, and sometimes allowed his own cleverness to obscure the cleverness of those he wrote about. Perhaps his bizarre personality was always at variance with his sentimentality and the result was sometimes a flawed man telling others how to be perfect without total conviction. What saved him was the force of his enthusiasms, for he praised, as he damned, at the top of his voice. Tynan has the ability to describe a performer or performance he admires or detests more vividly than any other contemporary critic I have read, though the discerning reader can sometimes detect the smouldering embers of envy. He remains, in his see-sawing relationship with the theatre, an outsider asking to be let in, and he consorts with his victims, always a fatal mistake.

We live now in the age of instant reputations and a leisurely quest to trace the origins of a unique personality goes against the tide. A generation has grown up which believes that the sum total of human experience can be potted into a single episode of *This Is Your Life*, and that a four-part serialisation in one of the Sunday newspapers will pass muster as authoritative biography. What follows here will necessarily disappoint those who have been schooled to expect more from the private lives of actresses than their public performances. Admittedly, some of the talents currently on display who cause themselves to be described as stars are more able to make themselves heard in the bedroom than at the back of the stalls, and in discussing Edith Evans we will leave them out of the reckoning.

It was Edith's wish (and, as many will testify, her wishes frequently reached us as commands) that I should apply to the writing of her biography those standards of honesty she had set such store by throughout her long life. She had no illusions about herself: 'I don't need a mirror,' she once said, 'to look at my own warts.' In her last years she rediscovered herself, for she had the enforced leisure—a unique experience for her—to look inwards and back. She did not always care for what she saw, but she never, to my knowledge, concealed the evidence. There was to be no last minute lifting of the carpet and sweeping the unwanted dust out of sight. That was not her way. She was fully aware of what I was writing, for I visited her most weeks and she liked me to read work in progress. 'That's right,' she would say, 'she *did* do that, that's what she felt, we're telling it truthfully.' It wasn't the self-conscious and often nauseating use of the royal 'we' so constantly employed by pop singers when announcing their next number, it was a lady of advanced years looking at the reflection of a young girl she had once known intimately and then grown apart from. I had become the go-between, turning the pages of a book she had once known by heart, refreshing the memory that fame had clouded. Some passages she returned to time and time again as though seeking assurance that nothing had been left out. I do not think I am being falsely sentimental when I say that I believe the writing of this book prolonged her life; the one sadness is that she did not live to see it completed. She died knowing the 'shape' of it, and 'shape' was a word she used frequently and with an emphasis that denoted respect.

Chesterton said that the test of a good biography is one in which the book vanishes and the subject of the biography remains, so I have tried my best to obliterate myself whenever possible. My sources are many, but where I have been unable to track down written or remembered corroboration of a particular incident, I have relied upon my own actor's instinct for what I felt to be the heart of the matter—an imperfect method no doubt and likely to offend some purists. However, having read deeply all my life, I am convinced that much of history is necessarily conjecture of the worst sort. I hope my occasional conjectures stem from knowledge rather than inspired ignorance and I accept full responsibility for them.

My primary source has been Dame Edith herself and taking full advantage of the cassette recorder wherever possible I have been able to use her own words verbatim. My knowledge of her was such that I cannot believe she ever misled me about herself.

Garrick once asked Kitty Clive her opinion of the acting of Mrs. Siddons. She replied, that 'it was all truth and daylight'.

'I don't think there's anything extraordinary about me except this passion for the truth.'
—Dame Edith Evans

I

The title was hers alone.

I had first thought of calling this book *Mad About The Truth*, taking a phrase she had once used when describing her philosophy of life. Nobody thought very highly of it and several of my friends felt it sounded like a song by Noël Coward. Edith did not dismiss it out of hand, but pondered between my weekly visits. Then one day she greeted me with, 'I know exactly what I want to call our book. I want to call it *Ned's Girl*. That's what I was at the beginning and probably still am. Ned's girl. Nothing really changes.'

Edward Evans, her father, was known as Ned. Edith told me that when she was first making a name for herself his cronies noting her billing on the posters, would nudge each other with second-hand pride and say, 'That's Ned's girl', and this pleased her and continued to satisfy sixty years later.

Her life began on February 8th, 1888, in Pimlico, an irregular triangle of no-man's land including the Ministry of Works neatness of Buckingham Palace and the Gothic sprawl of Parliament at Westminster. Victoria Station lies within its boundaries and to the casual visitor it gives the feeling of impermanence and anonymity, a place to travel through rather than settle in. The Pimlico of today, fallen foul like much of London to the regimentation of our concrete-obsessed planners, retreats even further from the individuality it might once have possessed. Its true boundaries are now obscured—so much of London overlaps, for history has made her streets incestuous—and the section of Pimlico where Edith Mary Evans was born fringes on elegant Belgravia.

The Abbot of Westminster once had a residence here on marshy, derelict fields, and later there were scattered cottages known as Neat Houses and a pleasure garden where Pepys sat in a box in a tree enjoying the favours of a harlot and incurring his wife's displeasure. Nell Gwynn's mother is reputed to have kept a bawdy house in the area and was 'drowned in a pond, having taken too much of her own refreshments'. Certainly there was once a tavern known, charmingly enough, as

Jenny's Whim, but by the beginning of the 19th century the romanticism suggested by this name had given way to a harsher reality and the place was renamed The Monster Public House, becoming, in due course, the starting point for the 'Monster' line of omnibuses. In all probability 'monster' was an intentional Cockney corruption of 'monastery' stemming from the site of the Monastery or Convent belonging to the said Abbot of Westminster who, in 1368, leased the whole of the Manor of Chelsea from one Robert de Heyle in return for the sum of £20 a year, a daily delivery of two white loaves and two flagons of convent ale and an annual gift of a robe of esquire's silk, a most reasonable and civilised contract between landlord and tenant.

The history of the area suggests constant change: now it was fashionable, now it wasn't, and the fluctuation continues today. In 1888 Ebury Square, Edith's birthplace, had been partially torn down. Those residents who had escaped the rebuilding were mostly those with aspirations to be considered middle class.

Edith's father was a minor civil servant employed in the General Post Office—'very conscientious, very good'—according to his daughter, and much respected. 'He wasn't an educated man. He went to what was called a Ragged School and was put out to work at an early age, but he was a gentleman. He knew how to behave to people. I don't really know what his birth, his background was, but he had innate good manners, an innate sense of what was fitting and right. Tall, slim, *delicious* manners and, oh, the charm, the gentleness of him. A quiet man, he could talk about politics, he could talk about anything, and his letters—beautifully written and constructed, right to the end of his life. I don't think he ever made a mistake in his letters. Where did he get it? He'd got something in him, you see, but where did he get it?'

Her mother was a Miss Caroline Ellen Foster before her marriage. They had one other child, a boy, called Edward after his father, but he died at the age of four when Edith was two.

'My mother had the good old-fashioned country upbringing—the real thing, you know, going to church and all that.'

Miss Foster came from a family of nine and was brought up on Bookham Common. 'She told me they used to all play games with a lot of running. They loved running. I was only me because my little brother died. But they were nine and they ran like mad.'

Edith's voice when she told me this evoked something which I can but inadequately convey on the printed page. When she said the word 'ran' she stretched it out, it seemed to hang suspended in the air . . . 'r-a-a-a-n' . . . with a dying fall to it, giving the listener a glimpse of halcyon days she had cherished and which no amount of later fame could ever compensate for. 'Oh, dear,' she continued, 'they were very healthy. I don't think one of them died until . . . until they were quite grown up.'

(I must be careful not to give the impression that Edith 'acted' ordinary conversation. That would be totally false. But at the same time, and for benefit of those readers who never heard her voice or lack the facility for remembering the cadences of speech, I must attempt to reproduce some echo of that extraordinary instrument, her voice, which was capable of infinite variety both on and off stage, and which often gave to the most mundane utterance a mystery and significance I have never encountered before.)

Talking of her parents, she said 'they had to have a funny daughter between them because they were both such individual people.' Her mother had been a nurse at St. George's Hospital and it was there that she met her future husband, he being a patient at the time. The impression given is that Edward Evans was more keen than she was. Her mother once confessed to Edith that she would have given herself 'more freely' to an intellectual man. On their marriage day she made a pact with herself: if she was in time to catch the train she would marry Edward Evans; if she missed it, she wouldn't, and that would be that. She caught the train. Not the best of auspices for a happy married life, but the relationship prospered and endured.

Edith's father, whom she revered to the end of her days, seems to have been the most easy going of men, a far cry indeed from the popular depiction of a Cockney, with little or no bombast about him. His wife, more of a stoic and possibly a frustrated woman in that her life was not as fulfilled as once she had imagined it might be, never fully recovered from the loss of their small son and even in old age could not speak of him without tears. Her origins were those of country folk, peasant and gypsy stock (her father was a cowman who could neither read nor write) but she had spirit and resolve and it was these qualities that she passed on to her daughter.

'Father wouldn't read a book, but Mother used to eat them, *eat* them,' Edith said. From her father she took the calmness that set her apart in a crowd. At rehearsal or on a stifling film set she conserved her energies for the job in hand—not aloof, for she was always approachable to discuss her craft, but impatient of small talk that could fragment her concentration. From her I got the impression that this, too, was the routine of her father; a diligent man, a careful man who gave of his best in those areas he had conquered to his own satisfaction, content to let others shine in more flamboyant fashion if that was their way. Edith never claimed to be an intellectual woman, only that she had an instinct for people and things.

When she was quite young the family moved a few hundred yards to No. 109 Ebury Street, a thoroughfare consistently described as 'uninteresting' in the surveys I have consulted. This surprises me. It

3

may have been true from an architectural viewpoint, but it certainly seems to have held attractions for a variety of fascinating characters. The infant Mozart lived there for a time, so did the young Noël Coward, who had No. 111 as his address, George Moore resided at No. 121 and later in this century Sir Oswald Mosley occupied a house in Ebury Street. Whole sections have been demolished since the end of the Second World War, but Edith's old address remains and when last I visited it there was a dentist's nameplate by the side of the door. George Moore wrote what I have always found to be an incredibly obscure book called *Conversations in Ebury Street* and it was from No. 121 that he first wrote to Edith. Until he sought her out she had been unaware of his proximity and fame.

After the move to Ebury Street she was enrolled at St. Michael's Church of England School, which was within walking distance of her new home. It maintained a reputation, if not for academic brilliance, then for solid Victorian qualities of decency and purpose.

It was in this building that Edith received her formal education. She was not compelled to wear a uniform, the only clothes regulation carried down from the original founders being the requirement that 'each child shall have a pocket handkerchief'.

She once ran away from school and was eventually recovered from Gerald Road Police Station by her distraught parents. Admitting that she often used to take the lead in games and transgressions, she once told me that her teacher had said, 'If you are naughty, all the class is, naughty.' She recalled her first 'boy friend', acquired at age six, one Georgie Cray, who became her accomplice in a short-lived life of crime. They apparently stole some marigolds from a neighbouring garden and were swiftly apprehended. Young Mr. Cray immediately turned Queen's evidence and blabbed. 'Edie made me' was his unsporting defence.

She did modestly well at her studies and in later years when her place in theatrical history was secure the Governors were anxious to claim her as a star old pupil, but it would appear that she left no lasting impression on the staff or her contemporaries.

The Principal of the school in Edith's time was a Canon Fleming and doubtless (from the very name of the school if nothing else) great emphasis must have been put on religious instruction. Yet her parents were not religious in any orthodox sense: 'they were not going-to-churchy-people'; and Edith had no memory of ever passing through that childhood phase, which approaches mild religious mania. 'Oh, no, I was too much *alive* for that,' she said with curious deliberation. 'I used to like boys to play with. My mother was always catching me on the sands at Bognor, playing cricket with the boys. She used to pull me away . . . but I liked it.'

4

Bognor seems to have been a persistent holiday Mecca, extremely popular from Victorian times until the Second World War. (It was to Bognor that George V went to convalesce after his first major illness and there is an apocryphal story told of his terminal illness when the Royal physicians whispered their pious hopes to the dying King that he would undoubtedly recover and live to enjoy the invigorating airs of Bognor once again. The King is said to have mustered his remaining strength and uttered the splendid reply 'Bugger Bognor' before lapsing into his last coma). As with Weymouth, another South coast resort, royal patronage would have bestowed a certain added attraction to Bognor for the Evans family; and it is a characteristic of the British that they not only take their pleasures seriously, but they also find comfort in familiarity. Edith told me that most of her childhood holidays were spent on the sands of Bognor and with the persistence of such youthful memories, almost Proustian in their tranquillity, she recalled nothing but sunshine. 'I remember so well, the lodgings we stayed in. They belonged to an old fisherman . . . Daddy Hyde, his name was.' She stopped and stared at him across the years and then turned to me: 'Fancy me remembering his name, just like that. Daddy Hyde. I can't remember lots of the people I acted with, but I remembered him.' Then it was back to childhood again, back to the 'wonderful times'. 'My great idea of luxury was Devonia toffee. Oh, I thought it was heaven, all gooey and sticky. You used to buy it in slabs and they broke it with a hammer. Another thing I remember were those three-cornered jam pots. I thought they were divine. I can't think why I thought that, there was nothing special about them, but there it is.'

Her father was entitled to three weeks holiday a year, then the high-water mark of a civil servant. She learnt to swim in the grey and uninviting waters of the English Channel and once swam a mile. Conscious, perhaps, that Edith was an only child, her parents once took another and less fortunate family with them on holiday, but the experiment was not a success and never repeated. Again the impression is of a solitary, isolated existence, a girl protected but not smothered by the affection of doting parents. She had no offensively ambitious 'stage mother' later to be immortalised in song by her Ebury Street neighbour as Mrs. Worthington. Edith was not pushed onto the stage, nor was she pushed into life. She was treated 'like porcelain, rather. I mean to say, if I wasn't in by a certain hour they were out looking for me, in the street, down the station. Father was out searching for me in a sweat of anxiety. It was terribly . . . like Royalty. D'you know what I mean? Sort of cherished, an only child, cherished. Consequently, the care that was put on to me because I was me. They were terrified I might go like my little brother. Children, lots of children, went quickly in those days. But I didn't. They *clutched* me so, but I was an old tough.'

5

Somewhat strangely she was once taken by her mother to a phrenologist in Ludgate Circus. The pronouncement was 'she has a great sense of mimicry. This could take her very high or very low.' Then the expert added an ominous aside: 'She might go so low she could never get back. This child hates monotony.'

Gradually, the picture builds up. An upbringing without affluence yet without poverty—that peculiar no-man's land of the lower middle class who have no pretensions. Edith, 'the old tough' surviving all the childhood illnesses without apparent harm: 'I had everything. You only had to mention the complaint and I'd get it. I suppose, being destined to become an actress, I had to have them and get them out of the way.' She was lucky, luckier than most from the same environment, for the diseases of childhood were many and the mortality rate for that period still agonisingly high. She came to believe that she survived because she was supported on 'floodtides of love'. This expression, which she often used in later life, owed little to conventional religious beliefs. She never thought much of 'your gentleman with the beard sitting up there in the clouds. I believe in God most terribly, but a spiritual God, the Spirit of Good and Love.'

Although she was to become a convert to Christian Science she was never an overtly pious person. She never forced her beliefs on others, nor did she suffer those who attempted to mould her beliefs in their own image. That enthusiastic crusader Lord Longford once tried to convince her of the superior merits of Roman Catholicism at a public luncheon they were both attending. Seeking to establish his case, he told Edith that all great actresses were or had been Roman Catholics. 'Well,' said Edith, 'there's one that isn't' and that was the end of that.

The headmistress and headmaster of the girls and boys at St. Michael's rejoiced in the names of Miss Chalk and Mr. Bottle and Edith confirmed that they were both outstanding personalities. Mr. Bottle was apparently a most convivial, Pickwickian character, seldom parted from a beloved top hat. Miss Chalk, somewhat strait-laced, insisted that, above all else, her pupils spoke well and without the hideous excesses of broad Cockney, giving Edith a grounding that her mother elaborated upon at home.

'My mother had a beautiful speaking voice. My Sunday school teacher once said this to me and I ran all the way home to listen. I'd never noticed before, you see. To me she was just mother, and I'd never really *heard* her. You don't, you see, you don't. It was a lovely, cooing voice and until then I'd taken it for granted. Perhaps that's where I got mine. There must have been some voice, somewhere in the family.

'Mother wouldn't stand for anything that was in the least bit not true, because she was frightened . . . She was frightened I might turn into a

6

sort of liar, you know. I was brought up in this passionate behaviour for the truth.'

It was a theme she constantly returned to, a thread running through her personal and professional life. I have the feeling that it was drummed into her, a single chord that she was made to play over and over again in her formative years. Children inherit fears: if a parent betrays unease when night falls, then the child will demand a light at bedtime. With Edith there is no doubt that Truth was her religion. Her mother was the dominant partner in the marriage and although Edith was careful to share her remembered love and affection when talking about her parents, she could not totally conceal an extra note of pride whenever she mentioned her father.

'If you met me now for the first time and we chatted away, you'd think I was the conventionally brought up girl by the ordinary things I say. I do say ordinary things most of the time. Well, behind me . . . I've got depths and depths and depths of good behaviour. I mean, when people talk about the old days, they perhaps will say, "She had very humble beginnings" . . . "Humble" was one word you'd never use in our home. My mother and father . . . well, there aren't people like them today. My father had a Cockney accent, but it wasn't anything like the accent you hear now. Gentle. And he never used the wrong words. Absolute principles, the highest principles I've ever struck, my old man had.'

So, no humbleness, no real deprivation—'I always had a bedroom to myself. So many privileges, I had'—and such loneliness as from time to time must have entered into her life was conquered by a Beatrix Potter-like escape into a world of her own making, and it was only with hindsight that the theatricality of her solitary excursions struck her as part of the eventual pattern of her life.

'When I was a little girl I used to pretend to be people. I used to say, to myself of course, "Now I'm being Dolly Turtle" or whatever her name was, walking down the stairs. Nobody was there, but suddenly I'd be Dolly, Dolly-whatever-her-name-was, walking down the stairs. Nobody saw me, nobody, but I used to enjoy being somebody else. I never wanted to be me.'

Nothing about Edith smacked of the conventional, the expected. Children who dress up and play act usually crave an audience: relatives, gathered together for Christmas reunions, are dragooned into witnessing some prolonged amateur performance; kind uncles bestow gifts of make-up and then pay the price of their indulgence. Edith was the exception. She did not seek an audience for her impersonations. She had no theatrical longings, she was not an *enfant du paradis* hugging herself in the gallery while watching an idol: indeed to the best of her recollection she was seldom if ever taken to the legitimate theatre. She

7

herself had no idea of the genesis of her talent. Where did it come from? What was the secret origin of her gift for speaking verse, of giving to a variety of poets, both classical and contemporary, interpretations which were so unique that the meaning of the words were illuminated with a clarity that the authors could only have dreamed of? She was given a book of poetry as a child, a prize at some end of term, but cared little for it at the time. 'I suppose they thought I ought to care about something, but I didn't. I was rather naughty.' Poetry was something you got when you were good, an adult favour more pleasing to the giver than the recipient. It wasn't until much later in life that she became consciously aware of the shapes of words. 'I began to see funny angles.' she said. (Her own choice of words when describing everyday events was frequently disturbing, challenging the listener to think anew.)

'When I was a little girl I remember thinking words were the funniest things in the world. I remember once, and I can't think why, I remember thinking the word "basin" was such a funny word. I kept saying it over and over . . . "Basin" . . . What a silly thing to say. But it amused me. I've always loved words, speech, and I fell in love with people with beautiful speaking voices more than good looks. They thrilled me.'

Again one searches in vain for the source. Edward Evans had a sweet singing voice as a child—'right on note'—and it was suggested that he take lessons and be trained, but he rejected the idea as being 'rather soppy'. Edith's mother, it is true, insisted on good speech, but her motives sprang, I suspect, more from maternal aspirations of gentility than the usual material ambition to see a daughter shine as a future actress and breadwinner.

To have escaped from peasant or gypsy stock and then to have one's only daughter take, as it were, a step backwards into the 'profession' with its uneasy similarity to an even older profession could not have been what Ellen Evans dreamed of for her child.

Edith told me that her mother longed for her to become a 'proper lady'. 'How she used to watch me walking up the street, watch me going and when I came back. She'd say, "Swinging those arms!" You see, ladies didn't swing their arms and she wanted me to be a lady, a nice, quiet, well behaved young woman and I was the exact opposite.'

Edward Evans, the quiet man, content with his lot, his limited ambition franked and neatly pigeon-holed like the mail he handled at the General Post Office, was equally puzzled by his offspring. 'I nearly sent him mad with all my energy. I was a raving lump of a girl. I just flew about the place like a lunatic. All that energy. I've always had it.'

To an extent it would seem that the majority of actors, far from being the indolent creatures of the night that novelists and gossip columnists would have us believe, are possessed of these extra stores of energy. One

8

of the prime requisites for survival in an actor is robust physical health, coupled with the ability to push pain to one side when that health is suddenly challenged. The legend of the understudy who never gets a chance to go on is, in ninety cases out of a hundred, true. There has always been too much unemployment in the profession, with too many actors waiting to fill too few roles. Vitality, creative adrenalin, sheer bloody-minded refusal to acknowledge any limitations which could possibly stand in the way of self-advancement, are more the characteristics of the average actor than long hair, frayed cuffs and a copy of *My Life In Art* clutched under the arm. The main concern is not the fear of failing to succeed, but the fear of not being given the opportunity to fail. And for such pursuits a robust constitution is mandatory. The profession demands a form of continuous courage—not the spectacular variety that earns medals, but an exercise of mind over matter. I don't believe that this kind of courage, this demoniac energy has any connection with the old adage that 'the show must go on.' More often than not the show comes off if it ever goes on at all, and in Edith's early days it very often came off without the actors getting paid a penny. It requires a special quality to retain stamina and a belief in one's own destiny when the ghost does not walk for weeks or months on end. Many actors are too proud, even now, to seek welfare benefits during those inevitable periods of unemployment they like to term 'resting'. It is considered professional suicide to admit publicly to a total lack of offers: actors are never 'out of work', they are 'considering a script' or 'just about to do something if the money is right'; attitudes doubtless foolish to outsiders, but accepted with the minimum of cynicism by those on the inside. Failure is, after all, part of an actor's make-up and few are strangers to it. Constant failure, the lot of so many, burns energy fast. An actor carries his vocation like a disease, contaminating his fellow players, asking for no permanent cure, only that temporary salve known as applause.

2

'There weren't any beginnings'

Edith must have been an unsuspecting carrier of that disease from an early age. Yet nobody in her immediate circle diagnosed it. There were no premonitions. She completed her schooling, such as it was, collected her leaving prize of a Bible, still consumed with an energy she neither understood nor could control—swinging her arms as no lady should as she walked, not hand in hand with destiny, but towards the genteel drudgery of an apprenticeship as a milliner.

Edith had just turned fifteen when she left school in 1903 and was immediately indentured to a local court milliner, a Mr. Blackaller who made hats 'for ladies of quality' in Buckingham Palace Road. She went out into the world, but not too far, for her place of work was but half a mile from her home.

'I wasn't very good at making hats. I liked it, I liked working with lovely materials, lovely colours—colours have always fascinated me. I see colours in words.'

Her choice of occupation was as haphazard as the rest of her life until that point. Girls of that period did not have careers; if they were born rich they languished within the strict confines of the social round until a suitable husband had been found; if they were poor they were required to supplement the family income from a tender age without thought to their health or welfare and if, as in Edith's case, they came from the lower middle class the necessity of finding employment was equally urgent, though the choice was more constricted. Edith had been educated up to a point, but she had no obvious qualifications and could therefore be considered lucky to have landed a job in an establishment such as Mr. Blackaller's immediately she left school. It was a cut above a shop assistant and the fact that she was 'indentured' bestowed a certain false dignity satisfying her mother's aspirations that she become a lady.

After putting in her required quota of hours doing all manner of menial tasks for Mr. Blackaller, Edith would return home to help her mother take care of the lodgers, for by now, doubtless in an effort to sustain a standard of living and provide for a few extra luxuries, Ellen

Evans was taking in a few selected 'paying guests' at the house in Ebury Street. Edith made it quite clear that her mother would only admit gentlemen of good character, who were almost certainly drawn from the ranks of commercial travellers. Ellen allowed her daughter to take their evening meals to them on a tray in their rooms—a degree of intimacy which was considered just permissible. There was a thin dividing line between a 'lodging house' and a home where carefully scrutinised guests were given accommodation, and Mrs. Evans set great store by the proprieties; what Mr. Evans thought of the arrangement is nowhere recorded, though it is probable that his wife took all the domestic decisions. The world of Somerset Maugham's *Of Human Bondage* is echoed here—the quiet backwaters where single men sacrificed a major portion of their meagre earnings to keep up a facade of respectability. (Noël Coward's famous Aunt Ida had kept such a lodging house in Ebury Street for many years and towards the end of the first World War his mother leased No. 111 for the same purpose, Noël occupying a tiny attic in the great tradition of La Vie de Bohème. With that attention to detail which typified his whole approach to life, the young Mr. Coward called the lodgers Lodgers and insisted that his mother did the same. As his biographer Cole Lesley puts it 'Paying Guests, like true-blue Englishmen in the jungle, changed every night into evening dress for dinner'.)

Edith lacked the sophistication to make such distinctions and confessed that she enjoyed her evening chores. It was another part to play —a welcome diversion from the routine of life at Mr. Blackaller's. As she grew more experienced that gentleman allowed her to make deliveries to favoured customers. On one such occasion she had to go to a fine house in Belgrave Square. The butler directed her to wait in the hallway while he advised his mistress of her presence. After an interval the lady of the house made her appearance and was quite startled to be confronted by Edith. 'Oh,' she said. 'And who are you? I was told there was a little milliner drudge waiting to see me.'

Edith curtsied and presented herself.

'How odd,' the woman remarked. 'I never thought they would send a lady.'

'I'm not a lady, ma'am.'

The woman gave her a Gioconda smile. 'Ah, but we *know*,' she said.

Despite the fact that many of Edith's recollections of this period in her life were fragmented and hazy, she recalled this particular incident with absolute clarity and attached great importance to it, as though the early admonitions of her mother had been burnt into her memory.

It has been said that childhood is a novelist's whole capital—a theory open to challenge in many cases—but to the best of my knowledge the same supposition has never been advanced for the child actor. Edith certainly never forgot her origins and drew upon childhood memories in later years when called upon to portray certain eccentrics. I remember that she once stoutly crossed swords with an interviewer who stated he found Wilde's Lady Bracknell artificial. 'Such women *existed*,' Edith told him. 'I won't say that she was typical because Wilde was an artist and artists are selective, but to dismiss her as artificial is quite wrong.'

True to her own self-description as 'a raving lump of a girl' she survived more than the occasional encounters with upper-strata snobbery. 'One day, I'd not quite finished my bit of sewing and the other girls had all gone to lunch. They didn't notice I was still there, so they shut the door. Locked it, locked me in. So after I'd finished, I thought, Oh, no, now I can't get out. How can I get out? I looked around and then I decided, well, I'll just get out of this window and walk along the ledge a yard or two and get in the next one.' She paused with an actor's relish for delaying the punch line. 'I fell through the roof. I didn't know it was glass. I thought it was tin, you know—what they used to call Humphrey's iron roofing, I think. I fell through this glass roof and they were so angry with me. Fortunately the people who owned the building, Trollopes, I believe, they realised it was just one of the girls who'd fallen through by mistake. Didn't charge me anything, hardly. My bosses would have made me pay out and they were the ones who were angry with me. I did everything like that. It seemed to me sensible. Get out of one window, walk along and get in the next. Why make a fuss?'

Although, as we have seen, her parents were over-protective in certain areas, they were not puritanical and allowed Edith to have young gentlemen 'callers' who were always welcome to share a meal with the family in Ebury Street. Shortly after she started work in 1903 she was introduced to a young ledger clerk from Woollands, a large general store of quality in London's Knightsbridge.

His name was George Booth, though he was always known as Guy. He was five years older than Edith, the son of an Army school teacher, and one of a family of nine. They immediately became, in the purest sense of the word, sweethearts—an apt if now somewhat derided and out-moded term. The story of their relationship has always seemed to me a romance by H. G. Wells rewritten by Somerset Maugham, with perhaps a touch of Kipling thrown in for good measure. In a sense it is the pivot, the triumph and the tragedy of Edith's life, a love story seemingly made for fiction rather than for fact.

The timing of their first meeting, the separate circumstances of their lives, the epoch in which their love first flowered are so perfectly dove-tailed, so dramatically correct that they appear to have been devised and shaped by an author rather than by chance.

Edith said that she had never been considered a beautiful girl. 'I had something, but I wasn't pretty. Even so I used to attract a lot of attention and that was all I could cope with.'

Attitudes have totally changed since the turn of the century and never more so than in the past two decades, and whilst it would be foolish to suggest that the basic physical attractions between two young people of the opposite sex have ever differed very widely, the conventions of every new age determine the *pace* of any relationship. Within the budding groves of each succeeding generation fresh conventions are established, previous lines of demarcation are obliterated, the very language of love is altered, and it is always difficult to define the exact moment when one set of conventions is replaced by another. Wars inevitably accelerate the process of change, the possible death of a loved one being perhaps the most potent aphrodisiac of all. Therefore, in telling the story of Edith and Guy, I feel it important to establish the setting, historical as well as personal, for there were outside forces at work which greatly determined the future of two innocents.

Edith put it this way: 'We were queerly undeveloped. Full of everything, but tight.' They met, they were obviously mutually attracted and it appears to have been taken for granted by both families that in due course they would marry. That was the order of things. They went bicycling together and spent weekends in Cobham, a favourite beauty spot within easy reach of central London. On such occasions Edith stayed with her maternal grandmother and Guy put up at a nearby cottage. It was all open and above board, as they used to say.

Guy, one feels, was the more serious of the two. He was handsome, not excessively so, easygoing, and in all probability, being a male, had received a marginally better education than Edith. The very fact that he had gained employment as a ledger clerk in Woollands gave him a modestly superior station. There were prospects of promotion— tortuously distant, but nevertheless within the bounds of possibility. There was an element of security, a factor which impressed Edith's father, for he had a civil servant's pride in a regulated society. Being five years older than Edith, Guy was more versed in the ways of the world, more conscious of its injustices and anomalies, and his conversation was spiced with more wit than the banter she exchanged with the lodgers or her fellow-milliners at Mr. Blackaller's. He could match her gaiety with his own and from the very beginning he caught a glimpse of that 'something beyond the evidence' that nobody in Edith's immediate circle had suspected. He encouraged and nurtured her individuality throughout his life. Despite his advantage in years there must have been times when she baffled him, for the strength of young girls in their teens is that curious mixture of innocence and carnality against which only the murderer has the ultimate answer.

'I was never starved for affection,' Edith said in talking of this period in her life. 'But I was a little aloof, a little bit sort of 'don't touch me', do you know what I mean?'

Most men, recalling their first fumbled encounters with the opposite sex, will know exactly what she meant.

In 1904, England was basking in the new Edwardian optimism. The 'wonderful century' was past, soon to be mourned, and for the moment people enjoyed the 'long and extravagant garden party'. Few had yet had a vision of a civilisation falling to chaos and fewer still wished to reach below familiar layers to uncover the preposterous vanities of the age. In spite of all appearances to the contrary the *Pax Britannica* was passing its zenith when the old Queen died. These later, self-evident truths were either hidden from most contemporaries or ignored by them. For most Europeans life was work, work with heads down from dawn to dusk, and any escape from the harsher realities of existence, however transient, however false, was better than none.

England had a popular King, but a King who had waited too long in the wings: the entire cast of European crowned heads, learning their lines from the same prompt copy, ordering their uniforms and decorations from the same costumiers, parading the same stage in routines as ossified as any grand opera, performed like actors who, accustomed to a captive and well-disposed audience, are no longer able to differentiate between comedy and tragedy, caring little whether they move the spectators to laughter or tears but concerned only with *being*. The British were more fortunate than their neighbours across the Channel for Edward VII at least tilted the crown at a jaunty angle, spurned the obvious use of his father's name and thus by implication his father's unyielding formality, and was prepared—taking the theatrical comparison a jot further—to ad-lib his technique for a monarchy which owed more to the Tudors than the Hanoverians. The British people, having waited for him, welcomed him, perhaps seeing in him the larger-than-life living excuse for their own smaller peccadillos.

Sir Harold Nicolson's stricture that 'one can never forgive the Edwardians their fundamental illusion, for it never dawned on them that intelligence was of any value' is curiously devoid of any compassion (in a man so personally compassionate) for that limbo-climate of transition which existed in the few years between the death of Queen Victoria and the outbreak of the 1914 war. The Edwardians cherished many illusions which we can now see in sharp focus, but they were hardly different from succeeding generations, and who is to say that an Age of Illusion is not preferable to an Age of Cynicism?

I believe that Edith and Guy were true Edwardians rather than latter-day Victorians, for they met in the fullness of their formative years and there is no better recipe for a change in attitudes than the coming together of two young people in love at a time of general flux.

The comfortably disreputable standards propagated by Edward VII rubbed off on his devoted and loyal subjects (ordinary people generally feel more comfortable when their leaders or figureheads are 'characters'). Not that their lives changed materially until after his short reign ended, but there was a kind of freedom in the air. The dream of the majority may not have been one with Elgar's recently unveiled *Dream of Gerontius* —nothing as generally exalted as that—but it was nevertheless a dream that ended on a note of hope. The Boer War came to its Pyrrhic end a month before the intended coronation and although the promised spectacle of all the crowned heads making the pilgrimage to London was denied because of the King's illness on the eve of the celebration, his recovery was another omen for good. The fragile calm was there to be enjoyed while it lasted, Income Tax was little more than a shilling in the pound for those who had to pay it and

Hats were hats of startling size
And waists were waists and thighs were thighs.

The world that Edith and Guy inhabited, later to be popularised as 'a Garden of Eden just made for two' by George Robey and Violet Loraine, held few premonitions of disaster for the great mass of the population. Such undecided prophets of pending doom as from time to time made their voices heard above the general gaiety were patronised by the Establishment when they weren't totally ignored.

There was no hint in 1904 that Edith's life would change course so abruptly within a few more years, or that because *her* life would go off at such a tangent, Guy's whole future would undergo an equally traumatic change. They could not have deciphered the code of their future lives because no message had been received. Edith believed that she would go on making hats of startling size until marriage, and Guy doubtless intended to apply himself diligently to the ledgers of Messrs Woollands as befitted a man who meant to take a wife and set up home. Meanwhile they could explore each other in unhurried fashion, for they looked no further than themselves.

None of their love letters survive from this period—perhaps they wrote none?—nor did Edith keep a Journal or scrapbook. The courtship flourished. Edith moved from Mr. Blackaller's establishment and found employment with a Madame François in Burlington Street. Although but a short distance from Pimlico, the fashionable shopping areas of Regent Street, Piccadilly and Mayfair must have taken Edith into virtually a foreign country. As J. B. Priestley has written, the accents of high society in Edwardian times were 'so extraordinary that they might well have been foreigners.' Because, in the same author's words, these golden days were 'on the other side of the huge black pit of war' most writers of the period have coloured them with bolder tones than they deserve. Yet to a young girl still in her teens they must have appeared cloudless, devoid of any menace, her only outward emotion sadness that they must necessarily end.

Whatever pleasures they devised for themselves, a shared love of theatregoing was not amongst them. 'I never played with a toy theatre, I never collected stage stars' autographs, in fact I was not in the least bit stage struck or interested in the theatre at all.'

Can there ever have been a stranger start to such an illustrious career in the theatre? Edith went on to remark: 'There weren't any beginnings. The only thing I remember saying when I was asked what I wanted to be was, I think, a rather significant one. I said: 'I don't want a job that I can see the end of.' That is a very ungrammatical sentence, but I was never very good at grammar. I'm pretty sure that is how I phrased it, and that little maxim more or less stayed with me all my life.'

At some time during this period, between 1904 and 1912—Edith could not pinpoint the date with any accuracy—she started to attend evening classes. These were run by a Miss E. C. Massey, one of those remarkable women who dedicate their lives to the betterment of others without thought of personal gain. She remained one of Edith's closest and dearest friends; Edith never forgot her debt to her and they corresponded for nearly sixty years. 'She taught me the value and the hidden meaning of words. I didn't take the classes all that seriously at first. Guy came with me sometimes, though I think it was mostly to see me, and I met other boys and girls, and we all had quite a lark together.'

They studied Shakespeare together and Miss Massey encouraged her part-time students to act out the plays for their own amusement, a method of teaching which boldly went against the accepted form of teaching Shakespeare in the schools, a form which practically guaranteed a life-long hatred of the Bard rather than the devout appreciation it was intended to instil. Even so, 'to take up acting seriously never for one moment entered my silly head, and if it had my parents would have discouraged me, I feel sure. When Miss Massey once told my father that I had a very definite gift for acting, he said: "Now please don't drum any of that nonsense into her. She probably stands out among all the other boys and girls in your class, but with professional players she'd be nowhere."'

Since there is no evidence to suggest that Edward Evans was an avid theatregoer, his sweeping dismissal of Edith's latent talents (which his daughter accepted without rebellion or hurt) presumably stemmed from prejudice rather than a considered evaluation. Guy kept silent on the subject. Miss Massey had fired the first shot, the referee had ruled a miss, but that indomitable lady reloaded and prepared to work around the flanks and sight the target from another angle. To her must go the undivided credit for discerning that embryonic something which set the young Edith Evans apart from her fellow amateurs. Although Edith was content to abide by her father's decision, she continued to attend the evening classes. She was earning 35/- a week from Madame François (a not inconsiderable wage for a girl of her age in those days), she was in love and she liked having a larky time in her spare moments.

Once a year Miss Massey felt sufficiently confident to mount a programme of Shakespeare at the Streatham Town Hall, presenting her mainly amateur casts in public performance. A strong amateur tradition had taken hold during the latter half of the Victorian era, and standards were sometimes impressively high. The mania for amateur acting straddled the classes—the leisured gentry often providing the money and facilities and being prepared in the common artistic cause to lower the barriers of snobbery. The tradition persists to the present day (readers will recall that the tragic protagonists of John Braine's celebrated first novel *Room At The Top* were introduced through amateur theatricals, and it was an important plot point that Joe Lampton could further his relationship with the girl from 'the Top' at rehearsals while being denied access to her in his everyday existence.)

Following Dame Edith's death in October 1976, a Mr. Roderick L. Eagle wrote a letter to the *New Statesman* in which he stated he produced *Twelfth Night* for Miss Massey at Streatham in October 1910. Edith was cast as Viola on this occasion and if Mr. Eagle is correct this predates what was hitherto her first recorded appearance on any stage by some two years. Before I had sight of Mr. Eagle's letter all the evidence at my disposal, and indeed Edith's own recollections, had led me to believe that her debut took place on Saturday April 20th 1912. On that date the Streatham Shakespeareans 'under the direction of Miss E. C. Massey' presented a Shakespeare Anniversary performance at the Town Hall. The programme was divided into two halves. Part One consisted of the Queen Katharine episode from *King Henry VIII*, with Miss Massey claiming the role of Queen Katharine for herself.

The second half of the bill was more ambitious in scope, consisting as it did of five scenes from *Much Ado About Nothing* with specially composed incidental music by the Musical Director, Mr. W. Hayes Hill. Edith appeared as Beatrice. Reginald Denham was also listed in the cast of both plays: he was then eighteen and made his professional debut the following year at His Majesty's Theatre; Miss Massey obviously knew how to pick them.

Edith's performance that night made no impression on the theatrical profession as a whole and might have slipped into oblivion with the rest of her delightfully named companions—Miss Adeline Motabhoy, Miss Gertrude Grebby, Miss Kitty Breeze and Miss Hilda Pratt to note but four—had not William Poel been present in the audience.

Today the name of Poel evokes little interest, for the British have always found perverse satisfaction in ignoring men of genius until it is too late, preferring instead to honour mediocrity prematurely. Like Edward Gordon Craig whom, in method and approach he so closely resembled, Poel was a passionate innovator in the theatre. As with Craig he was more often than not preaching to empty houses where the commercial theatre was concerned. No actor manager of vision ever came forward to provide him with a permanent home and adequate funds: it was less trouble to dismiss him as a crank—less trouble and certainly less expensive, for Poel's lasting obssession was the then (and to an extent now) revolutionary notion that plays written for the Elizabethan stage could never be fully effective inside the picture frame convention of the proscenium arch.

The late Robert Speaight when he wrote his scholarly and engrossing biography of Poel in 1954, a work commissioned by the Society for Theatre Research (an organisation that claimed Edith's interest until her death), found it necessary to pose the question 'Who was William Poel?' In paying tribute to Mr. Speaight's major piece of detection and urging my readers to seek it out for themselves, it is worth answering the question in abbreviated form here, and worth it for this reason alone: the majority of present day directors of Shakespeare, whether they are aware of it or not, are disciples of Poel's.

Prophets usually disconcert people. W. A. Darlington, for many years the senior dramatic critic of the London *Daily Telegraph*, reviewing Speaight's book, stated: 'Almost by definition they are fanatics and Poel carried his holy zeal to lengths which, to any but the elect, must have seemed absurd.' Darlington had no doubts: Poel was a crank. I feel that this is too convenient a verdict even from a practitioner of the noble art of instant opinions. The term crank is commonly used to describe people who are monomaniacally obsessed by impracticable projects, but Poel proved his point in at least one hundred productions he was responsible for in the fifty-two years from 1880 to 1932. Such a body of work, so sustained a mission, cannot be tossed aside by a single word verdict. That Poel was ahead of his time, that he antagonised succeeding theatrical establishments throughout his career cannot be denied. Having turned his back on the stifling respectability of a life in commerce during his middle twenties, he accepted the lonely dedication to his cause as readily as he accepted his chance change of name (his real name was Pole, but a printing error in the programme of the first provincial touring company he joined as an actor transformed him into Poel overnight and Poel he remained). Whilst allowing for the fact that he must have been irritating and pedantic to anybody who did not embrace his vision, I have more than a sneaking regard for his singleness of mind and nothing but admiration for the way in which he persisted with little or no recognition. Lesser, grosser talents became household names. Some of his contemporaries, dramatic pygmies by comparison, were revered and honoured; such disciples as, on occasion, deigned to sit at his table, frequently betrayed him by going forth to preach an expurgated version of his gospel. Shaw praised him, Max Beerbohm denounced him, the majority ignored him.

He merits retrospective recognition in these pages for one simple reason: not only did he seek out and make the unfashionable pilgrimage to the Streatham Town Hall that April night in 1912, but he also had the perception to act upon Miss Massey's prior judgement where Edith was concerned. Miss Massey had provided the key, Poel unlocked the door. He plucked the young milliner from obscurity and placed her firmly in the centre of stage, and for this act alone deserves a measure of the praise so long denied him. His critics, and there were many, frequently accused him of lacking judgement, but on the evidence of a single performance by an unknown player in an amateur company, his instant decision reached beyond the modern conception of 'talent spotting' with an accuracy that none can question.

He wrote to Edith (for he had the good manners of the age and would not have barged back-stage to overwhelm a complete stranger) and presumably by sheer force of personality, enthusiasm and conviction, he was instrumental in overcoming parental misgivings and persuaded Mr. and Mrs. Evans to allow Edith to take the next step. True to form and by way of illustrating that streak of perverseness that set his enemies' teeth on edge, he launched his new discovery in a revival of a sixth century Hindu classic called *Sakuntala* by the poet Kalidasa. Further to daunt even the most avid theatrical pedant, he presented this at the Cambridge University Examination Hall. The cast included Nigel Playfair (later to make Edith the central jewel in his Lyric, Hammersmith company) and Miss Irene Clarke. History records that Poel was somehow able to mount the production on 'a multiple stage which showed, simultaneously, the forest jungle, the King's palace and the Elysian fields.' Edith played a minor role, but she had been given her first taste of the living theatre.

It is easy to mock from afar, and if now the choice of play suggests a Monty Python-like exercise in Hindu obscurity, we should not forget that the theatre was not only the temple of Poel's art, but his entire life's work. Present day Broadway and Shaftesbury Avenue is mostly a grotesque imitation of what the theatre used to stand for, but other latter-day prophets, other fanatics, equally irritating to the purveyors of mediocrity on both sides of the Atlantic, are leaving the diseased woodwork of the commercial theatre and making new homes off-Broadway and in the hinterlands of London. These new pioneers are in many cases—presumably by instinct rather than education—embracing some of Poel's theories which were etched into the tablets nearly a century ago.

Edith was to have first-hand experience of another of Poel's eccentricities, that of casting women as male characters, a curious inversion of the Elizabethan habit of having young boys portray women. Doubtless some critics could speculate as to the Freudian implications behind such a departure from normal procedure, but I am inclined to the belief that Poel was motivated by a desire to extend his performers by forcing them to come to terms, in public, with situations beyond their previous experience. Some thirteen years before his discovery of Edith he had audaciously cast another unknown young actress, Margaret Halstan, in a major male role. Again he has to be credited with a bullseye, for Miss Halstan went on to a distinguished and long career, as I can personally testify, for I acted with her some sixty years later in *The Holly and The Ivy* and she was still an actress of exquisite subtlety and the very epitome of feminine elegance.

Edith's first appearance under Poel's direction took place in August 1912. Poel then shifted his tent to the King's Hall, Covent Garden. There he supervised a production of *Job* (dramatised by the Hon. Sybil Amherst) before preparing a major revival of *Troilus and Cressida* for December of the same year.

Edith had had her first taste of . . . what? Not success, for it goes without saying that the commercial managements of the day had not flocked to the Cambridge University Examination Hall to bid against each other for the privilege of bringing *Sakuntala* to London. Nor, it must be added, had the public at large betrayed any awareness that history was being made. No, what Edith had tasted was a mouthful of real as opposed to mock caviar for the first time. The effect must have been bewildering. On the one hand she felt pulled towards that mystifying country of injustice and glory which is the professional theatre, yet against this came the counter tug of caution. Her inheritance voted for security, marriage with Guy, a sensible, happy solution where personal choice was sublimated to the needs of a partnership. She was being tested. Her love for her father and Guy, the two dominant male figures in her life—both at that point tolerant but not over-enthusiastic—was finely balanced against her first experience of a passion. Poel was a mature man, sure of his instincts, urbane, tortured with a vision he wanted desperately to share with others and, above all, theatrical. He dressed theatrically, he spoke rhetoric and he had singled her out from the crowd. The glimpse of Elysium he had given Edith must have presented a startling contrast to the back-room, small-time chit chat of a millinery workshop where the highlight of any week was the approving nod of a satisfied customer.

It would be a gross distortion to paint Poel as some sinister Svengali-like figure intent upon seducing the young hat-maker away from her childhood sweetheart and the family hearth. He was too wrapped up in his own destiny ever to stray from the chosen path on purely sexual grounds. In Robert Speaight's definitive description, he was 'a man of the theatre who never really had a stage' and his struggle for recognition consumed all of his energies. He was certainly a kind man who helped many, but they had to keep up with him once he had extended a hand. I can well understand Edith's dilemma. She had no means of comparing Poel's opinion of her with others of equal experience. What, after all, did she know of the real world? She was not academic, she was not intellectual, and to be confronted and flattered by a man with such an obvious gift of the gab as Poel must have been very disturbing. Added to which, Poel was an underdog—always a devastating attraction to the young. And yet . . . Edith did not throw her bonnet over the moon as she might well have done.

There was a hiatus after her appearance in Cambridge, but after he had finished with his production of *Job* Poel sent for her again. It was only now that the family crisis was faced. Her parents began to perceive that this might not be the passing fancy they had previously indulged. Other relatives raised pious hands when they called to commiserate; there is nothing like the hint of scandal to unite a family. To their credit Edith's mother and father refused to be panicked; from what Edith told me I formed the opinion that Ellen Evans saw the escape route that had been denied her opening up for her daughter and could not bring herself to close it. There was gipsy blood in her and unlike her husband she had read enough to know that there was something more rewarding than a lifetime of ordinary domesticity.

Poel baited the trap. True to his reputation for startling people he offered Edith the role of Cressida. It is important to put this development in proper perspective. Here we have a man who was not only proud of his ability to shock, but also someone who demanded intolerably high standards from those who worked with him. He would never have been guilty of giving Edith Cressida merely to confound his critics. He must have believed that, under his tuition, she could rise to the occasion. He risked all, because he believed there was something there worth risking.

And what of Edith? Did she hesitate? Nor for long apparently. Poel believed in her, therefore she would start to believe in herself. It was no longer a lark, the pleasant interludes she had enjoyed with Miss Massey bore no relation to the fiery dedication that Poel demanded and which Guy would no longer be able to share. It was to be a move away from familiarity. Her resolve at first puzzled Guy and then scared him. 'I don't think he recognised me. At times I didn't recognise myself, but he had great courage, my sweetheart, the best kind of courage, the sort of courage you take from yourself and give to others.'

One strand of caution still remained; she elected not to give up her job and continued to work at Madame François' during the day (a decision Poel could not argue against, for his actors were poorly paid) and in the evenings took herself off to rehearsals to grapple with a major Shakespearean role.

Today it is difficult to appreciate the amount of sustained effort and enthusiasm that must have been required from all concerned to mount what was in effect a series of 'one-night stands'. *Troilus and Cressida* had three spaced performances at the King's Hall in December 1912. Esme Percy, who was the same age as Edith, played Troilus with Poel himself taking the role of Pandarus.

A fortnight later Edith wrote to Poel.

> 109, Ebury Street.
> December 29th 1912

I should have written to you long ago to thank you for allowing me to play Cressida for you . . . I thank you now and say everything is dull and uninteresting to me since the play is over. I can't make my hats, and although I try hard, my thoughts seem to wander and I'm afraid I shall have to give them up . . . I have not heard anything further from Mr. George Moore, so I expect he is too busy to write.

I can't make my hats. The decision, the final acknowledgement, is there in that painfully simple statement. The honesty her parents had instilled in her was transparent on the page. She had made a conscious choice.

The plaintive reference to George Moore stemmed from a correspondence which began the day after the first performance at the King's Hall.

> 121, Ebury Street,
> Pimlico, S.W.
> December 11th

Dear Miss Evans,

I could not help myself last night from asking Mr. Poel to introduce me to you. I should not have slept if I had left the theatre without trying to find words to express my admiration for your more than realisation, your creation of the part of Cressida. And now I cannot sit down to go on with my ordinary work till I have written to tell you that you seemed to me to take the part as a musician takes one; your acting was as music, for it expressed moods emotions and instincts—acting like music goes deeper than words can go: and your acting in Cressida enabled you to present to us the winsomeness of the pure animal redeemed from thought, ideas, prejudices and conventions. Your Cressida goes from one man's arms to another's with the urgency of a child—and the *instincts* one might almost say of a flower. I could go on writing to you for a long time telling you how spontaneous was every motion and gesture, how instinctive and how expressive, and I could praise you for your stage appearance which was in itself a creation. You seemed to take yourself as a sculptor takes clay and to mould Cressida . . . I break off though I have not said everything.

Very sincerely Yours,
George Moore.

Heady stuff indeed for a young lady who had yet to become a professional actress. There is an element of farce conjured from the close proximity of the two addresses: one almost expects the front doors of Nos. 109 and 121 Ebury Street to pop open and reveal the two principals in attitudes of shocked surprise as they recognise each other. Again the long arm of coincidence seems to have been bent at the elbow, for it is doubtful whether a novelist of Moore's calibre would have risked his reputation by devising such a plot development in one of his works of fiction.

The letter suggests an older man smitten, infatuated, for his language sometimes assumes a shade of purple. I could not discover whether Edith showed the letter to her parents or to Guy; the chances are she did, and the chances are that they were amazed by it—it is not everyday that a famous writer describes your only daughter as having 'the winsome-ness of the pure animal redeemed from thought' and 'the instincts one might almost say of a flower.' Here the novelist is obliterated by the elderly masher, and many fathers would reach for a shotgun. On the other hand it would be difficult to better his description of Edith's technique . . . 'You seem to take yourself as a sculptor takes clay' for this was true to the end of her career. Edith several times told me that had she not been an actress she would have liked to have been a painter. She came to each new character she played with a bare canvas, or a dollop of wet clay, and no preconceived notions. Then the first bold brush strokes, the prodding into rough shape and afterwards, as the rehearsals progressed, the gradual process of elimination, of refinement, simplifying, always taking the most difficult route to the ultimate obvious destination, making sure that her audience, her spectators saw only the finished work, never the technique that produced that work. The true object of technique, she used to say, is to conceal technique and she would take infinite pains over a single line. Peggy Ashcroft has told how Edith once admitted that she prayed about a certain line in *Romeo and Juliet*, her reading of which Dame Peggy considered perfection. Perhaps the absence of any theatrical background enabled her to dispense with the trappings of convention from the very beginning. Perhaps the fact that she hadn't seen any performances of the great classical roles ensured that despite the prediction, she did not commence her career as a mimic. She also had the advantage of being taught by Poel, who despised theatrical tradition.

First Poel and then George Moore: the foundation stones were laid by master builders. It would appear that Moore's fever and fret did prevent him from sleeping, for he wrote again the following day. (This second fan letter was typewritten).

121, Ebury Street
S.W.

12/12/12

Dear Miss Evans,

After writing the letter which no doubt you have received, complimenting you upon your acting in *Troilus and Cressida* I turned to the play. I had not read it for a great number of years and turned to it with some misgiving, for my memory of Cressida was a sprightly, witty young woman, and you turned her into a young woman so instinctive that she was nearly witless. My memory did not deceive me. Cressida is a witty young woman in the first acts and I continued to wonder how you arrived at your extraordinary reading until I came to the fourth act. Then a little light broke in upon my darkness. Cressida seems to me to lose all her wits in the fourth act and to be what you represented her, a purely instinctive creature, and it struck me that you said to yourself 'I shall have to be against the words at the beginning of the play or the end' and you decided to be against the words in the beginning and in agreement with the words at the end. The play reads to me like one written in a dream. While Shakespeare was asleep his pen seems to have dipped itself into the ink and written the play for him. It is as instinctive as your Cressida and quite as unreasonable; an interminable rigmarole with here and there beautiful passages. And what is it all about?

Troilus and Cressida interests me very much, and I should like to write something about it, but before doing so I should like to hear from you how your singular interpretation of Cressida was arrived at. Would it be too much to ask you to come some afternoon to tea and have a little talk about it?

Very sincerely Yours
George Moore.

Without wishing to take away from Edith's undoubted personal triumph, it does seem a little hard that Moore chose to ignore Poel's contribution—the credit in his bedazzled eyes belonged to Edith alone. I also note how, with the skill of a born writer, he moves from his evaluation of the play to a subtle invitation to tea for two.

24

He wrote again forty-eight hours later and once more the letter was typewritten.

Dear Miss Evans,

It would surely be pleasanter for you to come to dinner than to come in after dinner. I dine alone three or four times a week, so you can choose any day you like. Or shall we say Monday next? We can talk of Cressida after dinner. It is possible I shall write about the subject one day and I should like to hear how the interpretation was arrived at. But there is no use my broaching that subject since we are going to talk it out.

Very sincerely yours,
George Moore.

Even allowing for the fact that the GPO could then be depended upon to deliver a letter on the day it was posted, thus making it possible for Edith to have replied to his of the 12th, she had no recollection of having sent such a reply. She remembered a feeling of anti-climax after the performance, and I discovered a postcard from Poel, written in haste and delivered by hand, which was obviously a kindly attempt to comfort her.

I hope you will not be depressed by anything you read in the papers about your acting of Cressida. It was perfect and the only possible conception and treatment which could be consistent. The critics of the daily papers don't read the play and only look for something theatrical and unreal. They would have liked to see a Cressida with the real side of her nature hidden, but this the text does not allow of. Reading between the lines, I gather the critics were impressed but they are afraid to admit it because the profession doesn't like these kind of plays that need imagination and talent to become popular. Thank you very much for being so entirely the artist in your impersonation.

W. Poel.

This generous, spontaneous gesture to his fledgling contradicts those who insist that Poel had little time or compassion for anything or anybody outside his narrow field of vision. He did not seek, as many in his position would have done, to draw attention to her inexperience, using that as justification for the lack of perception amongst his critics. He, Poel, thought she was perfect: she had satisfied him and he, not the critics, was entitled to the last word.

Poel's fears as to the possible critical reaction were realised in part. One critic did have the honesty to admit that, being a stranger to the play, it was quite a long time before he could grasp what it meant, who was who, or why anything was happening. True to form, Poel had cast several of the male characters with women. 'A strange, uncanny, disquieting affair', wrote another of the daily sages and pronounced it decadent. All in all 'Mr. William Poel's curious revival' was not accounted a triumph and Edith received very mixed reviews. Several of the critics remarked on her artificial sing-song voice, and prancing gait in this 'quaintest of productions', but to balance she received two qualified tributes to her skill and nobody, as far as I can detect, had any awareness of her total lack of experience which I find the most revealing aspect of all.

After the three performances, a vacuum; any actor will know the feeling well; life seems to lack any purpose. Edith told me just as she told Poel, that the making of hats was no substitute. She confessed that she was wary of Moore. He was then a man of sixty with a deserved reputation as a womaniser. Some of his contemporaries (including some who called themselves his friends) described him in less than flattering terms. Lytton Strachey met him around this period (February 1913) and wrote, 'He reminded me of one of those very overgrown tabbies that haunt some London kitchens'. Of course Strachey was something of a tabby himself, motheaten rather than overgrown. Gertrude Stein was also present at this same meeting (at the house of Miss Ethel Sands) and her view of Moore was that he looked like 'a very prosperous Mellon's Food Baby' and was not taken with him. Not that Miss Stein's indifference should be held against Moore: she was hardly his type. Others have written of Moore's 'attitude of aloofness' and I suspect that like many grand old men of letters he was impatient in the presence of other writers who might—sometimes with justification—steal his declining thunder. Jacques-Emile Blanche insisted that Moore 'to the day of his death was a spoilt child' but Blanche had a cold, de Gaulle-like personality on his own printed pages and his *Portraits of a Lifetime* and the sequel to it read like the Goncourt Journals with all the juice extracted from them.

Edith's reaction to Moore was purely instinctive. She knew who he was by now and after questioning others, was suitably impressed by his literary pedigree, but she had not read any of his books. When such a distinguished stranger writes three highly flattering letters in the space of as many days to a girl he has seen but once from the other side of the footlights there is usually reason for caution. G.M., as most of his intimates came to call him, liked beauty. He had been attracted to young women many times in his life, notably to Nancy Cunard with whom he had an Alice In Wonderland relationship, a sideline to his lifelong devotion to her mother. He was in the business of 'free thought' a dedicated anti-bigot, not always reliable in assessing his nearest rivals and who said of himself (to his selected, but reluctant biographer,

26

Charles Morgan) 'I have two interests in my life—art and women—and, though no woman has directly influenced my art, they are woven together.' Morgan, that stylish Abelard of prose, was denied certain vital papers after Moore's death and declined to write an incomplete biography but had learned enough from personal observation and consequent research to form a firm opinion of Moore's sexual fancies. Morgan viewed him as a 'voyeur and tactilist' and I take that latter description to mean that G.M. liked to fondle the goods without necessarily wishing to purchase outright. This would seem to be confirmed by Nancy Cunard's own admissions to Anthony Thorne late in her own life. She described in great detail a number of occasions when G.M. begged her to let him see her naked. She finally granted him his wish in 1925 when G.M. was in his seventies. Gratified, he exclaimed: 'Oh, what a beautiful back you have, Nancy. It is as long as a weasel's!' which was, I suppose, a compliment worthy of a sexual poacher. Nancy Cunard also talked of his impetuosity as a lover in 'yester-years' and that he liked to remind people that he had been a 'great dab at making love' in his prime. There were persistent rumours that G.M. was Nancy's putative father and on one occasion she confronted him with them, demanding the truth, but received only an enigmatic answer. It was an age when 'love-children' were much in vogue and though G.M. was doubtless flattered to have been attributed with the physical authorship of somebody as remarkable as Nancy, and thus reluctant to scotch the gossip, all the evidence points against it.

Edith's behaviour towards him was ambiguous. Her letter to Poel complains that Moore was probably too busy to write to her, and yet he appears to have done little else but write to her. It is apparent that she did pay a call at No. 121 for there is an unsigned note from G.M. which, from the handwriting, suggests it was penned in some agitation and is full of sorrow.

Dear Miss Evans,

My maidservant told me this morning that you called last night but would not come upstairs. I was very vexed with her for not telling me that you were here—I should have gone down and fetched you up if I had known.

You will find me in tonight after dinner and glad to see you—my dinner consists of soup and cold beef. If you like to share it come to dinner.

Such a menu would hardly entice a gourmet, so G.M. must have felt that his company was food enough. Edith professed to have forgotten the incident and one can only speculate as to whether her nerve failed her at the front door or whether the maidservant took one look and decided to protect her innocence. Then again, perhaps both these possible explanations are unfair to Moore. It is possible that he was only interested in furthering Edith's embryonic career and had no ulterior motive whatsoever. Certainly she made a profound impression on him, one he was not to surrender easily. He continued to write to her and although Edith could not pin-point the dates with any accuracy, they did meet on several occasions. I reminded her that the author of *A Mummer's Wife* had earned a place in various anthologies of quotations for his remark that 'acting is the lowest of the arts, if it is an art at all.'

Edith savoured this in silence for a few moments. 'Well, he didn't say that to *me*'.

I can understand why Moore was intrigued by Edith on many levels. For one thing she would have provided material for a story or novel particularly suited to his school of writing. A young milliner taken from obscurity by a neglected prophet and given an opportunity to shine in a major Shakespearean role was a plot too good to miss. It is also quite evident that, although not conventionally pretty, Edith attracted men. On her side, the attention she received from men such as Poel and Moore must have had a considerable effect upon her. They inhabited with ease a world she scarcely knew existed, a world where things *happened*. The day-to-day sameness of her life as a milliner must have seemed intolerable once Poel had unlocked the first door and pointed the escape route. She had been allowed out for a few hours under supervision, as it were, now she wanted to escape again and the question was not so much *how* but *when*?

Poel, who I suspect preferred to be a benevolent jailer rather than an emancipator of his discoveries, came to the rescue. *Troilus and Cressida* was reproduced for a further performance on 12th May 1913, this time at the Shakespeare Memorial Theatre, Stratford-upon-Avon. On this occasion Ion Swinley replaced Esme Percy as Troilus and Hermione Gingold played Cassandra. (This was some five years after her much quoted debut in *Pinkie and The Fairies*. She was far more experienced than Edith although Edith's junior by nine years). The cast performed for love rather than money. Edith recalled that 'when I went to collect my fee—I can't remember, two or three guineas or something—he said to me: "Ah, she ran away with all my tunes." Course, he was noted for giving people tunes, which is the way we all talk really. Most people talk up and down, but I had a lot of *natural* tunes.' (She chuckled as she said this, being well aware that she had always been the impressionists' favourite target.)

'Poel thought he'd got a gold mine in tunes when he found me,' Edith said. 'He adored them, you can imagine, can't you? A nice old man, really sweet to me.'

In later years she was to tell me that she didn't care much for her celebrated voice. 'Some people like it, some people don't. Me, I don't think much of it.' Throughout her career there were many who found her method of delivery intolerably mannered and she was philosophic about this. The beginnings of her life in the theatre were so improbable —chance dealt her a series of aces early in the game—that I have every reason to believe that the rhythms of her speech patterns were moulded by her first experiences with Poel. He was inclined to run his theories to excess and insisted that his players performed to his precise instructions.

Edith's relationship with Moore progressed to the point where she met and talked with him about her future. An element of jealousy existed between Moore and Poel which is hinted at in Moore's letter to her of February 6th 1913. (Although this does not appear to be in his own handwriting, the signature is authentic).

121 Ebury Street,
Pimlico, S.W.

Dear Miss Evans,

I was sorry to miss seeing you the other night, for I enjoy a talk with you and the best thing will be for you to come to dinner, or come in after dinner, as soon as you have a free evening I will tell you all the pleasant things I said about you to Mr. Granville-Barker, he would like to see you.

Troilus and Cressida interested me very much, but now I have read the play and it is my own ideas about it that interest me, and not Mr. Poel's. You know how much I appreciate him, but I want to write something about the play myself, and were I to listen to another's explanation I should lose interest in it.

Sincerely yours,
George Moore.

Harley Granville-Barker, an actor turned actor-manager and author, was a quasi-disciple of Poel. A more flexible man than his teacher, he exerted a profound influence on the production of Shakespeare at the turn of the century when the British theatre was still married to Irving's school. Now he is best remembered for his *Prefaces To Shakespeare* which many dramatic students still consider their Bible. He could not stomach all of Poel's theories and was honest enough to admit as much, but he remained loyal to Poel. Poel was reluctant to appreciate the real worth of the *Prefaces*, possibly because he sensed that Baker had outdistanced him and was not a man 'stiffened by fanaticism', which was Robert Speaight's description of Poel.

Moore applied his own double standards. Here we have him writing (presumably) to impress Edith with mention of Granville-Barker's name, yet a few months previously Arnold Bennet had noted in his Journal that Moore denounced Barker's production of *The Winter's Tale*,

29

saying he had made the stage look like a public lavatory. Professional jealousy in the Arts is more potent a force than many outsiders realise. At least Moore had the honesty to admit that he wasn't interested in Poel's ideas, only his own.

The important thing as far as Edith was concerned was that a small group of marginally influential people were now aware of her existence. It did not solve the central problem of her life, but it meant that she had established a different, if still tenuous, identity. The reaction of some of her relatives has been noted, but it is worth considering the attitudes of her parents and Guy. If her mother and father cannot be said to have encouraged her (and given their backgrounds and character this was understandable) then credit must be given to them for not actively opposing her. There were no *East Lynne* scenes in Ebury Street. Guy was a more positive factor. He loved her with great perception and in an age not noted for its indulgence towards the ambitions of women, he had the foresight and courage to urge her forward. Subsequent events proved that this was not weakness on his part. He must have feared losing her—what young lover wouldn't? To see your intended wife tear up the existing maps and announce that she intends to journey alone in a country you cannot comprehend must give cause for concern. Guy knew nothing of the theatre. We are told that he liked going to the ballet on occasion, but there was nothing remotely theatrical in his make-up, and he had no yardstick by which to gauge Edith's chances of success. I daresay he had been amazed by her sudden authority on Poel's stage and had enjoyed sharing the pleasure she brought to the audience. That would be natural enough, a bright burst of colour in an otherwise routine existence. The chances are that at the beginning he did not take it all that seriously. It was an episode, nothing more, something to boast of to his fellow clerks at Woollands: his girl friend was a 'bit of a card', a character. Nothing would come of it, of course, but this strange old bird William Poel was apparently quite struck with her, and that novelist chap George Moore was also encouraging her. There was even talk she might take it up seriously. Only talk, you understand, because of course they were going to get married. . . .

Yet when she made her decision, he accepted it. He did not stop loving her, he did not attempt to change her mind, he faced the fact that he had chosen to commit his life to somebody he would never completely understand. True to her own character, Edith asked him whether he wanted her to abandon the idea of following a professional career in the theatre. He replied, 'I'd rather have you twenty per cent alive than eighty per cent dead.'

It was George Moore rather than Poel who forced the ultimate decision. He had dusted off and repolished a comedy he had had on the stocks for some eight years. The plot was based on an engineered piece of mistaken identity. In direct contrast to Moore's own life, the central character, a famous author, has no interest in the love letters written to him from female fans and allows his young cousin and private secretary to assume his identity and visit one of his more persistent admirers, a Countess von Hoenstadt. Moore's infatuation with Edith, whether professional or sexual or a mixture of the two, was such that he was determined that she should play the Countess. He first told Edith and then informed his associates. The play was to be presented by the Stage Society at a special matinee at the Haymarket Theatre. His associates were not enamoured of his casting idea and finally talked him out of it. Their decision was probably kinder to Edith than Moore's good intentions, since she was patently not ready for such prominence. Moore was forced to write to her again, softening the blow with an offer of the much smaller role of Martin, a melancholy housekeeper. Edith accepted and the performance took place on an afternoon in June 1913. As a debut on the West End stage it had fairy tale qualities. The small part of the housekeeper was 'made an astonishing lot of by, as one believes, Miss Edith Evans. Considering the slight materials at the artist's disposal this was one of the cleverest studies seen for a long time.' There was more in the same vein. In fact every single critic made flattering reference to her. She was 'the noteworthy success of the afternoon', 'carried off the honours', giving 'a remarkable thumbnail sketch'. Miriam Lewes, the actress who played the Countess joined the ranks of those now forgotten while Edith began her journey into legend. Messrs Vedrenne and Eadie who were then in joint management of the Royalty Theatre in Dean Street offered her a contract for a year's engagement at a salary of two pounds ten shillings a week, with an option for a further year at three pounds ten shillings a week.

'The moment I stepped through the stage door and found myself on a professional stage, I knew that was where I belonged. I didn't feel unduly excited, but I was absolutely and completely at home. All the things about my character, and my temperament that had previously been odd and remarkable and out of key, simply went click into place. That was the real beginning and I can truthfully say that I have been at home in the theatre ever since.' These were her words to me sixty years later when she had just faced the realisation that the time had come when, finally, she would have to vacate that home.

3

'*God was very good to me. He never let me go on tour.*'

In 1913 a man of no importance called Charles Brookfield was the natural enemy of J. E. Vedrenne, Dennis Eadie and other advocates of the New Drama. Brookfield had been recently appointed the Lord Chamberlain's Examiner of Plays, a pretentious title for a powerful position which, denuded of its Gilbert and Sullivan undertones, meant simply that he was the official Censor. To his shame Brookfield had once been an actor of moderate talents and a dramatist of sorts—his most popular work being *Dear Old Charlie*, a risqué farce adapted from the French (sex in translation was considered acceptable). The play of ideas which Messrs Vedrenne and Eadie wished to champion was not only beyond Brookfield's limited intellectual comprehension but also, in his protocol-blinded eyes, a danger both to society and the commercial theatre. From all accounts he was well suited to the post. He had made no attempt to conceal his loathing of Wilde at the time of that unfortunate's downfall, though it is true to say that few people with any influence in the theatre behaved with much courage towards Wilde. I suppose it takes a peculiar mentality to accept the position of Censor, especially if you are a practising member of the craft you are now empowered to thwart and obstruct. It is more than possible that the Lord Chamberlain selected Brookfield with conscious irony: it would have been in keeping with the humour of the times to license the author of *Dear Old Charlie* to sit in absolute judgement over the works of Ibsen and Shaw.

Vedrenne and Eadie were two gentlemen of integrity and perception, especially Vedrenne who although seldom in the public limelight was a man with a better claim to theatrical immortality than many. At the turn of the century when he was manager of the small and unfashionable Court Theatre in Sloane Square he gave a home to and entered into partnership with Granville-Barker. It was an auspicious marriage and bloomed for three years which, in stage terms, amounts to a triumph. Their names swiftly became synonymous with all that was most vital in the otherwise conventional British theatre. They entered into battle with Brookfield's predecessor and the Court became the rallying point for all those who believed, in Shaw's words, that 'Drama is no mere setting up of the camera to nature; it is the presentation in parable of the conflict between man's nature and his environment; in a word, of problem.'

Shaw was an admirer and close friend of Barker and of the thirty-two plays presented during the Vedrenne-Barker reign, eleven were by Shaw, including *Candida, Man and Superman, Major Barbara, The Doctor's Dilemma* and *Captain Brassbound's Conversion*: these five alone would have sufficed most managements for a lifetime. Galsworthy's first play, *The Silver Box* was accepted with an alacrity that astounded the author. Here was a play concerned with social problems, a 'trenchant criticism of the ideas which still govern the relations between the well-to-do and the needy.' Yeats, Laurence Housman, Maurice Hewlett, John Masefield, Maeterlinck and Schnitzler were amongst those given a hearing during the three dazzling years. It is a record worthy to stand beside the George Devine reign of later years: once again the same theatre, removed both geographically and in purpose from the mixture-as-before commercialisation of Shaftesbury Avenue, found a guiding spirit with the courage to explore new horizons. Barker, like Devine, was an actor of subtlety. Unlike Devine he was given an opportunity to put his idealism to the test while still a young man. He was fortunate in having as manager a man of the experience of Vedrenne—too often innovators in the theatre are devoid of any business sense, failing not for any want of imagination but because they don't know the price of the nuts and bolts. Their backer was a wealthy amateur actor, J. H. Leigh, and with Vedrenne watching the budgets the venture not only satisfied those critics perceptive enough to realise they were witnessing a revolution, but also gave Mr. Leigh his money back.

Edith went to the Royalty unaware of this heritage. She was not seeped in theatrical tradition and folk-lore, nor was she a true revolutionary. Poel, one of the first to assume the role of *director* as we know it today, had shown her that it was possible to defy established conventions. Acting came to Edith by instinct, not by formal training. She was flung in at the deep end and once she had recovered from the shock, she swam with confidence, using all manner of techniques to keep afloat, content so long as nobody asked her to leave the water.

'That's where God was so good to me, because he put me in the right company. Not going on tour, not learning a lot of naughty tricks which I would have learnt quicker than anybody. He put me in a first class company with ladies and gentlemen, all speaking good English, all behaving properly, all acting beautifully. Of course I caught it . . . I caught it like the measles. Poor Dennis Eadie used to send messages and say would we not make so much noise. We were always laughing and acting the goat, you know, in the understudy room. . . . Oh, it was a happy time. They were so sweet to me, all of them. I think they thought, this lump's got something in her.'

This is so patently the language of remembered bliss, and I can well imagine the feeling of exultation she must have known, suddenly released from bondage, earning a regular salary which albeit modest was nearly double her wages in the hatshop, accepted by real actors, sponsored by a responsible and well-respected management, and able for the first time in her life to make use of those terrible energies she had for so long kept sublimated. No mention, no thought—and why should there have been? —of gathering war clouds. The theatre isolates its inmates.

There is no Royalty Theatre in Dean Street today: like the old Gaiety it became derelict before the Second World War and later disappeared altogether. It has long been taken for granted by both public and government that the British have never hesitated to neglect or destroy their heritage. Few mourned, few noticed and practically nobody recorded the passing of the old Royalty. It wasn't until that lovely, atmospheric St. James' Theatre felt the crunch of the demolition ball that the public conscience staggered to its feet. Today, as I write, there is a continuing campaign under the banner 'Save London's Theatres'. It is true that after the St. James' affair certain safeguards were written into the planning legislation designed to prevent other theatres suffering the same fate, but like most legislation concerned with culture it was a compromise—that brilliant British invention, a net that can catch the sprats but allow the mackerel to slip through.

Dean Street cuts through Soho like a dirty knife and runs from Oxford Street to Shaftesbury Avenue. Today, like most of Soho, it seems to be inhabited by a stateless population that expects to be forcibly evacuated within the hour. A few respectable establishments struggle to maintain an identity with the old atmosphere of Soho, an atmosphere of cordial sleaziness that persisted from Edith's time until the end of the Second World War. Now the sleaziness is triumphant and the cordiality has vanished, for only the saddest amongst us could find any pleasure in the proliferation of sex shops and strip joints.

The Dean Street of 1913 that Edith discovered forced her 'to see people as they really were.' Her new home had begun as Miss Kelly's Theatre at No. 73 Dean Street. Dickens once acted there in 1845 in a performance of Ben Jonson's *Every Man in His Humour*. Miss Kelly had originally intended it as a school for acting, but it was later enlarged and renamed the New Royalty. Dean Street enjoyed a reputation for theatrical associations until the middle of the twentieth century and includes Mrs. Thrale and Madame Vestris amongst its former inhabitants. An interesting street, constantly changing, giving shelter to painters, thespians and 'characters': totally different from the genteel sameness of the terraced houses in Ebury Street. It was here that she observed, assimilated, stored experience; watching those she admired, taking from them what could best be fitted into her own personality and discarding anything that lacked truth. Nobody told her to do this, she didn't study books on the subject or attend lectures, but she gradually developed a diamond-cutter's eye for knowing where to place the chisel. Dean Street was her Hatton Garden, the place where she collected the uncut stones.

She was twenty-five years old, which is late in life to begin a career in the theatre. 'I had to first of all learn to behave myself. I had no control. Just flew all over the place. I didn't know any better, you see. I had friends who used to say, 'Can't you hold it back a bit? When you come on stage the whole place goes up.' But those character parts I played taught me. That was what was so marvellous. Marvellous, that God should have put me into character parts, because I was going to play the beauties, the lovelies, later.

'I always remember seeing a race. It was one of those military ones, and the horse flew back into the stable. When the race was over he was brought back to the starting point and made to run the race again. No nonsense, you see. I think that's the sort of training you need if you're a person who naturally kicks over the traces. And so many of the young ones did. They had no discipline at all. They didn't come with any discipline, they didn't learn any discipline, they didn't *want* to learn any. So of course they never knew what they were doing. And that's what made me. I made myself accept discipline. I wasn't born with it, I didn't like it, but I accepted it. I had to learn to play all those old girls and I enjoyed them. It was marvellous training, because it taught me to *conserve* . . . Oh, darling Nigel Playfair, he used to say, 'I don't know whether I like it, but there's an awful lot of it.'

In the past twenty years so much emphasis has been placed on methods of acting that completely spurn discipline that Edith's advice to the players will strike many as heresy. She once said: 'I don't know what you *ought* to do, there's no *ought* about it. I did what seemed right to me and that's the only excuse I can make for my acting. I could never be taught how to do it. You see, words weren't words to me, they were people. I had to be the person. That's what Shaw said to me one day. He said, 'You have that quality of turning yourself into the person, and the words then are the person speaking.' I could never recite. I didn't know who I was if I recited. Was I the person in the recitation, or was I me? I always had to be the person and although it got me my living, in a way it was a very great disadvantage. That's why the Almighty never sent me on tour, I think. Anything more marvellous than the way my career was handled by the powers above would be hard to imagine. Whoever would have taken a milliner and put her straight on the stage?'

She remained loyal to Poel and got permission from Vedrenne and Eadie to appear in three performances of a version of the Second Quarto *Hamlet* which Poel produced at the Little Theatre in January 1914. She was reunited with Esme Percy who played the Prince, Edith taking the role of the Queen. It is interesting to note how often at the commencement of her career she was cast in roles better suited to actresses of more mature years. She went back to Poel whenever she could and he constantly gave her unlikely roles, pushing her, it seemed, into a career of male impersonations. In 1919 she played the raffish Knight, Sir Randall, in an Elizabethan curiosity Poel had unearthed called *The Return* and which he presented at the Apothecaries Hall. In May of the following year she was performing Captain Dumain for him in *All's Well That Ends Well* at the Ethical Church, Bayswater. Her companion male impersonator on this occasion was Winifred Oughton who was cast as the other French lord and it is recorded that she and Edith played one of their scenes in a total blackout. Poel certainly commanded dedication from his actors and audiences. Perhaps because he was always struggling, he cared little for his surroundings. I may in ignorance be committing an architectural injustice, but at face value the Ethical Church, Bayswater has a certain depressing ring to it.

During Edith's first season at the Royalty, she was a willing maid of all work. She understudied, she played a variety of character roles and gradually lost all traces of her former life. Her contract was renewed for a further year a few months before the 1914–18 war began. By then she had left Ebury Street and was living at No. 17 Claverton Street in the City of Westminster, a bare mile from her previous home, but much closer to the river.

Her contract now guaranteed that she would receive not less than one hundred and fifty pounds a year. There was a further option for a third year at the management's discretion which would boost her salary to five pounds a week. The management also had the right to close the theatre on Ash Wednesday, Christmas Eve, upon the death of any member of the Royal Family or other reasons beyond their control, and in the event of such closures no salary would be paid.

'We didn't squabble about money then. I thought it was such a lot. I'd never seen so much money in my life and all of it was mine, just for doing what I liked best. I couldn't get over it.'

The letter confirming her second year's employment, signed by Vedrenne, was dated Monday June 8th 1914. It was the start of that magic, burning summer, the last summer of peace.

Actors, as individuals, seldom reflect the times they live in. They do not originate trends, but are mostly forced to follow them. Their personal attitudes are, of course, quite a different matter: the public face they present is determined by forces over which they have no control. In times of war theatregoers seem to demand a certain type of entertainment; playwrights respond and the actor performs; unlike the writer, painter or composer he is in no position, by the very nature of his craft, to be anything other than an interpreter of material supplied by others. These are hardly original observations, but the truth of them is often ignored by historians and actors are frequently criticised for standing outside world events.

The young Edith was not consciously political, though as her lifestyle changed and her horizons widened she was not unaware of the worm within the bud. She lived within the boundaries of the principal battle-field selected by Mrs Pankhurst and her followers, and she must have been concerned at their suffering, but she did not commit herself to the cause. The demands of her new calling were too urgent and exciting to permit of any added involvement: she had chained herself to the theatre.

The Season of 1914 was one of singular brilliance and half the world, as Walter Sickert said, 'dined out for Art'. Theatrically it began with a series of climaxes in April 1914. That month saw Melba singing Mimi in *La Bohème* at Covent Garden, the opening of a memorable new revue called, somewhat prophetically, *The Passing Show*, and the first night of Shaw's *Pygmalion* directed by the author with Sir Herbert Beerbohm Tree as Higgins and Mrs Patrick Campbell as Eliza. (After the final rehearsal and having endured two months of almost constant bickering between Mrs Pat and Tree, Shaw went home to Adelphi Terrace and wrote letters to both of them. His remarkable *Final Orders* epistle to Mrs Pat happily survives, but its counterpart to Tree, which consisted of eight closely written pages of abuse and cheerful insults, was lost to posterity. Perhaps Tree deliberately destroyed it, preferring to let future generations remember his own comment on the letter without distraction from the original. Tree said: 'I'm not saying that insulting letters of eight pages are always written by madmen, but it is a most extraordinary coincidence that madmen always write insulting letters of eight pages.')

The theatregoing tourists who flocked to London that Spring were perhaps made more aware of The Word spoken by Mrs Pat than they were of the external forces shaping their future destinies. They can be excused, for the popular Press, although hypocritically coy about printing the actual word themselves, encouraged a positive avalanche of controversy regarding Eliza's 'Not bloody likely' tag-line, and once the mountain of self-righteousness began to slide there was no stopping it. The boys of the Eton Debating Society, who could not have been total strangers to grosser vulgarities, solemnly considered the motion 'This House Deplores The Debasement And Vulgarization Of The Commercial Theatre'. From the Secretary of the Decency League came the anguished cry, 'Where was the Censor?' With that consummate lack of humour which has so frequently distinguished those elevated to the highest offices of the Church of England, the Bishop of Woolwich told the *Daily Sketch* 'I certainly think The Word should be banned'—an utterance which to those missionaries toiling in the far flung outposts and deprived of current theatrical gossip must have seemed curiously baffling, not to say downright disheartening.

The Silly Season, which arrived earlier than usual that year, thrived on such ludicrous material. Doubtless preparing himself for the more moral task of blessing the war later in the year and not wishing to be outshone by his Brother Woolwich, Bishop Weldon delivered a sermon in more specific terms: 'I dislike vulgarity on the stage. It is not *nice*, for an actress and in particular a married woman with children to have to speak The Word in public.' Alas, Mrs. Pat, a very recently married woman as it happened, did not reply in kind. She was content with the House Full boards and every week took home £130 as her wages of sin. Shaw, at age fifty seven, woke to find himself a legend, while Tree—a richly paradoxical character worthy to trade blows with Shaw—found the enormous acclaim for the play irksome. 'This horrible, relentless success is killing me,' he remarked. 'Oh, damnation to Art.' The Princes of Religion and Theatre had swopped roles.

The continuing furore over Shaw's play threatened at times to obscure other events in the stage calendar.

Removed from the mainstream of theatrical activity, defiantly impoverished and in direct contact with God was another 'first-class Cockney', Lilian Baylis. She remains one of the most improbable figures ever to achieve theatrical immortality and those readers wishing to explore the unvarnished truth of this remarkable lady should turn to Richard Findlater's admirable biography which contains many pleasures. Lilian and Edith were destined to come to each other's rescue in a memorable partnership some eleven years later, but in the months remaining before the outbreak of war, Lilian was almost certainly unaware of Edith's existence. There was little if any cross-pollenisation between the Waterloo Road and the West End, for Charles Kingsley's 1833 description of the Royal Victoria Hall as a 'licensed pit of darkness' still lingered despite the heroic efforts made by Lilian's aunt, Miss Emma Cons, who had leased the building from 1880 until her death in 1912. Handed the flickering flame on her aunt's deathbed, Lilian quickly discovered that it needed to be constantly shielded from the economic winds. 'Theatrical management,' said Shaw, 'is one of the most desperate forms of gambling. You must disturb a man's reason before he will even listen to a proposal to run a playhouse.' Even coming from Shaw's pen the idea of a thirty-nine-year-old spinster running a theatre would have seemed outlandish, yet here was Lilian Baylis, an under-educated woman, a one-time child violinist, to whom Art was 'a kind of medicine dispensed to the poor and needy' daring to attempt it single-handed. She began her reign as she intended to continue: meeting opposition head-on, going down on her knees to God when public indifference to her cause proved too much to keep to herself, as often as not grousing to Him rather than praying—for she was a firm believer that God, like actors, needed a prompt in order to share her vision.

In the Spring of 1914 she had the first of many fights for survival on her hands. Aunt Emma had bequeathed the passion but not the cash and the continued existence of her beloved Royal Victoria—the Old Vic as it had become known—would have been dismissed as hopeless by anybody who relied on orthodox methods. Like many of the generals who were shortly to become household names, Lilian was ill-equipped, relying on her eccentric instincts on an hour to hour, day to day basis. Fortunately for the British theatre her instincts proved superior to those of the Imperial General Staff. We shall return to her in more detail when Edith's path leads to the Waterloo Road a decade later, and I have introduced her here but briefly to illustrate that history, whether it be on a global scale or confined within the narrow boundaries of theatrical prejudice, is seldom if ever tidy. Edith and Lilian, strangers to each other in 1914, were using the same maps. Both owed a debt to Poel, both were pushed towards a career in the theatre by accident, both held less than conventional religious beliefs (Lilian felt that God was on the staff and should always be in when the Half was called). Edith on the other hand found a form of religion that satisfied her *after* she took up a theatrical career. Her well-thumbed copy of Mary Baker Eddy's principal work contains a quotation in Edith's handwriting on the fly-leaf. 'Be not afraid, Take no thought for the body.' It is dated June 26, 1918). Before Poel Edith had been unaware of Shakespeare as a controversial force. Dear Miss Massey had proved he needn't be boring, but it was Poel who opened her eyes. Lilian was a very reluctant convert: her ignorance of Shakespeare was remedied by commercial expediency rather than the sudden discovery and appreciation of his genius. Both, in 1914, were just beginning to relish their liberation, both felt a need to 'rise out of all that was low and sordid and ugly.' One was destined to become the brilliant exponent, the other the brilliant administrator. What they did share, in their ignorance of the more worldly aspects of theatrical life, was the ability to discern and reject the second-rate. Both gravitated towards those who knew. Patriotism brought Ben Greet to Lilian's tattered door and she flung it open for him. Edith found her way to Ellen Terry. They were two originals unhampered by pride, two revolutionaries with old-fashioned ideals, two reactionaries consumed with the need to overthrow the system.

4

'If I could just give God a hand, I'd like my hair to be long. I've also got a slightly crooked eye, but it doesn't notice as much as it did. When I was a girl, I used to wear my hair all on one side to hide it.'

When the war came Edith was playing in *My Lady's Dress* by Edward Knoblock at the Royalty (the author's surname is spelt Knoblauch on the programme in my possession). The cast included Lynn Fontanne—who was born in Woodford, Essex, not in America as is often assumed—Beryl Mercer, Edmund Goulding and the ravishing young Gladys Cooper. Exactly the same age as Edith, Gladys was already launched on her spectacular career and responsible for a flourishing picture-postcard industry, the demand for her photograph being so enormous.

'She was the great leading lady, and of course just imagine seeing somebody as beautiful as that! I nearly went mad. I'd never seen anybody beautiful like that before. I used to stare at her at rehearsals, in the wings, on stage. I couldn't take my eyes off her. I think she thought I was crazy. I'd never seen such beauty in my life. It was long before people made-up a lot, you see. And Gladys' beauty was the real thing—straight out of the bath. Lovely golden hair and beautiful eyes. She always kept those lovely eyes, right to the end.'

(When Edith related this story to me I was much taken with her description 'straight out of the bath.' I remarked that I had never heard such an expression before. 'Well, that's right,' Edith replied. 'You wouldn't have done. I just made it up.')

Edith and Lynn appeared together again later in the year in a revival of Arnold Bennett's and Edward Knoblock's *Milestones*, first produced with success two years previously. Edith played a character role once again, Lynn a juvenile. The revival did not repeat earlier triumphs and Bennett's entry in his Journal for November 5th 1914 notes that Vedrenne intended to close the theatre if he couldn't take £400 a week (present day managements will envy such a modest 'get-out' figure). The run ended on November 28th.

Just as Edith's life had been re-routed by outside forces, now it was

40

Guy's turn. He volunteered for the Army and in due course was commissioned into the Gloucesters. Few of his war-time letters to Edith have survived: such as remain are written in pencil on scraps of odd paper torn from exercise books, and the years have faded them. They reveal that he carried his love for Edith to the trenches and one fragment, written when he had just moved up to the Front Line for the first time, makes it clear that Edith had not forgotten him, for he begins:

> Sweetheart, your almost daily letters have been a great boon in black days at first experience of front line work and I am so grateful to you. If I could but express it to you personally darling . . .

Several times he mentions receiving packages of food and 'other good things' from her.

> The choice was such as only you would make and the 3 that are left thought it all perfect. We were out of water and had only iron rations and whisky to go on with. It took us right out of ourselves.

He wrote very much as R. C. Sherriff was to write in *Journey's End* in later years. Nowadays it has become cynically fashionable to decry the simple Stanhope-type dialogue, so easy to parody by those either too young or too warped to appreciate the attitude of those horrendous times. The promise of greatness denied to so many of Guy's generation was recorded in some of the most poignant poetry in the English language, and when one considers how men existed in the trenches the wonder of it is that they retained any sanity at all. Guy's letters touch upon the sadness of time lost, yet like so many of his generation he somehow managed to refrain from communicating self-pity.

> Oh, you cruel darling, how could you draw such pictures of times we'd have together if youth but might and dared!

We will never know what 'cruel pictures' Edith described in her letters to him, for they did not return from Flanders. There are passages where the countryman that Guy longed to be and was only to achieve in his last years surfaces through the images of war.

> Disturbed some partridges today and if they had only known how pleased I was to see them, they'd have entertained small fears . . . The new line shows up a row of hills a wondrous soft blue in the bright sun today, picked out by captive balloons at intervals. Thank you dearest for each day's charming pick-me-ups and so much for un petit violet. It is now doing its utmost to adorn the face of France in a snug corner of a garden here with some barbed wire to protect it.

Reading these scraps I was constantly struck by the quality of Guy's imagery; his choice of words belong to a born letter-writer, for he obviously wrote as he thought and spoke, making no attempt, as so many people do, to project a false personality on the page. His letters to Edith come so obviously from the heart, with no artifice, no excuses.

The life of a junior officer in the trenches could often be reckoned in mere hours. Guy describes the death of a fellow subaltern, killed beside him the day they moved up to the Front Line.

Poor little chap, he was a merry companion . . . I had slept with his arm under my head, huddled together on the floor of the dugout for warmth and you will know sweetheart how shocked I feel at his loss. For myself a cut and the after effects of the shell shock—about 10 feet separated us—is all I picked up, but I must confess that as I write you, wet to the waist with mud and water, bloodshot eyes and generally shaken and unwashed I feel rather miserable.

In the simple, flat sentences of Guy's scribbled love letters, one can discern the gradual depersonalization of an ordinary young man forced to experience the abyss. There is a sense of sorrow without end, a sense of the 'death of belief' that the generation of 1914–18 suffered. If cynics now find cause for smirking amusement in the triteness of the pencilled emotions trapped on the mud-stained pages, then they are the losers, for in failing to comprehend the causes they also fail to comprehend the effects.

One must carry on from hour to hour and not let the men see one's feelings . . .

He wasn't a product of a public school, nothing in his background had prepared him from birth for such leadership; he was a complete stranger to the responsibility of preparing men for almost certain death. In one letter he mentions that most of his Company had seen far more action than himself and asks:

What would they think of me if they could but look into my mind or interpret the flickering of my eyelids?

He had the courage to reveal himself to Edith.

Do you think me a coward, dear, for feeling as I do? It will be best to let you know it all, that you may form your own judgement accordingly.

This is not the language of cowardice. He did tell her all, often with humour, that gentle private humour that flows between two people in love, and one can read between some of the lines and discern the panic that always overtakes those in love who, although loved in return, are yet fearful of being forgotten.

A parcel has come addressed quite clearly from a 'Mrs' . . . but there, unless you doubt me, I have no idea of the name or supposed name of the sender. Now really Miss Evans, this sort of thing must cease and that instanter. Am I to understand that staying in a small town in certain (or uncertain) circs, the trade folk can only conceive of you to be of married estate?—I like that last—or is it a deliberate, malevolent, not to say libellous attempt upon my present standing and future welfare? Before drawing my own conclusions I shall want your full explanation and withdrawal in at least three 3 halfpenny papers, none of which must be read by either the profesh or the Harmy!

Again I am at your feet with great joy and all the other emotions capable of abbreviation . . . Bless you and may the Gods continue to smile.

Through roseate hues, Yours and all . . . Guy.

Their separate worlds could not have been further apart, for the make-believe atmosphere of the theatre is always intensified in times of war. Governments recognise this and go to great pains to ensure that the troops are entertained in the actual theatres of war, and if one stops to think about this a certain savage irony infiltrates. Those who are about to die are not saluted, but feted with diversions, usually of a nostalgic nature. Places of entertainment usually prosper during such periods; soldiers on leave flock to the timeless unreality of musical comedy, feasting on women who are both desirable and untouchable, remote, brightly painted, beautifully dressed, moving in a world that can be recreated every night. When the next leave comes round, if it comes round, they will still be there, the scenery unchanged, the dialogue identical, a glimpse not so much of paradise but of permanence.

Edith continued her career at the Royalty, building on small roles for which more often than not she was too young, but managements seem to think she was better cast in character parts. Her enthusiasm was such that she accepted everything offered gratefully and without complaint. By July 1916 she was playing a Miss Myrtle in a patriotic offering called *The Man Who Stayed at Home*, an immensely successful piece which satisfied the national fervour for dramas about German spies and the like. (Some of the titles of the period given a authentic taste: *Seven Days Leave*, *The Female Hun*, *By Pigeon Post*, *The Freedom of the Seas* and *Jolly Jack Tar*. The drama of ideas had been submerged by the drama of naked propaganda, which sometimes appeared under the guise of social comment—witness the turgid, flat-footed and almost

43

unactable *Damaged Goods*, only licensed by the Lord Chamberlain because it was deemed expedient in time of war to admit the existence of V.D. It was again revived during the 1939–45 war; between the wars V.D. is put into official cold storage and flourishes accordingly.) *Chu Chin Chow* opened at His Majesty's (Tree was in America at the time) in August 1916 and was still running there when the war ended, becoming not so much a play, more a way of life. On Armistice Day Oscar Asche, the leading man, took his curtain call dressed as John Bull and a white dove of peace was released into the auditorium.

Classical revivals were few. Lilian Baylis, consumed with the desire to keep her frequently mocked head above water, allowed Ben Greet to present his own bowdlerized versions of Shakespeare's plays. The productions were crude and lusty and as the war dragged on casting the male roles became increasingly difficult. Lilian dispensed with such formalities as auditions, taking whatever turned up at her doors and lack of experience never concerned her. By 1918 the Old Vic had become the spiritual home of male impersonators with actresses like Sybil Thorndike and Winifred Oughton playing all manner of gentlemen with apparent gusto. Lilian somehow kept her tattered flag flying through weekly financial crises, air raids and the newly imposed Entertainments Tax (Let the people sing, but by God don't let them sing for free!). Her own legend became more secure than the building she inhabited, for she cursed, cajoled and commanded her way to immortality, demanding as much from her audiences as she did from her underpaid actors. 'I'm ashamed of you all,' she once shouted during a rehearsal that had been interrupted by bombs dropping nearby. The cast had understandably dived for cover. 'If you have to be killed, at least die at your job.'

Luck, which plays such a vital role in the development of any artist and is divorced from merit, came Edith's way again in 1917: luck in the guise of the first lady of the British theatre, Ellen Terry. By the time Edith met her, Ellen Terry was already past her zenith and had published her autobiography *The Story of My Life* in 1908. Like everything else connected with her it bears the imprint of an extraordinary personality, somebody who could not only portray the characters created by others with penetrating insight, but who could also bring that insight to bear upon herself. It is a book of considerable literary merit, far removed from the usual theatrical memoirs, so patently ghosted whatever the fly-leaf purports. In later years the publication of her correspondence with Shaw established her literary talents anew and her old fame as a great actress, cast like others before her into the press-cutting tombs of Fleet Street, was rekindled by her obvious abilities as a writer. Her daughter Edith Craig, in the Preface to a new edition of the autobiography issued four years after her mother's death, gave a most perceptive explanation for the neglect of this aspect of Ellen Terry's genius.

The memoirs of all celebrities who are not professional writers are approached with a certain prejudice. It is considered extremely unlikely that they will have any literary merit, and, such is the power of preconceived notions, when they possess it, it is often not perceived. Critical opinion of the memoirs of actors or actresses is further biased by an old tradition that the greatest of them are stupid outside their own art.

Ellen Terry was by no means stupid, and she was fortunate in that from an early age she met everybody who was anybody, and they were fortunate, as they recorded in print, photographs and paintings, in meeting her. Shaw said that her face had never been seen in the world before, and when we study Julia Cameron's photograph of her taken shortly after her first marriage at age sixteen (posed it should be noted in Tennyson's bathroom) it is impossible not to be ravished by it. Her first husband was the fashionable painter George Frederick Watts and his many portraits of her reveal a beauty puzzled by an innocence she was never given time to enjoy. Lewis Carroll also focused his camera on her, for he was a close friend of the Terry family and given his now closely scrutinised predilection for photographing nymphets, it was not surprising that he was drawn to the four Terry daughters and to Ellen in particular.

The image of innocence denied fits the facts of her early life; she had worked ever since she was a child of five or six. At nine she was acting with Charles Kean's company, at a time when child actors were exploited just as grossly as the more documented child factory workers, often rehearsing fourteen hours at a stretch and then performing after that. Back-stage conditions were, and continue to be, a shabby disgrace and it says much for the tolerance and dedication of actors that in many cases they endure an unpublicised squalor which in other spheres would provoke an immediate outcry. In Ellen Terry's day, when stage illumination was provided by gaslight, the actors must have felt they were inside an oven.

Her early marriage to Watts, a man thirty years older, was, as might have been expected, a disaster, lasting a bare ten months. The alliance was the subject of obscene speculation among some of Watts' friends, for the double-standards of Victorian times—noble attitudes as rigid as any classical statue concealing the sexual worm within—were most prevalent in the fashionable society that Watts aspired to: the maximum opportunity being combined with the maximum hypocrisy. From all accounts Watts, despite his success as a painter, was a self-tortured and somewhat pompous character. In a letter to a titled lady friend just

45

prior to the nuptials he confided that 'to make the poor child what I wish her to be will take a long time, and most likely cost a great deal of trouble, and I shall want the sympathy of all my friends.' The language seems to belong to a bereavement rather than an impending marriage and reveals that Watts, while casting himself in the role of the do-gooder had also learnt the lines for the part of the reluctant seducer. Perhaps he did himself a rare injustice, for two of his biographers are of the opinion that the marriage was never consummated and there is some evidence to suggest he was incapable of normal sexual relations. His self-importance is nowhere better illustrated than in his fervent belief that in marrying the young innocent he was rescuing her from a life of iniquity and bestowing upon her the accolade of becoming Mrs. George Frederick Watts. He convinced himself that the marriage was not so much an emotional necessity but rather a moral duty and openly solicited admiration for the sacrifice he was making.

In a passage suppressed when the Shaw-Terry letters were first published, Ellen reveals the extent of her innocence—a touching anecdote which confounds the then popular image of young actresses as little better than prostitutes. Watts made the first approach at the conclusion of a posing session. 'I'll never forget my first kiss. I made myself such a donkey over it . . . Mr. Watts kissed me in the studio one day, but sweetly and gently, all tenderness and kindness, and then I was what they call 'engaged' to him and all the rest of it, and my people hated it.' The expurgated passage continued later: 'Then I got ill and had to stay at Holland House—and then—he kissed me—*differently*—not much differently but a little and I told no one for a fortnight, but when I was alone with Mother . . . I told her I *must* be married to him *now* because I was going to have a baby!!! *and she* believed me!! Oh, I tell you I thought I knew everything then . . . I was *sure* THAT kiss meant giving me a baby!' (The italics are her own).

This was the child Watts felt compelled to save from a life of debauchery. She cried after the wedding ceremony and true to form as a dedicated artist Watts' first concern was for her future as a now captive model. 'Don't cry,' he told her, 'it makes your nose swell.' She was carted off, without a honeymoon, to become the proxy mistress of Little Holland House, Watts' household being run after, as well as before, his marriage by a formidable lady with the daunting name of Mrs. Thoby Prinsep. Removed from the 'temptations and abominations of the stage' Ellen seems to have been required to pose until she fainted. Watts felt that in bestowing upon her immortality on canvas he had no need to grant more human favours. Even Dickens might have hesitated to invent such a situation, although Mrs Thoby Prinsep could well have stepped straight from his pages.

The amazing thing is that Ellen was not completely broken by the

46

Edith inscribed this to me with the words: 'I was always told I was a plain girl. I don't think so.'

George 'Guy' Booth, Edith's husband. Taken while he was a serving officer in the First World War.

Polly With a Past, St. James's Theatre, 1921 (L to R) Henry Kendall, Noël Coward. Donald Calthrop, Edith, Alice Moffat and Edna Best.

Back to Methuselah, Birmingham Repertory Theatre, 1923. Edith, as the She Ancient, standing to the right of Shaw. On the extreme left Cedric Hardwicke and next to him Barry Jackson. Sitting at Shaw's feet is Gwen Ffrangcon Davies.

Tiger Cats at the Garrick Theatre, 1924. Arthur Wontner disposing of Edith.

Left: Edith as Florence Nightingale in *The Lady With a Lamp*, first produced at the Arts Theatre, London, January 1929.

Right: Orinthia in Shaw's *The Apple Cart*, with Sir Cedric Hardwicke as King Magnus for Sir Barry Jackson's Malvern Festival, August 1929, and subsequently at the Queen's Theatre, London.

Below: Irela in *Evensong* with that gifted actor Wilfrid Lawson in an uncharacteristic pose as the diva's manager. Queen's Theatre, London, June 1932.

The three ages of Edith's Nurse in *Romeo and Juliet*:

Top left: with Katharine Cornell at the Martin Beck Theatre, New York, December, 1934.
Top right: last appearance in the role, Stratford-upon-Avon, 1961.

Below: with Laurence Olivier as Romeo and John Gielgud as Mercutio, New Theatre, 1935. In this production the two actors alternated the roles.

experience. In later years she was able to look back on this bizarre episode without malice. Indeed, she spoke of worshipping her, then, new life 'because of its beauty' and stated that in many ways the marriage was happy. 'I was in Heaven for I knew I was to live with those pictures.' The only thing she shared with her middle-aged husband was an exceptional and individual talent, and it is significant to note that Watts entered into his most productive period of painting at the time of the marriage. Ellen's restless and impetuous nature could not be chained for long and within a year a deed of separation was drawn up whereby Watts agreed to pay his wife £300 annually 'so long as she shall lead a chaste life.' It was a condition which only a man lacking in sensibility could seek to impose and was presumably inserted to make sure his circle of friends would allow him the benefit of his own doubts.

For the ten months they lived under the same roof Ellen had been introduced to some heady company—Gladstone, Disraeli, Mrs. Cameron, Tennyson, Holman Hunt and Browning amongst them—and had taken the first hesitant steps towards her self-education. But the humiliation of failure is real enough whatever the justifications and her return home to her family was a return to familiarity without comfort, and she hated it. 'I hated my life, hated everyone and everything in the world more than at any time before or since.'

There were some redeeming features in Watts' eventual attitude towards his child bride. In later years he became convinced that he had ruined her entire life. He begged her forgiveness. 'If you cannot, keep silence. If you can, one word "yes" will be enough.' She answered him with the one word.

Two years after the marriage had ended she was 'driven back' to the stage by her parents. She had no enthusiasm for the old way of life. This was in 1867 and on the Boxing Day of that year she appeared in Garrick's shortened version of *The Taming of the Shrew*, playing Katharine to the Petruchio of a twenty-nine-year-old actor called Henry Irving. It was their first appearance together and contemporary reviews show no awareness that history was being made. They were not reunited until eleven years later when she joined him at the Lyceum.

There are echoes of Edith in these early years. Like Edith she could not refrain from giggling and larking about off stage and was frequently reprimanded, but at this point in her career she lacked Edith's passionate commitment. She no longer cared whether she acted or not. By her own admission she was more interested in love and life than the theatre. The cause and the measure of her discontent was an architect called Edward Godwin, somebody she had first met and admired as a child. In the summer of 1868 she abandoned family, friends and a career to set up house with Godwin. They decamped to a life of rustic simplicity in a

47

small cottage on Gustard Wood Common in Hertfordshire. She confided in nobody prior to the elopement and if her behaviour towards her family seems callous one must remember the moral strictures of the times. Godwin was a widower, they intended to live in what was quite definitely considered to be a state of sin. She was still legally married to Watts and still in receipt of his annual largesse. Charles was not. In these more permissive times it is difficult to imagine complexity and enormity of the step she and Godwin took. The situation was further complicated by a macabre coincidence. Shortly after her flight the dead body of a young woman—a presumed suicide—was taken from the river. The similarities were sufficient for her father to identify the corpse as Ellen. Her sisters went into mourning. It was only by chance that Ellen learnt of the tragic misunderstanding and rushed back to London to console her distraught parents. Again a Dickensian twist to the plot of her life.

Godwin proved to be her one great love and was the father of her two children. Neither child was baptized during the time Ellen and Godwin lived together. Godwin tired of her after a few years and married another younger girl. They parted, in Gordon Craig's evocative description 'by mutual misunderstanding.' Ellen eventually made a second unfortunate marriage, this time to a soldier-cum-actor named Charles Wardell who used the stage name of Charles Kelly. The children assumed the name Wardell for six years until Ellen had them christened and confirmed as Edith Geraldine Ailsa Craig and Edward Henry Gordon Craig—the surname chosen on an impulse by Ellen because she thought it had a good theatrical ring to it.

Edith's path first crossed Ellen Terry's in 1917 when she received an invitation to appear with Ellen in scenes from *The Merry Wives of Windsor* at the London Coliseum. The first indication Edith had that her talents had been noted by the great lady was when Edy called in person at Claverton Street. 'Darling Edy' as Edith called her, arrived in a brougham with the request that Miss Evans should accompany her to meet mother. Edith set off, as well she might, and was duly ushered into the presence. The discussion soon got round to the question of terms.

'What wages do you want, child?'

'I like my answer nearly as much,' Edith told me. 'I've never had more than five pounds, Miss Terry,' I said.

Miss Terry, no stranger to the financial fantasies of actors, was suitably impressed with Edith's artful honesty.

'I shall give you fifteen and take it off the man.'

(The man in question must, I think, have been Mr. Roy Byford who appeared as Falstaff. Edith later discovered that he was getting twenty pounds a week, but admired Ellen Terry's counter-subterfuge and was well content with her elevation to double figures. 'We played an extra

48

matinee during the run and that week I got seventeen pounds ten. I nearly fainted. That was over fifteen pounds clear, because I paid my dresser two. And all of it mine!')

In the excerpts Ellen played Mistress Page and Edith Mistress Ford, the dramatic interludes coming in the second half of an amazingly divers bill. Appearing with them were Baisen 'The Talking Comedy Cyclist', Pierce and Roslyn 'In A Whirl of Melody', Miss Ina Hill the Operatic Prima Donna in 'Selections from her Repertoire', Cyril Clensy in 'Impersonations', The Delson and Good Trio 'Comedy Acrobats' and perhaps most surprising of all an item called 'The Fringes of The Fleet' —four songs from the work of Rudyard Kipling set to music specially composed by Sir Edward Elgar who conducted in person. The leader of the orchestra—then mostly composed of women—was a Miss Nellie Fulcher, who also acted as deputy conductor when Alfred Dove was absent from the rostrum with gout. Miss Fulcher wrote to Edith in 1961: 'Edith Craig produced and insisted that the fanfares for the entrance of the Doge should last until he had crossed that big stage and was actually seated on the dais. 'Dovey' deputed me to write them for trumpets and trombone and I twice lengthened them to get the timing exactly right. Then one day 'Dovey' took it into his head to conduct the fanfare which took the curtain up for the Doge's entrance. He afterwards said to me— "You've altered this, haven't you?" "Yes," I said, "it wasn't long enough." And he said, "You mustn't pamper these artists like this; he must get across the stage quicker."

'What a delightful Nerissa you were! and not the least attractive feature was the way in which you so unobtrusively and tactfully 'insinuated' the missing word when dear Ellen's memory failed her for a moment! She celebrated her 70th birthday during these weeks at the Coliseum and there was a little ceremony on stage, during which Bransby Williams claimed a kiss which, he said, she had promised him as a boy, if and when he accomplished something or other—I forget what—anyhow he asserted that he had done it and helped himself to the kiss, whereat Ellen was quite taken aback! On this occasion she tipped the orchestra £2.'

The patrons of the Coliseum could hardly complain they weren't getting their money's worth; the cheapest seats were priced at 6d. with tuppence tax added. The Royal Box which held fourteen, could be had for six guineas, with a guinea tax in addition and this included the use of the luxurious retiring room. A copy of the programme which I have before me as I write also lists other mouth-watering prices: dinner at the Criterion or Frascati's was advertised at 5s. 6d., which in today's currency will just about buy two cups of what is generously termed coffee in a motorway drive-in. Ladies were urged to avail themselves of the opportunity to purchase 'The Doreen' Afternoon Gown, combining exclusive style and finest quality crepe-de-chine at $5\frac{1}{2}$ guineas from Peter Robinson's of Oxford Street. Afternoon tea during matinees was served in four separate saloons, cost 8*d.*, and for that you got bread and butter, cake and your own pot of tea. On the inside back cover of the programme a wistful photograph of Miss Gladys Cooper (so famous that she was not named) endorsed the excellent qualities of Messrs Schweppes mineral and Malvern waters.

Later in their association Edy was to remark 'Edith is the only one who can stand up to mother.' And what an enchanting first association it was—Edith and the great Ellen Terry 'on the halls' together; for that is what the engagement amounted to, sandwiching Shakespeare between a talking cyclist and Sir Edward Elgar. Circumstance and then a little patriotic pomp. For Ellen Terry it must have seemed a far cry from her gilded years at the Lyceum with Irving.

They played other dates after the Coliseum and then parted company in Bristol. Ellen Terry scribbled a note in pencil to Edith, and to my experienced eye it looks like the hasty goodwill tokens that actors exchange with each other on the last night of a play before dashing off to catch the train.

Mistress Ford—from Mistress Page—Bristol 14 Dec 1917. Goodbye—for the present at least—'I wish you your heart's desire'

Their separation was short-lived, for less than a month later, on January 3rd 1918 Ellen wrote again, from a temporary address in Dunmow, her London home at that time being 215, King's Road, Chelsea.

Dear Mistress Ford—

Are you at work again? I ask because it is now settled that we do the trial scene (from M of V) at the Coliseum on the 18th February—for 3 weeks and as I told you I could only offer you the tiny part (2 lines!!) of 'Nerissa' with a letter to read thrown in—I don't like to tell you the absolutely tiny salary—but the part only carries the small sum, and there are so many expensive parts—Shylock, Antonio—Bassanio, Gratiano—etc etc and so on. If you have something else in your eye for goodness sake take it, but if not let me know. I hope you are well and jolly and with all my heart I wish you a Happy New Year.
Yours sincerely, Ellen Terry.

(The handwriting for this, like all the other notes to Edith in my possession, was bold. Ellen Terry appears to have used a heavy black crayon and some of the words seem formed from brush strokes rather than by a pen. They were not letters anybody could ignore.)

It is interesting to speculate as to the extent of the influence Ellen Terry had on Edith. Some legends are a disappointment to meet in the flesh, some actually repel. It is safe to say that Edith was not dis-illusioned. Although Ellen Terry was past her prime as an actress when she and Edith met, she was by no means a burnt out case. Her memory was not what it had been—the classic nightmare of any actor of advanced years, and indeed of some of less advanced years—and she was sometimes forced to write out her parts on pieces of paper and pin them up at strategic points around the stage. Again Ellen differed from Edith in that she was never consumed with a reverence for an author's text. Her son has told us that she was not above rewriting her lines when it suited her, and even accorded Shaw this treatment in *Captain Brass-bound's Conversion* which must have tested his adoration.

A great actress forced by economic circumstances, or simply because she cannot bear to relinquish a lifetime's dedication, to continue beyond the point of no return is always a sad sight. Not that I am for one moment suggesting that in 1918 Ellen Terry belonged to a geriatric chorus line, but when she and Edith worked together in what was, bluntly, a semi-music-hall turn, she was undoubtedly past her prime. In a sense her career had come full circle, for her serious theatrical legend can be said to have started with her portrayal of Portia in the Bancrofts' production of *The Merchant* in 1875. The undertaking was a failure for the Bancrofts, but Ellen's performance set the town buzzing. Her last appearance on any stage with Irving was also as Portia when they were reunited at Drury Lane on 14th July 1903 for a charity benefit. Now, as the Great War entered its final year, she completed the circle with scenes from *The Merchant* in London and subsequently in provincial music halls. Obviously she still had charisma and to the end she never lost her hold on the public imagination. Her needs were, happily, not financial. Although not a rich woman, she was nevertheless well off by the standards of the profession, for actors do not, by and large, die rich. She was seventy when she acted with Edith and there are few professions which allow their giants to go on performing at that age. (I would like to think that most surgeons are lecturing to students rather than wielding a shaky knife at seventy; and in a sense that is what Ellen Terry did in her remaining years; she gave a series of illustrated lectures, illuminated every so often with those shafts of inspiration that had distinguished her original interpretations.)

I believe that what Edith took from Ellen Terry was moral strength. I think she sifted through the sacred and profane remains of a once unique talent and found there materials she could graft onto her own life and career. In forging her own legend, Edith was able to build upon the foundations laid down by Ellen Terry. Until they met the major influences in Edith's life had all been men. Now she was suddenly con-fronted with the example of a member of her own sex who had sur-mounted all: unhappy marriages, scandals, personal tragedies; who had

51

become synonymous with beauty and success and who retained to the last a dignity that routed her critics, few though they were, and continued to confound her many admirers. She was not a private person like Edith, her personality was more theatrical, her emotional gestures more flamboyant. She painted the canvas of her life with bold and confident strokes.

Edith was in awe of her, and for the best reasons. The offer of two lines and a tiny salary was hardly irresistible: there had to be something else, and that something else was the personality of Ellen Terry, courage allied to audacity. In one letter Ellen Terry wrote to Edith during this period she talks of being crippled with neuritis which was 'eating up' her right arm. Edith accepted the pittance of a salary without too much hesitation, for the deal was concluded by 17th January. Even so it would appear that she was kept waiting for her last salary cheque. Writing from Chelsea on 12th March, Ellen Terry apologised to:

My Dear Nerissa,

Here at last is the *remainder* I owed you of your small cheque.
Yrs affectionately
Ellen Portia.

I found only one other letter, undated and penned from an address in St. Martin's Lane this time. In it Ellen said how delighted she was to see from the papers how Edith was 'going it'. That and a torn piece of ordinary brown wrapping paper with the words 'Miss Edith Evans with love from E.T.' Fragments of an impulsive, warm and altogether fascinating woman, who was obviously drawn to Edith and whom Edith revered.

Edith was to remember their brief time together for the rest of her days; having seen what the course could be, she commenced her own marathon. When Edith reached seventy she was still in full possession of her own remarkable gifts (she was appearing as Mrs. St. Maugham in *The Chalk Garden* and her film career was only just beginning). They both shared a love of work, and in Edith's case the dedication was complete and without compromise. Her eventual marriage to Guy produced no children and unlike Ellen Terry she resisted all pleas to tell the story of her life. For Edith there was nothing but the theatre, sixty years of uninterrupted work; no deviations from a career that came to her by chance but, once embarked upon, was embraced with a dedication that is perhaps unparalleled.

5

'I can't imagine going on when there are no more expectations'

Guy survived the war. Like so many of his generation who, young in 1914, returned middle-aged by the experience, he found it was not only a long way to Tipperary, but an even longer way back to the life he had left behind. Being a civilian again was unreal. The fear of death had been lifted from them, but the fear of 'the long littleness of life' remained and for many it was more potent than the familiarity with and eventual contempt for the black angel of the trenches. The soldiers came back speaking another language and they were quickly made aware of that core of disillusion contained within any victory. Those who came back in 1919 were rightly derisive of any touch of rhetoric for they were conscious that they had been 'the unwilling led by the unqualified to do the unnecessary for the ungrateful'. The currency of life in the trenches was valueless in the post-war world; it could not redeem the past nor buy the future.

None of Edith's letters to Guy during and immediately after the war have been found, possibly he destroyed them by choice, not wishing to hoard any trace of those four wasted years. Edith told me that she found him changed, unsettled, lacking concentration, his previous sense of humour scarred. She described it as being like a tree that still stands proudly, but the bark has been damaged wantonly. 'Some of the sap had bled,' she said. His whole outlook on life had undergone a profound metamorphosis; there was no question of him meekly accepting a lifetime of sedentary compliance behind the ledgers at Woollands. He had not only to wrestle with his own destiny, but to come to terms with a greatly changed Edith. Their love had survived the war, but he was no longer the dominant partner. The world Edith now moved in with ever-increasing confidence was a world he could never fully share—not because Edith wanted deliberately to exclude him—far from it, she was always concerned to ask his guidance—but because he was like a child who has missed many terms at school through illness and who, when he finally rejoins the class finds himself unable to decipher the changed codes of conduct that have sprung up in his absence. The comradeship of the trenches could have nothing in common with the isolated friendships that exist in the theatre. The girl he had loved and left was now a woman with a separate existence of her own. He was amazed by her, proud of her, perhaps even a little frightened of her and the world she was willing to share with him was more alien than anything he had imagined.

The old order of things had gone forever. Guy felt, like Richard Aldington, that he was one of the old men—'some of us nearly forty'— who could only anticipate the title of Robert Graves' classic auto-biography and wish for goodbye to all that. He felt deeply: his letters reveal that, and he had a poet's instinct and a poet's way with words. Politically, he started to move away from the old shibboleths, for the sense of injustice was rising to the surface in him as in so many others who returned to find that nothing had really changed and would not change unless they caused it so.

Edith had gone to France—her first trip abroad—a few weeks before the war ended. Under the auspices of the Y.M.C.A. Lena Ashwell ran a repertory company in Le Havre. The manager and resident producer was a Mrs. Penelope Wheeler and plays were presented for members of the British Expeditionary Force on leave or in transit camp. Edith had appeared in a three act play by Githa Sowerby called *Rutherford and Son* with that fine actor Herbert Lomas in the leading role. The cast was a mixture of civilian and army personnel and the programme denotes that Captain Millar, Private Grosvenor North and Sergeant Baker took part. Lomas produced on this occasion. He was a very simple man and immensely gifted, and because he was tall, naturally nicknamed 'Tiny'.

He wrote to Edith after she had returned to England and I quote a section of that letter to show that she affected him as she affected so many: she may not have been born with Gladys Cooper's looks but she 'had something' as she said.

> . . . Havre is very dull and the time drags wearily. But the sea is still here and that light is still going round. Thanks to you I retain delightful memories, for which I am very grateful.
> The few minutes that I have been associated with you, for it only seems a few minutes, has made a deep impression on me, and it's a better 'little feller' I am in consequence.
> With Love to you and abundant happiness now and all time.
> Gratefully yours for Ever,
> Tiny.

I introduce this passage into the text without thought of innuendo, but because, putting myself in Guy's shoes for a moment, this is the sort of instant friendship that the theatre spawns and which outsiders find impossible to understand. The backstage language employed by actors is not necessarily insincere by virtue of its flamboyance; I believe it is used to bridge the gap between reality and make-believe. It is always difficult, though by no means impossible, to sustain a relationship between two people, one of whom is in the theatre and one outside. It is doubtless easier if the outsider knows from the beginning what he or she is taking on, but in Guy's case he fell in love with a milliner, not an actress. He was not even present during the transition. It would have been difficult enough for him to have returned to the status quo. Life cannot be changed with the ease of a slide projector: now a picture of horror, next a picture of peace. Even if he had come home to find his milliner as he left her, they had lost four years.

Guy was a quite remarkable man, for he somehow surmounted these multiple difficulties. He had enough compassion left to understand Edith, the changed Edith, Edith the stranger. Their relationship was never conventional and the mistake would be to smother their unconventionality in bogus sentiment. They were both realistic about their separate and joint lives: Edith was searching to release the truth she now sensed was within her reach, and Guy was intelligent enough to know that he would never forgive himself if he thwarted that truth. The fact that they loved each other made it more rather than less difficult. It was not a change of heart that separated them again but a change of circumstances.

Neither Guy nor Edith seemed to set much store by marriage at this watershed in their lives. Perhaps his pride in her success, which never faltered and which never ceased to thrill him, hardened his resolve to prove himself in *her* eyes. He rejected his old life and although his years in the Army had robbed him of his youth, something had been given in exchange. Balancing the ledger he could read with such a practised eye was an item carried forward: goodwill. As an officer he had been introduced to another section of society—not the caricatured world of the Blimps, for the life of a junior infantry officer in the trenches bore no resemblance to that—where men not unlike himself questioned the purpose of life whilst living in the closest proximity with death. Friendships were made, bonds were forged and promises exchanged. Guy redeemed one of those promises and from contacts made in the trenches he found his own escape route. He took the decision to turn his back on England and try his luck abroad. I do not believe that this was the self-sacrificing gesture so frequently used by novelists of the old school, although all the ingredients were there. Edith told me it was a decision they took together. Again it would be a mistake to imagine that, like so many others in the same situation, they opted for a trial separation designed to settle the outcome once and for all. This was not the plot they invented for themselves.

Dearest Wife of mine,

Help me to stick up my head and find a way to success, a success which is going to be a hard fight to obtain and establish.

Let me think of you giving up to me a few moments each day, not to being unhappy but rather in a strong impetus towards better work and firmer hope: this will be of great assistance and bring us so close to each other in all we do. My sympathy and love you know are all yours and I feel no lack of yours—it just wells up to me through your letters and for the time I feel like a king, one who has found the greatest Thing of all.

This letter was written from the British Controlled Oilfields in Maracaibo, Venezuela, his final destination. He had arrived there in December 1919 after a sea and land journey which, en route, took him to the United States for the first time. He had found 'Lil Ole Noo Yoick' amazing, although he noted that

... the Pankhurst Comm. has so put the wind up the youth of N.Y. that a girl never looks at a boy and the gentle art of 'clicking' is unknown.

Writing again soon after his arrival in Maracaibo, anxious to set down his first impressions and share them with Edith, he pronounced them

... very favourable. Once they learn you are Inglesia and not Americano they are charming and tender all kinds of help ... On being introduced to a local magnate I was informed that his house, wife and family were mine, but so far I have not ventured to collect the goods!

Really it was all very charming, the only fly in the social ointment the presence of large numbers of large Boches, who sat in a circle in the coolest balcony of the club where we had been put up, a baron at the head, the rest according to rank, talking shop as has been their practice for the past 29 years.

What a race!

This was the recent soldier writing, suddenly reminded of all he wished to put behind him. The 'Dearest wife' he wrote to was appearing as Nerissa again, this time in J. B. Fagan's stylish revival at the Court. There were forty-two theatres open in London in December 1919, but little that was new or notable on view. Shaw, still in the shadows because of his unpopular stand during the war, was represented by a revival of *Arms and The Man* (and I find irony in that) which Robert Loraine was presenting. There was the annual production of *Peter Pan*, of course, and nine musicals, including *Chu Chin Chow* in its fourth year and *The Maid of The Mountains*. Maugham had *Home and Beauty* running, a moderate farce by his standards and there was something called *Lord*

Richard In The Pantry which as the title suggests was a long way from Ibsen. Arnold Bennett who, on the day after the Armistice was capable of writing in his Journal 'Raining now. An excellent thing to damp hysteria and Bolshevism'—an entry which does much to explain why Guy and others found little they could relate to in post-war London—had dramatised an old novel, *Sacred and Profane Love*, an enterprise which did little for his reputation although he made money from it.

The quality of mercy dished out to Guy and Edith by fate was of a curious variety. In charting the course of their love story I am conscious of the need to employ the same honesty in the unfolding of it as they both brought to the living of it. Their was no smugness in their relationship, a great deal of self-inflicted sadness and from time to time a hint of pathos which even their united resolve could not keep hidden. That they managed to sustain their love for each other at such a distance and for so long a period is unusual enough—absence has been known to weaken the heart—but the unlikely happy ending of two childhood sweethearts finally coming together and finding true happiness (and I use trite language to make my point) did in fact take place. What fascinates me is the *consistency* of their feelings for each other when, by the book, they should have drifted further and further apart. The plot of the unknown young milliner who achieved fame and went on to be considered the greatest actress of her generation is in itself sufficient to satisfy most romantic tastes, yet when one adds to this the war hero who departs his native shores to seek his fortune abroad, the structure is in danger of collapsing from the sheer weight of improbability.

Edith and Guy, though 'queerly undeveloped' before the war came, had both changed by the time the war ended. They had become lovers before Guy departed for Maracaibo. When Edith made this admission to me with gentle honesty I asked her whether this development had made their decision to go their separate ways that much harder. 'Well, it certainly didn't make it any easier,' she said. 'But, you see, what we felt for each other, the love that flowed between us wasn't like other people, I don't think. It's all a long time ago now, and while one doesn't forget dates, one forgets emotions. Guy didn't want to hold me back, and I wanted him to find himself. It was the war, you see, the war did terrible things to men, terrible. You couldn't expect . . . You didn't have the right to think that everything could be exactly the same after that. I don't know who was to blame, if anybody was to blame . . . We just loved each other. Perhaps not wisely, all the time.'

There is a gentle simplicity of language in Guy's letters to her of this period immediately after their separation.

Lordy, Lordy, how I miss you. Yes, my sweet you must permit me to let rip just this once and I'll promise to be good hereafter. My vanity and pride all melt when each hour I think of you, and the struggling waggon driver can only just discern the star to which he has hitched all for the future. I live on one letter for about three days then I have to call up the reserves and re-read all to get back my pluck and carry on.

This is selfish and weak and ungrateful so be assured that I can still say my thanks to the Gods for your love, and all that you have brought to me, and help me to stand for. My best thoughts live with you, all my loyal regard and delight in your art and the spirit you interpret each night is with you during each appearance each new venture, and much more all my warmest love is for the dear girl who, despite of all, trusts me to be her man, accepts as her lover and Husband.

He typed this letter because he was in a hurry to catch the mail boat, but the word 'Husband' was written in ink. Some of the phrases he used are food for parody, fifty years after the event: Lordy, Lordy, To let rip, Get back my pluck—it is easy to smile whilst forgetting that each generation provides material for the next generation to ridicule. I find them touching, just as I find his confessions of weakness touching. Alas those return letters from Edith he lived on for three days at a time are lost to us. (I retained hope of their discovery until a few weeks before this book went to press, but every trail proved false. Their absence is a great disappointment which Edith shared with me.)

Whatever temptations Guy resisted during his long stay in Maracaibo (and it would be presumptuous of me to allege that he had none to resist and equally presumptuous to ignore the possibility that he did not resist all, for he was a passionate man and it is doubtful that he inclined towards total celibacy), these were paralleled by the temptations that growing fame introduced to Edith.

By 1920 a great number of influential critics and writers were becoming increasingly aware of her as an actress and as a woman. She was no stranger to compliments, both public and private. Because she was working consistently, going from job to job with hardly a pause, enjoying herself no end, she became emancipated both in her personal and professional lives. 'I lived the life of old Riley,' was an expression she used. She loved dancing and confessed that she had always had a secret desire to shine as a tap dancer. Her home life was still simple and she cared little for current fashions; good taste, yes, but nothing avant garde—her conversion to high fashion came much later in life. Against the high jinks she was capable of and delighted in, we must set her curiosity towards Christian Science. It was not a subject she would ever discuss in great detail, but she believed in the Christian Science teachings most passionately. I am not qualified to evaluate her personal interpretations of that particular religion, but there were some members of her circle who felt that she strayed from the chosen path. In religion, as in so many other things, Edith's beliefs were never conventional. There was something paradoxical in her very nature and she applied it to all things.

In the sullen aftermath of the war which was to lead to the General Strike of 1926, the theatre underwent many subtle changes. The style of acting was changing, easing its way towards a quieter, more naturalistic approach which, in turn, demanded a different type of play for the performers. That dedicated and sometimes under estimated chronicler of the theatre, J. C. Trewin, describes this period of transition with characteristically informed humour. 'It became the most infamous of sins to be "ham", though users of the word often had no idea what they were condemning. It was simply bad form to attack, to lash out, to plaster the gallery wall, to do anything that might win reproach as "theatrical", or might allow an audience to understand that you were acting. Yet two players, Sybil Thorndike and Edith Evans, who conquered the theatre of the twenties, used a method that was against all fashion.'

Shaw, who had not given the world a full-length play since *Pygmalion*, anticipated the changes and was ready for them. During the war years, in addition to a constant stream of journalism, most of which was ill received because of the unpopular sentiments he wished to propagate, he had been working on two major plays—*Heartbreak House* and the mammoth *Back to Methuselah*. Both of these translated his 'notes from the madhouse'—his deeply-felt aversion to everything about the war— into dramatic form. In *Heartbreak House* he moved in his own way towards the Tchehovian technique. He felt it to be his greatest play and although it was published in 1919 he had to wait until 1921 before it was performed in England. At first he was content to describe it as 'a fantasia in the Russian manner upon English themes' but in later years he identified it as his *Lear* and there is no doubt that the play has more affinity with Shakespeare than with Tchehov despite surface appearances to the contrary.

The 1921 production took place at his old address, the Court Theatre, and the reviews were condescending when they weren't downright abusive. Edith created the role of Lady Utterword for English audiences. It was her first chance at a major character in a contemporary play by a great dramatist, and the first time she had any contact with Shaw. She fared better than the author, for whereas the play was variously described as 'a private lunatic asylum with many patients and no keeper', 'Jawbreak House', 'an overwhelming ordeal', Edith was acclaimed. Her 'captivating' Lady Utterword was, in the words of one critic, 'even as Miss Ellen Terry might have been in her prime' which, to Edith, must have been praise indeed. She was talked of as 'one of the few actresses on the English stage who can act'—a statement I am sure Edith, with her sense of proportion in everything, thought absurd even though flattering—'astonishing in the range of her powers and the complete absorption of her personality' and 'one of the wonders of the evening.' St. John Ervine, on the other hand, writing in the *Observer* failed to mention her at all, which is curious for a few years later he was professing an unrequited love for her in private and writing paeans for public consumption. During the course of his long and pithy review he took his friend Shaw to task, laying down Ervine's Absolute Law that a Bernard Shaw play 'must be acted as swiftly as Mr. Shaw thinks. "Speed, in the name of the Lord, speed", as Henley sang after Lord Northcliffe had taken him for a motor-drive.' But of Miss Evans he made no mention.

The play was a failure in London and Shaw for once stepped out of character and allowed his mortification to be seen. He had been a pungent critic himself, but even he could not shrug off the damning reviews and the indifference of the general public. He was no stranger to attack from many quarters at once, but to have what he consistently believed to be his greatest dramatic work abused in terms such as 'As a play of course, it is about the worst there ever was', 'four hours of it if we were quiet and possibly five if we dared to laugh or applaud', eroded his usual fortitude.

For Edith, on the other hand, it was the beginning of a new and important friendship, and if her relationship with Shaw was never to climb to the same heights as enjoyed by Mrs. Pat and Ellen Terry, it was yet a rewarding experience for both of them. Edith was intrigued by him, was willing to be instructed by him and anxious to serve him as an actress, but was never taken in by his undoubted personal charm which, with women in particular, he blatantly employed to get his own way. He flirted with her and enjoyed her company and in recounting certain episodes to me Edith remembered him with affection. 'He kissed me once,' she said. There was a long pause. 'But I derived no *benefit* from it' —choosing and delivering the line like a young Daphne Laureola. She remembered him best for the advice he gave her. 'He gave a lot of advice. Some people resented it. I didn't. He was a born *ad-vise-er*. You see, I've never tricked an audience in my life. If I can't do it truthfully, then I don't do it at all,' she said. 'Because Shaw once told me, "You're not worth ten pounds a week in a mechanical play, because the minute you come on we see all the works. You don't mean to show them, but you can't help it'. And he was right, you know. He was always right about actors, though not always right about his own plays.'

They were not to work together again until two years later, in 1923, when *Back to Methuselah* finally gained its first British production at the

Repertory Theatre, Birmingham.

In the interim Edith consolidated her position, an anonymous profile-writer in *Time and Tide* putting it thus: . . . whether you find her personality pleasing, or repellent, she compels your attention . . . She comes 'with fan spread and streamers out', sometimes flamboyant and bouncing, with superb self-confidence. There are no half-tones, timidities, little awkward gestures. She appears certain of her effect, of her charm and her ability, in love with herself and the audience . . . She has nothing in common with the modern intellectual actress, as, for example, Cathleen Nesbitt. She is more akin to Mrs. Patrick Campbell, but whether she will ever achieve the fame of Mrs. Campbell is uncertain. She has, too, very marked peculiarities of face and voice . . . a flamboyant person with a beautiful and supple figure, a curious, irregular, rather heavy face, with prominent eyes and heavy lids, and a full, well-shaped mouth; altogether a boisterous, rather overpowering individual . . . without being a beauty, she can look striking and oddly attractive. Her greatest singularity is her voice . . . She is now—if one may believe the Press, which has well nigh lost its head over her—the greatest English actress of comedy.

Edith said, 'I can understand people, if they like what I do, being pleased to see me perhaps, but I never can understand why anybody should ever be in awe of me, because I think I'm such an ordinary person. I'd have to be much grander than I am to be in awe of me. Much. I've never understood it. It's nothing to do with me at all. That's what God gave me and I can't tell about that.

'I could manage beauty. Yes, I jolly well saw to that . . . and dresses and things. All that. But I would never play a part if it depended entirely on absolute physical beauty. Because that I couldn't do. I could *as-sume* beauty and did very often. My face took the paint well. I'm not talking about charm. I'm not talking about fascination. I'm talking about pure physical beauty, the sort of thing Coral Browne has—lovely features, lovely style, everything about her excellent. Cathleen Nesbitt's another very beautiful woman, and Gladys was, of course, and Dorothy Dickson. All right, I never attempted to do anything they did. But I had my own little nonsense, if you know what I mean. I'm quite accustomed to people saying 'Oh, you look so beautiful on stage'. That's all right . . . yes, I arranged that. I meant to look beautiful . . . but . . . don't kid yourself!'

She rather scoffed at the idea of being a 'great' actress; she didn't like being put into quotes. 'I sometimes think when I'm on the stage "What do they mean? Is this great, what I'm doing now?"'

I was also fascinated to learn that she never saw herself as a tragedienne or wanted to play in tragedy because she did not really believe in it. She thought it was a lovely form, but that it was not true. Predictably she was asked to play Lady Macbeth several times during her career, but always refused. 'Don't think much of her,' she said. 'She's not complete, I can't play people who are only half-finished. Shakespeare never finished her.' She never elaborated on subjects that she had considered and dismissed; she stated her opinion and that was that. One old friend, Muriel Adams, to whom I am indebted for many items of interest concerning Edith, advanced the theory that Edith's attitude towards tragedy was in some way related to her religion. It is a supposition worthy of serious consideration: tragedy, the misfortunes of friends, death, made her unsettled, edgy. She said she cared too much about everything.

Edith and Cathleen Nesbitt had shared a dressing room at the Court during the run of *The Merchant* and Miss Nesbitt has since noted in her autobiography that she felt Edith was too much for the role of Nerissa, and tells an anecdote she remembers from their tea-parties in between the matinees and the evening shows. Edith had told Cathleen and Nigel Playfair that if she wasn't a star by the time she was forty (she was then thirty one) she would give up the stage and try something else. After she left the dressing room Playfair turned to Cathleen: 'Star?' he said. 'Poor girl, poor girl, what a hope.'

He had to eat his own words within a few years. I find the story intriguing not because Playfair was so hopelessly wrong, but because of what it reveals of Edith's character. A few years before the incident she had no thought of a stage career, and yet here she is giving herself a time limit to achieve stardom. The revelation strengthens my conviction that the girl Guy returned to in 1919 bore no resemblance to the girl Poel discovered and Guy first fell in love with. She had learnt to take care of herself and if she had illusions she had also calculated the exact moment when she would kill them.

As far as the purely commercial theatre was concerned Edith can be said to have arrived with her performance as Kate Harding, a domestic servant, in Roland Pertwee's *I Serve* which opened at the Kingsway Theatre in September 1922. The *Illustrated London News* critic remarked that 'when she came on there was hardly a hand; when she finished there was an ovation which betokened a reputation made.'

James Agate confessed that he only attended the play 'for fun' one afternoon, and took his seat in a non-professional capacity in the sparsely-filled pit. 'I had no programme and knew nothing of play or cast. A forebodingly comic plumber was mending a grate, while a maidservant—arch and coy, I felt sure, as soon as she should turn round was 'answering the door' upstage. (I have a rooted dislike to plays which begin like this.) Suddenly my heart gave a great leap; I recognised that the actress was Miss Edith Evans. From that moment this exquisite player held not only me but all that handful of an audience in thrall . . . I have always found it difficult to keep my admiration of Miss Evans within reasonable bounds. Her catty old ladies were creations after the heart of Louis Wain; her Cleopatra according to Dryden was a Lely, her young woman in *Heartbreak House* a Sargent. Her Kate is the most finished piece of acting on the London stage today. . . . It is the portrait of a great artist who possesses the gift of observation, a fine sense of comedy and the pathos of Mrs Kendal. The end of the play found the little house in tears, with one exception. I had shed all mine in earlier acts, in sheer joy at so much beauty and felicity.'

You can't, as they say, have much better than that! Herbert Farjeon, who with his sister Eleanor was to become dear friends later on, headed his notice OUR BEST ACTRESS? then reprinted it the following day with the question mark removed (Ah that our present day critics were allowed such luxuries of space!) Farjeon also sent her a bold gypsy's warning.

THE WEST END
IS A DANGEROUS PLACE FOR ACTRESSES WITH A VIRGIN
GENIUS. MISS EVANS MUST REGARD IT AS AN ENEMY TO
FIGHT AND CONQUER AND SHE MUST SUSPECT NOTHING MORE
THAN SUCCESS.
IT MAY BE A FINE FEELING TO SIT ON A THRONE—BUT NOT
WITH GYVES ON YOUR WRISTS.
                                                —Herbert Farjeon.

The other performances that Agate referred to had been given in a rag-bag collection of plays, ranging from *The Witch of Edmonton*, *Out to Win* (also written by Pertwee in collaboration with Dion Clayton Calthrop), *The Wheel* by James Bernard Fagan and Dryden's *All For Love*. She had also appeared with the young Noël Coward in *Polly With a Past* by George Middleton and Guy Bolton—Edith 'greying-up' for a character role and Noël playing a juvenile lead. I have unearthed a photograph which shows Noël complete with white trousers and tennis shoes holding hands with Henry Kendall while Edith, Donald Calthrop and Alice Moffat react to a piece of over-acting from Edna Best. Noël's latest biographer, Cole Lesley, relates how Edith and Noël would walk home from the St. James' Theatre together discussing their future careers. When I asked Edith to elaborate on this she was vague on the subject: 'Perhaps we did, I can't remember'.

Agate praised her in *I Serve*, others were not so enthusiastic, finding her 'not always convincing' 'she has a showy part and plays it showily, without conviction'. The upshot of it all was that the play was withdrawn after a run of just over two weeks. This was doubtless heartbreaking for Mr. Pertwee but fortunate for Edith, since there is nothing more calculated quickly to advance an actor's career than a personal triumph in a play that flops. It means that while the praise is still fresh in the minds of those who count, the actor is immediately available for something else. To be a success in something that runs forever may be of comfort to one's bank manager, but more times than is healthy, it blights a career.

By November of 1922 she was at the Globe playing Cynthia Dell in *The Laughing Lady* by Alfred Sutro. Again Edith was singled out in a cast that included Marie Löhr, Violet Vanbrugh, Henrietta Watson and Godfrey Tearle, the *Evening Standard* predicting that 'Miss Edith Evans, who one of these days, with her astonishing intelligence and versatility, will be a star with a theatre all to herself' and added that she was the only player called for by name when the curtain came down. *Punch* felt that Mr. Sutro had treated her well and that she had repaid him with interest and 'her unfailing sureness of technique'. A visiting French critic, a M. Raymond Recouly, was given unlimited space in the *Manchester Guardian*; having shown that he was a much travelled man of the world by comparing Sutro's play to a little known river in the extreme South of Algeria called the Zousfana, he went on to pronounce Edith 'above all a mistress of the *sous-entendu*: what she does not say, what she implies by intonation, a movement of the head or a gesture, becomes by virtue of this gift far more important than what she says.' A notice guaranteed to enchant Mr. Sutro.

Did Edith heed Farjeon's advice and suspect nothing more than success? I suspect she did. Most contemporary readers, denied from ever having seen Edith when her star was rising, knowing only *Dame* Edith Evans (the honours title that women are saddled with and which could only have been the invention of a man) are perhaps dubious that there was ever a bright young thing using the simple name Edith Evans. A study of the press-cuttings that fell thick and fast in the twenties would convince them otherwise, for the young Edith was treated as the Press has always treated actors in the ascent: she was asked her opinion on a variety of subjects beyond her ken, and having given an opinion, mocked for it. She was photographed, cartooned, profiled, dissected, praised and criticised—not by the dramatic correspondents, but mostly by diary and gossip columnists.

'Since', said I, as I sat down, and Miss Evans continued to apply the local colour, 'I have seen you at your incomparable best in *I Serve* I shall not mind the deception of make-up seen too near.' Notice the subtlety. The technique is to get into the dressing room by invitation, start with praise, and then imply that the subject of the interview needs every artifice of Messrs Leichner, the well-known makers of theatrical cosmetics. This from the diary correspondent of *The Pall Mall Gazette*.

A. Esdaile Macgregor, writing in the *Evening News* had another approach. He (or she) tried to draw Edith out on the subject of 'other actresses'. This is known as the Comparison Gambit in the trade and is a much-used trap by the poachers of privacy. 'I mentioned a young actress whom she had not seen, and said 'I am afraid that when her youth and beauty go there will not be much left' 'Unless something happens to her,' added Miss Evans. She did not explain what she meant, but I gathered that at some time Miss Evans had a new vision of what essentially matters in life and art, had summoned all her powers to realise and express it, and meant to hint that without some such vision an artist must miss lasting success.'

It is revealing to note how Edith's polite and simple reply has become meaningless conjecture in the hands of Mr. Esdaile Macgregor.

In February 1923 Edith appeared in a comedy of Welsh village life, *Taffy*, at the Prince of Wales Theatre. The author was Caradoc Evans (no relation) and the play was presented at a special single performance on a Monday afternoon. It aroused mixed feelings of a nationalistic and political nature and the matinee was punctuated by fervent protests from the supporters of Lloyd George and the counter applause of the author's friends. The *Morning Post* critic, in sardonic vein, noted that 'Mr. Evans' characters were a mass of mud from head to foot before he finally let the long-suffering audience out of the theatre. We believe the performance was public. If so, some of his dialogue was in the worst taste, and a gratuitous insult to those to whom holy things are holy, and not blatant hypocrisy.'

The correspondent of the *Sporting Times*, writing well below the belt, stated that if he had been a Welshman on this occasion he would have gone out and stolen a brick ('Stolen it, mark you,' he emphasised) and heaved it at the author. He was of the opinion that a riot was only prevented by 'the superb self-possession and finished artistry of Edith Evans.' Like others before and since, the *Daily Sketch* critic made the wrong assumptions as to Edith's origins. 'That brilliant person, Edith Evans, who is, I suppose, Welsh, has never done anything that isn't perfect and her emotional scenes are a revelation.'

Edith learnt from these early skirmishes and retreated—becoming, over the years, the most private of public people; asking few favours of the Press, taking its praise for her work, but making sure that when she was judged, as judged she must be, only the actor stood in the dock.

6

'My life has been a sort of D. H. Lawrence book.'

Apartado 232
Maracaibo.
29th August 1924

My Dearest Edith,

Surely there must be some mistake, it cannot be a year since I last
wrote to you or poured out my soul; yet methinks it's a long long time
and you are very dear to overlook my moral, physical and literary
turpitude. There is no excuse for I follow your doings and success and
one or two friends keep me posted from time to time here, with
cuttings from the Press. So that you are constantly in my thoughts
and my feelings exactly as when I sailed, and I can truly say I have
not changed one iota beyond having aged perhaps.

The remnants of energy and brain left to me are concentrated on the
job, excluding time for games and jollifications, though the latter is
contradicted somewhat for having a hard head in a beer fight!! I go
out nowhere, avoid entertaining as much as possible, and, it will be
obvious where so many conflicting interests are centred, make few
friendships. So that in effect one just lives for the work which is
endless, and awaits the disappearing date of the homegoing steamer's
sailing.

When I cabled you at the New Year I had decided to leave in March
and Marriott, a director, had instructions to drag me home in his
train; however it became impossible. Now each month, Dr. Andreae,
our M.D., expresses fears for my health and demands my return.

For the rest I think you may realise me better in the catechism form:
I am your Friend. I will always be your Friend because I love you;
I will write to you though I won't promise how often, it's no use; I do
not 'want to drop you' that's obvious, and I ain't drifting away; I am
not married to someone else, nor have I any intention of so doing,
how could I? Shall I add one or two for myself? I thank God that
after twenty years (or is it more) shush, that we are still great friends;
I also thank Him that I did not make a fatal blunder and that you
have been free to develop along your best lines even at a sacrifice;

I joy in recalling that I at least did not try to discourage your desire to act, also in that I was often a brute to you, it did you good, my dear; for the rest perhaps I should not have claimed so much of you, dearest, but so our lives opened to us and it is mine for all time. Tell me, Edith, would you alter it an you could?

What a gift to have just 24 hours all to myself. I have most of the things man can want here, house, horse, car, launch, a few friends, a little power, a lot of 'pull', plenty of work and the 'guts to do it, little leisure and lots of longings and more money than I care to spend. But…

With a decent interval to get some clothes and a bath after landing, I shall present myself at your door round about Easter and claim such 24 hours of you, and accept no refusal. So look out and look your best for you are comprometido for one whole day. You will now reread the second paragraph on page 3, double its significance, and believe all to be true. For I do love everything about you, and love being able to tell a sweet woman so.

Your letter tells me that you are well and may all be well with you. My best love. Guy.

I must be careful, possessing only half the puzzle, not to complete it out of my imagination. The clues are scattered throughout Guy's letters. Some things are self-evident, others need joining together, relating what appeared feasible to Guy in the British Controlled Oilfields on Lake Maracaibo in Venezuela to what was actually taking place in England.

Self-evident: the correspondence between them had petered out for a whole year. Guy seemed to have accepted that the fault, if any, was mostly on his side. He hinted at his own moroseness, and revealed that he had tried to sublimate his feeling in work and beer. He could not resist adding that his health had suffered.

Edith had been the one to break the silence. From the paragraph he set most store by and asked her to reread, we can extract the essence of her letter to him. In it, she must have written her fears: he had either married someone else, or he had deliberately neglected her because he wanted the relationship to end. His reply refuted both these allegations. Edith once described her life to me as being something out of D. H. Lawrence: 'all bits and intimate developments of one's character and growing up and sex and everything. I've done the most extraordinary things, masses, amazing things.' The language Guy employed in his letters reminds me of Lawrence. His attitude towards women, and to Edith in particular, is a curious mixture of morality and earthiness. He talks of their lives 'opening' which is pure Lawrence. He seems trapped between an inherited morality and the desire to cut loose. In the descriptions of his lonely existence he manages to inject a certain swaggering tone, harmless enough, but indicative, as though wishing to impress Edith from afar. They were divided by choice and yet both wanted the reassurance that they were not forgotten. 'Double its significance,' Guy writes, as he makes a date for seven months hence. He has already revealed that he follows her every doing, congratulates himself on not making the 'fatal blunder' of standing in the way of her success, and rejoices in that success. 'I will always be your Friend because I love you.' It is a cry from the heart.

He was writing in August 1924 and by that time Edith's career had soared; the promise of greatness had been realised a bare decade after her debut on any stage and in a way that made Nigel Playfair's well-intentioned pity seem totally superfluous. The press cuttings and news items that found their way to Guy in Maracaibo could have given him no real inkling of what was happening to Edith.

In the latter half of the previous 'lost' year she had renewed her association with Shaw for the first British production of *Back to Methuselah*. She was invited to join the stock company of the Birmingham Repertory with Cedric Hardwicke and Gwen Ffrangcon-Davies as her co-stars for Parts I, IV and V of the *metabiological pentateuch* as the author called it with his tongue in Moses' cheek. The complete work had already been presented in America, but commercial managements in England, aware that the Theatre Guild had spent $20,000 on the venture in New York, were reluctant to reach for their wallets. The Birmingham experiment, an act of singular courage by Barry Jackson, followed over a year later. Several of Shaw's biographers assert that he described Edith and Cedric Hardwicke as 'provincial nobodies' but I find this hard to believe. In the first place Edith told me that Shaw was always unfailingly courteous to her and, secondly, he was too intelligent and too knowledgeable about the theatre to have put such an inaccurate tag on her. Comparative newcomer she might be, provincial she most certainly was not. It is true that Hardwicke had yet to make his mark in the West End (which he did shortly afterwards in *The Farmer's Wife*) but again it would seem totally out of character, not to say insane, for Shaw to have deliberately insulted his Birmingham leading man in this fashion.

Shaw stayed away from the rehearsals, but made his presence felt nevertheless. He was particularly concerned, during the month of August, with the suggested appearance of Edith as the Serpent for that segment of the play entitled 'In the Beginning.' H. K. Ayliff, the producer, put forward his own views and was smartly corrected by Shaw.

68

Parknasilla,
Kenmare,
Co Kerry
29th August 1923

Dear Ayliff,

No property head that the clumsiest pantomime property man could perpetrate could be half as fatal as Edith Evans's torso offering itself as the voice that breathed on Eden.

You must get an artist (or get Sir Whitworth Wallis to choose one) to design a very slender snake's head and neck to rise out of the Johnswort and quiver there while Edith, sunk in the cut with her head just above the level of the stage, and hidden by the Johnswort, speaks the lines. She must stand on something resonant, not on anything solid, and lick out her words with deadly distinctness in a tone that suggests a whisper, but isn't.

(And here Shaw made two small drawings to illustrate what he wanted. One looked like everybody's idea of the Loch Ness Monster and the other was Shaw's version of a Cobra head spread.)

The hood may be practical or may not. The serpent's neck should be vibrant, not rigid. It is impossible to say more without experiments on the spot, and a real artist doing the design and colouring and lighting.

If I had known Edith was to be in it I would have written in a proper part for her. Why don't you make her play the Envoy's wife? She would lift it to a leading part at once. *Anybody* can play the oracle. She is going to play Lady Utterword in *Heartbreak House*, I hope. Ever, G.B.S.

Edith and Ayliff both replied the following week. They both employed different tactics with Shaw, Edith selecting the role of a contrite, saddened woman who has caused her author to be cross with her and wishes to make flirtatious amends.

4, September 1923

Since hearing that you want a property snake to act the part, and me to speak it from below, I am almost broken-hearted.

Of course I must do as you wish but oh I beg beg you not to be definite until you have seen a rehearsal. Your direction about the licking voice was exactly as I had seen it in my mind and I have been supple-ing myself in order to give the impression of a serpent body and oh everything. I haven't looked or thought about my part since yesterday morning. The way dispirits (is that the word?) me so. Don't bother to write to me, I know you are terribly busy, but come as soon as you can. It will be so good to have you there. I don't want to be tiresome but I can't recover from the blow. May I send my love?

Edith Evans.

69

Ayliff, in that most difficult of positions, betwixt author and leading lady, tried a different tack. He wrote as the brisk professional.

September 4, 1923

Dear Mr. Shaw,

Your letter has caused severe attacks of discouragement and Miss Evans reports complications in the shape of a broken-heart in addition. Perhaps this is as it should be.

Of course, if you insist, we'll make the property snake's head and neck. That presents no difficulty; our workshops are efficient and our scenic artist and designer is a 'real' one—in fact quite first-rate. But if you saw Edith Evans coiled round a rock rehearsing, I think you'd find her convincing as the Serpent of Eden. Your directions for the delivery of the lines exactly describe the way she is speaking now, but she protests that she could not feel or speak the part standing erect with her head emerging from a trap and herself out of contact with the other characters of the scene. Our idea is for her to be right in the snake's skin up to her head, which will be surrounded by the cobra hood.

We didn't know that Miss Evans was coming till just before I last wrote to you. She is lifting the Oracle into a leading part and I don't know anyone else who could touch the She Ancient.

Miss Hope had already been engaged for Lady Utterword before we were advised that Miss Evans might be willing to leave London, so I fear that casting must hold.

These letters had the required effect on Shaw and he gave in.

He wrote Edith an amusing and illustrated letter during rehearsals for *In The Beginning*. Although they had met before, his method of address was still moderately formal, given his personality.

Great Southern Hotel
Parknasilla-on-Sea.
17th September 1923

My Dear Edith Evans,

Why do you want to look like this? I leave this place tomorrow, and shall be at the Malvern Hotel, Great Malvern until I come over to see what on earth you are all doing with poor old Methuselah.

I should have written before; but I had to finish a new play; and when that was done I had a bad fall on the rocks and drove a camera through my lungs and ribs something horrid.

I had no idea you were abandoning London for Birmingham or I should have been tempted to revive a discarded section of Methuselah with a good comedy part for you in it—the wife of Barnabas.

I have half a mind not to meddle with the rehearsals at all: I am rather afraid of upsetting you at the last moment and doing more harm than good. Authors are not really necessary evils.

However – – – – – !

I wonder can I buy a big enough notebook in Birmingham. One of the large red royal quartos: they are so impressive.

ever G. Bernard Shaw.

Nothing would have kept Shaw from the rehearsals had he not trusted Barry Jackson. He was amazed by Jackson and had asked him whether he meant to take his wife and family to the workhouse and die there on the straw when Jackson announced his intention of reproducing the entire cycle of plays. Jackson replied that he had neither wife nor family, and was prepared and willing to take the risk. In his biography of Shaw, Frank Harris depicted Jackson as a sycophant, but as his book is about as reliable as a British Rail timetable, and is riddled with envy for anybody who had Shaw's ear. I stand convinced that Jackson acted from courage. There are many plays of Shaw one could produce as an act of sycophancy; *Back to Methuselah* is not one of them.

Alas, the Birmingham experiment was also a commercial failure, losing £2,500 during a run in which the plays were presented four times. This must have been a major disaster for a company operating on a shoestring, but Jackson never regretted it and Shaw found in him a worthy successor to the Court Theatre partnership of Barker and Vedrenne. Jackson later founded the Malvern Festival with Shaw as his star attraction.

Although many of the critics could not resist prefacing their notices with laurel wreaths to themselves and the Birmingham audiences for sheer stamina, they also declared themselves enriched by the ordeal. The gentleman from the *Empire News*, obviously at a loss to understand what he had sat through, contented himself with social notes from all over, saying that Adam and Eve (played by Colin Keith-Johnston and Gwen Frangcon-Davies) were 'semi-nude, with vegetable coverings. I have often seen 'show ladies' less modestly attired.' He also thought that the 'Welsh actress' Edith Evans was the hit of the entire production and claimed that the combination of Shaw's marathon and the iron-masters conference had made it difficult to get sleeping accommodation in the city.

In his Preface to the play (and many of the London critics swotted up on the text before venturing as far North as Birmingham—they seldom journeyed into the provinces without an extra layer of intellectual armour) Shaw wrote that all his efforts as a playwright had been to disabuse people of the belief that the theatre is only a place of shallow amusement, somewhere to go 'to be soothed after the enormous intellectual strain of a day in the city'. Then with the mock humility he increasingly employed; 'I am doing the best I can at my age. My powers are waning, but so much the better for those who found me unbearably brilliant when I was in my prime.'

It was theatrical history in the making on the heroic scale, written by the outstanding literary voice of the time, a man of sixty-five and boundless ambition, whose longing to write a masterpiece sprang from his disillusionment with contemporary politics and his lack of positive influence as a political figure. In his detailed examination of Shaw's major dramatic works, *The Cart and The Trumpet*, Professor Maurice Valency puts forward the theory that Shaw half believed that *Back to Methuselah* had been dictated to him as the Koran had been dictated to Mohammed. If he could not be a political messiah, Shaw was determined to be remembered as a quasi-religious prophet.

The strange thing about actors is that the significance of any given play seldom enters into their reckoning when they evaluate its worth to them. They are educated, as it were, *after* the event; at the time of accepting the engagement they are more often than not primarily concerned with such parochial details as salary, wardrobe and the pecking order. It would be churlish to criticise them for this, and the modern emphasis on over-intellectualising what is basically an emotional craft frequently banishes excitement into the wings and substitutes boredom instead. It is the playwright who should be the intellectual: the artist called upon to interpret him must give the colour and movement and bring the argument to life. A great exponent like Edith takes possession of the role during rehearsal and then, in turn, is possessed during the actual performance. It matters not one jot whether the actor achieves his ends by some convoluted, private intellectual process or by instinct. What matters is that when the results are revealed on stage to an audience, that audience is held and moved.

Edith told me that she was never conscious of 'making history' when she tackled her major roles. She was what is known in the theatre as 'a slow study'; that is to say she never came to the first rehearsal word perfect; she liked to find her way into the part by stages. Obviously any artist of reasonable intelligence can differentiate between the dialogue supplied by an author of Shaw's stature and the dross supplied by some hack: a great dramatist does not necessarily make the task of the actor any easier—frequently it is the reverse—but he does ensure that the blueprint he hands over to the actor contains all the vital information; the actor still has to physically build the house. Poor dramatists provide the walls and the roof, but neglect the plumbing.

Take the case of *Back to Methuselah*. It is doubtless an interesting experiment in absurdity to ask students at a dramatic academy to imagine they are a serpent if it helps them shed their skins of inhibition. But to ask an actor who is ultimately going to appear before a paying audience to *intellectualise* himself into the state of being a serpent would produce the theatre of embarrassment. The response to such a problem must be emotional. Being a down-to-earth person who was always content to thank God rather than Stanislavsky or his less-talented imitators for her inspiration, Edith approached her various roles in *Back to Methuselah* as she had, and would, every other role. She was being paid for the luxury of doing what she adored—surely, as she said, one of life's greatest hand-outs. And it is worth recording that Shaw anticipated her instincts and kept away from rehearsals. Edith always regarded the text as sacrosanct, she didn't alter the words to make her own contribution easier, but while she was 'making the bread' as she liked to call it, she didn't want too many other people in the kitchen. Times have changed, of course, and the modern method is to have the entire cast sitting around for days prior to the cut and thrust of the actual rehearsals analysing themselves and the play into near oblivion. I have not observed that the results justify the agony.

After the limited run of *Methuselah*, she returned to Shakespeare, appearing in *The Merry Wives of Windsor* again, this time in its entirety at the Lyric Hammersmith. On this occasion she was the Ellen Terry, playing Mistress Page to the Mistress Ford of that fine actress Dorothy Green. This revival opened in the last days of 1923. It was produced by W. Bridges Adams who in a letter to a friend nearly forty years later wrote an appreciation of Dorothy Green, saying that he felt she had never had the recognition that was her due but that 'she had at least the satisfaction of knowing that for critics of discernment she had set a standard in the great tragic parts of Shakespeare by which more celebrated people must be judged. So good a trouper, too, that I have seen her carry a brilliant but less experienced comrade (Edith Evans) to triumph by playing for *her* instead of herself.'

Nigel Playfair presented the play for the Christmas holiday season, from Boxing Day until January 5th 1924, and the words 'jolly romp', 'merriment and vitality' and 'bustling farce' were sprinkled throughout the reviews. Honours were neatly divided amongst the three leading players (Roy Byford was once again playing Falstaff) and it would be monotonous to list the superlatives laid at Edith's feet. One observation from the critic of the *Yorkshire Post* is worth quoting, however, in that it gives substance to what I have said earlier concerning Edith's method of tackling a role. 'She seemed to be creating Mistress Page from moment to moment.'

And so we move into the fateful year of 1924—fateful for a variety of reasons. The relationship with Guy reached its low water mark, but the tide of success in Edith's career was in full flood. She could do no wrong, it seemed, and if she was troubled in spirit her audiences were unaware. The gossip tipster of the *Sporting Times* made his selection as early as

November 1923, writing 'Nigel Playfair will probably add to the Fortunes of Nigel by his 'cute' engagement of Edith Evans for the great character of Millamant in Congreve's *The Way of the World* at the Hammersmith Lyric—Edith having been born to play the part.' How did he know, I wonder? If his racing tips were as good, he was obviously a man to follow.

Edith's interpretation of Millamant was a performance not of a single opening night, or of a season, but of a period. In front of a first night audience that included George Moore, John Drinkwater, Lytton Strachey, Arnold Bennett and Eddie Marsh, she shot Congreve's masterpiece into fragments. It was, we are told 'an amazing achievement', 'the finest and rarest acting', 'perfect', 'Miss Evans came triumphantly through that last hoop of the great comedy actress, the playing of Millamant', 'the joy, the ecstasy of this *Way of the World* is Edith Evans,' 'nothing quite as brilliant has been seen on the stage for decades.'

James Agate, scorning discretion, stated: 'Let me not mince matters. Miss Edith Evans is the most accomplished of living and practising English actresses. Leaving tragedy to Miss Thorndike, she has a wider range than any other artist before the public, and is unrivalled alike in sentimental and heartless comedy. Miss Evans has simply got to be dinned into that most insensitive of auricular appendages—the ear of the West End Manager. They say that, by the tape-measure, this actress has not the fashionable type of feature, for all the world as though her business was to grin before a camera. But if she does not possess rare beauty in the highest sense then I know not that quality. Her countenance is replete, as was said of Congreve's style, 'with sense' and satire, conveyed in the most pointed and polished terms." Her acting is "a shower of brilliant conceits, a new triumph of wit, *a new conquest over dullness*". You could hang any one of this player's portraits on the sky, and challenge the Zodiac.'

There was more in the same vein, for Agate was not the man to water his enthusiasms. Did any of Guy's friends send him this particular cutting, I wonder? If so, how could he have taken it in? What price the childhood sweetheart now? One can well imagine why he neglected to write: he could hardly top the praise she had received from strangers, and must have felt inhibited by past intimacies with a woman who was now, so obviously, public property.

Edith had her critics as well. Several of them found her 'too modern', but the few dissenting voices were drowned out in the general fervour to climb aboard the latest fashionable band-wagon, that of claiming to have discovered her first. Success on this scale in the theatre often sends quite ordinary, conventional people off their heads. The artist will be invaded by the lunatic fringe of casual acquaintances, would-be playwrights and fame-maddened fans. Old enemies turn up with creased-smiles at the dressing room door. Mashers send flowers and cryptic notes. Mothers beg for advice, convinced that such success should, by rights, rub off on their own progeny. Success can come too early or too late (it is always capricious) and in both instances it is seldom an instrument for good in the development of an artist. In Edith's case the Gods were on her side. She survived the experience.

I think what she always valued most was the response she evoked in ordinary people. She kept all their letters and was touchingly proud of them. They were letters from total strangers for the most part and they came from all walks of life. From time to time, and, I hope, not to excess, I will quote from them, since it was Edith's wish that I should. I particularly like the sentiments expressed by George Bealby: Dear Miss Evans, I have not paid the overdue gas account, but have paid for a Box tonight to see a *very great Artiste*'. Mr. Bealby was in no doubt that he had got his priorities right.

In arriving at my own conclusions as to why Edith remained un-dazzled by her sudden fame and notoriety, I considered anew the influence of her parents. 'My mother and father came to the first night' (of *The Way of The World*) 'They were so proud and quiet and well behaved. I'd apparently made a most terrific success as Millamant, you see. Or so everybody said in the dressing room afterwards. I didn't know. I said what the part said and somebody remarked to Mother—"Mrs. Evans, Edith is wonderful, isn't she?"—it was somebody quite famous, I believe, and Mother replied, "I think they're all very good." That's for you, famous or not! I was doing my job and that was quite enough, thank you. Mother always said the right thing. She was the comic, of course. Father used to look at the way the theatre was run. He was more interested in whether the brass was cleaned than in me. I'd go home sometimes after a performance when they'd been in front and Mother would say, 'Your voice was a little high, dear.' That's enough, no more than that . . . pressing, shunning away. She didn't know how to trip it properly, you know, didn't know the right terms, but "a little high, dear", thank you very much and say no more.'

Her leading man in *The Way of The World* was Robert Loraine, a veteran of Shavian leading roles, who during the war had listed Shaw and Mrs. G.B.S. as his next of kin. The childless Shaws accepted him as a surrogate son and when he was hideously wounded Shaw behaved with an affection and generosity that he kept well hidden from his public. Loraine was wounded again before the war ended, but resumed his career nevertheless and was a much sought-after leading man with a considerable public following.

Edith paid tribute to the help Loraine gave her at that time. It is worth stating that whilst some theatrical feuds have passed into legend and certain leading players have rightly been attributed with a strain of bitchiness of particular virulence, there is another side to the coin. Edith remembered Loraine and Nigel Playfair with enormous affection and gratitude. 'Playfair told me I'd got the character of Millamant right, but said, "It's all this business".' She waved her arms around to demonstrate what he meant. '"Superb", he said to me. "Remember she was *superb*, always superb. You can be as larky as you like, but remember . . . *su-perb*." Because she was cosseted and all that sort of thing.' She sat very still, as though still in wonder at the profundity of this advice. 'Fancy somebody saying something as marvellous as that to you, just when you needed it.'

(I am forced to query Edith's recollection of this incident, for I have a well documented alternative version given to me by Cole Lesley. Mr. Lesley recounted that when Edith paid a visit to Noel Coward's Swiss home some forty years later, Noel asked her what or who had been the most important influence in her life. She thought for a while and then told the story of the advice given her after the dress rehearsal of *The Way of The World*. She did not reveal the identity of the man who had given her the advice, but the following morning when they were out walking in the village, Cole Lesley happened to ask if she remembered a playwright called H. R. Barbor. 'She stopped and put her hand on her heart—the great actress, you know,' Cole said. 'Why do you ask me that? *He* was the man I was talking about last night. He was the man who told me to be superb. I owe him so much.' Mr. Lesley explained that his question had been an innocent coincidence, because he had known Barbor years before and had once been directed by him in some amateur company. Edith couldn't get over it and thereafter often talked of Barbor whenever she and Mr. Lesley met. Certainly the timing of the incident gives credence to this version, for, as I will shortly demonstrate, Barbor was laying siege to Edith at the time of *The Way of the World*.)

Arnold Bennett—'notable in a stage box' on the opening night— went home to write up his Journal. 'Friday, February 8th 1924. Last night, 1st performance of *The Way of The World* at Lyric, Hammersmith. I have seen two rehearsals and the performance of this play, and still do not know what the plot is, nor have I met anyone who does know . . . The performance and production last night were admirable. The play will fail, but it must add to the prestige of the theatre. Edith Evans as Millamant gave the finest comedy performance I have ever seen on the stage. I went behind afterwards, told her so. "How exciting," she said,'

George Moore who, according to the *Evening Standard* 'created a minor sensation' on the opening night 'by moving slowly across the stalls during an interval' (they must have been hard up for news that night) also rushed home to his typewriter.

Dear Miss Evans,

I shall be very pleased to see you again, for I want to tell you what a great artist you showed yourself to be in a play that bored me incredibly except in the few moments that Congreve kept you on the stage, and then it was not Congreve that interested me, but you. It would have been well, I think, if Mr. Playfair had accepted the excellent judgement of the eighteenth century (which knew so much more about the aesthetics than we did that it booed *The Way of The World*) and if Congreve's own judgement had been considered. The unaesthetic century we have the misfortune to live in accepted Congreve's impassioned utterance that he would never write again, the public not being worthy of his wit, the true truth being that Congreve had said all he had to say and knew that his refined sawdust would no longer animate his bucks and belles. Did it ever really animate them? Yes, in *Love for Love*, a comedy that I admire as well as another, belike. In Millamant there is a flicker of the talent that wrote *Love for Love*, and you were exquisite in these episodic flickerings of a dying talent. Mrs Bracegirdle, your predecessor, did not speak, I am sure, that pretty analogy: lovers and curlpapers, as exquisitely as you did, and she did not make all the audience love her, as you did. One more criticism and I have done. You were the nearest thing in the cast to the eighteenth century, and as near to it as the twentieth century will ever get. The rest of the cast presented us with samples of almost every kind of acting: we had realistic comedy, we had romantic comedy, and there was knock-about farce. I am an admirer of Margaret Yarde, but she needs low life, as Clare Greet does, for the exhibition of her talent.

When will you come to see me? You owe me a visit. Come to luncheon or come to tea, but let us see you again. And will you ask our friend Mr. Playfair who was the colour-blind scenic artist that designed and painted that purple room. I had to sit through all those acts with my eyes closed. It was really too flagrantly twentieth century.

Very sincerely yours, George Moore.

It was still the age of letter writing, thank God; the age of studied invective, when people had the leisure and the inclination to commit their opinions to paper. With the notable exceptions of politicians and civil servants who put down in writing those verdicts they are curiously loath to voice in public, much of current social history is flung to the winds over the telephone. Edith hoarded her correspondence, thus not only making my task an easier pleasure, but ensuring that all manner and variety of trivia as well as documents of importance were preserved. I select a passage from an exuberant letter written by a woman friend shortly after *The Way of the World* opened. 'Dear Genius, dear Greatheart, how you have worked. Do you know that you sail across the stage, you don't walk? . . . The other actors, alas for them, are porridge after meat, chaff and bran. That man spoils your last scene by the fat way he leans over the end of the couch.'

Poor Robert Loraine! Theatrical legend has it that he was not the most generous of actors, but he had suffered a great deal in the war. Photographs of the production show that the lady was quite correct: he did lean over the edge of the couch in a fat way. It is an unlikely, but brilliant description.

Bennett was also right. The play did not enjoy a lengthy run and by the end of June 1924 Edith was launched in the highly controversial *Tiger Cats* at the Savoy. Between these two vastly different plays she managed to sandwich an appearance for the Stage Society in Elmer Rice's *The Adding Machine*. This was given two special performances at the Strand and was described by *The Times* critic as 'a curious, sordid, symbolical play' and treated by his colleagues as a theatrical novelty 'almost inconceivably tiresome and tedious,' the *Irish Times* stating that 'the general level of the acting was high, but I could not help wondering why all these clever people waste so much time on a play that is designed to be profound, but only succeeds in being aimless.' It was now becoming commonplace to praise Edith 'whose name when seen in a programme gives a thrill of anticipation to most intelligent theatregoers.'

It was inevitable that other men than Guy would fall in love with her. One of her most determined admirers was a young dramatist called H. R. Barbor. From his letters it is transparently obvious he had what used to be termed 'a bad case.' Reminded of this, Edith seemed slightly amazed. 'I certainly didn't know he was in love with me like that. I knew I'd made a tremendous impression on him from the first time he met me . . . I suppose I did that to his whole life. I used to do that to people without knowing it. We went on some sort of trip together and afterwards he said nothing was the same any more, all the streets looked different. I remember that, the way he put it. But it wasn't like today, where the moment you had any feeling like that you popped into bed together. Never touched each other . . . I don't know what it was.'

One of Barbor's letters dated May 1924 begins:

My Golden Girl, I have to submit to you a very humble apology . . . It is not that my intention was wrong, but that I clumsily phrased the emotion that was at my heart . . . I love you and want only your presence, only your nearness. What I do as a playmaker shall be for you. Don't think of me, think of yourself—as I do. I don't matter. But God help me, I love you and it is a blend of anguish and ecstasy to love you as I do now. At present all the real world, this humdrum traffic of near things, seems to be parting away from me. I am lonely, unstabilised and battered . . . Is it any wonder that I am mad? . . . But I'll buy 'em all out yet, and steal you, Marie Ediste! . . . All my heart's love, dear . . .

In 1924 he sent her copy No. 1 of his privately printed play *Jezebel* with the inscription 'Edith, Here's for you, if you will. A labour of love.' Alas, such labours of love, however well-intentioned frequently disappoint, for the talent does not always match the passion that inspired them. Barbor's description of Jezebel within the text holds up a mirror to Edith.

'Jezebel . . . is a splendidly built, full-figured woman of thirty' [Edith was thirty six at the time] 'black of hair, and with a heavily moulded face. Her eyes are large and rather sad, her mouth fulllipped and sensual but strong. Gracious in everything but her commands, she is a great queen and a great woman, and the air of poignancy and disillusion—of impending tragedy—enhances her majesty.'

The play which followed was written in indifferent blank verse and Edith never performed it. Her rejection of it did nothing to dampen his ardour. Later that same year he wrote: 'I cannot see the wood, friendliness, for the trees, love. My darling, I am simply drowned in this allcompelling passion. You are all loveliness, all desire, all hope . . . So you will forgive the incoherence that must of necessity follow the revealed desire of a lifetime.'

Barbor was to die, aged forty, in 1933.

Back to Methuselah had been brought to London, to the Court Theatre, in the February of 1924, but minus Edith, for she was then storming the citadels in *The Way of the World*. Her original roles were played by Caroline Keith who enjoyed the dubious privilege of being compared unfavourably to her predecessor.

Tiger Cats was first presented as a series of matinees at the Savoy. As though determined to exhibit her versatility, Edith was also appearing in the evenings at the Everyman in Hampstead, playing a revival of Shaw's *Getting Married* with Claude Rains. Of the two, *Tiger Cats* promoted the greater interest. Mr. Barbor crops up again in different guise, this time in the role of critic for *The New Age*. Understandably not the most impartial of observers on this occasion, he told his readers that Madame Karen Bramson's play 'would have taken up no space in this column but for the fact that Miss Edith Evans has, for some reason (?)

seen fit to appear in it.' After giving the bare bones of the plot, Barbor ended by saying 'that this superficial clap-trap should be distended into the semblance of beauty by the art of our finest actress is a disgrace to the English theatre that does not find her a better occupation.' Uncharitably, one is forced to the conclusion that poor Mr. Barbor was thinking of his *Jezebel* as the better occupation. He could not resist one final puff for Edith: 'Miss Evans played the part magnificently, as she does every part . . . When you try to confine a gale in a pill-box, the only thing that suffers is the pill-box'.

Not that Barbor was alone in declaring *Tiger Cats* something less than a masterpiece. Herbert Farjeon stated that Edith had been asked to play a monstrous part in a monstrous play (the greater part of his review being taken up with an account of his efforts to raise enough money for the Old Vic to be able to entice Edith there for the next season. The fund stood at £170 at the date he wrote).

Controversy is frequently box-office in the theatre. If a play is controversial *and* a work of distinction, so much the better, but in a pinch most managements will settle for the former quality. The matinees of *Tiger Cats* whetted the public appetite and it was subsequently moved to the Garrick for a normal run. There, for a time, it became a fashionable debating point. Another set of reviews prolonged the argument. The *Daily Graphic* didn't waste much ink. 'To make this play successful, it would have to be cut down to one act and one actor. Edith Evans was magnificent. Had all the others been invisible it would have been better. I, for one, found it hard to bear watching Robert Loraine breaking pencils to express nervous tension.' Agate tempered his second notice with the lightest rap on the knuckles for Edith. 'Miss Evans made a little speech at the end, a thing I have never heard her do before, and which I beg her on my bended knees never to do again. Sarah never did it throughout seventy years. But then she had a very acute sense of what constitutes and what destroys mystery. Miss Evans spoke charmingly, but that is not the point.'

The anonymous 'Domino' of *Horse and Hound* practically needed a saliva test by the time he came to the end of his review. '*Tiger Cats* is simply naked sordidness . . . it is impossible to believe in the characters. They are not, you feel, human beings at all. They are monstrosities . . . An ugly, unpleasant play . . . but the acting of Miss Edith Evans almost makes it worth while. The character (of the wife) is shown as utterly carnal, a creature that is loathsome beneath a mask of beauty. Her smile, so near a leer, her sneer, which is half a snarl, her movements so full of sensual suggestion make up a thing to hate. In its ugly way Miss Evans' performance approaches greatness. But the play makes one feel the need of a mouth-wash when the curtain falls.'

THERE REALLY ARE TIGER CAT WOMEN was the headline in the

Daily Sketch, August 14th 1924. '"There are thousands of homes like mine, thousands of wives like ours", declares the desperate husband in *Tiger Cats*, and at that the audience stiffens and frowns as though human nature has been insulted, as though, indeed, the sensual parasitic woman, married to the highly-civilised and vulnerable man, and tearing out of his life all that was nobility and fineness, were a wildly exaggerated fantasy of the dramatist.

'And all the time the great cats go about us, ravaging, stealing, corrupting, always in the softest places, and with the finest fur and the thickest cream, bringing consternation and despair to really human beings, and especially to really civilised and non-predatory women.'

The author of this hysterical rubbish was a woman, and if we are to believe her the audiences at the Garrick were nightly frozen into Madame Tussaud-like attitudes by Miss Evans, the Super-tabby. Edith told me she didn't much care for the play. 'You see I didn't know it was about what they said it was about. Just a play, duckie, with a good part. Sometimes you can't ask for more.' Mr. Agate paid another visit and resumed his familiar rhapsody on the theme of Edith.

He was writing in a vintage year for the women. Sybil Thorndike was now popularly known as 'St. Sybil' after her great triumph in Shaw's *St. Joan*, Athene Seyler dominated *The Mask and The Face* at the Criterion and Margaret Bannerman, described, somewhat oddly, as 'the most improved actress in London' was bringing them in for *Our Betters*. The friendly rivalry between Edith and Sybil—often distorted by the gossip writers—was to persist for the rest of their lives. Each had a host of camp followers, passionate in defence of their separate heroines, who found some perverse delight in formenting an emnity that existed only in their imaginations. Though Edith never maintained a close relationship with Sybil—as she did with Gwen Frangcon-Davies and Ruth Gordon, for instance—this was mostly because their careers kept them apart. They were friends and respected each other. Sybil's son, John Casson, in his loving biography of his parents, confirms that Edith was a frequent visitor to the family house in Carlyle Square in the early twenties. 'It was best when she was the only guest. Lewis' thrusting logic and disciplined thought underpinned by immense artistic sensitivity and insight, Sybil riding her bounding imagination like a battle-charger galloping over everybody, but making them get up and gallop too, and Edith's gorgeously orchestral voice commanding attention by its more smoothly flowing magic, was all like watching and hearing not a play but a kind of Olympian circus'.

Various theatrical historians have deplored the fact that Edith and Sybil only acted together on one occasion, and that towards the end of their careers, in 1951 in *Waters of the Moon*. The fault, I fear, lay with the dramatists rather than the two ladies concerned. It is rare enough in the

British theatre for there to be one thundering good female role in a new play, let alone two. I cannot improve on John Casson's description that any stage partnership between Edith and Sybil must have been rather like having 'Circe and Brunnhilde in the same cast' though with admirable discretion he did not elaborate as to who was Circe and who Brunnhilde.

Sybil, with her distinguished actor husband and her family, was a more outgoing person than Edith. She involved herself with the outside world far more than Edith ever did; was active in politics as Edith never was; and by nature she was more flamboyant, her personality flashing round theatres like a lighthouse beam. I think Edith envied Sybil her lack of loneliness, surrounded as she always was with the regenerating energies of children and grand-children. Each in her own way provided great theatre, for they were both larger than life, and were content to eye each other, not with malice or petty jealousy, but wary, interested, intrigued: champions in any field have a healthy respect for quality. Sybil had a more gregarious romance with the theatre; she mixed more with her colleagues off stage. Both retained an extraordinary vitality throughout their long careers and both professed to strong, uncomplicated religious beliefs, especially Sybil who married God and the Drama into a theatrical evangelism that few could resist. The beauty of that epoch when they were both bestriding the London stages was not that one was forced to choose between them, but that one had the choice.

(Interestingly enough, a letter from Leon M. Lion to Edith expressing his 'grateful appreciative thanks for all the splendid work you devoted to "Suzanne" under the most unfair and irritating conditions' revealed that originally Sybil had been going to play the role, but, wrote Lion, 'from the first she had declared there was none like unto you.')

The actor's art, they say, dies with him. An old photograph (and that perhaps ludicrous in our eyes, for the techniques of photography today emphasise past inadequacies, and never more so than in theatrical poses), a few lines of praise culled and reprinted from newspaper mortuaries are all that furnish draggle-tailed testimony to yesterday's glories. How, then, does a writer rescue a great performance from the grave? I have tried to quote selectively from the best and worst critics of the day (for they both tell us something), to give the modern reader some faint idea of her accomplishments, but I am ever conscious of the inadequacy of this, the only method open to me.

In struggling with this problem, I chanced upon an item quoted by W. Macqueen Pope in his book *Ladies First*.

'There was a Miss Evans who danced to the town's delight at Lincoln's Inn in Betterton's time. Her death was particularly regretted by Vanbrugh. He said in a letter to a friend: "Miss Evans, a dancer at the new playhouse, is dead. A fever slew her in eight and forty hours. She's much lamented by the town, as well as by the house who can't bear her loss; matters running very low with them this winter. If Congreve's play don't help 'em, they are undone. 'Tis a comedy and will be played about six weeks hence. Nobody has seen it yet." The play was all right. It was *The Way of the World*.'

In 1924 another Miss Evans made Millamant her personal property and so far nobody has challenged her freehold. I have not the years to do justice to the remembered excellence of that landmark performance. Perhaps Herbert Farjeon anticipated my present dilemma. Writing on the eve of Edith's last performance as Millamant at the Lyric, Hammersmith in June 1924, he said: 'And when we tell them how wonderful she was, they'll never, as the song at the Winter Garden goes, believe us'.

7

'*I was born like a nun*'

Back to Methuselah was brought back to the Court Theatre again in September 1924 for eight matinee performances, but prior to this Edith had appeared in another Shaw play, *Getting Married*, at the Everyman, Hampstead. In this she took the role of Mrs. George and Shaw could not resist sending some advance stage directions.

> Ayot St. Lawrence
> 28th May 1924
>
> The Everyman writes to me about playing Mrs. George (in *Getting Married*) 'straight' or otherwise. I always want her to be made up like the Queen, who is obviously the original and only Mrs. George; but in your case she should be played straight. Fanny Brough, for whom the part was planned, was much older, and had a tragically wrecked face; but you have happily neither of these qualifications; and it would be absurd for you to simulate them by padding, lining, or any such nonsense. Play it just your own way; and it will come out a regular dazzler, much more brilliant and fascinating than Millamant.
> G.B.S.

The revival of *Back to Methuselah* was confined to Parts I and V only, but London finally got a chance to see Edith as the Serpent and the She-Ancient. Shaw went to one of the matinees without revealing his presence to the cast, and afterwards sent Edith a postcard. There was a photograph of him on one side of the card and Shaw obviously felt he needed to apologise for it.

> This is me considering a prologue, and finding that it is ridiculous and can't be done. At least I can't do it.
> Ask Lawrence Binyon: he might get away with it.
> On Thursday last the serpent hissed in the wrong place. This hiss is a stage trick to make the audience look at the serpent *before* it moves. Except for this, the reptile was very fascinating. G.B.S.

During this period he was employing all his guile to persuade Edith to appear in the title role in *Mrs. Warren's Profession*. Today it is difficult to comprehend that it had been denied a public performance in England for thirty one years. New York had seen it in 1902: there, on the first night, Arnold Daly and his entire company were arrested when the final curtain fell. In England the Lord Chamberlain had banned it on the flimsy grounds that it was concerned with incest (the only evidence to support this absurdity being an incidental reference to the possibility that Vivie Warren and Frank Gardiner might be half-brother and sister). It may strike modern readers as surprising that the censorship had nothing to do with Mrs. Warren's profession. Shaw refused to delete the few short speeches in which the possibility of incest was hinted at and the ban remained in force for three decades.

Frank Harris has it that when the ban was finally lifted in 1924, Shaw was dismayed at the prospect of seeing the play performed so long after the creative act of writing it. Harris quotes from an interview Shaw gave at the time. 'Now that I have reached the venerable age of sixty-eight years and am in the odour of sanctity, if one may so put it, the Lord Chamberlain has let loose this awful piece of mine, written nearly thirty years ago when I was only a young tiger believing in neither man nor God: a play which this terrible censor now authorises to prevent me from ending my days in peace. I cannot forbid the production, because it is as true and necessary now as in 1894; but if one wants my personal impression regarding the necessity of producing it, I would say: 'No, frankly, better never than late.''

This is Harris, quoting Shaw. But against this we have a postcard from Shaw addressed to Edith at 17, Claverton Street. There is no date or postmark, but the information it gives pinpoints that it must have been written in 1924.

> Edith:
> the Lord Chamberlain has most unexpectedly licensed *Mrs. Warren's Profession* for Charles Macdona after thirty years obduracy. Have you ever read it? If not, I will write to Constables to send you a copy. I have told Macd. that there is nobody else who could do anything with it. It is as old fashioned as Ibsen, and much cruder; but Mrs. W. has two very powerful scenes.
> But fancy my feelings at having this horror shoved on me when I am in the very odor of sanctity after St. Joan.   GBS.

It is interesting to note that he uses the phrase 'odour of sanctity' in both cases (though Shaw's spelling was different from that used by Harris). Was he serious, or was he being roguish, at this sudden concern for his new and holier reputation? After all, the play was in print for anybody to read. What is one to make of this contradiction? In the first place Shaw could have prevented production; the fact that the

Lord Chamberlain had licensed it for public exhibition did not negate the author's rights and controls over his own work. Any playwright can, with the protection of his copyright, withdraw a work from *authorised* presentation. And if Shaw truly felt it was an 'awful piece' why did he write as follows on 8th September 1924 from the Gleneagles Hotel in Scotland?

My Dear Edith,

Your age has nothing to do with it. If you were a man you would play Lear without waiting to be eighty: in fact if you were Lear's age you couldn't play him. The same thing is true of Mrs. Warren: a woman such as Mrs. Warren is supposed to be in the play couldn't play her. Poor Fanny Brough, a wasted wrecked genius who had drunk herself all to shreds, never could play her all through at the same performance. The first time she pulled off the second act and made nothing of the finish. The second time she was afraid of forgetting her lines in the second act and made nothing of it; but pulled off the fourth act in a transport (stimulated I suppose) in which at one point she seized a chair and whirled it round her head. There was no third time. Only a woman at her physical best, as you are, could have the staying power—the second wind—to come back after the first big scene and do another.

Consequently I shall have to give the part to a young woman anyhow; and I think the young woman should be you, and not Edyth Goodall or another. After Millamant it could not compromise you by classing you as a matron. Of course you cannot make your neck join on at the back as Mrs. Warren's did; but the audience will not think of that.

Besides, Mrs. Warren, who may be supposed to have become a mother by her first escapade or thereabouts (it is a sterilizing profession) cannot be much over forty, and might be less. I have described her as an old blackguard of a woman; but that was by Victorian reckoning, which put women on the shelf in caps as matrons and called them old the moment they were married and mothers. Victoria lived and reigned 7 years after Mrs. Warren was created. You may make Mrs. W. a battered old devil in point of experience; but she should be physically very far from being decrepit. You are not too old to play Vivie; but you are too 'heavy' in the theatrical sense. You could play the part on your head; and nobody would find you too old for it, *but*—you would play Mrs. W. off the stage and upset the balance of the play.

As likely as not, the Vivie will be older than you are. But she will not carry your guns.

I think you have a bit too much devil in you for Lady Cecily, who is a sentimental comedian; and you would be a terrible Ann: Tanner would be a trodden worm; but it is extremely difficult to guess what would happen. I should have said that you were too heavy for the girl in *The Adding Machine*; but it was perfect. When you have the true dramatic imagination, the most incredible transfigurations take place. You can act anything you really want to; the difficulty is to distinguish the fancies and interests that lure you to the wrong parts from the genuine response to it which overcomes every apparent unsuitability.

Think again about Mrs. Warren. It is not the mere dread of the drudgery of looking for someone else that makes me hesitate to take No for an answer: it seems to me that you are capable of as great a success in it as the wretched old play will hold; and it will last all your life as one of your repertory parts.

Ever.   G.B.S.

Shaw's lengthy defence of his 'wretched old play' shows that he had not lost his touch when it came to flattering an actress he wished to snare. The original is four hand-written pages and he used all the weapons in his considerable armoury. Perhaps he lost his case in the very last line, for to suggest that Edith might be grateful to have a *tour de force* up her sleeve to bring down periodically when nothing better was to hand, was to misunderstand her temperament. Edith never wanted to play the same part over and over again; her energies directed her to constant change; long runs bored her, and she had tasted the intoxicating wines of her own versatility. She was no longer the grateful ex-milliner feeling her way. She was a crowd-drawer, a personality in her own right with half a dozen managements anxious to employ her and most of the critics already at her feet. Famous playwrights, including A. A. Milne, sent humble suggestions and often went away empty-handed.

Shaw returned to the subject in another letter a week later. He was still in Scotland and by now seemed to have accepted that he had failed to sway Edith.

> Gleneagles Hotel,
> Scotland.
> 16th Sept. 1924.

My Dear Edith,

Nobody could want to play Mrs. W. in her soul: it would be a *tour de force* of acting, and probably a draw. But you are quite right to follow your instinct in the matter; and far be it from *my* soul, worn out as that article is, to violate it.

I note your admirable suggestion: it would be a hard and masterly performance, but not a sympathetic one. I doubt if the audience would feel sorry for the old devil. Claire Greet, now – – – – have you ever played with Lady Claire? *Man and Superman* is a play somewhat damaged by time and Loraine's attempt to revive it with Ann left out. It is a case for an experiment to try how cold the water is. If Macdermott were to put it up at the Everyman for a fortnight with you, and say, Nicholas Hannen (for you must not try with Tanner left out), I should be interested. I am packing for my departure tomorrow. I am coming home by easy stages, and will hardly arrive at Ayot St. Lawrence, Welwyn, Herts (my country refuge) before the middle of next week.

ever   G. Bernard Shaw.

A fascinating footnote to the saga of the newly-liberated Mrs. Warren is contained in a news item published in the *People*, December 1924. The heading was G.B.S. LAUGHS, and the story which followed was that Alfred Butt and Tony Prinsep had expressed an interest in presenting the play.

'You can have the play on one condition,' Shaw is reported as saying. 'There is only one woman in England who can play the part of the Mother. That is Ivy. St. Helier.'

(The two managers were somewhat astounded: Miss St. Helier, primarily a variety artist, was chiefly famous as the composer of 'Coal Black Mammy'.)

'I don't mean the only one', Shaw corrected himself. 'There are two others—Sybil Thorndike, who doesn't need a manager, and Edith Evans, who wouldn't play the part.'

On this occasion one can agree with Frank Harris who labelled Shaw 'ever the coy Victorian lady, contradicting himself in the same breath, saying "no" when he means "yes".'

In the event Edith gave a polite refusal to Shaw and started rehearsals for a new production of *A Midsummer's Night Dream* at Drury Lane, in which she was cast as Helena.

This was not to be a conventional Shakespearean happening. Basil Dean, the producer, had conceived it on the grand scale, using the Lane's unique facilities to the full. He was determined to work from the uncut text, have the Mendelssohn music, two ballets by Fokine and aimed to make it 'the premiere Christmas show' with the first performance on Boxing Day evening. His partner in the venture was the somewhat sinister Sir Alfred Butt, a one-time accountant at Harrods who, by 1914, had bought or gained control of many of the leading theatres and music halls in London. From all accounts he was not an attractive figure and Dean, as managing and artistic director of the Lane, found he was constantly in disagreement with him. Butt was Chairman of the

Board and everything Dean suggested he vetoed on the grounds of cost. Their wrangling, in this instance, centred on the choice of cast. Like others before and since who have had to take part in the unequal struggle between art and finance, Dean was at a disadvantage. He had a vision of *The Dream*, Butt could only visualise the balance sheet. If Dean finally persuaded him on a particular actor, Butt then objected to the salary being offered (he included Edith in this respect, which shows that she had come a long way from Ellen Terry's fifteen pounds a week.)

Rehearsals were conducted in an atmosphere of hostility, and I am quite sure that some of Dean's rancour towards Butt was transferred to the cast, for Dean was not noted for his sweetness and affability even at the best of times. The pitch and toss between him and Butt continued to the first night.

It would be poetic justice, since I am determinedly in Dean's camp and by temperament and experience opposed to the Butts of this world, to be able to record that the production proved an unqualified artistic success. The irony is that it was a financial success, Dean being taken to task by several of the critics who viewed his lavish inventions in less than festive spirit. Herbert Farjeon, who didn't even like Edith on this occasion, found it 'an aesthetically vulgar and vainglorious affair, a shopkeepery production, the sort of thing a rich man would buy on sight in Bond Street, and then tell you how much he paid for it.' This smacks of early literary Kung Fu rather than dramatic criticism. Farjeon had the honesty to admit that 'I did not expect to like the production, because I knew that Mendelssohn's delightful but dramatically devastating music was to be employed; because I knew that there was to be a great deal of dancing, and dancing is the last ditch of fairyland on the stage; and because I knew that Mr. Dean was partial to pictorial splashes, and memories of Henry Irving and Beerbohm Tree have convinced me that Shakespeare's pictures should be heard, not seen.'

The critic of the *People* considered Edith a failure. 'She whined. She showed that Shakespeare is not her line.' What surprised me most was that two or three of the critics commented on her *lack* of voice, hardly a verdict to be expected. *Punch*, for example, found her Helena 'a brilliant failure, which would have been a brilliant success on a smaller stage. . . . Her voice however would not carry—the Lane is a daunting place for intimate method.' She was playing a mortal in a play primarily concerned with immortals and as the year ended, a year in which her two extraordinarily contrasted performances in *The Way of The World* and *Tiger Cats* had been extravagantly praised, she was reminded of that mortality, and the fact that critics can damn as often as they commend.

It seems fitting to conclude this episode with a quotation from the review in *The Lady*, a periodical much favoured by the British Nannie.

The article was unsigned, but it is fairly safe to assume that the author was a woman. She thought herself lucky to be taken to the first night of *The Dream*, made a few polite remarks about the cast, hated some of the sets, and saved her gush for an appreciation of the audience.

'In one of the boxes I saw Lord and Lady Curzon of Kedleston with Lady Cunard, and, you know, Lady Curzon had to postpone her holiday trip with her own young people to St. Moritz, because her daughter Miss Marcella Duggan has to have an operation for appendicitis, which probably will have taken place before this letter is in your hands . . . In the stalls I saw Sir George and Lady Marjoribanks and their daughter Miss Monica Marjoribanks, who, however, had to leave early, as that dauntless young lady was catching the night train to Scotland in order to hunt the following morning . . .'

The General Strike was eighteen months away.

8

'After Basil Dean's production of A Midsummer Nights Dream, *in which I played Helena to the satisfaction of very few people and certainly not to my own, I felt it necessary to find out how to play Shakespeare'*

Guy returned to England in 1925, as he had promised, though he did not make it for Easter. He and Edith had corresponded erratically during the latter half of the previous year—'we'll catch up with the old days and ways' he wrote from Maracaibo just before Christmas 1924, and thanked her for two photographs of herself she had sent him. 'Of course you will have changed during the past fifty years of my exile, but you are always you and so saith the photo. I was somehow glad to learn that you do not like your "Tiger Cats" part, and hope that the real opportunity will soon come to you.' It is obvious from this extract that he was not up-to-date with her news and this particular letter, in contrast to most others, is curiously muted: an uncharacteristic reticence had crept in, perhaps the result of their 'lost' year.

After her less than triumphant appearance in *The Dream* Edith's career suffered a hiatus for the first time. We know there had been no shortage of offers, but although she had declined *Mrs. Warren*, A. A. Milne and others, she seemed at a loss to make up her mind and for a short period her life lacked its usual impetus. Her single-minded dedication ran out of steam and there was nobody to whom she could turn for advice. She prayed for guidance, for there is no doubt that she took the failure of her Helena very much to heart and did a great deal of soul-searching. Guy could not help; he was removed both in distance and professional understanding. The answer had to be found within herself: she had failed and there was a reason for that failure. Her voice, which so many had praised and held up as an example, had proved inadequate. Right, she would take care of that. She made enquiries and was told that there was only one voice teacher to go to: Elsie Fogerty. Edith set out to meet Miss Fogerty. She wore her best hat for the occasion and her finery offended the redoubtable Miss Fogerty, who thought her flighty, not the sort of pupil she wanted to teach. This was a set-back that Edith had not anticipated, but she rallied some friends to her defence and they persuaded Miss Fogerty that she was in earnest. Having conquered the London stage with ease, Edith went back to the drawing board.

Parallel with this she decided that her Shakespearean salvation could only be found at the Old Vic. She asked Lilian Baylis if she could join the company for the next season. She had tried before, six years earlier, using the good offices of Sybil Thorndike to effect the introduction. Lilian rang Sybil a few days later and complained: 'How dare you send me such an ugly woman' (or at least that is how the legend has it, and the story may well be true since Lilian seldom had time to be as polite as convention demanded). She was later to regret her hasty and hurtful rejection, admitting to Sybil that she had acted foolishly on the earlier occasion. 'I ought to have engaged her then, but she didn't look the leading type.' It is revealing to note that even such a renegade as Lilian Baylis was not immune from the commercial considerations of 'type-casting'. Leading ladies were supposed to have a spurious, chocolate-box attraction whatever their talents, and there are few, even today, who break through this stupid barrier without a struggle.

Edith felt that her success as Millamant would count in her favour and help remove the stigma of *The Dream* in Lilian's eyes, but the call never came. Without a great deal of enthusiasm, and perhaps in some panic, she accepted a leading role in a new play written by Princess Bibesco, Lord Oxford and Asquith's daughter, called *The Painted Swan*. This opened at the Everyman, Hampstead in March 1925 in front of a first night audience described by the *Daily Express* as the most distinguished ever to be drawn to a suburban theatre. Some of the critics found the piece amateurish, 'a sort of schoolgirl effort', the author being handicapped 'by a fatal fluency in writing smart dialogue which runs away with her', giving her audience a 'rapid fire of second-rate epigrams.' The major honours went to Edith who, in the character of Ann, Lady Candover, had the pleasure of seeing her critical admirers return to the fold. Agate found her 'exquisite . . . not a shade of subtlety escaped her throughout the whole piece.' The cast was worthy enough to satisfy society making the trek to the suburbs, for it included Felix Aylmer, Elissa Landi, Clifford Mollison, Robert Harris, Allan Jeayes and Frank Cellier and it says much for the standards established by the producer Norman Macdermott that he could gather together such a group in a small, out of the way theatre. It is doubtful whether the play extended Edith and one wonders whether Edith was wise to spurn Shaw's *Mrs. Warren*. The final impression is that she gave a clever display in a theatrically effective, but ultimately slight play which kept her name before the public but did little to surprise the already converted, and nothing whatsoever for those who expected nothing less than greatness every time she appeared.

In this period of restless transition Edith felt the need to return to her theatrical origins and was next seen in the Renaissance Theatre's revival of Beaumont and Fletcher's *The Maid's Tragedy*, one of three productions mounted to honour the tercentenary of Fletcher's death. Her erstwhile companion in *The Painted Swan*, Frank Cellier, was the producer and she joined Ion Swinley, Baliol Holloway, Stanley Lathbury and the Chinese actress, Miss Rose Quong. *The Maid's Tragedy*, with its glut of murders and suicides, borders on Monty Python parody, but if one can stomach the plot, the poetry is noble and it forms an interesting example of the sort of entertainment that moved our ancestors to 'tatters and tears'. Curiously, Sybil Thorndike had played the same role—that of Evadne, the accursed mistress of a libidinous king—only four years previously. Thus for the first time the rivalry engendered by sections of the Press could be put to a practical test. The character of Evadne demands big guns; she cannot be played by halves. Sybil, with Hecuba and Medea behind her, had almost cornered the market in these outsize ladies and comparisons were inevitable. Once again, as the senior dramatic citizen, it was left to Agate to pass sentence.

Writing in his *Sunday Times* column on 24th March 1925, he donned his literary black cap. 'England is a free country, and there's no divinity round dramatic critics. I may be quite wrong about this play. It just didn't happen to impress me. Neither did Miss Edith Evans, and there I venture to think that I am not wrong. Nobody will accuse me of a prejudice against this actress, but she must not play tragedy. I respect fully suggest that Miss Evans is the most brilliant comic actress of our day, with a good turn of domestic pathos. But the tragic mask, voice and manner are not hers, and she will never acquire them. Miss Thorndike showed us how much can be done in the part. Miss Evans how little. And now if the former artist will produce her Millamant I shall be delighted to apply sufficient balm to any wounds which the above may have occasioned to the foremost *comédienne* of the day.'

This was Agate's best bedside manner: pronouncing a terminal illness while at the same time slipping the patient a pain-killer.

In the teeth of this devastating rebuke, Edith persisted in her efforts to persuade Lilian Baylis to change her mind. She wrote to her and pleaded her case anew. Andrew Leigh had been appointed producer for the new season and his enthusiasm to include Edith in his first term of office appears to have tilted the scales in her favour. Lilian Baylis finally agreed, not without argument as to terms, naturally, and Edith was offered no less than thirteen roles, including Portia, Rosalind, Cleopatra, Beatrice and the Nurse in *Romeo and Juliet*, a varied list containing many notable challenges. The announcement of her joining the company was greeted with widespread enthusiasm in the Press, and her obvious financial sacrifice commented upon in approving terms, but her friends were dubious.

'Everyone, or nearly everyone, thought I was mad. But I had to find out how to play Shakespeare. I was, I believe, the first 'West End'' actress ever to go to the Vic, and this might explain Lilian's reluctance to employ me and the regular Old Vic audience's apprehensions as to my motives. Most people could only think of the money I was turning my back on, but money never worried me. I like money, but it has never dominated my thinking. I knew where I ought to be and so I went there. It was as simple and as complicated as that. I was terrified, but I had to get over that.'

One person who did not think she was mad was Herbert Farjeon. He broke the unwritten law and wrote to her.

> Camden Cottage,
> Round Hill, S.E.26.
> Saturday May 30th.

Dear Edith Evans,

I have this morning received a letter from the Old Vic telling me the best news I have heard since I was a dramatic critic. And I cannot refrain in all this aloofness from writing to thank you and to congratulate you and to tell you how, for once, I am actually looking forward to the winter. Don't believe the gentleman who says you are not a tragedienne. I don't, anyway. And remember, through all the doubts and disappointments and worries you may have, that you are in the direct line of descent from Shakespeare and he needs you badly.

From what text do you learn your parts? I believe (with Poel) that all Shakespearean players should learn their parts from the original text—there is a flavour in the spelling, the typography and the punctuation that adds something important. If you haven't a First Folio reprint, I should be pleased to lend you a copy of such plays as you may be wanting to study.

Yours most expectantly, Herbert Farjeon.

You will find Andrew Leigh a darling—I know him well and much admire his acting. Baliol Holloway is a good choice, too—he makes Elizabethan plays 'go along'—a wind that bellies out the sails.

The first play of the new season was to be *The Merchant of Venice* with Baliol Holloway as Shylock. Edith spent the entire summer studying all her roles (reading some of them for the first time, she admitted, from copies supplied by Mr. Farjeon) and naturally devoting much of her attention to Portia. 'Portia really terrified me. Not only was she to be my baptism at the Vic, but everybody I spoke to talked about Ellen Terry in the role. I was meant to understand that I had no chance of approaching her brilliance.'

It was during this time that Guy returned home to England.

It is always satisfying in this cynical, unromantic age to record a genuine happy ending, and as I approach the telling of the central core of Edith's private life, so different from the public image projected over fifty years, I am anxious to do justice to a love story that, from my first discovery of Guy's letters—letters, I might add, that Edith feared she had lost—has gripped and stirred me. The mode for biographers in such matters is to maintain a discreet distance, but Edith urged me to approach closer. Perhaps there was a sense of time lost, a sense of guilt, in her insistence; she welcomed the discoveries we made together, and there was pleasure in her pain. Their romance was such a 'queer mixture' as she put it, surviving as it did so many improbables; old-fashioned in its completeness, for it had a beginning, a middle and an end, those now despised components of a good story; and if the end was ultimately tragedy, there was at the centre of it a relationship which enriched two extraordinary people.

Guy returned a successful man. He was well thought of by the directors of The British Controlled Oilfields and held a responsible position in the field which, had he so wished, could have advanced him further. He had invested his savings wisely, taking advantage of his technical know-how, and he had frequently written to Edith to follow his tips. More importantly he had achieved what he had set out to do: namely prove himself to Edith, for he never wanted to be a burden to her and felt it vital, once her life had shot off at such a tangent, that he retained his own identity and independence.

Their reunion was not a disappointment to either of them. Whatever else the separation proved, it certainly hadn't diminished their need for each other, and without belabouring the point it is abundantly clear that the physical attraction they felt for each other was at least as important as the rediscovered delight of companionship. Edith was still living in Claverton Street and it was there that Guy went when he landed. He seems to have been gifted with a quite amazing understanding of Edith's personality, for he arrived at the very moment when she had taken her decision to join the Old Vic, yet he was able to put aside his own pleasures, so long awaited, in order to accommodate her fears and help resolve them for her.

He had only a short leave due to him and knew that he must return to the oilfields by the middle of September. By then Edith would be in the final stages of rehearsal for *The Merchant*. Their separate lives were controlled by external forces so vastly different as to baffle the ordinary imagination. Knowing they had to part again, they decided never to part. Twenty one years after their first meeting, Guy's proposal of marriage—by no means his first—was accepted.

Yet once again the plot takes a twist. Shortly before the date they had agreed upon Guy went off on his own to stay in St. Ives, Cornwall, ostensibly to look for a future home for them both, but in one of his letters to her from Cornwall in August 1925 he lets slip a further clue to his sensitivity towards Edith. 'You my beautiful will be wise to study daily, for I shall return starving for you . . . By then you will have had lots of freedom for your own quiet thought and to regain your purely own perspective and for this I can be glad. . . .'

(The expression 'your own quiet thought' crops up time and time again, and pertained to those periods of meditation that Edith felt to be so necessary. She urged others to do likewise, and in a letter written from the Playhouse, Liverpool in 1924, Herbert Lomas, told her he was trying hard to 'hold the right thought' and that, as a result of their talks in Le Havre at the end of the war, he had embraced the teachings of Christian Science.')

Guy understood Edith better than anybody. He had waited for her, he had finally claimed her and he was not going to panic her at the eleventh hour.

In another letter written from Cornwall he poured out his heart to her, as though twenty-one years of love could no longer be contained.

Ye Gods how I want you, you, the inspiration of you, your love and trust, your whole being, form, future, passion, hopes and doubts—the entire whole of you.

Thus and only in this way can you come to me, my Woman, my first and final love, my other half, my Everything.

No little incident in my life has or ever will touch this ruling passion for you Edith and this you must know and make your decision upon. Anything else, any retention of the smallest part of you, any measuring of your love or surrender could and would wreck us: such a possibility I cannot, dare not court, for you know and I know that our failure—gloss it over, cynically make light of it as we both might attempt, would harm you dreadfully; you the woman, and do infinite damage to your fine soul and your art.

For my part I feel that I understand you more, mentally, morally and your physical self as well, and I know that as a man I can be more patient and strong than the average fellow. I see our life and our whole relationship through your eyes and to so live, yet retaining my own man's right and status is my function—horrid word—and to help you largely by curbing my own desires of and for you, to keep you truly free, but Mine: that is my life. Your life's work, the greatest end, the greatness that is within you must be envisioned and has so been by me for years, because I love you. If I must sacrifice for this end I am willing, so willing to do so always, but I too must discuss with myself the normal wisdom of the abstentions, the givings, the

96

ultimate results of our intentions and acts upon our joint being.

With your marked individuality this is more vital than in ordinary relations between life lovers, because your Woman's way of thinking from the personal standpoint is so developed, and necessarily so from out of your life's experiences. We are ourselves and must not fail, or entering ever fear failure. It is at all times hard to put aside our own wishes, the outcome of habit and ideas absorbed in the past, and these when they have become almost convictions ruling our life and thoughts must be reckoned with and applied, corrected or effaced. Now, my dearest, it is your time for looking within yourself and throwing out the old apparel which has shaped and coloured your thought, guiding your past actions, and choosing that which is worthwhile. No easy thing my love, when we realise that nature wars on ideas and ideals, often making of bright aspirations little else but dark acts, clouding serene skies with doubts sufficient to decide our temporary choice of intellectual garments.

I do not preach, my angel, all I try is to prompt, not even guide— now. And this because I have had time for quiet thoughts here, especially during the radiant silence of these beautiful moonlit nights. It is then that life seems such a fine thing, so fair and clean down to the small details of the day: it is at such times we are not confronted with the unsympathetic; the greed of this material world, which has almost made of me a cynic to laugh at its vaunted aims and reality and to wish to withdraw to a position of complete separation, freedom—which you can see at once can only spell negation. What of it all, my dearest girl, apart from the vanities! Soon I hope to hold you in my arms and to tell you again I adore you you and your happiness. Keep me in your thoughts 'till then. Your Guy.

They were married on September 9th 1925 at St. Saviour's Church near Claverton Street on the only free day Edith had from rehearsals. There was no hope of a honeymoon, and the marriage itself was a secret they kept from most people. Edith wrote to her parents, who by now were living in Eastbourne, Edward Evans having retired.

'We have done the deed. 9.30 this morning at St. Saviour's so that's allright. Blessing on you both and love from Edith and Guy.

P.T.O.

On the reverse of the page, Guy had added:

'Well, Edith hasn't left me much to say, except that we are very happy notwithstanding the rain and that I now can subscribe myself Your affectionate Son   Guy.

(If it now appears somewhat out of character for Edith to agree to marry in a rush between rehearsals, one should not forget the forbidding presence of Lilian Baylis who treated romances within her company in the same way as she had treated air raids: they were unfortunate and were to be ignored as far as possible. There are many stories to support this, the best known being perhaps the account of the young couple, both members of the company, who went to her office one day, hand in hand. Lilian was working at her desk and didn't look up. They waited. Finally, she gave some sign that she was aware of their presence. 'What is it?' she said. The young actor, giving possibly his worst reading of the lines, replied: 'We're in love, Miss Baylis, and we want to get married.' 'I haven't got time to listen to gossip,' Lilian said, and went back to her work.)

I return to the long letter he posted to her from Cornwall prior to the marriage, for it contains Guy's whole credo. She was his 'first and final love'; there is no doubting the naked truth of this statement. At the time of writing this letter his proposal of marriage had been accepted, but Edith still wanted time to 'look within' herself. She did not question her love and affection for Guy, it was herself she questioned; whether or not she had the ability to sustain a relationship that must, by its very nature, challenge her vocation. Conditions had been made, discussed and accepted between them and Guy makes passing reference to them: 'I too must discuss with myself the normal wisdom of the abstentions, the givings'; he felt he was capable of being stronger and more patient than the average fellow—she was to be allowed to be truly free in spirit while remaining his wife in the eyes of the outside world. He made the offer of sacrifice, while at the same time admitting that it was hard to put aside previous convictions. Edith was a simple woman with complex emotions; it was not until long after Guy's death that she faced up to the sacrifice she had made in the service of her art, and by then it was too late to reverse anything. If anything she had too much self-discipline. She could always sublimate her personal feelings if they appeared to stand in the way of her professional dedication, but in so doing she deliberately trampled on her heart, giving, to strangers, the impression that she was a cold person. This was not so. She was always at war with herself. There was Edith Evans the great actress who constantly tried to isolate herself from Edith Evans the woman, and for many years the contest was uneven.

Edith's debut at the Vic was three days after the marriage, on September 12th and by the 17th, Guy was writing to her from Aldershot on the eve of sailing to America, the start of his long journey back to Maracaibo. He had accepted the terms of the contract.

Edith's first night at the Vic in front of a packed and curious house aroused great excitement; all the old loyalists were there for the start of the season and their ranks were swelled by those who had come to see what the new girl would do. Edith was under no illusions. 'I wouldn't say they were what you would call impartial to me as a "West End" actress. Maybe they thought I was coming to teach them something; actually I had gone there for them to teach me a lot.'

The Old Vic audiences of those days were fiercely partisan. The house held 1200 and it was Standing Room Only for Edith's debut, which must have gone some way to placate Lilian Baylis' doubts as to the desirability of employing her. Edith confessed that, at first, she was at a loss to know how to make contact with this vast and committed audience. They were not against her, but they weren't for her: it was too early for that—she had to prove herself and measure up to their standards of what was acceptable. She had, in her own words, to find a way to make her performances 'larger and simpler (not necessarily louder) than I had been used to.' She found her experiences in *The Merchant* 'a very strange affair.' She was acting alongside an old hand at Shakespeare, Baliol Holloway—'that taut, spare greyhound of an actor' as J. C. Trewin has described him—and the character of Portia is one of those over-familiar roles that audiences can quote by heart (sometimes more accurately than the actress up on the stage). It was a testing debut, especially when one remembers that she was also in the midst of a personal drama, for the prospect of parting from Guy so soon after their marriage could not have lessened the tensions leading up to that opening night.

Many of the critics were guarded in their praise; several of them observed that she had yet to find 'the pitch' of the theatre. Final judgement was reserved, for the season was young, there were many other major roles to come.

In the last letter he wrote on English soil that year Guy had said 'while you grace Padua I shall be hustling for the Spanish Main, and days are full of hope and romance and lovers' work. What would you like when I get there, the scalp of a Jabberwock, a Margueritan emerald or a letter from Your Lover?'

He was burdened with his own sadness at their parting.

I love you and love you the more that you love me and will outdo you in both . . . You are quite right when you say that you could not love a failure, and that seems an absurd paradox, doesn't it? . . . I shall sail away tomorrow with a stiff lip to be a better man, and learn to be a better oilman and still more to learn those graces which should become you in your man . . . Soon, then, the time will have flown by and this interval will appear a mere short passage in our lives like going to school for a term. Have I been blind and selfish that I did not realise how much you are to me, or is it that only now are we becoming fitted for each other?

The next time he wrote the letter was postmarked New York.

We arrived in glorious weather and, do you know, the first, almost the first question I was asked was "Haven't you brought Mrs. Booth?" I not unnaturally explained that I had left her at home with the children. That nettles you, doesn't it? and "wises" you to what a loose-tongued man you have got, *no*, not to contend with.

With that pleasing superiority of the newly-married man, he went on to tell her:

I gathered during my drive to the hotel that marriage seems to have been forgotten almost, and that almost all the girls and wives have their "sweetie" on the side putting up for them. Ye Gods and what a mark it puts on them all.

He told her that he intended to go and see 'our old friends Nervo and Knox tonight at the Hippodrome so I shall enjoy sitting in imagination with you again,' but then the letter switched from the mocking facetiousness of the opening paragraphs and tenderness took over.

You seem so near, so gentle and sweet and I can feel your soft hair against my cheek, feel your heart beat under my hand as I stoop over you and adore you. Surrounded by a gregarious horde of nearly 14 millions, these become a mere medley of sounds as I think on the dear youness of You that day we spent wandering over Windsor and the Castle. It is nearly five—ten o'clock with you and a delighted audience "In Front"—so I must away to my appointment and leave you to conduct Justice and Happiness along their appointed paths. Au revoir, my dear, and a happy ending to your play.

Edith was still playing Portia, since for the first time Lilian Baylis and Andrew Leigh had done away with the old repertory system and substituted limited runs. When not performing she was preparing for the next ordeal, the role of Queen Margaret in *Richard III* and again 'there was the same fight and struggle to get into touch, to get used to long speeches, and again in this play I would say only a modicum of success was achieved.' Herbert Farjeon, for one, did not agree with her self-evaluation, correcting Agate's confident dictum that Edith could only play comedy. He found her performance 'so commanding, so powerful, so large that it reduced all the other actors on the stage, with the exception of Mr. Baliol Holloway, to the level of pygmies.' Agate himself was content to praise her in general terms: 'Here is an actress who can walk like a queen and rant like one also.' Though pulling himself up just short of the word 'genius' he found Holloway's Richard 'undoubtedly fine' but was not over-enthusiastic about the whole. Lilian Baylis had apparently saved money on the minor roles, and many of the critics drew attention to the fact that standards were low. Across the border, with all the confidence of a man assuring Lindbergh of the feasibility of flight, the *Edinburgh Evening News* critic solemnly advised his readers to 'keep your eye on Edith Evans.'

Nobody was keeping more of an eye on her than Edith herself. She was far from satisfied at the rate of progress and applied herself to the third play, *The Taming of The Shrew* with renewed dedication. Discussing the attitude of the Old Vic audiences towards her, she said, 'I felt that in every new play I had to convince them, not now of my integrity, but of my performance. In *The Shrew* I began to get the hang of it, and for the first time the audience and I became friends.'

She struggled with the problem of how to deal with the long speeches and eventually arrived at her own solution. Years later she confided it to Michael Elliot. 'What you must do, dear, is to take the last line of the speech and pull it towards you.' Cyril Connolly once asked 'how many books on painting did Renoir write?' and if one applies the same criterion to the mystery of acting it is difficult to think of any book, any acting manual that in any way approaches the heart of the matter. Edith, although not an intellectual woman, who never dissected her work or lectured others on technique, was yet capable of talking brilliantly about acting in an epigramatic way. The image she conjures up in that simple statement—'take the last line . . . and pull it towards you' is indeed a shaft of lightning illuminating the darkness that, like a miner, the actor accepts as his natural lot. Michael Elliot has also said that 'she knew, better than any other actor I have ever met, that obscure, mysterious, organic process whereby you give birth to a performance which is highly delicate, extremely vulnerable, especially in early rehearsal, which has to be produced afresh for every audience every night.' Edith was to struggle to find the truth to the end of her days; it was never easy for her. What she presented to the public may have looked easy, but the finished performance held days and weeks of anguish. She was always concerned for her audiences, concerned not to cheat them, and she found her own way of ensuring that, during a long run, those who came towards the end got the same value as those who had attended at the beginning. 'You have to think of it as riding a different horse round the same course every night,' she said.

She played her Katherine in *The Shrew* in 'a shouting auburn wig, and simulating the pangs of hunger so powerfully,' wrote Horace Horsnell, that 'the very chocolate-sellers in the auditorium fled to cover as at the approach of a rapacious army.' She had found the key she was looking for, and once she had unlocked the first door there was no looking back.

She was writing regularly to Guy and keeping him fully posted on her various ups and downs. Back in Maracaibo at the beginning of

November he was able to write:

I am so delighted that you are having such success with your work
and congratulate the audiences on their taste. It is a joy, too, to me
to know that thus that rather silly domestic atmosphere—or was it a
flavour?—doesn't have much scope for developing at the Old Vic;
has it more or less disappeared or been pushed back into a corner?
My blessing and a kiss for one "Katherine" and may she be just the
delightful creature you outline to me. *You* could so easily and so well
play the part as done in the past by those of lesser imagination and
look such a ruddy lady withal. Yes, I overheard what you said . . .

Congratulations came from many sources. The playwright Henry
Arthur Jones wrote to her on November 5th 1925:

Dear Miss Edith Evans,
I had a most enjoyable evening. There was a true Shakespearean
spirit in it. I am glad you have deserted modern comedy. You had an
assured career before you. But you won't be sorry you put it aside.
Nor will the public. We moderns can't offer you parts that are
comparable with Shakespeare!

It had taken Guy nearly seven weeks to arrive back at the oilfields.
He wrote frequently and was full of plans for the time when he would
return to England for good and they would have a home of their own.
In his mind's eye he had already selected the spot where his dreams
would become reality. Recalling the journey he had made to Cornwall,
he wrote:

Oh, my darling I saw such a pretty nook, a little green bank all
ablaze with autumn sun, and set in reddening oaks and hazel, and
washed by a sea of scarlet haws: what spot a to take my love to,
and what a store of dreams it holds.
Somewhere near Itchen Abbas will one day bring us our bliss, or
I am an oaf.

He was also concerned to give her advice about her career and urged
her to obtain a copy of Stanislavsky's *My Life in Art* from the nearest
library. He hadn't read it himself but 'I gather you will find it both
interesting and helpful.' Edith duly obtained a copy, but was not
impressed by it. Stanislavsky's whole approach was too intellectual for
her. 'Too much explaining,' she said. 'I couldn't be doing with all that.
I have to find the truth of a part—that bit I agree with—but the rest,
crikey, I didn't know what he was getting at.'

Guy had charted his route across America on the journey back to
Venezuela, posting written bouquets whenever he made a stop. 'Each
day you are more and more my beloved and again how I wish "you

were along". I kiss your hands and carry the gentlest thoughts of my only girl into the West' was the message he sent her from Ponca City, Oklahoma. He next wrote from Summit, California.

This morning awoke at 5.40 looked through the compartment window out on to a pretty little Arizona station and noted the station name "Bagdad": murmured "liar" and off to sleep again. . . . I get little joy out of it all without You. It all seems rather hollow, one cannot get away from tongues and twang.

On notepaper headed The Biltmore Hotel, Los Angeles, he mentioned something which obviously occupied him—the possibility that they might have left it all too late—'so many opportunities lost'—and that it was somehow entirely his fault.

I have met a happy couple here married two years, he is 53 and she just ten years younger who have a fine babe; you never met such a surprised and happy couple in all your days. So we will count old man Time our good friend.

From Pittsburgh (and I should perhaps explain that his route back to the oilfields was not a direct one; he darted back and forth across America, attending to business on behalf of his company, visiting the Tulsa Exhibition and making contact with other oilmen) which he found 'another Birmingham' and where it snowed continuously, he commented:

Like everywhere else the place reeks of money, and I am convinced that these large cities have a big potential for good art, who will appreciate and pay high for what they want and do not get, and that one day not too far distant my Edith is going to supply the one and collect the other.

This was one rare instance where he failed to understand Edith. She never set much store by conscious talk of Art; in some curious way it embarrassed her, and she suspected those who wanted to use Art with a capital A as a bargaining point. Nor did she ever care overmuch for money or material possessions. She liked to be paid well for what she did, but money was never a status symbol with her. By show business standards today she was always a long way down the money tables even at the height of her drawing powers, and she denounced some of the fees paid to the superstars as obscene. She liked what money could buy, but her upbringing ensured that she retained common sense in her own housekeeping and to the end of her days she remained convinced that she was on the edge of poverty. Apart from good clothes and, very late in her career, a stately second-hand Rolls Royce which she greatly prized but constantly half-apologised for ('I bought it because the rail fares were so expensive.'), she never surrounded herself with the more obvious trappings that usually accompany success. She owned very little jewellery, for instance, and that which she did possess she seldom wore, her favourite adornments being two simple silver bracelets. She worried about money, yet gave it away to many a worthy cause and a great number of old friends who had fallen on hard times. In going through her papers after her death I was amazed by her numerous acts of genuine charity—unheralded, discreet and unfailingly generous: an old stage-door keeper to whom she sent money every Christmas, a friend who needed helping through a dull patch, another who had asked for a private mortgage, others still from days gone by who needed some assurance that they were not forgotten. But with herself she was far from generous; the act of treating herself to a comfortable armchair two years before the end caused much soul-searching; could she afford it? and even if she could afford it, should she spoil herself with such a luxury? Her nephew by marriage, John Booth, who managed her affairs during the last decade of her life, was constantly chided for allowing her such extravagances. Fortunately he was able to humour her away from self-recrimination when, after much debate, she finally agreed to 'lash out' on a new dress. Perhaps she had too many memories of her contemporaries ending their lives in poverty or in the actors' Denville home, dependent on the charity of others. The example set by her parents died hard, yet once again we are confronted with two Ediths: one who seldom hesitated to help others in genuine need, and the other who denied herself much. In truth, her fears concerning money were groundless: with Guy's help she had invested well and although she professed a total ignorance of the vagaries of the stock market, she was canny enough to employ the best professional advice. Like most of us she was constantly outraged by the demands made upon her by Her Majesty's Collectors of Taxes. People, she felt, were being raped—hard-working people, that is, like herself, who were rewarded for their efforts by ever-increasing penalties. She often put pen to paper in this connection.

Doubtless Guy meant well, but she never took him up on his suggestion that she should take Art to Pittsburg for material gain, and during the course of her long career made very few appearances in America. There is no doubt that had she crossed the Atlantic and deserted England for good, as many of her contemporaries were persuaded to do, the rewards would have been generous. She was often asked, but the thought of leaving England appalled her.

Without being able to quote from her letters to Guy, the record of their love for each other is necessarily one-sided. We know from many references that she wrote to him almost as frequently as he did to her, but what language she employed remains a mystery. She often told me that she considered herself a poor letter writer; I think she over-stated her inadequacies, for such letters of hers that I possess have an unconventional verve to them, but I think it is true to say that they lacked the roundness, the fluency and the passion of Guy's.

'I grow tired,' he wrote from Pittsburgh, 'and want you so in this big warm room, just to be real and to love you as you ought to be loved, as my dear shall be loved in the days that now seem so distant. I would kiss your hands and lips and breasts, your lovely arms and hair, crush you into protesting, discover you to be slimmer, more creamy white, even more lovely to be loved and look for the passion in your eyes to put out mine. Keep me for your true kisses.'

He also wrote to his mother from Pittsburgh, and she replied to him on November 12, 1925 from Aldershot, addressing him as *My Dear George*. It was a letter mostly concerned with ill health, her own and other members of the family, but contained a revealing reference to Edith. 'Yes Edith wrote to me some time after you had gone but I have been so unwell and have had so much trouble that I have not answered it yet, and I don't know quite what to do or how to address her, as she said in her letter that she saw no reason why her marriage should ever be made Public. I suppose I must not address her as Mrs. Booth, and I don't feel like addressing her as Miss Evans, so perhaps you will tell me what I am to do.' I have not been able to discover any mention of this in any subsequent letter from Guy to Edith.

He had returned to New York for a brief spell before catching the boat which took him, finally, to Maracaibo. He stayed in what was then advertised as 'The largest hotel in the world'—the Pennsylvania, with its 2200 rooms and 2200 baths—and was delighted to find a letter awaiting him and with it a new batch of photographs (presumably taken of her various triumphs at the Old Vic).

My darling, my darling, . . . I will not confess how many times I have gone over your perfect letter and kissed each of your charming pictures.
I had so hoped to have them before I sailed and here they are, beautiful beyond any words of mine, dear, even if you do look rather sulky in one of them. Did the photographer escape with his life?
How fine a thing Life is when I can read that you love me and can wait until my job is finished. At times it is hard, very hard to go on, but more often it is otherwise and I have so much to do to deserve you. Have learnt such a lot for your sake, not only about my work but more of charity and gentleness to the other; you can and I trust will inspire me to do more than my little best and you always ring so true.

105

This latter is wonderful always to me for I used to think that through your work you might be influenced to express more than you felt. Do you understand just what I mean? There are those who in the act of expression are carried on the tide of their own words, voicing in spite of themselves ideals or views or sentiments quite other than their real convictions or feelings.

This last sentence is almost worthy to stand alongside La Roche-foucauld. Time and time again he returned to the theme of making himself worthy of her. His letters are a strange mixture of carnality and prudishness (on the train to Pittsburg he had observed: 'And it is no little, well, upsetting, to see the outwardly charming girls on the trains pair off with the men after preliminary skirmishes and disappear into corners and compartments where amorous "petting parties" are staged. There would seem to be a thin dividing line severing the hussies who openly drink their men's spirits from one hip and hang on the other during dances, and the college minx who takes her fling talking cheap biology—this will go down as the "biological period" here—and claim full "freedom" and is equally messy. They all wear bright silk bloomers, and for the rest, are expensively if scantily draped. The men are either hugely handsome or horribly Hebraic, are horribly hung with "bespoke" garments, and, as I have plenty of opportunity of noting make love? spare the mark, like unto the buffoon, the bear or the beast. Enough, Jorge, you are hipped!').

For the fourth production of the Vic season Edith was given a short breather; after *The Shrew* the company moved on to *Measure for Measure* and in this she played the minor role of Mariana. She needed the rest, for the greatest challenge was next on the list—Shakespeare's Cleopatra, as opposed to Dryden's which she had already played for the Phoenix Society in 1922. It was not to be one of her unqualified successes, though she had made much preparation for the role and was conscious of the need to convert others to her interpretation. Shakespeare's Cleopatra has defied many a fine actress, for there is almost too much for anybody and everybody—'the whole of womankind just won't go on a stage', said George Cukor, the American film director, when asked his opinion of Vivien Leigh's performance in the role. It is my belief that because, like Napoleon's Josephine, Cleopatra is synonymous with love on the grand scale in most people's minds, they approach any new attempt with a pre-conceived notion not only of the physical attributes they think the lady should possess, but also, by the same sub-conscious process, a notion of how they would react, were they Antony, to the passion the words are intended to convey. Audiences and critics seem to demand not a single character but an amalgam.

Guy and Edith had discussed the way in which she was going to attempt Cleopatra: the letter he wrote from Maracaibo on December 1st 1925 confirms this in detail.

I did pray for you last night on your first presentation of Cleopatra and can hardly await the news of your success: I hope you still have your original conception of the character—to smooth out the frowns and overdone scowlings of Katharine and delete the smack of harlotry from Cleopatra's memory.

The man who wrote that was married to the actress and although not necessarily totally blind to her faults, was naturally disposed in her favour. Alas, the deletion of 'the smack of harlotry' was not what Agate was waiting to see. One man's meat, etcetera. Agate felt that Edith did not have enough passion and vulgarity for the role, that she was too fastidious: the actress, he pronounced 'was simply not suited.' His idea of the perfect Cleopatra was Janet Achurch, yet Shaw was on record as saying that everything Miss Achurch did as Cleopatra was mistaken. Where does one look for the truth? Perhaps it is asking too much, as Cukor said, to hope that any actress could live up to the descriptions that Shakespeare scatters throughout the text. Alan Dent in his bouquet-cum-memoir of Vivien Leigh lists them all, and a forbidding tally it is. I will mention but half a dozen to make the point. 'Cunning past man's thought', 'this great fairy', 'a cow in June', 'triple-turned whore', 'most noble Empress' and 'yon ribald nag of Egypt.' Take your pick as you stare into your dressing room mirror on the first night. Perhaps Agate was in sour mood that particular evening for little about the production pleased him. He observed that as far as he could see 'Alexandria and Rome only possessed two pieces of furniture between them, and the population of these cities was about three to the square mile.' He objected to the cold quality of the lighting and the fact that Edith curled up on the sofa and died 'like a naughty consumptive in the reign of Dumas fils' instead of sitting bolt upright on the throne for the final occasion.

It was hardly to be accounted the success that Guy had prayed for. He was plunged into his own repertory of work.

Now that the fireworks and dinners in camp are past and I have eaten all the indigestible food of friends here, I am making desperate efforts to set 'abaht it': if only those flowers and the picture of you admiring, and stooping in gentle attendance over them, would play fair and give me a chance I might sleep soundly and forget you a bitty. This latter of course is the only one that will see me through, so think of me daily banishing you into outer darkness and concentrating on staffs, rations, politics and crooked lawyers, railway construction, damming rivers, buying land and putting up new quarters and listening to everybody's complaints and ills.

I have a black eye and torn throat but it is not as bad as it would appear. Riding a restive horse at dusk back from our new area, I got hooked up in a vine by the neck and thrown against a tree trunk. But it's all in the game and the real irritation I feel is from bites of numerous "garapatos" or small ticks, which find me juicy eating at present.

God is in His Heaven and I still love you my dearest as I never thought possible. Each day is yours and all that is best in me. Keep jolly and teach *Everybody* to love you (But do not particularise!).

He was still in ignorance of how Cleopatra had been received when he wrote again just before Christmas. Apparently he gleaned most of his news from home from copies of the *Tatler* passed on by a friend in New York with the engaging name of Boggs.

I am so impatient for the November 30th issues and to read of your rendering of Cleopatra. By the way you never thanked me for my wise, not to say, heavy writing from the "Lapland" all about the life, habits and correct conception of this interesting and delightful lady. Sorry if you thought it all tosh, and I hopes your sandal comes off, or the asp refuses to gormandise. Oh happy asp, could I but bribe him out of one short show.

(Unhappily his advice to the player did not survive amongst his papers).

In the same letter he advised Edith to buy 500 shares in another oil company which had doubled its production, but urged caution where his own company was concerned. He was anxious to tell her 'there has been no hestitation in the bosoms of certain candid companeros to inform me that marriage has much improved me, made it almost possible to live in the same town with me.' It was with a trace of embarrassment that he related he had been kissed on both cheeks 'in a crowded public place' by the German-American General Manager of the Standard Oil Company, but went on to confess 'what a lot of kindness and goodness there is in this bad old world, often expressed in the quaintest fashion.'

Did his 'candid companeros' really comprehend who it was he had married? If, like Guy, they were self-exiled from the post-war sullenness of Europe, they could hardly appreciate the extent of Edith's triumph in the theatre. Possibly to them Guy had merely married *an actress* which would have been fuel enough for gossip when the gin and whisky came out after work was finished. Although he was obviously flattered that his colleagues found him 'much improved' by marriage it was not in his character to have discussed her with them. His intimacies were confined to the letters he wrote her, but for the rest he convinces me as an introspective man, 'deep' as they say in country parlance, a man who kept himself to himself. Despite the changed status that marriage had brought, they were still hesitant with each other and the vital factor remained Guy's inability to gain a real intimacy with Edith's professional existence. Here was a man who loved to excess; who was capable of putting as many expressions of love to Edith as his pen had ink for; who could articulate on paper from a distance what, perhaps, he found difficult to tell her face to face. She had let him know that she was unwilling to love a failure, and one can sense the urgency of his desire to convince her that she had chosen wisely after so long a hesitation. He was jealous—and who can blame him for that?—but too intelligent not to realise that he must conceal that jealousy, for Edith resisted being possessed even by the man she loved and had married.

The reason Guy plays such a vital role in Edith's life and career is not immediately apparent. Many of her contemporaries in the theatre were scarcely aware of the marriage and to this day there are still some who are surprised to learn that she was ever married. I believe that Edith craved love but was afraid of the divided responsibilities that love brings. In one of the most revealing pieces of film she allowed me to include in my television documentary, she said: 'I think I was meant to be a nun. I'm a sort of loner, you know, really. I attract the wrong sort of people for me. I have to get rid of them, do you know? Then the people I do love and attract always die. So I was sort of meant to be alone, I suppose. I don't know.'

I had asked her if she relied on God and she replied: 'I do, terribly. I'm afraid I worry Him a bit. But He does look after me. I wouldn't have anybody else, you see. I can't understand it. Everyone I've loved has always died. One's parents . . . well, you have to lose your parents . . . then I lost my husband . . . I've got a funny thing about me I don't awfully like. I attract people . . . I think it's something to do with the theatre, I think and they go raving mad about . . . wanting to look after me . . . and I'm not like that, I'm an independent person. I love my friends, my real friends I've had for years and years, but there are certain people who want to be the *only one*, and I'm not the person who likes that. Yet I'm not really self-sufficient. Circumstances have *made me sufficient*, because if there's nobody else to help you, you've got to try and find out how to do it. I've done it mostly by my faith, my religion. If I hadn't had that I wouldn't be here at all.'

Did Guy's extraordinary patience spring from his awareness of Edith's innermost fears? I think it more than likely. No novelist can out-invent the workings of the human heart, and perhaps Edith and Guy found the only solution possible to their joint and several needs. Their long separations, both before and after marriage, may not have been of Guy's choosing, but he accepted them as the price he had to pay if he was not to lose her. Patience and trust had paid off once, and now he took out a second mortgage.

9

'Do you realise that your work and spirit gets into the minds and pens of the critics and that they quite noticeably write of you in a different way?'

—Letter from Guy, 31st January 1926

'That tiresome woman from the West End', as Edith sardonically described herself, had finally become a favourite of the Old Vic audiences, and once they had given their blessing she was theirs for life. Writing of her first season (in an anthology of tributes to Lilian Baylis published just before the Second World War) she revealed how she dealt with Lilian's notorious, if often necessary, stinginess.

'The Wardrobe at the Vic was a very interesting experience for me. I had quite a lot of fun with them, because they'd obviously said to themselves "Here comes a New Actress—she'll want new clothes and if we can say she must have them the tight-closed fist of Lilian will have to open'. So I was rather artful. I wanted new clothes, too, but I didn't want Lilian to think that this tiresome new girl, whose value as a Shakespearean actor still had to be proved, was insisting on unusual expenditure. Consequently, when the question of clothes was mooted I asked very politely if they would telephone down to Miss Baylis to come to the Wardrobe and discuss the matter. She came, rather surprised, but she came, and before the session was finished she was wanting new clothes as much as I was. Later on she used to boast of the beautiful dresses made for the season of 1925–26.'

More's the pity, therefore, that none of them has survived. Visiting the Ellen Terry Museum at Smallhythe, by contrast, one can still see many of her famous costumes, notably the one she wore for the Sargent portrait of her Lady Macbeth. However, it must be remembered that Ellen Terry would have paid for most of her own clothes at the time, whereas in a company as close to the poverty line as the Old Vic was in Lilian Baylis' day, they would have been returned to the Wardrobe to be adapted and altered to fit another actress in a production of a different play. Doubtless aware of this and not wishing to give a brand new performance in second-hand clothes, Edith drew upon her early training as a milliner when she was exposed to the intricacies of fashion, and, with those considerable powers of charm and persuasion which were never lacking when the occasion demanded, turned the tables on Lilian Baylis. It is curious how so many actresses lack any sort of personal dress sense, both on and off stage. Although Peggy Ashcroft has told me that in her early and mid-career Edith did not care over-much how she looked in private life, she was always meticulous and demanding of high standards for her stage appearances. In later years she cultivated a personal style that became as distinctive in its own way as that evolved by Queen Mary. She found her way to Hardy Amies' door and thereafter remained faithful to his house style, confessing that it was her one persistent vice. 'I go out to buy a loaf of bread and come back with an expensive hat or frock. I don't know what comes over me. It's rather shaming.'

1926 was another year of change. Nationally it has passed into folklore as the year of the General Strike—a sad and painful exercise in betrayal, a peculiarly British form of revolution which highlighted those contradictory aspects of our national character that so often confound our enemies. Both sides in the struggle retain, to this day, their own memories and fantasies of those nine days in May. To some it was a lark, a welcome relief from the monotony of the daily grind; to others it symbolised the emasculation of the Labour movement, especially of the then Labour leaders. The humiliation was to persist for two decades, the slate only being wiped clean in some minds by the General Election of 1945 when Churchill was landslided into shock oblivion—a further demonstration to outsiders that patriotism is seldom enough.

It is impossible not to be semi-isolated in the theatre. Outside events obviously have an effect on the profession, but by and large actors are uneasy political animals. This is not somehow sinister or reprehensible: any artistic community dominated by a particular political belief, bound by the dogma of that belief, circumscribed by the limitations of that belief and fearful of criticising anything that remotely challenges that belief, is doomed for early sterility. In the histories of the General Strike that I have studied there is little to suggest that the Theatre, as such, or actors as a body, played any significant part. Individual lives were disrupted, but there was no concerted effort, for actors were not organised as a single entity and unemployment is so familiar to the majority of actors that they find it difficult to comprehend why others are compelled to take to the barricades.

In those uneasy days at the beginning of 1926 when the sounds of the growing discontent were muffled to her ears Edith was living within a closed community, a flamboyant nunnery, austere, tightly disciplined, run by a Mother Superior of commanding presence, and with a work schedule that left little room for active participation in the outside world. There was no time for anything else, not even time to be shy, according to Edith. 'A season at the Vic can do more than anything I know to break down the shyness and inhibitions that are such a holding back to an actor's development. You launch one big part one night and the next morning you start work on another. What can you do but plunge again? An actor said to me once, 'You don't seem to mind making a fool of yourself at rehearsal" and I could only answer "I haven't got time to mind". That is only one of the many reasons why, from an actor's point of view, we must always have a living theatre, call it the Old Vic, the National, or what you will, where actors can go to learn their job.'

She was learning all the time. After Cleopatra came an oddity, The Angel in *The Child in Flanders* by Cicely Hamilton, and then Mistress Page. That was followed by Goldsmith's Kate Hardcastle in *She Stoops to Conquer*, then a different Portia, the wife of Brutus in *Julius Caesar*—all leading to the performance that was to be talked of in the same breath as her Millamant: her first Rosalind in *As You Like It*.

Reviewing George Alexander's full four hour production of *As You Like It* at the St. James' in 1896, Shaw found it difficult to understand how anybody over the age of seven could take any interest in 'a literary toy so silly in its conceit and common in its ideas' and pronounced 'an Eskimo would demand his money back if a modern author offered him such fare.' As a consequence subsequent and lesser critics of the drama had felt somewhat inhibited when they came to judge the play. Shaw had also handed down another tablet: 'who ever failed, or could fail, as Rosalind?' His influence remained such that most actresses must have approached the role with some misgivings. If they succeeded, then they were merely showing off in a foolproof vehicle, and if, God forbid, they failed they would be establishing a new low. Edith approached the role for the first time in her thirty-eighth year.

She once said: 'When I came to my lovelies, my Millamant and Rosalind, I'd learnt to control myself. It was marvellous that God should have put me into character parts first, all those little aunts and old ladies and fat women—they all taught me something. That's where I was guided, because I was going to play the beauties, the lovelies, later.'

It is a curious fact of theatrical life that few actresses succeed in the major roles at an age which coincides with the age of the actual character. Teenage Juliets are sometimes touching (and obviously more so on film) but lack that command of technique that can borrow from and expand experience so that the performance soars beyond simulation of emotion to the thinner air of remembered anguish. Edith, we know, had never been a conventional beauty and at thirty eight was considered by many to be too old for Rosalind—a young girl masquerading as a boy and wildly in love. (Even more amazing was the fact that she played her again eleven years later in a still more memorable performance, when the same arguments as to her suitability were once more demolished by her artistry.)

I advance the theory that Edith drew upon her love for Guy, remembering perhaps those adolescent, halcyon days before the war when they besported themselves in the Surrey woods and life had been one long continuous lark. It cannot be denied that her own far-distant Orlando thought of her 'always as perfection' and who wrote in the Spring of 1926 'Bless you my Ladye Faire, think of me often as I feel you must—one could not be so loved and remain conscious at any distance.'

I am not suggesting that Edith's art was lifted straight from the pages of her own life—that would be insulting to her—but I can substantiate my supposition with her own words. She once said to me: 'If I'm supposed to be a good actress, I couldn't act as well as I'm supposed to have acted if I didn't know a few things, could I? Because that's what somebody once said to me. Michael Gough's mother once said to me "You answer my questions, up there." And then she said, "Some of the women I watch on the stage don't know as much as I do." Frightened the life out of me. But she was right. I know as much as they do and I know a lot more than some of them.'

This was Edith talking in her eighties, but she had always lived her life to the full; not as a self-conscious rebel aiming at an effect to draw attention to herself or to hide her inadequacies, but because she was born to be different. Here we have the case of a mature woman, recently married to and instantly separated from a lover she had known from the age of sixteen, surely of itself sufficiently unusual as to be note-worthy in any examination of her character. It was a situation which might well have confounded many people, given the circumstances of her public life, but Edith appears almost to have welcomed it. Despite the tragedy of her lost letters to Guy, it is abundantly clear from various asides in his letters that it was not a one-sided arrangement, but some-thing they had both agreed upon and somehow drew strength from. It would be fatal to suppose that it was a marriage such as was enjoyed by Harold Nicolson and V. Sackville West, for the freedoms that Edith and Guy granted to each other did not include the freedom to love and tell outside the marriage. Both had ample opportunity to cheat had they so wished, for the very distance between them would have ensured that the deception went undetected. There is every reason to believe that their relationship was consistently a love affair rather than a marriage and the actual wedding ceremony made little or no difference. Guy wrote to her in sublime happiness, confident that they had all the time in the world still ahead of them. He had waited twenty one years to marry her, and now he seemed content to endure further years of separation and celibacy without qualm. I cannot believe that, given this situation—a spur to the imagination of any actor—Edith did not make use of it in shaping the performance that captivated audiences and critics alike. She produced, according to Herbert Farjeon 'one of the divinest pieces of comedy this astonishing actress has yet given us.' In a sense, he answers my question for me when he stated 'has there, I wonder, ever been an actress more sunnily in love?'

His sister, Eleanor, echoed his wonder. She wrote to Edith, 'if, like my brother, I were a critic, you would long ago have learned to know a little of the joy you give me. Many times this season you have heard me as part of the big voice of your audience; but now your heavenly Rosalind has put me too much in your debt, and as I can't take to print I must to pen and ink—in the shape of a letter, because there are no trees in the Waterloo Road on which to hang my verse . . . When I was little and began, at the age of four, to go to plays, there was for me and my brother a distinction in our theatregoing—there was going to other plays, and going to Shakespeare. Shakespeare for us meant Irving and Ellen Terry and Ada Rehan, and the times we saw and heard them were golden times that gave life and air and light and shape to our imaginations. What they gave me of course has never been lost, but I never believed those times and gifts could come again! . . . you have set a new light in my world of dreams.'

Farjeon himself believed that one of the great charms of *As You Like It* was 'that it succeeds in making us feel that very rare thing, a love untouched by agony. Most love is purgatory, but Rosalind, devising sports, knows all the time that she has got Orlando safe as houses, and nothing less than a lioness can give her a moment's anxiety.'

It is dangerous for a biographer to carry conjecture too far: having searched the evidence, he can but surmise. There is evidence in abundance in the letters Guy wrote during 1926. On New Year's Day, for instance: 'If we could have but one hour together occasionally this game would be really a game and bearable.' The jury might be asked to take note of the use of the word 'game'. In the same letter he made reference to the passing of time:

Well, I am 41 today, and you will arrive at the 36th milepost, is it, next month, no the 35th*, and it all means just nothing in my scheme of things which way the tail is wagged. Buddy if you had seen me the other night all dressed up escorting a bushous† bridesmaid up the aisle of the R.C. Cathedral at 9.30 p.m. helping out at a weddin',

* It would appear that Edith had concealed a couple of years from Guy. She was 37, approaching 38 in January 1926.

† Possibly phonetic spelling of a private word between them—perhaps 'beauteous'.

you would put me down at 25 *and* single! Dirty work somewhere, I ween, but I couldn't help it without hurting a lot of feelings. *She*, my bridesmaid, not the bride—don't think I noticed her—wore a silver tissue flop or leghorn hat, and a pannier frock of old gold shot silk which she assured me was very becoming. It was, but the stockings were quite out of the picture, due no doubt to local shopping difficulties.

Social notes from all over, as the *New Yorker* might put it, but perhaps containing some clues—fingerprints of regret, a smudge of conceit?

'My Dearest One,' he concluded, 'if we get but a tenth out of life as I foresee it, why we shall possess a live Paradise of 24 hours each day of love and hopes and action to carry us on into the eighties. My love and all my thoughts are yours, yes, often to the exclusion of all else. Benedicto es.'

This letter was typewritten, but he added in ink the enigmatic question: 'Who can strike a blow?'

On the last day of the same month he wrote again, relating a significant anecdote.

A young Englishman, a representative of the Caribbean Pet. Co., came to the house the other day, and shyly produced a picture from the *Tatler* of you and Anthony in *juxtaposition* asking if I uugghh— had uugghh! a very particular interest in the original of the photo, and was I not very jealous!! I was delighted with him and later recalled the spontaneity of my reply and the freedom it evidenced.

This half-mocking, half-serious, perhaps not entirely truthful retelling of the event, prefaced a passage that got closer to the heart of the matter.

One's self is but one's self, a poor brief thing, an 'opinion' and it seems to me that if one is on rare occasions permitted to reflect the good things of life, to be associated with worthwhile achievements one has lived, and holds a fund upon which to draw in times of weakening. One much used and perhaps abused constant phrase here is 'It's a great life if you don't weaken', and the sting is in the tail.

Yes, sweetheart, I too think it well that we could see light enough to part and carry on 'as was' we should (sic) now have a sounder perspective and be nearer happiness one day for having foregone the customary way of man.

Cutting across their private lives and discussed by Guy in some detail, was the take-over and reorganisation of the British Controlled Oilfields by Standard Oil of New Jersey. He had just been instructed by his new masters to place himself, staff and properties at their orders.

I am informed that my services are to be retained—my wishes are not discussed in the matter. . . . At present rumour has it that I am to take charge of the management of the Standard's interests in Western Venezuela, but this is rubbish . . . Standard cannot and do not hope to equal our results, nor can they by virtue of their mentality and methods get the work done so economically . . . the moment they discover to their own satisfaction that it is sufficiently productive . . . they will by weight of the $ push out B.C.O. and then as is usual their own men from U.S. will be installed. It is a position of some nicety and, being an Englishman and an old B.C.O. man, I shall have to tread carefully . . .

By 6th February 1926 he was writing to tell her that he was 'more or less a "creature" of the Standard . . . which not unnaturally did not please me muchly, and on top of this the new Board is hopeless and has to be daily taught *by cable* elementary lessons of the oil business . . . I have been guilty of several cold blooded murders during the past few days, and had it not been for you, *You You*, always You should have probably put my foot in it.'

His fears for his own future were increasing all the time and he included long passages of self-justification for his past efforts and talked of trying to gauge the right moment for 'getting out. I have some nice profits now, but they are but paper.' He felt that his prospects, if he remained, were 'dullish' then, as though suddenly catching himself out, apologised for monopolising the letter with his own woes and finished in more familiar style. 'So far I have not seen any notices of the Merry Wives performance by the most wonderful wifelet that ever was (a wifelet is one who may still flirt with her husband with a clear conscience). . . .'

The expected crunch came a few weeks later. He was instructed to make all the local arrangements for the transfer of power to the officials of Standard Oil. It was a classic example of the man on the spot being manipulated without prior reference while paper wealth changed hands. Hc told Edith he felt 'rather like a mother bereft of her child,' and asked her to overlook his weakness, 'but it is no little of a shock and I cannot foresee what will now ensue. Personally I don't much care what happens, nothing matters but to get on with the unpleasant task before me, which, I fear, will not be to the advantage of staff or shareholders.'

He made an effort to put aside his own problems and in his next letter concentrated on Edith. She had obviously asked his advice as to whether she should cut her hair for the Forest of Arden.

What can I say to your haircutting wish? Of course cut your locks if you are sure you wish it, though my preference is to have you as you are. As it means a photo of you, I shall smile, but I shall on my return exercise the right you give me to 'raise a howl' if I am not convinced it becomes you. If it makes for your present happiness, so let it be.

In her 'two dear letters' Edith had obviously broached the question of her joining him at the close of the Old Vic season, but Guy did not think it would be wise.

The voyage is neither interesting or pleasant and you would get little from it by way of experience and after such a visit from you and days of completion here I do not think I should have courage to stay. I want you God knows, I want you here every day, almost every hour, to love you, kiss you, take you; to be proud in the privilege of having and monopolising you, to spend the glorious night in the worship of my lady.

Oh, sweetest of women to have you close clasped and to kiss your fair form from head to toes, just to kiss your lovely throat as your head sank back in generous giving. But wait I must, and live and carry on in the big hope of coming to you in proper time, when we are both ready for each other and have won through.

There is a sense of desperation in the letters of this period. The nightmare of failure—that failure which, alone, he felt, menaced his love—was ever present. He was firing cables into the no-man's land of the Board Room, fighting a lone rearguard action. London, he told Edith, doubted his word. London was 'inconsistent and silly' and although he had corrected this slur on his character with 'no loss of prestige' he admitted that he had suffered a heavy financial loss as a result of a fall in the share price. 'I feel a ruined man, but shall hope that they'll come back one day.'

His first intimation of her enormous success as Rosalind was a letter in an old copy of the *Observer* which apparently said that such a delightful presentation should not be lost. 'Of course it will not be lost, for have you not promised to play it again that I may see you and love you in it.' Alas, although she kept her promise to play it again ten years later, Guy was not alive to see it. He wrote that he was hunting for St. John Ervine's notice ('larking through the forest, but remaining entirely feminine' was St. John Ervine's description of her Master Ganymede; echoes of Edith the child once again.)

One of the dangers of playing Rosalind is that she can so easily become principal-boyish, and I have witnesses several thigh-slapping performances which would have been more at home in *Puss in Boots*, but every contemporary critic of note found nothing but enchantment in Edith's portrayal. She had slimmed, she had cut her hair and her enjoyment of the part was lyrical and real. Agate, as usual, had the last word. In a BBC broadcast (given, curiously enough on the first day of the General Strike) he told his listeners 'One may safely say that there has never been a more versatile actress than Edith Evans.'

Writing of Martita Hunt later that year Agate made what I consider an odd statement about Edith. 'I see red when I remember Edith Evans' long fight against lack of appreciation'. Without in any way detracting from Edith's talents I can think of few people who had an easier route to the top. Agate had been writing about her unique qualities for years, she had been constantly in work and, even when the plays she appeared in were accounted failures she invariably emerged from them with her reputation enhanced. It is difficult to discern any lack of appreciation and Edith herself confirmed this. 'Many kind and well intentioned critics have stated that recognition has come to me on leaden feet; that I have struggled for too long in obscurity. Their friendliness has blinded them to the facts. The truth is I have been amazingly fortunate ... Premature recognition of an actress is a deadly thing, and it is a matter for congratulation rather than consolation that it is only four years since I began to play leading parts.' She said this in an interview for *John O'London's Weekly*, March 1927.

Edith's final Shakespearean role in that Old Vic season was as Beatrice in *Much Ado About Nothing*. By coincidence the opening night was May 3rd and because of the General Strike it came and went without, if I may so put it, much ado. Between Rosalind and Beatrice she had played Dame Margery Eyre in Thomas Dekker's *The Shoemaker's Holiday* and had given an impressionistic sketch of what was later to become her definitive Nurse in *Romeo and Juliet*. It was, by any standards, a remarkable gallery: thirteen totally conflicting roles in just under eight months. Her decision had been vindicated and Lilian Baylis' early hesitation forgotten. Apart from the final production the box office returns had reflected the courage and versatility of the season. More importantly, Edith had not only conquered her critics but also her own fears regarding her lack of experience in tackling some of the major Shakespearean roles. She had gone to the Old Vic to complete her classical education and at the end of her first term had graduated with honours. And we know now what her public did not know then: that in the midst of this feat of endurance and memory she was not only trying to find her rightful place in the theatre, but was also attempting to unravel her future relationship with Guy. She had always possessed the ability to grasp the essentials of a dramatist's conception and then, after cogitating, recreate them in terms of her own personality, working by instinct rather than by any textbook method, and by so doing transforming Art into life.

It was a time of national unrest, a year of sullenness and spite, a year of weak decisions taken by weak men, giving the lie to what remained of the Gay Twenties. On the one hand there was a nation of self-confident middle-class strike breakers, and a second nation of desperate, un-employed, underpaid men improvising a solidarity that for nine days in May surprised them as much as it surprised the Establishment. All the old values were turned inside out. Guy, on the other side of the world, had already learnt at first hand how men and companies could be gutted by strangers, and the events of 1926 changed his way of thinking. Writing of the strike, he agreed with Edith that,

> the policy of ending a difference with 'Shan't play then' is pathetic at this time of day, and it would seem hopeless to overcome the long legacy of mistrust and illwill, the outcome of the shortsighted policies of employers of the past who blindly refused to see or accept new conditions and their demands reducing the labour class—particularly the skilled—to fighting for every concession which might make for better living. Now God knows what will be the outcome, but I anticipate a similar mess to that which followed the close of the fighting in 1918.

As an afterthought, he added, in brackets, the word *Optimist!*

His own worries were still with him. He confided that he had offered his resignation to his new masters, but it had been refused. Knowing of the mass unemployment at home and that he had scant chance of landing such a well paid and responsible post if he returned, he tried to make light of his fears to Edith, but had to admit that he grew ever more homesick—'it is fast getting to be a constant hurt: unless I get my way of things here and if this constant gnawing interferes with my work, I shall just pack my little gunny sack and pull my freight.' He found his new superior in the field 'bloodless' and went on to detail a chapter of disasters: 'There is little to excite one here, one of our porters has chopped up the other with a machete and now has twelve years in a fortress before him; the State president has been suddenly changed which means a change in all the local offices here, and a tanker collided with our loading pier and put it out of commission. Nothing else of interest'.

In 1976 I received a letter from Mr. V. H. Cheyne, a former oilman himself, who had worked with Guy during this period. 'Colonel Booth was our Manager and all the staff and native workers found him to be an extremely nice person to work with. He was efficient and unassuming, but could show a hasty temper at times and flare up. I think he resigned to the regret of all, because of this.

'I remember meeting him for the first time; he was kindness itself and after a good dinner he showed me his album, full of Edith Evans' photographs, of which he was obviously proud. He remarked, 'She is not very pretty, but has a lovely voice.'''

One senses that Guy was making a conscious effort to be light-hearted, for in his next letter the old angst returns. 'I just live from one to the other of the messages at the close of your letters, and yet hate sometimes the longing that draws me to you. Living is still a good thing without your presence while I know I have you, that you are mine to love and that your lips will meet mine when I come questing for them.'

He wrote to her several times in June, once to urge her not to buy a car before he got back, and once to say, in reply to a request from Edith, that he would try to learn more of dancing 'though I get so little opportunity and grow so tired at the end of the long working days in the field.' Edith took one of her rare holidays before starting rehearsals for a revival of Maugham's *Caroline* at the Playhouse, in which she played Maud Fulton. She wrote and cabled Guy frequently, and he made many references to the comfort her letters brought him.

Your last letter was the finest and sweetest you have ever written to me, and is badly crumpled from much reading. How lovable you are, my Edith, and how you seem to be right inside of me. I am so glad we did not marry each other years ago, it always seems that we should have missed much, certainly the heights would have been reached at a lower altitude. Bless you, Angel.

His line of reasoning is difficult to follow. Loving her to distraction as he undoubtedly did, there seems to be a strange contradiction when he congratulates them both on not marrying earlier. The only explanation that makes sense to me is that he believed that had he pressed her into marriage sooner, the relationship would have burnt itself out by now at the 'lower altitude'. Yet even when he did claim her and his long patience had been rewarded, they still agreed on further separation. He once wrote 'I too think it well that we could see the light enough to part and carry on "as was".' His language was often old-fashioned—beautifully moulded phrases, but curiously dated, and yet he was not a man who lived in the past: most of his spoken thoughts were concerned with plans for the years ahead. He hated the injustices of big business, but he bought stocks and shares and watched the market very carefully, urging Edith to do the same. He was no stranger to adversity and his experiences in the war had brought a new awareness of the transience of human life and the need to live it to the full when the opportunity came. What, then, caused him deliberately to delay the start of his own complete happiness? Was it only the fear of failure in her eyes that made him accept the situation with such seeming enthusiasm, embracing it with the fervour of a religious convert? There is some evidence to suggest that Edith wished he could find contentment within the teachings of Christian Science, but his replies smack more of duty than conviction. He was not attracted to any religion as far as I can detect; no doubt the horrors he had witnessed in the trenches had exploded the myth of God's boundless mercy. Like Edith he was a loner, capable of surviving with his own company. To be consistent, such an arrangement as existed between them would point to a relationship devoid of any physical passion, yet this is patently not so. They had been lovers before marriage and his letters to her after marriage are hardly those of a man who has settled for married celibacy. The contradictions abound. 'We will . . . be nearer happiness one day for having foregone the customary way of man.' This would seem to denote that they had never known happiness together, but again this is a false trail to follow. Apart from the one year when their correspondence faltered, they had always been satisfied with each other and in Guy's case his letters show the growing intensity of his love for her over the years. He was aware that Edith attracted other men and that the nature of her chosen profession granted frequent opportunities for a change of male scenery. He was proudly jealous of her and of her situation, and did his best to conceal this. When his guard dropped, the references were playful; witness his remarks about her first Orlando, Frank Vosper: 'Of course if the Old Vic management provide you with such handsome lovers it is but natural that your wonderful conception of such parts should possess an addi tional edge in the interpretation.' He was not to know that he had nothing to fear from Mr. Vosper, whose sexual tastes lay elsewhere.

Outsiders to the actual daily workings of the theatre are often guilty of imagining that life on the boards is one long round of licentious and riotous behaviour; and whereas it would be absurd to claim that when attractive people are thrown together in romantic situations they never transfer the stage make-believe to their own lives, it would be equally false to contend that every stage romance automatically leads to an off-stage affair. I have no means of telling what Guy thought of Edith's various leading men, for he was reticent on the subject. Likewise Edith could never be bothered with back-stage intrigue, seldom if ever repeated any gossip and was at all times supremely vague about what was going on around her. It wasn't that she considered herself above such mundane things, but purely that she was genuinely not interested. If, on a film set, during the hours of boredom that inevitably occur, a fellow actor tried to engage her in conversation and switched, as actors do from chat to gossip, Edith quickly turned the dialogue in another direction. Kenneth More was one of the rare exceptions, for he has always been able to relate the most preposterous and scandalous stories without offence, and he even succeeded in making Edith laugh at his harmless bawdy. I have the feeling, though, that even Kenny would have been put in his place if Edith hadn't respected him as an actor. She could forgive good actors anything, but had no time to spare for the others. 'I don't think I ever had anybody as a great friend who was a bad actor . . . I don't much care for bad actors, I don't understand them'. That is not to say that Guy, thousands of miles away, was ever in a position to comprehend such niceties; a lover separated from the object of his affections can find much to resent in mere companionship; there are some who find less hurt in adultery than in the holding of hands.

It is an incomplete map for the biographer to follow. Guy longed for their reunion, yet the moment Edith suggested she should journey to join him, he put forward various arguments why she should not. His work in the oilfields assumed the proportions of a penance—yet, penance for what? What compelled him—what compelled them both—to endure such agony? I can understand, just as Guy could understand, Edith's need for periods of isolation in order to 'recharge the batteries': there is nothing unusual or untoward in this, it is common enough amongst those whose vocations sap the not inexhaustible powers of imagination. But Edith was never a recluse, nor was she a Meggie Albanesi: in between intense bouts of creative activity, she was gregarious, sometimes strangely childlike, given to 'bread fights' in the dressing room and other unsophisticated diversions which, I have noted, often attract the energies of artistic people when they relax. Guy could have been no stranger to this side of her character.

Those who surrender themselves to an intimate relationship with a partner possessed of genius always have to face the fact that they will be excluded from the process that gives birth to such genius. They may wholly comprehend the results of that genius, they may be wholly responsible for nurturing, guiding and presenting that genius to the world at large, but in the last analysis they can only share the effects, not the causes. All the evidence points to the truth that Guy was the ideal man for Edith. She knew it and, without conceit, he knew it. Nobody ever replaced him in her affections, and she never remarried. That is what makes their voluntary separations so inexplicable: two people who had such desperate need of each other, who loved each other with such intensity and yet spent most of their lives apart.

10

'*I don't look back much*'

So in the summer of 1926, while Guy wrestled with his conscience and the manoeuvres of The Standard Oil Company of New Jersey, Edith enjoyed the relaxation of playing Maugham's moderate farce—batting his smart lines across the net to Irene Vanbrugh and Marie Löhr: three Wimbledon seeds coasting through a village tournament.

A curious little episode took place during these summer months; it concerned the playwright and critic, St. John Ervine. Edith remembered meeting him for the first time in May 1913. 'I was in the gallery of the Court Theatre and I believe the play was *Jane Clegg*, and a young, fair young man came up and talked to some people, and later on when I got to know him I realised that that was St. John Ervine.'

Jane Clegg was St. John Ervine's third play, and the London cast included the young Sybil Thorndike, who once described the piece as 'a Cockney poem, a Greek tragedy in Cockney. There was not one word you could misplace.'

St. John Ervine was an emigrant from Northern Ireland who was quickly caught up in the various intellectual currents of Edwardian London. An early member of the Fabian Society, he was soon critical of Sydney and Beatrice Webb, later picturing Sydney as being 'as automatic as it is possible for a human being to be.' Whereas the Webbs thought art and the theatre insignificant in comparison to such riveting subjects as 'the incidence of sickness in married pregnant women', Ervine was immediately drawn to Shaw, Granville-Barker, Galsworthy and the rest of the Court Theatre group. Unlike the Webbs he had little or no interest in tabulating people into neat columns of figures, he wanted to dramatise the human condition and put his non-revolutionary, social democratic views into dialogue that actors could speak; converting by entertaining his audiences rather than overwhelming them with incomprehensible statistics. When he became a dramatic critic he swiftly established a reputation for dealing ruthlessly with anything mawkish or 'refained' and frequently aroused very fastidious people to extraordinary fury by saying exactly what he thought. He set out to annoy, he meant to excite and arouse and was never too concerned with the finer subtleties of criticism, but his column in *The Observer* gave strangers a completely false impression of his real character. In private life he was genial and amusing, but he didn't like people who had no heart in what they were doing. Sybil Thorndike felt that he had sympathy for human creatures first and foremost 'and a deep understanding of human troubles and a love of human beings.' She compared him to Shaw, saying she thought Shaw always put his arguments first and his concern for human beings last. 'I never knew how much Shaw loved human beings. He was a humanist, but not human.'

Edith was never as gregarious as Sybil and even after her marriage and the eventual time when she and Guy found a home of their own, their circle of close friends was always small in contrast with the Cassons. 'When I was young, I thought it a great mistake for actors to mix with people outside the profession, and especially critics who although they would never admit it, are more outside than most. So one day when Mrs. Ervine asked me to lunch I said, "I'll come if St. John isn't there." He always told that as a very amusing story. I did go to lunch and he went out. But I still do think, I've always thought, it's a great mistake for them to meet us. They ought to think of us as a rather mysterious proposition and not know what we're going to be up to when they see us act.'

She went on to tell that she had only really got to know him when she played in *Robert's Wife*. 'But that was different. I was meeting him as a playwright, not as a critic.'

Their second meeting, which was probably by sheer chance, took place in Trafalgar Square during the General Strike.

> Garrick Club,
> W.C.2.
> 16.6.26.

EDITH EVANS!
You have shamefully deceived me! When I poured out my young love to you in front of St. Martin's Church during the General Strike, you did not tell me you were already the property of another man. Oh, woman, woman, what a thing to do to your broken-hearted

> St. John Ervine.

P.S. Blast you!

Edith must have written some form of apology almost immediately, for Ervine picked up his pen three days later.

> Garrick Club,
> W.C.2.
> 19.6.26.

Cruel Edith Booth!
Not only do you trample on my young love for you but, with super-

fine contempt, you address me as St. John Irving when the pride and joy of my life is that I am St. John Ervine! Oh, Edith! and me ready to lie down and be a doormat to you!

Outside the damned sun is shining, indifferent to my love.

More broken-hearted than ever,

St. John Ervine.

P.S. Gawd!

Since Ervine was a happily married man there is no reason to suppose that this episode was anything more than a mild flirtation. On the other hand even a flirtation, however short-lived, has a certain significance. Miss Evans obviously concealed the existence of Mrs. Booth. Perhaps St. John Ervine was not entirely blameless, for I have since learnt that he enjoyed a reputation as a 'taxi tiger', as they used to be called. It is almost certain that this chance encounter took place before the invitation to lunch from his wife, and I therefore deduce that it was not only the critic Edith was reluctant to meet socially, but also the man.

Maugham's brittle dialogue for *Caroline* was possibly out of tune with the spirit of that uneasy summer; at any rate the revival did not survive for long and in September Edith appeared as Rebecca West in a new translation (updated and set in an English manor) of Ibsen's *Rosmerholm* under Barry Jackson's management at the Kingsway. A photograph taken at the time shows her dressed in pleated skirt and cardigan, her hair still shorn and now worn in a fashionable bob, sitting on an ugly wooden chair. The critics were divided. Some found her performance too intense for the attempted naturalism of the production. Ivor Brown observing that she 'kept wrenching the play up to a different theatrical level.' She earned Shaw's approval however, for he sent her one of his photographic postcards (post-marked 25th October 1926) to her address in Eccleston Square.

I'm immersed in lawsuits and all sorts of preoccupations—worse than rehearsals. 6.30 on Friday next seems the only moment this week when I shall certainly be at 10 Adelphi Terrace. It seems about 10 minutes since your note made this heart jump; but the date says it is 13 days! Impossible.

I appeased my own longing by going to *Rosmerholm* when I returned from Italy. Rebecca very memorable; but the rest mostly ill chosen.

G.B.S.

After the prolonged excitement of the Old Vic season, Edith seemed to be in second gear and the year ended somewhat tamely for her, her only other performance being a Drury Lane matinee in aid of the Memorial Theatre, Stratford-upon-Avon, in which she played Katherine in a scene from *The Shrew*. Perhaps she needed a pause, for her versatility was not to everybody's liking in a profession that by and large prefers its stars to be predictable. Managements are never more content than when they are given the mixture as before, tried and tested. Or again perhaps she felt like Sybil: 'I don't seem able to do anything at the moment,' Sybil wrote in a letter generous in its praise of Edith. 'Nothing comes as I hear it—do you ever get like that? I suppose sometimes a full stop comes to me just to get me quieted or fallow or something. Damn acting!'

I like the use of the word 'fallow', especially coming from Sybil who, one felt, was always ploughing, ploughing and sowing anew.

On Christmas Eve Herbert Farjeon penned a short note 'to wish you many fine performances in many commercial failures during 1927, so that I may see you on the stage again and again and again.' Not the sentiments to gladden the hearts of managements!

1927 began with a Restoration splash. Edith returned to Nigel Playfair's Lyric, Hammersmith; familiar ground and a familiar period, for Edith always seemed a resident rather than a visitor to Restoration comedy. Her Mrs Sullen in this spirited revival became another legendary role in her career, for she took Farquhar's *The Beaux' Stratagem* and, to use J. C. Trewin's words, 'set it to her own music.' His mock-broken-heart presumably soonest mended, St. John Ervine enjoyed telling his readers that Edith moved 'like a triumphant army. The dying Farquhar creating Mrs. Sullen in his ultimate illness, must have revived had he seen Miss Evans perform the part: no man could go to his grave without a terrific struggle to live long enough to write another part for her.' Prophetic words, as it happened.

Edith was surrounded by a remarkable cast, including James Whale as Squire Sullen, Miles Malleson, Carleton Hobbs, David Horne, Winifred Evans and Dorothy Hope. Playfair himself appeared as Gibbet. Many of the critics felt that 'the language of eulogy' was inadequate to describe Edith's latest inventions, and to quote them here at length would be to risk overkill as well as go against Edith's wishes. However it is worth including a passage or two from a long article on her career to that date, written by Horace Horsnell in May 1927 which appeared in *The Outlook* under the heading SOME OF OUR CONQUERORS.

(Her) reputation owes little or nothing to hearsay, adventitious aids or the dubious arts of publicity. It is one of sheer merit. Miss Evans recommends no beauty preservatives; her appearances in public places go unchronicled; on the burning questions of the moment she preserves, so far as the popular press is concerned, a discreet silence. I doubt if she is even good copy. True, there was a slight flutter in Fleet Street a year or so ago when the news leaked out that she had quietly married. But since she is neither a flapper's delight nor a subaltern's dream—is admired less for what she is fondly supposed to be than for what she actually does—sagacious news-editors let the fact pass without inflating it. Yet of all contemporary actresses she is probably the only one of her generation to whom the adjective 'great' may eventually and without absurdity be applied; the one above all others about whom posterity—should posterity share with us so agreeable a weakness—may conceivably be most curious.

Ivor Brown also thought it likely that 'years hence we shall bore posterity by quoting this magnificent performance to incredulous and careless youth, as we, incredulous and careless, have been bored by Victorian legends of vanished and, no doubt, authentic magnificence.'

It was a triumph on a scale that even Edith had not experienced before, and the out-of-the-way Lyric, Hammersmith became *the* theatre to visit. Curiously, around this time, Edith posed for one of her rare 'pin-up' photographs. The issue of the *Sketch* dated May 25, 1927, has a photograph of Edith captioned 'The Reflections of Mrs. Sullen.' It shows a bare-shouldered Edith, twisted in an unnatural position and admiring herself in a hand mirror. She is wearing a string of pearls wound round one wrist in slave-girl fashion, and the draperies have been lowered as far as decency allowed. Any suggestion of cleavage has been carefully air-brushed out, giving a curious unreality to her otherwise admirable bosom. By contrast, a portrait exclusive to *Theatre World* taken by G. Mannell on more conventional lines is totally ravishing. A porcelain figurine of Edith in the character of Mrs Sullen was struck at the time (a charming art which, alas, has all but died out) and I am fortunate to have one of the edition before me as I write; Edith left it to my wife Nanette when she died.

During the run of *The Beaux' Stratagem* she received an enormous fan mail, and I have selected one, an amusing letter from her first Orlando, Frank Vosper, who was not only an actor of considerable style and authority, but also the author of several extremely good plays.

Theatre Royal,
Haymarket.
Sat. January 22, 1927.

My Dearest Edith,

I must write and tell you how delighted I am at your great triumph in *The Beaux' Stratagem*. Bravo! and really truly sincere congratulations. I met my old friend Major Belchington-Currie of the 96th Punjabis the morning after your first night and he was in ecstasies about your 'Spankin' fine show'—he said—'I should like to ask the little memsahib to a bit of tiffin one day—you know, just the odd pheasant and a spot of bubbly—she puts me in mind of the District

Commissioner's wife up in I.D.K. who ran away with a feller in Jacobs Horse, broke the poor old D.C's heart—*She* was a damn fine little actress too,—you should have seen her when we did *The Marriage of Kitty* at Poona in '97—or was it '96?'

So you can see how impressed the Major was. Once again congratulations.

Ever Yours   Bandy Face.

Although never the one to let praise go to her head, Edith was not immune to the siren call of appearing under her own management and during the run of *The Beaux' Stratagem* snippets began to appear in the press that she was contemplating a season of plays 'old and new' which she would present on her own account. In the event she shared the risk with Leon M. Lion, a much respected actor-manager and dramatic author. They chose for their debut— and it was a strange choice, especially for Edith—a little-known farcical comedy, *Maître Bolbec et son Mari* by George Berr and Louis Verneuil, translated from the French by Bertha Murray under the English title *The Lady in Law*. Edith cast herself as Maître Bolbec, 'a lady barrister of great eminence' and perhaps for once she was persuaded to ask herself to accept the role for reasons that were not entirely artistically pure. She engaged a first-rate cast— Frederick Leister, a fine and gentle actor, was her leading man; and she had the added talents of O. B. Clarence, Margaret Halstan and Ann Codrington—but the result dismayed her admirers and sent the critics searching for excuses. 'Although the first play produced under this combination has an air of hesitancy between the highbrow and the popular, our faith in Miss Evans and her own mentality will almost inevitably guide this management in the way it should go,' were Mr. Horace Shipp's well-chosen words, though he could not resist adding that he felt Edith had 'shirked her affair with destiny and chosen something which we might have had—had we wanted it—from less intelligent managements.' It was another way of saying that the fact that somebody is a brilliant pilot does not automatically ensure that they are an equally brilliant navigator. The applause at curtain fall on the first night was 'less than frantic' and at least one member of that opening night audience felt the play would go better with people who came to the theatre 'after an unhurried dinner.'

Guy had returned to England in May 1927 and was present at the first night, 'standing most interested in a box' according to the *Daily Express*. The same news item had it that he had been living ninety miles from the nearest white man during his term in Maracaibo, which was a typical journalistic fantasy and the author of the article mixed gossip with dramatic opinion, ending with the statement that 'theatre management is something like the oil business. You sink a lot and only now

128

and then is there a spurt.' Never the newspaper to leave a story half-eaten, the *Express* returned with added salt for Edith's wounds the following day. 'With the exception of Lady Ottoline Morrell, I did not see many notable people at the first night of *The Lady in Law* . . . One of the sensations of the evening was caused by an object dropping with a crash from a second tier box on the head of a lady in the stalls. The victim of the accident merely patted her hair and smiled with a heroism worthy of a better play.'

Edgar Wallace also wrote in jugular vein. 'People refer to Miss Evans vaguely as being clever; and I suppose she is. She is also terribly inaudible, and is a graduate of that restless school of acting which has so many interesting exponents on the English stage.'

Giving his SECOND THOUGHTS ON FIRST NIGHTS under the pseudonym 'Sir Topaz', Agate reluctantly gave a characteristic thumbs down. Writing in *Eve, The Lady's Pictorial* he remarked with a certain sadness that 'I don't believe that six Edith Evanses, standing in a row and acting this part along the lines of Lord Beaverbrook's community singing, could have made anything of it . . . Let her take this consolation to herself, that Sybil would certainly not have fared better in this piece. But would Sybil have appeared in it? Only, I may think, over Lewis's dead body.'

Other admirers also found it impossible to give words of comfort. Herbert Farjeon could not divest himself of the belief that 'Edith Evans into modern costume won't go . . . many people seeing her for the first time, may wonder what we have been making such a fuss about.' But it was left to Anne Doubleday of *Time and Tide* to administer the *coup de grace*.

'What is Miss Evans thinking of? She could act this part if she chose to take the trouble—of course she could—and it is because she does not trouble to act that the play falls down . . . The truth is that Miss Evans today is standing at the parting of the ways. If she takes one road, the fine road, she will go a long way, she may even, for surely she has it in her, become a great actress. If she takes the other road, the easier, she will be a great popular favourite, she will draw her thousands, but she will not be a great actress, she will not be an actress at all, she will be a masquerader.'

Whatever became of Anne Doubleday?

It was not an auspicious homecoming for Guy, and since he was not a Lewis Casson and had little or no first-hand experience of the vicissitudes of theatrical fame, he must have been bewildered by the spectacle of his fallen idol. While abroad he had received nothing but good news of Edith's prowess, and yet on the first occasion after his return he was shown how fickle is public and critical taste. The play died an early death, taking its toll of Edith's savings, and Guy was ever more convinced that his proper station in life was that of the homemaker, the bastion of reliability who stood aloof from his wife's professional existence.

Fortunately Edith had in abundance that quality of resilience without which no actor can survive. She made a return dash for the safety net of familiarity—back to the Restoration for the second time that year, to the proven queen of coquettes, Millamant, and all was forgiven. There were important changes from the previous Hammersmith cast—notably Godfrey Tearle as Mirabell—but Nigel Playfair 'sitting critically in a box, looked on it all and saw that it was good. So, too, did the stalls, and more rapturously the pit and the gallery.' Edith and her partner only had the lease of the theatre for six weeks, but the renewed success of her 'glove-fit' Millamant did much to retrieve her self-confidence and repair her bank balance. Until now she had been a stranger to such savage personal failure, and she was too aware of her own capabilities not to realise that she could not rely on endless revivals whenever in doubt or in trouble. But where were the great new roles? British dramatists have always been more generous to men than to women and for any one female star role in a decade there are twenty for the males. Shaw was never to come to her with an Eliza Doolittle or a St. Joan, which is cause for lasting regret.

And although in 1927 Henry Arthur Jones sent Edith a copy of his play *Whitewashing Julia*, with the inscription 'To Dear Miss Edith Evans, with great admiration for your splendid gifts, and hoping they may continue to meet with recognition from playgoers and critics', he was near the end of his life and no longer capable of a major dramatic work. He added a fascinating postscript to his inscription: 'These privately printed old Chiswick plays are beginning to be valued by the booksellers on account of the fine printing, no longer now to be obtained in an age when Democracy is coming into its own, to the great discomfort of us all.'

The greater the classical role, the more it serves to remind us of contemporary lost opportunities. Coward never wrote directly for Edith, nor did Maugham, or Rattigan, Lonsdale or Osborne. From this list, Coward surprises me the most, for the Master loved excellence and professionalism above all else and they are the first two qualities that come to mind whenever anybody, friend or foe, talks about Edith. When one adds to them her undisputed gifts as a comedienne of genius, the absence of any tailor-made star role from the Master's pen becomes all the more inexplicable. One possible explanation is that, despite their early association in *Polly With a Past*, Edith was never an intimate of Noel's; she never felt really at home in his volatile circle. Noel admired her, was lavish in his praise of her, but was never persuaded to write especially for her. Likewise Rattigan, who was always capable of creating a modern Lady Bracknell. Again, although they both lived in

Albany, Edith and Rattigan were never close friends. Tracing the pattern of her life one finds that, as her fame grew, she deliberately removed herself from the kind of life that is mostly associated in the public eye with a great leading lady. Scandal did not touch her; she wanted to be known through her work and only through her work. A great number of people were in awe of her from an early age, and in our strange and often bitchy profession, awe is sometimes uncomfortably close to envy. Edith's aloofness, which was genuine and not an affectation, was misinterpreted by many: they mistook it for grandeur and were put off by it. Obviously, in the theatre, she demanded and rightfully was granted great respect. She was an imposing figure and to that extent, within the confines of a theatre, a law unto herself. But great art seldom survives without self-discipline. Since she demanded so much of herself, since her dedication was so complete, Edith found a lack of it in others hard to understand or forgive. The world of the theatre that Edith inhabited in the twenties, thirties and forties was a far cry from the theatre of today. The strictures and abuses prevalent then may have needed loosening and correcting, but the freedoms under which art flourishes are not the freedoms that man strives for under political banners. Once the first step is taken to impose an industrial pattern upon a creative process, all that follows is a slow erosion of the basic need of the true artist: the ability to choose at will those routes he wishes to explore. When self-indulgence replaces self-discipline, when political considerations supersede artistic priorities, then art itself withers. The rule is without exception.

It is a paradoxical irony that Edith's very versatility led to her being type-cast. Certain roles were automatically designated 'an Edith Evans part' and since, in the theatre, imitation is often the cheapest and insincerest form of flattery, she was aped by many inferior actresses; and like most fakes they brought the original into disrepute, so that for certain periods it became fashionable not to like Edith. Perhaps some of the leading dramatists of the day were scared to pick up the gauntlet her talent hurled at their feet. Or else they felt that if they accepted the challenge they must always write something large than life. If so, they failed to appreciate that Edith did not need a role that was larger than life: her genius was that she could take normality and transform it. Whatever the reasons, history must record that she was neglected, forced time and time again by the laziness or timidity of playwrights and managements to fall back on yet another revival. Thus, in March 1928, with no major dramatist willing to grasp the nettle on her behalf, she was persuaded to return to the Royal Court and repeat her Serpent and She-Ancient in *Back to Methuselah*. Now there is nothing wrong in a great actor repeating past triumphs, especially if it allows him to bring new dimensions to a familiar role and affords an opportunity for a younger generation of theatregoers to evaluate the opinions of their elders. The real cause for regret is that the actor is forced to rekindle imagination, rather than light new fires.

Shaw was not enamoured of her performance on this occasion.

> 4, Whitehall Court,
> London, SW1
> 22nd March 1928

My Dear Edith,

You played the Ancient as an old woman and a very tired one, instead of as a bald-headed volcano. What is the matter?—a new love?—a baby?—or are you bored with the part—or with me? Can I sympathize? If so tell me.

> G.B.S.

The chances are she was bored with the part. The She-Ancient, beginning with the name, is a singularly unattractive character for a woman—'baldheaded volcanoes' are not every leading lady's idea of feminine grace, but Shaw, who gave naught for appearances, would not have thought of this. With the memory of Mrs. Sullen still fresh, Edith must have found the absence of elegance and wit under the grotesque bald wig a trying experience. There is some evidence to suggest that she had several times asked Shaw to write her a play that more accurately reflected her style and would give her an opportunity to shine for him. Shaw's reply on a postcard from Italy, was breezy and cold comfort.

> Aint in London at all, darling: I'm here. No plays, alas! The book on Socialism contains the equivalent in words of $12\frac{1}{2}$ plays! You cannot announce a new play by a Septuagenarian!! Therefore, though I wish you much glory, I cannot hope to share it.

> G.B.S.

Shaw had posed the all-important question: what was the matter with her? By this time she and Guy had found and bought their first and only home together, not the 'pretty nook somewhere near Itchen Abbas' that Guy had once prophetised, but Washenden Manor, a period farmhouse in Biddenden, Kent. It was set in the middle of rich farmland and hop fields not far distant from Ellen Terry's final resting place at Smallhythe. Guy finally had a place of his own where he could fulfil part of the dream that had sustained him all those years of exile. I write 'part of the dream' deliberately, for even in marriage their relationship remained unconventional. Edith still kept a London address and spent most weekdays there, especially when working, returning to Washenden after the last house on a Saturday. Guy, I think realised he could not compete with the theatre, was not at ease in theatrical circles,

132

and therefore withdrew from the race. He was content to farm the land at Washenden, look after the animals and be there for Edith's returns from that other world he had little inclination to explore in depth. He was drawn to active politics, becoming in time the first Chairman of the Tenterden Labour Party, but nothing suggests that Edith actively shared the involvement with him.

It was typical of Shaw the married bachelor to ask whether a child was on the way, or whether Edith had a new love. Edith always regretted that she and Guy never had a child, but was honest enough to admit that the reluctance to start a family had been all hers. It wasn't the fear of having a child that held her back, but fear of losing one. She repeatedly told me that although Guy's untimely death almost caused her to lose her reason, she could never have recovered from the loss of a child. Her mother's grief at the death of Edith's small brother persisted until the end of her days, and this had a profound effect on Edith. She referred to it many times and in a way that suggested that her mother's grief had been transferred to her. People she loved seemed to die. 'I've got nobody to run to now,' she said to me in 1976, the admission blurted out over lunch, a non-sequitur in the conversation which took me by surprise. 'Now that my parents are dead, and Guy, who can I run to?' There was no comforting answer that I could give, and the sense of loneliness hung in the air over the lunch table we shared like smoke from damp logs on the first day of winter. It seemed to me one of the saddest remarks I had ever heard, and in thinking of it now I am convinced that this was the persistent fear which moulded so many of her emotional decisions.

Shaw, with his bluntness—the bluntness of an old man who had always scattered opinions like chaff—came near to the truth. Edith did not have a new love, but she was unsettled by the old. She had been entirely on her own for so long, aware of Guy's enduring passion for her, needing it, leaning on it, returning it, but in a make-believe fashion. A love affair conducted mostly by correspondence avoids all the day to day peccadillos that human flesh is heir to, and by the time the marriage took place she and Guy were both too set in their separate ways to accept change easily. It was a happy marriage, nothing to regret but nevertheless something was always lacking: that intimacy that only comes from many years of growing accustomed to another person sharing one's entire life, and they had both allowed the locusts to eat those years.

'He had everything he wanted at the end,' Edith told me, but I felt she was reassuring herself rather than imparting information. We were sorting through and identifying a batch of old family photographs at the time, and she had come across a snapshot of Guy taken at Washenden. She peered at it for a long time before speaking. 'My old boy,' she said.

'My Guy, and so he'd rather be. He couldn't bear being old. There he is, on his own land, digging away in all the muck, and he'd stuck a leaf on his forehead, just to be silly. Oh, oh, he was such a nice man.'

She might have been describing a stranger.

II

'Work is my hobby'

One has to mark Edith's card 9 out of 10 for sheer courage. As her next venture she chose to appear in the role of an actress in a dramatisation of a novel by a theatre critic, and was directed in it by another actress!

The play was *The Tragic Muse* adapted from the Henry James novel by Hubert Griffith (described by a colleague as the 'intellectual' dramatic critic of the *Evening Standard*). The piece was directed by Athene Seyler and shimmered briefly at the Arts Theatre Club. Dog refrained from eating dog as far as Mr. Griffith was concerned, and after two performances given over a weekend, his muse retreated, tragically, into obscurity.

Next came *Napoleon's Josephine* by Conal O'Riordan at the Fortune Theatre, with Leslie Banks playing Bonaparte and Edith in the title role. Athene Seyler, relinquishing her recently-acquired status as a director to her husband Nicholas Hannen, appeared as Mme. de Staël.

J. C. Trewin's verdict was that both the play and her performance in it were without distinction. The Corsican honey pot provides an inexhaustible source for biographers and dramatists, the majority being trapped to drown in sweet sentimentality and one must conclude that this fate overtook Leslie Banks and Edith.

Edith said that she carried the script of Reginald Berkeley's *The Lady With A Lamp* with her for a year before the first performance, and that she read it through five times: 'Unusual for me. As a rule I scarcely think of a part until I rehearse. All my work is done at rehearsals. Work is my hobby. I do nothing but memorising at home. Once I start rehearsing I'm no good to anyone. I meet people hardly knowing who they are. I talk to people not knowing what I am saying. In the middle of a conversation I will suddenly exclaim, "Ah! now I see why she said that."'

Certainly her typescript of Berkeley's play has a suitably dog-eared appearance. Examining it I was struck by two things. Firstly Edith made hardly any personal notes; the odd line is scratched out and here and there she has made a cross in the margin, presumably to denote that she wanted to remember an emphasis. The other thing is that the

135

play originally started life with the title *Florence Nightingale*. This was subsequently scratched out and *Woman Power* substituted. Then the author had second, third and fourth thoughts and listed other alternatives: *Sex and Power*, *Sigh No More Ladies*, *Achievement* and *The Power and The Glory*.

Sex and Power would have been a very daring title in 1928. But *The Lady With A Lamp* was the final choice and the role of Florence Nightingale, although well written, was not an exacting task for an actress of Edith's capabilities. Ivor Brown called it her 'St. Joan of sanitation whose girlhood voices give one clear call to drains.' It was first produced at the Arts for a limited run of one week, proved a success there and was transferred to the Garrick. Rereading the play today it seems to fall into the category later made so commercially attractive by the partnership of Dame Anna Neagle and her husband Herbert Wilcox: potted history with neatly dovetailed highlights that pleased the public as readily as it offended the purists. What the play accomplished for Edith was to provide her with her best vehicle to date outside the classics. Appearing with her were Gwen Ffangcon-Davies, who was to become and remain one of her closest friends, and Leslie Banks. Neil Porter, an imposing actor of the old school who ended his days hissing and spitting the Bard to R.A.D.A. students, Richard Goolden and Henry Oscar took the other leading roles. The play was included in the 1929 edition of Victor Gollancz's *Famous Plays* series—six unabridged dramatic works in one volume for the now amazing price of 7s. 6d.

Leslie Banks relinquished the role of Tremayne when the production transferred to the Garrick and, at his suggestion, the young John Gielgud took over from him. Gielgud had never acted with Edith before, nor had anybody as yet discovered his potential as a classical actor. He was usually cast as a highly-strung romantic, 'not quite crude enough for his youth' in Granville-Barker's opinion, and the year before he joined the cast at the Garrick he had survived Ibsen's *Ghosts* with Mrs Patrick Campbell. Doubtless any young actor would be highly-strung after receiving a sample of Mrs. Pat's advice: 'Keep still. Gaze at me . . . speak in a Channel-steamer voice . . . speak as if you were going to be sick.' She had also admonished him for shedding real tears on stage, taught him how to eat snails and given a social commentary on who was sitting in the front stalls while he was playing his big scene. Edith must, literally, have been a Florence Nightingale to him after this theatrical Crimea.

It was during the run of *The Lady With A Lamp* that Gielgud was approached by Lilian Baylis's newly-appointed director at the Vic, Harcourt Williams, and asked if he would be interested in joining the company Williams was assembling. Like Edith before him, it was the watershed of his career, and it makes fascinating speculation to ponder what might have happened to both their careers had they not taken Lilian's coin—for coin it was, £10 a week being the average salary for the leading players, and £20 being the normal sum spent on the set and costumes of any one production!

Harcourt Williams was a brilliant teacher of actors rather than an inspired director, a man with a great feel for people, kindly, raggedly eccentric and dedicated to the pursuit of restoring the original *pace* of Shakespeare's plays, for he was determined to junk all the old garbage that cluttered every revival of the Bard. His smart West End company, which included Donald Wolfit, Martita Hunt, Adele Dixon and Leslie French that first season, found themselves directed by a vegetarian urging them to break what one critic termed 'another world's speed record', and managed by somebody who acted like a theatrical land-lady granting them bed and board and little else.

Gielgud was thrown into confusion by Williams' offer; attracted to it, but fearful of it. One afternoon, during the break between the matinee and evening performance at the Garrick, he went downstairs to Edith's dressing room and with that noted and much quoted facility of hurling himself where angels fear to tread, knocked on the door to ask Miss Nightingale's advice. It was a well-known unwritten law in the theatre that Miss Evans was never to be disturbed during her rest. The young Mr. Gielgud knocked again and roused her. She received him graciously, talked to him of her own past reasons for going to the Vic and urged him to follow her example. I have no doubt that Edith remained in period character while dispensing first aid, for there are few pleasures so keen as when we persuade others to make the same sacrifices as we have already made, and Edith, I feel sure, would not have relinquished Miss Nightingale's solicitude for her stage lover who nightly died in her arms, 'covered liberally in fuller's earth.'

The run at the Garrick was not very long and while Gielgud crossed Hungerford Bridge to the Old Vic (an aptly named route, it would seem, in view of the salaries paid at the end of the journey) Edith headed for Malvern to take part, during the burning summer of 1929, in the first of Barry Jackson's Festivals of homage to Shaw. It was announced that Edith, in addition to her familiar Lady Utterword in *Heartbreak House*, would also take the part of Orinthia, the King's favourite, in the first British production of *The Apple Cart*. Sub-titled 'a Political Extrava-ganza', the new play had had its world première in Warsaw, and the advance publicity from Poland (whence several special correspondents had sent back reviews) was hardly encouraging. The *Observer*'s man on the spot had described the play as 'dull as ditchwater, sadly empty of illumination.'

The Festival was to open on August 19 after seven weeks rehearsal for a mere two week season. Despite the reports filtered back from

Warsaw, the advance bookings were healthy. Shaw defended his new work with customary vigour, stating that he always measured his success by the shrieks of the wounded. Barry Jackson found it necessary to deny that his Malvern production would be performed by the Teatr Polski Company in Polish. 'Thank goodness for that,' commented the *Daily Mirror*, never doubting that the wogs began at Calais. 'You have only to look around on the blank faces when a company is playing in Italian, or even French, to realise the mental vacuum that would arise were the Shavian dialogue to be given in Polish.'

Shaw had seen Edith as Florence Nightingale and sent her a postcard: 'Fine, Edith. Great acting. My Blessing.' The role of Orinthia is a far cry from Eliza or St. Joan, a long argument dressed up in expensive female clothes and, as conceived by Shaw, nothing more than a bloodless puppet on the printed page. I cannot escape the belief that Edith accepted the role mostly from loyalty and affection, for it is difficult to see how she applied her criterion of 'finding the truth' in such a cardboard character. *The Apple Cart* is a curiously confused piece, intended to expose 'the unreality of both democracy and royalty as our idealists conceive them,' but the comic arguments that Shaw presents lack the tightness of construction that political satire requires above all. Edith's role was in the form of a duologue with the King (played by Cedric Hardwicke, to whom the major plaudits were awarded) which occupied the entire Second Act. It is 'heavy sledding' in Katharine Hepburn's phrase, even for an actress of Edith's capabilities, but one can see why Shaw wanted to write it for her. He describes the character as 'romantically beautiful' and once again the flirt in him surfaces, bobbing up on the placid waters of his dotage. He was a lover of the *idea* of beautiful women. He loved them all on paper, but perhaps could never bring himself to embrace that element of passionate vulgarity that even romantic love demands if it is to live off the printed page. Orinthia, for all Shaw's skill and intellect, remains an unreal creature, the invention of a man too far removed by age and habit from ordinary life, even the ordinary life of kings. Sections of the dialogue between Orinthia and Shaw's king skirted around the situation which was to precipitate the country into a major Constitutional crisis a few years later, but unlike the reality it anticipated, Shaw's version had no poignancy at its core: it was intellectual comedy worked over by the T.U.C. General Council, and contained a bad paraphrase of one of Wilde's best lines for good measure.

The critics made depressing reading. Most of them went to some pains to mitigate their disappointment. They were kind to Edith, but hardly lyrical. Exasperation at what might have been was the order of the day. The public, however, were not put off by the reviews and directly after the Festival ended the play was transferred to London, reopening at the Queen's Theatre on September 17th 1929. There, after receiving another full set of reviews far more favourable than the first, it ran until June of the following year. Indeed, studying Edith's scrapbook for that period, I am amazed how many critics had second thoughts: by the end of the run some of them were employing words like 'stupendous', 'glorious', and granting headlines such as 'Mr. Shaw's Flashing Comet.' Shaw had the last word. Addressing the Critics' Circle in October 1929, he said 'the dramatic criticism of today is not worse than the dramatic criticism of the nineties. It could not be. After all, there are limits to what can be done by incompetence, by ignorance, by carelessness, by irresponsibility, and in those old days several times a week they reached those limits cheerfully. Dramatic critics are never interfered with, as such; they are entirely irresponsible, and whether they are qualified or not is purely an accident. In such circumstances men must always do their worst.'

Being off the stage for two acts out of three even in a successful long run made Edith restless and she went into management again, presenting a now-forgotten play called *Wills and Ways* by Halcott Glover for two special performances at the Arts, which more often than not was a graveyard for experiments. This having failed to create any stir, she returned to the same theatre to appear in a comedy by the Poet Laureate, Robert Bridges, called *The Humours of The Court* which at least provided her with a role that allowed her to flex her talents. Edith was never happy, as some actors are, to be trapped in a long run. 'I can feel myself being blotted out. Not that I cheat my audiences, they still get their money's worth. But I cheat myself.'

The moment the run of *The Apple Cart* finished she treated her admirers and herself to another look at Mrs. Sullen when *The Beaux' Stratagem* was revived for a short season at the Royalty.

What of her home life during this period? The word is placid. She returned to Washenden at weekends and her life was neatly divided into two compartments. It is doubtful whether Guy wholly acquiesced in this arrangement and there were times when the marriage was tested. They entertained a small circle of friends, but unlike the house parties that characterised some of her fellow luminaries, her gatherings were not sophisticated or grand. She was faithful to old friends and these included people outside the theatre. Most of these seem to have had a great affection for Guy and speak of his sense of humour. There was an attempt to run Washenden as a farm on a paying basis, but it met with little real success since both of them were amateurs on the land and in Edith's case she could only give part of her mind to it.

In London during the weekdays she busied herself with good causes and socialised in an unostentatious way. London was her first love; she enjoyed the peace of the countryside, it gave her room to breathe, but

London was where she felt she belonged. James Agate noted in his Diary: 'Walking in Piccadilly, I met a superb creature some 6ft tall or so with eyes now sweeping the heavens, now raking the pavements for contumacious opposition.' The superb creature was Edith, probably on her way to buy an expensive loaf of bread from her dressmaker.

I don't think Edith ever had ambition in the conventional show business fashion, for she despised many of the trappings that fame brings. But she was driven. Nothing could ever stand in the way of her vocation. 'Variety is the soul of my existence,' she was reported as saying in an interview granted to the *Birmingham Daily Mail* during this period, and although I am sure that the sentiment is accurate, the language does not fit Edith. 'Some nights I feel as if I could speak for ever. It comes like water from a fountain.' She was driven and she was torn. 'I hate anything static.' Torn is the operative word. 'I am interested in doing odd jobs in the house and pottering about my Kentish garden . . . *On the other hand*, I am always interested in life in London.' (The italics are mine.)

She was constantly in demand to support worthy causes, being closely identified with the Cecil Houses project, a charity dedicated to the foundation of providing accommodation for homeless women where for one shilling a night, they could obtain 'a good bed, hot bath, tea and bread and butter.' She found time to appear in a one-act thriller by John Hastings Turner called *Plus ça change* in aid of the Oxford Preservation Trust. The Poetry Society also claimed her services on frequent occasions, and she often appeared in charity matinees to raise cash for the Actors' Benevolent Fund. Sometimes she was to be seen selling flags for the blind, but her major efforts were reserved for the formation of British Actors' Equity Association.

'I have finally, definitely and equivocally decided that a trade union is the only thing that can help us,' Godfrey Tearle told his fellow actors at the first mass meeting. This was in May 1930. The rogues and vagabonds had resolved to band together and organise themselves. They were led by the elite of their profession, and this is why they triumphed in the teeth of savage opposition within and without their ranks. The platform speakers were an impressive array: Dame May Whitty, Sybil Thorndike, Brian Aherne, Marie Burke, Dame Madge Kendall, Bromley Davenport were numbered amongst them, and the meeting, which was held in the New Theatre (kindly loaned by Mr. Bronson Albery, the well-known manager, which sheds some light on the divisions within the divisions) was presided over by Alfred M. Wall of the London Trades Council. Hannen Swaffer, the 'Dean of Fleet Street' as he became known—a deliberately eccentric and influential journalist who was noted for his ability to obliterate his clothes with cigarette ash—was also prominent at the historic inauguration and devoted his entire column to it that week. Athene Seyler once said of Hannen Swaffer: 'Whenever I see his finger nails, I thank God I don't have to look at his feet.'

There was fighting talk and emotional uproar. Edith told me of cheques for a hundred pounds fluttering down onto the stage from the crowded boxes, the theatrical aristocracy showing a lead to their less affluent colleagues. Godfrey Tearle, no doubt enjoying the fact that he had come to praise actors and not to bury them, answered his critics in admirable rhetoric. 'I've been accused of being a Tory, and I've been accused of being a Bolshie,' he thundered. 'This I know. I am an actor. My people have always been that. They have been nothing else, and I'm proud of it. If it means being a Tory, or being a Bolshie, or being a Trade Unionist when I want my profession put right, well, I am whatever they accuse me of being. There is our leader,' he continued, pointing to Alfred Wall. 'There is the man who is to lead us to Trafalgar Square, waving red flags. He is the man who will tell us to burn some manager on the monument. Well, if he tells us, I suppose we shall have to do it.'

The task of organising what Leslie Henson described as 'the world's most irresponsible people' (and personally I think he used the wrong word: actors are not so much irresponsible as careless) was a formidable one. The first aims were to secure a standard minimum terms contract and to ensure that managements could not do a 'moonlight flit' at the end of the week, leaving the cast stranded and penniless.

From such stirring beginnings, other meetings followed, and on one occasion the British contingent gathered to hear reports from Ethel Barrymore and John Emerson, two distinguished visitors who had been prominently associated with the already established American Equity. By an odd coincidence, neither was in perfect condition for public speaking: Miss Barrymore was extremely hoarse and could only deliver her speech with difficulty, and Mr. Emerson had such a bad throat that his speech had to be read for him—which introduces an element of farce when one considers that it was an actors' meeting.

The Americans had taken their early struggles to an actual strike, and although in the months to come the British were to threaten an all-out strike in order to bring the managers to the negotiating table, the ultimate weapon was avoided at the eleventh hour. The minimum wage they sought to establish was the princely sum of £3 per week, Sybil Thorndike delivering herself of the opinion that 'anyone not worth £3 a week ought not to be in the profession at all.'

Edith followed Sybil on the platform on this occasion. Somewhat inaccurately she began by saying that she had had a hell of a time trying to get on the stage, and continued: 'I am having a hell of a time trying to keep on it. What our profession wants is the law behind it. It's no use saying nice things to each other and wishing everybody success. Even in the marriage contract at the altar, when we swear to love and honour each other for the rest of our natural lives—well, you put it in writing, don't you?' This, according to the verbatim report in *The Stage* got Edith the laugh I am sure she had worked for. 'Equity is a beautiful word,' Edith said, 'and it cuts both ways. Actors must be protected against the managers, but, great heavens, managers have sometimes to be protected against the actors. Equity should help both parties.'

Actors make uneasy trade-unionists, their basic instincts rightly directing them away from conformity. It was necessary to form Equity to correct the many abuses that actors were subjected to, but the central debate continues to this day. In recent years Equity has been buffeted and brought to the edge of self-destruction by divisions within the ranks. The most strident group shake the banner of The Workers' Revolutionary Party like a tiny, angry fist. In 1975 Edith made the long journey from Kilndown to attend yet another mass meeting held at the Coliseum, called to block one of the frequent take-over bids by the militants, the majority of them hardly experienced enough to carry a spear let alone a conviction. Edith called me the night before the meeting and with that magnificent disregard for the realities of the situation which her advanced years had bestowed, asked me to reserve her a box. I tactfully pointed out that the house would be filled on a 'first come, first served' basis, but promised to keep a look out for her and see that she obtained a seat. She duly arrived dressed as though for a Royal occasion and a seat was found for her at the back of an already crammed loge box. She surveyed the packed stalls in silence for a few moments, taking in the serried ranks of the Redgrave army who, like all good revolutionaries, had taken care to secure the front seats. 'Who *are* all those people?' Edith demanded in a voice that would have shattered the glass on Lenin's tomb. 'I thought this was an *ac-tors* meeting?'

There was no fluttering of hundred pound notes that Sunday at the Coliseum, and the elite were jeered and shouted down, divided, on this occasion, by the hatred of member for member rather than the passion which had characterised the days of Equity's inception when the aim was to ensure justice for all. Actors of Edith's generation are bewildered and confused by the purely destructive nature of Equity's critics from within, for they sense that not only is the basic freedom of the actor threatened, but that freedom itself is on the rack. The struggle continues, and Edith is well out of it.

In 1930 the issues were easier to define and Edith played her part, for in the company of her peers she was mostly concerned with establishing standards of excellence. She must have been reminded of those standards when she journeyed from her 'moated cottage' to be amongst the

Edith 'assuming' beauty for a
rare glamour photograph, 1941.

Above: Agatha Payne in *The Old
Ladies* with Jean Cadell (left) and
Mary Jerrold (centre), New
Theatre, 1935.

Left: As Madame Arcadina with
John Gielgud in Komisarjevsky's
memorable production of *The
Seagull*, which Shaw hated so
much, New Theatre, 1936.

Above: *The Country Wife*, Old
Vic, 1936. Edith among the cast,
which included Ruth Gordon,
Michael Redgrave, Ursula Jeans,
Ernest Thesiger, Richard
Goolden and Geoffrey Toone.

Right: Edith as Lady Fidget with
Michael Redgrave as Mr. Horner.

Katharina in *The Taming of the Shrew*, with Leslie Banks at the New Theatre, 1937.

Same position, different play. *Robert's Wife* with Owen Nares, Globe Theatre, 1937.

Left: The famous Rosalind. Edith and Michael Redgrave (Orlando) in *As You Like It* at the Old Vic 1936 and subsequently revived at the New Theatre, 1937.

Top left: Antony and Cleopatra, with Godfrey Tearle, Piccadilly Theatre, 1946.

Top right: Lady Pitts in Bridie's *Daphne Laureola*, Wyndham's Theatre, 1949.

Right: With Sybil Thorndike in *Waters of the Moon* – the two Dames together for the first time in N. C. Hunter's comedy, Haymarket, 1951.

Left: 'Arise, sir, from this semi-recumbent posture'. Act I of *The Importance of Being Earnest*. Gwen Ffrangcon-Davies and John Gielgud confronted, for the first time, by Edith's definitive Lady Bracknell. Globe Theatre, 1939.

Rehearsing *The Dark is Light
Enough* at the Aldwych Theatre,
1954. From left to right:
Oliver Messel, James Donald,
Christopher Fry, Edith, and
Peter Brook.

audience for the festival at Smallhythe to commemorate the first anniversary of Ellen Terry's death.

Edith, though enjoying being the toast of the town again as Mrs. Sullen, was restless. At one point she announced plans for a South African tour, including Maugham's *The Constant Wife* and a Shakespearean tragedy in her repertoire, but nothing came of them. So once again she plunged into management. 'Don't ask my why. If you do I'll give you what men call a woman's answer, Because I want to. I shall throw all my heart and savings into the venture . . . and cross my fingers.'

Her fingers were crossed not only for herself but also for H. R. Barbor who had written the play of her choice. *Delilah* which Barbor had dedicated to her five years previously, was described as being based on the Biblical story of Samson and Delilah, but 'treated in the manner of a modern psychological study of the conflict between two races.' John Longden, an old Bensonian by now enjoying a new career as a film star, was engaged to play Samson. Surprisingly, Leslie Banks designed the scenery and the incidental music was specially composed by Leslie Bridgewater. Edith gave more than her usual quota of interviews before the event. 'It's not just a Bible story. It shows how a woman always wants to go on and on until she has found out a man's last secret. She wants to know what's in his inner soul, and when she knows she's often disappointed. That's why I cut Samson's hair.' The press conference was held during rehearsals at the Prince of Wales theatre and Edith was described as 'climbing over a colossal heathen god, vaulting a hand loom and narrowly evading collision with a lyre' in order to meet the *Daily Herald*'s correspondent.

'I am now "limited"', she told the *Observer*. 'At various times I have been in management with other people, but now I am on my own. I am putting all the wages I earned in *The Apple Cart* into Edith Evans Limited because I believe so thoroughly in this play by Mr. Barbor.'

Alas, her faith in the piece proved to be an error. *The Times* spoke of the 'insufferable flatness' of the author's style, not 'vulgar writing . . . not cheaply pretentious . . . an honest but misguided compromise between two manners of English, and between poetry and prose, which lies on the stage like a fog that will admit neither warmth nor light.' The majority of the notices were equally depressing. '*Film Star Brings Down The Temple—But Not The House*' was the *Daily Express*'s unkind headline.

Edith withdrew the play after only three nights, and took the blow philosophically, or at least gave that impression in public. She was not the first leading actress to discover that plays written by admirers are expensive gifts to receive. According to her bank pass book she paid out £5,082.12.3. on the venture, and the credit side of the balance sheet shows that the takings just topped £300.

'I backed the wrong horse,' she said in deciding to abide by the verdict of the critics. 'But I shall save up again and as soon as I have enough money behind me, I shall try again.' Her business-manager, Miss Honor Bright (which name is pure Arthur Marshall-ish in its aptness) gave that most familiar of theatrical explanations. 'We all thought we had a good play, but it seems we were mistaken.'

Much of the history of the theatre is contained in that one sentence.

12

'If you're an actor, a real actor, you've got to be on the stage. But you mustn't go on the stage unless it's absolutely the only thing you can do'

It was the only thing that Edith could do, but her run of bad luck continued into 1931. After the bitter and costly failure of *Delilah*, she next appeared in a conventional comedy by Reginald Berkeley entitled *O.H.M.S.* It was slender stuff and Edith played Mrs. Carruthers, the private secretary of the Governor of a far-flung outpost of our then Empire. (Carruthers, I have noted, is a name persistently used whenever a playwright feels compelled to parody British Colonial or Army life. The British cinema stole the habit and used it almost as a brand name. One can be fairly certain that any character given the handle Carruthers will be portrayed as a silly ass.) *O.H.M.S.* was set on a fictitious island in the South Pacific heavy with the scent of scandal, but apparently devoid of the sweet smell of success. Critical waters covered it from sight in less than a week. One critic, deploring the sad waste of Edith's comic talents, remarked it was like putting Cleopatra in charge of a whist drive.

With depressing regularity she was forced back into revivals, this time renewing a former acquaintance with the predatory vamp, Suzanne, of *Tiger Cats* fame. An act of desperation, since years earlier she had told Guy how she hated the role. Robert Loraine was reunited with her in the role of the husband, Edith received plaudits for returning to the role after seven years with a more masterful technique, but otherwise the resurrection was without distinction, though it marked the professional debut of Leo Genn in the role of an examining magistrate.

It was a sorry season for the leading ladies of the day. Herbert Farjeon noted that it was remarkable that Sybil Thorndike, Athene Seyler and Edith, all three possessed of unusual abilities and with famous names to help them, should be unable to establish themselves as permanent fixtures on the London stage.

'Miss Athene Seyler generally has something to do, but she has not taken the position that would certainly have been hers if she had lived in the eighteenth century. Miss Evans appears to be waiting for something to turn up without much more luck than Mr. Micawber. And

145

Miss Thorndike, too, is unable to find parts at once big and popular enough for her talents.'

An old friend came to Edith's rescue, not with a new play, but at least with a role she hadn't attempted before. Nigel (by now Sir Nigel) Playfair asked her to return to the Lyric, Hammersmith, always a lucky theatre for her, to appear in Congreve's *The Old Bachelor*. The gesture was well-intentioned, but the material was inferior, for *The Old Bachelor* is a cumbersome vehicle, written when Congreve was trying to rouse himself from illness and the role of Laetitia is no Millamant or Mrs. Sullen. The cast as a whole was worthy of better things, including as it did the young Eric Portman, Diana Wynyard, Roland Culver, Hay Petrie, Miles Malleson and Henry Hewitt. Edith's role had originally been played by the amazing Mrs. Bracegirdle in 1693 and of that occasion Lord Macaulay wrote: 'Nothing was wanted to the success of the piece. It was so cast as to bring into play all the comic talent, and to exhibit on the boards in one view all the beauty which Drury Lane Theatre, then the only theatre in London, could assemble.'

Playfair's production in 1931 failed to provoke any such excesses and although Edith collected her usual armful of critical bouquets there was nothing like the clamour aroused for both *The Way of The World* or *The Beaux' Stratagem*. It enjoyed a respectable run and Edith derived some satisfaction from the fact that she had at long last broken the spell of misfortune.

She made plans for her American debut, telling readers of *The Gateway* (a long defunct magazine) that 'I am taking *The Lady With a Lamp* to Broadway very shortly, and Florence is going to be different. More flame to her, more of a rebel at the beginning. I understand her better now. I am different, I understand more, I am reaching a new phase in my career, so Florence will be different.' In another interview she spoke of feeling 'like a sort of Christopher Columbus—going to discover America in order to discover myself.'

She went alone, sailing in the White Star liner *Majestic* on October 14th 1931. Predictably, she was asked whether she would seek to travel on to Hollywood and attempt to break into films. 'I don't think I have a film face,' she told reporters at Southampton. 'It moves about too much.'

Guy was left behind to mind the house and two stray kittens they had adopted. It seems odd that he did not accompany her; he knew America, they could have shared her discovery of the new world. Yet he stayed behind, waiting in the wings for a cue he was never given. Her scrapbooks for the period are beautifully kept, all the entries neatly pasted into separate columns and their origins noted in ink alongside. I suspect they were Guy's handiwork, for after his death the continuity of order is absent, all is confusion—bundles of yellowing cuttings tied into parcels

146

which remained unopened until I cut the brittle string forty years later.

New York treated Edith 'with something like the reverence given to Paderewski' and her 'magnificent performance' was said to have illuminated what the Broadway critics found an indifferent play. John Mason Brown spoke of 'England's admired actress speaking with as lovely and as caressing a voice as can be heard' and Edith's personal triumph crowned a season of success for imported London players.

Edith carried bad luck across the Atlantic like excess luggage and within the month there was a sudden slump on Broadway, which never does anything by halves and eleven shows were withdrawn in one weekend, including *The Lady With a Lamp*. It had survived for twelve performances only. Edith stayed on for a short while and joined other leading players such as Mrs. Pat, Beatrice Lillie, Raymond Massey and Douglas Byng in staging a cabaret in aid of the Emergency Unemployment Relief Fund. I find a certain irony in the unemployed helping the unemployed, but with actors it was ever thus. And whereas America is the best place in the world in which to be a success, failure is regarded as the bubonic plague.

She caught the *Majestic* again for the return voyage and Guy sent her three separate cryptic Marconigrams while she was at sea. In order of receipt they read: YOU OUGHT TO KNOW. MY DAILY LOVE. GUTS GALOREM. I questioned Edith as to their meaning and it appears that whenever they were apart he was in the habit of sending coded expressions of his affection, the most common being 'my daily love'. 'Guts Galorem' was his way of telling her to cheer up.

Arriving home on January 22nd 1932 she told everybody that she had adored New York. 'It's a city in which you can do what you want. If you want to drink milk, you may. If you want to stay up late, you may.' The availability of milk and the right to go late to bed are hardly exclusive to New York, and indeed they seem slender enough reasons to adore any city. Edith had taken stronger nourishment than milk during her brief visit, confessing that she had sampled a speakeasy. 'I think they expected me to ask for some difficult potion like Tokai,' she told reporters. 'So when I said I'd like a long orangeade and a chocolate ice they gaped with astonishment. I'm not sure if they decided I was a great genius—or merely dotty.'

Her homecoming held one pleasant surprise. An urgent letter awaited her from Gielgud and was beautifully timed, for in it he asked if she would join his production of *Romeo and Juliet* for the Oxford University Dramatic Society to play the Nurse. She had fourteen days before the announced first night at the New Theatre, Oxford.

The *Isis*, in frivolous mood, commented: 'the great mystery of the week is how the O.U.D.S. prevailed on Miss Edith Evans to accept their invitation to play the Nurse. It is not true, we learn, that Mr.

George Devine caught an express train to Southampton, bullied his way on to the boat and threw himself at Miss Evans' feet. Anyone who knows anything about it knows that he missed the train. It is known, however, that Mr. John Gielgud cabled to the captain of the liner and told him to put Miss Evans in irons until an O.U.D.S. representative could be hurried to the quayside.'

It was Gielgud's first production and he came to it while enjoying a year's run in Priestley's immensely popular *The Good Companions*. His coup in persuading Edith to accept (and I am sure that with an actor's instinct and sympathy he knew that his letter offer was timed to be psychologically potent) was further enhanced by his choice of Peggy Ashcroft to play Juliet. The young undergraduate poet, Christopher Hassall was the Romeo, with George Devine, then President of the O.U.D.S., as Mercutio, William Devlin as Tybalt and Hugh Hunt as Friar Laurence. Terence Rattigan had a single line to speak as one of the musicians who came to awaken Juliet for her wedding, a traumatic experience for him, one gathers, which in later years he was to make use of, for he built his one act comedy, *Harlequinade*, around a production of *Romeo and Juliet* in which his solitary 'put up your pipes' line was featured.

From top to bottom the O.U.D.S.'s *Romeo and Juliet* was a coming together of many embryonic talents centring around Edith. Gielgud's genius for discerning talent in others and his innate generosity towards such talent is a byword in the theatre. He is a vague man to be directed by, given to many changes of mind, but his rehearsal indecisions are excused by the fact that his casts know they stem from his search for perfection. On this occasion he discovered three art students who later entered the professional theatre under the collective name Motley. Their names were Elizabeth Montgomery and the sisters Audrey and Peggy Harris. They became his costume designers.

The first night was a splendid undergraduate occasion, well attended by the London critics who, at the request of the O.U.D.S., were prevailed upon to delay their reviews for twenty four hours; a request which the *News Chronicle* referred to as the Society's 'prehistoric inhibitions.' In his famed autobiography *Early Stages*, Gielgud recalls that the first performance was not without its disasters. The curtain fouled and by the end of the play his nerves were in such a state that he blurted one of his many legendary gaffes. 'The graceful compliments I intended to distribute circled madly in my head, and I referred to Miss Evans and Miss Ashcroft as 'two leading ladies, the like of whom I hope I shall never meet again.''' (Such 'Gielguds' have long been part of contemporary theatrical folklore and although many must be considered apocryphal, I prefer to believe that if they are not entirely true, they ought to be.)

148

The O.U.D.S. production was well received, though Mr. Charles Morgan of *The Times* erred when he wrote 'it was Mr. Gielgud's private discernment that saw the Nurse in Miss Evans,' forgetting she had already played the role during her season at the Vic.

We are told that she had the hands of an old woman, the walk of a sly one. It was a performance she was to build upon over the years, for she came to it again in two other notable productions. An earthy characterisation, full of innuendo humour, a portrait of a coarse old confidant, it surprised many people. In lesser hands the Nurse can be a thundering old bore, prating on and on, but Edith's great achievement was that she found hidden meanings which disguised some of the more tedious aspects of the character. There was a quality of stillness about Edith's major performances that few, if any, equalled. She *used* silence, she listened, and this to my mind is one of the hallmarks of greatness in an actor. A great actor has an ear for the pause and can calculate its bearable duration with the exactness of a scientist. In comedy, timing is everything. Edith had it, Rex Harrison has it to perfection; dropping the laugh line into the silence like a stone falling to the bottom of a well. Actors of the calibre of Edith conceal themselves even as they conceal their art. Gielgud has written that he remembers once saying: 'I wish I could have a photograph of Edith Evans. I can never recognise her when she comes on the stage. She always looks exactly like the part she is playing.' This was a verdict from a connoisseur.

Edith left little to chance. I particularly like the story of the young actor who once went up to her just before the red light flashed for transmission time on a BBC drama broadcast. 'Good luck, Dame Edith,' he said. 'With some of us,' Edith replied, 'it isn't *luck*.' At work everything was subordinated to the job in hand. She rested between the matinee and the evening performance. Knowing that she was not a Gladys Cooper with a beauty 'straight from the bath' she studied her face in the dressing room mirror until she knew its faults by heart, and by the time she appeared on stage she had 'assumed' that beauty she deemed necessary for the occasion. When her call came, her last act was to powder her hands. 'You'd be surprised how many people notice dirty hands on the stage. You watch next time. You see somebody come on, dressed to the nines, all airs and graces, and her hands! red raw, my dear, like something in a butcher's shop. Women should always powder their hands—those and their eyes are what people notice most. They're our tools, we have to take care of them.' These were the trade secrets, so often despised nowadays—a tradition of discipline which, like courtesy, is a devalued currency for a generation of performers spawned by television, where the audiences applaud to order and the laughter is canned.

'Illusion, madam, is one of the assets of the theatre,' Sir John Martin

Harvey once said in reply to an admirer's question as to whether he actually played the violin in a certain role. Edith guarded the illusions she created, preserving an aura of mystery which few dared to encroach.

Her pleasant interlude with the O.U.D.S. reawakened yearnings for the classical repertory and in the spring of 1932 she went back to the Vic to play Emilia in Harcourt Williams' production of *Othello*. Agate began his review in the *Sunday Times* with a long paragraph about Edith, but was devastatingly dismissive of poor Wilfrid Walter who played the Moor, and was equally scathing about the Desdemona of Phyllis Thomas. Ralph Richardson, who played Iago, gave a performance which, he thought 'was very good Richardson but indifferent Shakespeare.'

She stayed on at the Vic for Viola in *Twelfth Night*, receiving very mixed notices. There was no doubt that she was the chief point of interest, but several of the critics felt she was not suited to the role. 'Can a truly versatile actress be miscast?' one of them asked, while the reviewer on *The Star* told his readers that 'Edith Evans, on another night, may inspire the cast instead of overpowering it.'

A further revival of *Heartbreak House* followed in which that supremely gifted actor of spasmodic genius, Wilfrid Lawson, played the role of Mangan and Edith repeated her Lady Utterword yet again. An amazing number of column inches were devoted to a play that had already been exhaustively analysed on at least three previous occasions. Shaw's 'wordquake' seemed to inspire the critics to emulate its length in their reviews.

Shaw, elated by Edith's dedication to his cause, wrote the following postcard:

27th April 1932

Edith Evans

You had better be told—in case you don't know it—that your performance on Monday was Magnificent, Superb, Stupendous, Surpassing, Masterly, Delightful, Overwhelming, and Better-than-the-Part.

It saved us from shipwreck.

In short, quite good.

Bless you.   G. Bernard Shaw.

Now, unexpectedly, Edith found a new play and a star role 'in which one can swim'. This was the Edward Knoblock-Beverley Nichols adaptation of Nichols' novel *Evensong*. The plot concerned a temperamental prima donna in her sunset years who realises that her voice is fading. The principal character was Melba with modifications, many of the incidents in the drama having been lifted straight out of Melba's life, which was hardly coincidence since Nichols had at one time been the singer's social secretary. He went through the motions of denying that there was any resemblance to persons living or dead, but his protests carried little conviction.

(One Australian newspaper declared that Nichols 'himself is recognisable, in feminine disguise, as Irela's niece and general factotum, whose function is to bring an anaemic love interest to the piece. One closed the novel with a shudder.')

Edith was suddenly in her element. In one of her few bursts of public frankness, she announced 'it is in another category altogether from anything I have done before. It's a part I've been feeling towards for a long time, a *real* woman who isn't me. Selfish, and domineering, and full of petty faults, but *great*—driven by her genius. She has had the world at her feet. And if anybody so much as breathes the words 'eighteenth-century' to me over this, I'll murder them. There's an enormous gap between this and anything else I've done. For it, I've changed my whole technique. My method of speaking is different, my method of moving my hands. Even my figure is entirely different. Some people think that all we have to do is go on the stage and open our mouths. It makes me so angry I could bash somebody.'

Guy noticed the change in her and was amused by it. 'Who have I married now?' he asked her. She went about in a high fever and many of her friends asked him what had happened to her. 'She's having an opera singer,' he said. Some of her closest friends had felt she was always 'behind a veil' but now she widened her circle and gave large week-end parties at Washenden in total contrast to the life style she had hitherto been content with. She indulged her love of dancing and bought a new wardrobe with an apparently clear conscience for once. One can only assume that, consciously or not, it was an extension of the personality she had selected for the role of Irela. 'Something seemed to swell to bursting inside me.' she said, which ties in with Guy's pregnancy joke. 'It said to me, "let me out, let me out!" But I didn't know what it was. "What are you?" I asked. I could cut myself open to let it out, but I didn't know what it was. Then I was given this role, and the question was answered. You see, on the stage I'd made such lovely people that I couldn't live up to them. I felt that whoever had seen those beautiful people I'd made would be disappointed when they just met me.'

This outpouring illustrates the turmoil that she went through when preparing for a new role, but, more importantly, it admits that there was another side to her, one that she had kept hidden at considerable cost to herself and her marriage. It wasn't a question of all passion spent, but of all passion hoarded.

The photographs of her as Irela bear witness to the physical change. She explained further: 'When I begin working on a part, I always do what I *feel* first. I don't think the part: I feel it. I try to *be* the person I'm studying. I think and feel the way she would. I always check everything from the *inside*. I go digging down to where her foundations begin. Sometimes, when the words come out of my mouth wrong, I scamper after them with my technique . . . It's like cooking. You may put all the ingredients of a dish together quite perfectly, and then take it out of the oven too early, and it's not fit to eat. You have to work and wait, wait, wait. But once a part is made, everything drops into place naturally and the character becomes alive—exists by itself—is another me.'

The new Edith of *Evensong* was to everybody's liking and the play proved to be her first copper-bottomed commercial success. J. C. Trewin has written that until this time, despite the loyalty of her Old Vic following 'there had been a certain West End reticence. Possibly some people felt that Edith Evans had been the critics' find, the highbrows' prize; that she was now being forced on them with this talk of the contagious spirits of an Ellen Terry and the intellectual audacity of a Réjane.' *Evensong* changed all that. Her triumph in the role was total. She was surrounded by an enormous cast of distinguished names— Wilfrid Lawson, Henry Wilcoxon, Frederic Leister, Reginald Tate, Violet Vanbrugh, George Devine and Joan Harben amongst others— and on the opening night the audience were cheering her by the first interval. Mr. Agate deplored such excesses and interruptions, but was won over in the end. 'She walks the stage like Juno, and when, diadem'd and splendorous, she makes entry at her rival's party, her cloak of blue velvet has the majesty of offended heavens.' Others were slightly less purple but no less uninhibited in their applause. Edith relished her success, and who can blame her? *Evensong* had ended the long, dry season and here she was replenishing her lost savings in a smash, popular success, being compared openly to Bernhardt, running through the whole gamut of temperament like a Toledo blade dividing silk. Shaw had once said to her: 'Do you seek adventure?' and she had answered, 'No, but it follows me all the time.' Now she stood centre stage, gathering unaccustomed praise for qualities other than her acting. She was now told she had 'the finest carriage of anyone on the London stage, and a figure that the gods might envy, being not only better looking than any prima donna in her old age, but better looking than any prima donna at the height of her celebrity.' And nobody breathed the words 'eighteenth-century.'

Edith had her own views about artistic temperament. 'It's a monster that lies in wait to "have" us. It's not a thing to glory in and boast about, but to fight. For, whereas truly artistic persons—by one of the inexorable laws of compensation—are always obsessed by temperament or nervous tension, due to the anxiety to do justice to their art, I have found that those who deliberately cultivate such a state of mind or emotion are

152

nearly always placid pretenders, who take it out on others, while retaining their own equilibrium.

'It is unreasonable to demand or even suggest that an artist should have the power to hold thousands enthralled for an hour or so, and then slip back into the position of being just a casual onlooker. It isn't a question of conceit, or egoism, but of commonsense.

'Temperamental people think and live differently from anybody else and their perspective is adjusted accordingly. Whatever anybody may say in the way of criticism, artists in general take a broad view of life for themselves and other people. They do not ask for more than they are prepared to give. The only pity is that they so rarely have time to give it.'

This insider's description would be hard to better. She said it all in 1932 when she was still enjoying her greatest popular acclaim to date. Perhaps, with her usual cutting self-honesty she was conscious that success did not of itself bring total fulfilment . . . The only pity is that they so rarely have time to give . . . She knew the risks, but was powerless to alter things. In the mass of cuttings and interviews I could find only two references to Guy and her marriage, and those in passing. She was photographed in her London apartment (somewhat sparsely furnished, for she was no lover of clutter) but Washenden and the life she shared with Guy was never mentioned. Edith asked me to write the truth in this biography, but the truth is never simple. There is nothing really scurrilous to conceal, only a remembered sadness of days lost between two people who were constantly searching for each other, but consulting different maps. Sometimes the references crossed and there was joy and tenderness and companionship in the reunion. The compass of their emotional life always showed true North when they allowed it to, but there were many occasions when outside forces flickered the needle.

'People who labour under the disabilities of artistic temperament are usually very conscious of the fact and strain every nerve to appear completely sane and normal in public,' she said. She talked of them as 'unfortunates' and many times admitted to me that 'the strain of trying to be good' imposed enormous physical pressures. 'I put too much strain on my nerves under my skin. Some people don't mind anything, you see. They aren't affected. I mind so terribly, and I know I shouldn't. I know it's wrong to mind if people are unkind or forgetful or cruel. It's very hard to be a Christian. It's the hardest thing in the world, the Christian faith, terribly hard. You've got to forgive everybody, got to love everybody. I ha-ate it. I know I'm wrong, though. But when you feel somebody has been terribly unjust to you, really unjust, it's awfully hard to forgive them and love them, I think . . . Even just to like them a bit. I mind too much, you see. That's my fault, that's really all that's wrong with me physically. If I mind anything, then everything goes wrong. It was always like that.'

She was busy outside the theatre during the long run of *Evensong*—attending meetings of the newly-formed Equity Council, sitting for a portrait by Wyndham Lewis, taking part in a series run by the *Sunday Dispatch* called WHAT DOES THE LORD'S PRAYER MEAN TO YOU?, and appearing disguised under a sinister black wig as Irma, evil daughter of the villain in *Bulldog Drummond*, complete with foreign accent, for a Royal Charity matinee in aid of King George's Pension Fund for Actors. In addition, and somewhat oddly, she judged a fashion competition for corselettes and belts organised by the *Sunday Pictorial*. She was suddenly 'news' in a way she had never been before. Gossip columnists wrote of 'the Evans drawl' which annoyed her and she replied that she was now a reformed actress: 'I speak all my lines in modern plays in the approved quick-fire style. People apparently want short, snappy talk nowadays. I can't think why.' A lady journalist calling herself 'Miss Gossip' reported how Edith 'jollied up' a City luncheon by telling the guests that 'actresses are such very dull people off the stage. We are only delightful and brilliant when we are doing what we are told to do. Off stage we are awful chumps.' I have the distinct feeling that Edith was playing the columnists at their own game. Photographs of her appeared in all the glossies and she was presented as having assumed a totally different character. This is to be doubted. She was acting. The newspapers and the public having taken her performance in *Evensong* to their hearts, wanted to believe that the private life of Edith Evans mirrored the semi-fictitious life of Irela, the prima donna. Temporarily, she entered into the deception and, I have no doubt, enjoyed herself hugely.

She took *Evensong* to New York at the beginning of 1933, confident of success, but in New York the champagne went flat. As with *The Lady With a Lamp* Broadway audiences and critics applauded her performance but dismissed the play. Once again the letters from Guy resumed their old frequency for, as on the previous occasion, he did not accompany her. He wrote to give her sad news as well as the everyday gossip of Washenden.

> Ted Berman wrote me bad news for you about Barbor. The poor fellow has passed on, having succumbed to septic peritonitis at Port Said. I do hope his little wife and boy are provided for.

The actual date of Barbor's death was January 13th, 1933 and eight days later another old friend of Edith's also died a long way from home. George Moore's death took place in Toulon on January 21st and once again it was Guy who broke the news in a letter primarily intended to wish Edith a happy birthday 'wreathed in smiles, free of parrrrrties, crowned with success and the harbinger of many more.'

His letters of this period are a strange mixture of tenderness and small-talk.

> I love you so much dear and can sense your presence when moving around: sitting here it just becomes a pain . . .
>
> Cuckoo came yesterday and enjoyed a short visit . . . She told me they were worried about Leslie Banks' growing fatness and had decided to mention this defection from his worked grace. But Tippy Griffith blundered into his dressing room and spilled the beans all over poor Leslie's corpulence and spared them the strain. I learn he cannot now wear his original clothes for Act I, pity isn't it? Bunty is held up in the Red Sea, hold caught fire and exploded and they were taken off and the ship sank: some experience.

The news of the play's failure in New York distressed him.

> How grateful I am that you will not be depressed about it, instead I can see and hear your cheering some of the others of the Company who will not, perhaps, take it as well . . . I hate to think of you being wacked, you could do so much for them with a good part . . . Let Hope and Fulfilment spring. You will get the best out of living each day I know—nothing less for you, my girl. I kiss you so very much in spirit and love you always . . .

Here and there in the numerous letters he wrote are scattered asides as to his own condition. The brain tumour that was shortly to claim his life had not then been detected, but his letters reveal that he was conscious of something untoward. The old buoyancy was absent, he no longer outlined plans for the future, as though he sensed that his winter was upon him.

> . . . cripes what a lot to—it all has me rather beaten for the moment. Shall take a day off next week and go to the flat for a break. I miss you terribly dear, my only consolation is work in clean air and At Home . . . I am very tired. Lawks how I sleep . . . The doctor was very good, told me I was lucky to be clearing up so well—few really recover—and that, with care I shall go on to victory. Have got to go to him 2 months hence for a thorough examination and final clearances, so for the nonce we'll forget all about that. I will use all the care that's God's and your work 'require in air' and get over this rather washed out look, seeing things as they *are* . . .

His reasons for consulting the doctor on this occasion had no connection with the tumour. He appears to have been suffering from the smouldering after-effects of an illness contracted in Venezuela, though it is always possible that the tumour, as yet undetected, was beginning to make itself felt. Edith's attitude towards illness was ambiguous. Except for a few accidents and an occasional bout of sickness, she was a stranger to ill health, sustained by her faith and disinclined to visit the doctor. Many years later when she suffered a major heart attack she talked of illness as another stage role, a role she had never played before. 'I didn't know what you did when you're ill.' She believed most sincerely that most ailments could be cured through prayer and although I have been told, by people more erudite in these matters than myself, that her interpretation of Christian Science was a highly individual one, I can only report that her faith in the efficacy of the teachings of Christian Science seemed to me constant. With Guy it was a different matter. Out of love, out of loyalty, he went along with Edith's beliefs (his letters make passing reference to them) and when he was taken ill he was torn between Edith and orthodox medical treatment. She wanted him to believe as passionately as herself and he made valiant attempts, but his heart was not in it. Perhaps he suspected the truth about his own condition and concealed it from her. To a much greater extent than today cancer was the prime taboo, talked of in hushed tones; even when a loved one had died of it, relatives were often reluctant to say the word, as though by avoiding mention of it they could protect themselves; it was, inexplicably, regarded as something shameful by many. It was my firm impression that, to the end of her days, Edith held herself responsible for Guy's death. She felt that her faith had not been strong enough, that she, not God, had failed him and that she should have worked harder with her prayers.

'Tomorrow's abstentions are the trap of today! (Aphorism for 1933)' Guy wrote to her while she was still in New York. Perhaps in the context of their own lives he should have reversed the order.

A new dog, a spaniel, awaited Edith's return home from America. Failure in the theatre makes many a star react in the same way as a racing driver after a crash: they want to get behind the wheel again as soon as possible. Edith did just that. Instead of brushing up her Shakespeare, she brushed up her American accent and took over the role of a vaudeville performer in a Hollywood satire by Moss Hart and George S. Kaufman called *Once In a Lifetime*. She acquitted herself with style, but it was a poor substitute for the success she had anticipated and failed to achieve on Broadway.

By now British Equity had obtained formal ratification of its hotly contested 'closed shop' resolution. The Association now boasted a membership of 2,000, and no General Council of a fledgling trade union ever claimed a more illustrious roster of household names: Sir Gerald du Maurier, Gertrude Lawrence, Evelyn Laye, Gielgud, Bobby Howes, Nelson Keys, Lewis Casson, Raymond Massey, Dame May Whitty,

156

Leslie Henson, Marie Löhr, Arthur Wontner and Edith amongst them. Writing from her West Halkin Street address, Edith issued a personal statement.

> I joined my Trade Union because I love my country and wish to abide by its common laws.
> This—the only legal way of banding together with my fellow artists— enables us to obtain a fair contract and protection from exploitation, and provides a means of disciplining one's own people when they are naughty.
> Join your own Trade Union and take your part with others of your trade or profession in ensuring its Dignity.

The enthusiasm of those founder members of Equity was infectious. They earnestly discussed the dangers of White Slave Traffic, Mr. Wall, the Honorary Secretary of Equity, telling a mass meeting at the Garrick Theatre that it was a serious menace. He quoted a recent Scotland Yard enquiry into a management that had taken a number of girls to the Mediterranean under conditions which were 'not good.' At the same meeting Oscar Asche asked the platform whether, as members of a trade union, actors would now be called out to support a coal strike.

'Emphatically no,' replied Mr. Godfrey Tearle. (And before actors are accused of lacking in solidarity towards their fellow trade unionists, it is only fair to add that one doubts whether the coal miners would come out in sympathy with the actors if put to the test.)

Edith retained a splendidly practical attitude towards back-stage working conditions, which have scarcely altered for the good in the past forty years. Dressing rooms are still cramped cells, usually containing a few sticks of handed-down furniture; they are badly heated and ventilated and decorated to resemble an Orwellian conception of functional luxury. Some I have inhabited would tax the ingenuity of a Houdini, were he compelled to execute a quick-change. Even the so called 'star' dressing rooms suggest left-overs from a slum clearance scheme and all are distinguished by a lack of toilet facilities. Edith agreed with me. 'The real trouble is dressing rooms are always such a long way from the loo. That's the one thing in the world you want when you're acting—you want to be near the loo.'

During the run of *Once in a Lifetime*, a frequent visitor, welcomed and for once allowed to break all Edith's rules, was Emlyn Williams. During waits in the play he coached her in a Welsh accent since she was 'less to do with Wales than her name implied.' The reason being that Edith had been cast in *The Late Christopher Bean*, a play with a curious pedigree. Originally written in French by Fauchois under the title *Prenez-garde à la peinture*, it had first been translated into English and adapted for the American stage by Sidney Howard. Then, when Gilbert Miller decided to bring it to London, it was at John van Druten's suggestion that Emlyn was contracted to change the setting from a New England to a Cheshire village and make the central character of the maid, Gwenny, Welsh. Emlyn made the necessary changes in a week, and although Edith had fooled a previous generation with her portrayal in *Taffy*, she insisted that her accent was not good enough and thus Emlyn was recruited as schoolteacher. In the second volume of his autobiography he has described the forty-five-year-old Edith as having 'the eager enthusiasm of a young girl' and somebody who 'though she normally talked a great deal and fluently, when she came to discuss the part her vocabulary halted and she made me think of Epstein, feeling his way in an instinctive dark.' He found the transformation from 'the unlikely part of a wise-cracking American secretary' to humble pupil 'extraordinary to watch.' Emlyn relates that she repeated her lines back to him like a child, 'but behind the lines I could see starting a ferment of creation.' There is a hint of prophecy here: Morgan Evans and Miss Moffat from *The Corn is Green* with the roles reversed. I have no doubt that Emlyn was a superb teacher, for he has always been an actor's actor and an actor's playwright. It takes a very bad actor indeed to fail in a role written by Emlyn.

The Late Christopher Bean proved to be the long-running Christopher Bean, opening at the St. James's in May 1933 to the loudest cheers heard in the West End for many years, one of those glorious nights when triumph, like darkness, falls from the air, covering critics and audience alike. Edith's glory was shared with Cedric Hardwicke, and their joint playing ensured that the play ran until the summer of the following year, and the London production then went on an extended tour of the provinces. Hardwicke was knighted on the morning of a matinee day in March 1934.

1934 was a good year in the theatre, and Edith's performance as Gwenny was rated the top of a selected list which included Gielgud in *Richard of Bordeaux*, Flora Robson in *Mary Read* and Diana Wynyard in *Sweet Aloes*. Attention was also drawn to the young Peter Glenville for his performance as Marchbanks in *Candida* at the Manchester Repertory Theatre. The son of Shaun Glenville and Dorothy Ward, Peter had been President of the O.U.D.S. prior to his entry into the professional theatre and writing in the *Isis* in May 1934 on the subject of 'This Acting Business' he had extolled Edith as 'surely one of the best examples of the perfect actress. She can play the American flapper, the aged Florence Nightingale or the waning opera star without ever giving the faintest suspicion of a peculiar "Evans" style common to them all.'

If the shadow of Guy's failing health darkened her private life, she gave no indication in public. She told me that the tumour was not diagnosed. They were both made increasingly aware that something was seriously wrong, but lulled into a false sense of security by a variety of conflicting opinions. 'He thought he could run for a bit,' she said, 'and he did for a year or two, but they didn't have proper treatment in those days.' Just as the pain of childbirth is soon forgotten, which is just as well for the continuance of the human race, many people deliberately blot out rememberance of a loved one's terminal illness. Edith did this. Forty years after his death she would sometimes refer to it in isolation— a bubble of pain surfacing, but she could never bring herself to discuss it in any detail.

During the long run of *Christopher Bean* (which stabilised her fortunes once more, and prompted Emlyn to write from Wales that she was very popular in his family circle as 'that Miss Evans who is making Emlyn so much money') she also found the time and energy to rehearse another leading role, that of Sarah, Duchess of Marlborough in Norman Ginsbury's brisk comedy *Viceroy Sarah*. It was to be presented for a few special performances at The Arts. Edith was keen on the play and took the risk of talking about it before the event in an interview she gave to the *Observer*. 'It isn't the classic dialogue of Congreve—where people must have spent the whole morning thinking out a *mot*, and then waiting to fire it off with the greatest effect. But it is also not modern English dialogue. It is just careful, attractive English, and it takes some speaking.'

As always, she was loyal to her author. 'How historically correct it is I do not know. I have not read the latest researches on the subject. As an actress called on to interpret a play, I leave the historical reading to the author, and try to be as faithful to *his* idea as I can. I suppose his conclusions may be disputed; one never knows what theories develop about historical characters. When I played Florence Nightingale I got bouquets from one side of the family and rude letters from the other . . .'

Her views on the degradation of the English language are particularly fascinating. She was a Londoner, a Cockney—and they have never been noted for their slavish devotion to the Oxford Dictionary pronunciation of words—and she felt passionately about the feel and actual mechanics of speaking well. 'I think our vocabulary is getting smaller and smaller. It will probably end up as two words only, "Yep" and "O yeah". The dialogue of country people is still rich in lovely things. A countryman will look up into the sky and say that he sees "tempest" coming. How often do we use that word now? "The cattle look kindly" —meaning they are looking well. What a lovely phrase that is.'

The interviewer, Hubert Griffith, asked her views on the current health of the theatre in England. 'We don't take it seriously and we don't respect it enough. We give the world the very greatest dramatists; we've an enormous amount of acting talent among us, and then we say "O rats" and toss it away through lack of organisation.'

It was hoped—Edith hoped—that the special performances at The

Arts of *Viceroy Sarah* would whet the appetites of managements and ensure that the play would be represented when the run of *Christopher Bean* ended. 'I ought really to be in a decline,' she told Griffith. 'I've been playing Christopher Bean solidly for a year, eight performances a week, and now these rehearsals on top of it.'

Guthrie directed (and he, too, was looking for a transfer to the West End proper to further his own career); the reviews were highly complimentary to all concerned, the majority of the London critics urging that the play ought to be seen by a wider audience. One exception was the young Harold Hobson, then writing for the *Christian Science Monitor*. He found Edith's playing 'overbearing', thus proving that even faith will not save you from a bad notice.

Edith also made time to appear in a curious mock trial, one of many that season, staged in aid of King Edward's Hospital Fund. Mr. Norman Birkett, the eminent K.C., arraigned Dorothy Dickson, Heather Thatcher, Peggy Ashcroft and Edith on the grave charge of 'luring his Majesty's subjects from their ordinary occupations.' The case came up before 'Judge' Franklin, a gentleman who combined cricketing with the law. The oath was taken on a newly-bound book and the defendants affirmed 'I swear by the Irishman Bernard Shaw to tell his own inimitable truth, and anything but the truth.' When asked how she wished to plead, Edith answered: 'Cheerfully guilty, my lord.' Peggy Ashcroft went further, declaring, 'I should like to plead insanity—at least on the part of my counsel.' The sentences were varied, severest of all being meted out to Miss Ashcroft, 'a bad case' as the Judge remarked, who was condemned to play Juliet for two years in Wigan with Wallace Beery as Romeo. Edith got hard labour, a term in Wales to learn to speak English.

This frolic was set against the sadness of Sir Nigel Playfair's death in August 1934. Edith had much to thank him for. After Poel he had done the most for her. A man of great taste, his name would always be linked with the Lyric, Hammersmith, scene of some of Edith's earliest and greatest triumphs.

As the post-London tour of *Christopher Bean* came to an end in Streatham, New York and Juliet's Nurse beckoned once again. This time it was a production staged by Guthrie McClintic for his wife, Katharine Cornell who was then generally accorded the title of 'America's foremost actress.' It was to be a prestige occasion, with sets designed by Jo Mielziner, dances staged by Martha Graham and an all star cast. Basil Rathbone had been engaged for Romeo, Brian Aherene for Mercutio and Orson Welles for Tybalt. Edith sailed in the *Majestic* at the beginning of November, cutting it rather fine, for she had only left herself fourteen days rehearsal before the out-of-town opening. The short rehearsal period gave Miss Cornell some concern, but McClintic insisted he would have nobody else.

The *Tatler* published a picture of Edith on the deck of the *Majestic* posed alongside a fellow-passenger, George Arliss. There is a passing resemblance to Ethel Neve and Dr. Crippen and the caption beneath the photograph is a masterpiece of understatement (film division). 'Having finished everything in *The Iron Duke* film excepting the battle of Waterloo, the Iron Duke himself left for America.'

After the event, there were people who criticised Edith for not being by Guy's side during his last illness, but having pieced together all the evidence available to me (including, curiously enough, the few odd letters from Edith to Guy that have survived) I am convinced that neither of them had any real premonition that when she sailed away that November day they would never see each other again. Her mother and father wrote to her frequently, touchingly simple letters that they compiled together, her mother usually addressing her as 'Edith Mary dear' and certainly at the beginning of December 1934 they were writing to assure her that '*apart from his headache*' Guy was in good spirits and decidedly better. Edith herself wrote to Guy on Sunday 2nd December from Detroit.

> My Darling,
> We arrived here after quite a pleasant all night journey and open tomorrow. Went for a walk with Brian round Belle Isle.
> Quite pleasant and a little reminiscent of Barnes and Richmond and it made me home sick. I can't believe I'm here, but I'm not sorry I came, but oh so hoping that you will come out as soon as possible after Xmas . . .
> I feel sure that you are making progress with your healing. It all seems to me to be working the right way and I do miss you terribly at times. I do so want to share everything . . . There was a lovely sunset this evening at about 5 o'clock and then I remembered it would be about eleven with you and you would most likely be in bed. I must get a tiny rest now. All love, Edith.

> She added a postscript before posting this.
> Back from rehearsal. It's about 1 o'clock and I'm rather tired. Didn't sleep much on the train. Thinking of you constantly and longing for news.
> Edith.

Her parents' letter to her of December 11th made no mention of Guy's health and was mostly taken up with the news that Uncle Jim's Will had been sworn for Probate and that there were 16 residuary legatees, all cousins, with Edith amongst them. Uncle Jim was a recently deceased relative and Edith was to receive £444.16.6 as her share. 'We are very glad the dear little man's affairs are settled up so nicely,' her mother wrote. 'A pretty little spot in the bank for you when you come home. It nearly frightens me to know of so much money coming into the family.' She hoped this news would arrive by Christmas Day in New York.

Edith had written to Guy the day before, on December 10th, and by now she was in Cleveland on the second week of the tour. She thanked him for 'both your sweet letters'. Although few of his letters at this period were dated, I believe she was referring to one of two letters in which he wrote 'Naughty one, it is time I came to look after your figure that I too have more than a part interest in. Beloved, if that same adorable figure were nigh I'd crush it oh so gently, I ache to kiss it so. Heavens, how I ache for you.'

The mails were erratic, not only because it was the Christmas rush but also because Edith was travelling, and the various letters frequently crossed. The play opened at the Martin Beck Theatre on December 20th and proved to be another jewel in Miss Cornell's crown. Her perform-ance as the Nurse now consolidated and rounded off by three separate productions, Edith scored a personal triumph. Katharine Cornell found her 'an absolute dream to work with. It was the most thrilling thing in the world to play the garden scene with her—one of those things you were eager to get on the stage to do.'

Edith wrote to Guy on theatre notepaper, but unfortunately this again is undated, though it was obviously sent after they had arrived back in New York.

'I am so gratified darling for this healing and know that this is only the beginning of a larger life altogether. We are both going to become our real selves, and do fine things together. If you are able get Tom to finish quickly and then we can rest a little in our sweet home. A real home this time, before we start real activity. I don't need to know what. I just know it's there for you as well as me.
My dear love always Edith.
Write as soon as you can.

She knew that his condition had worsened, but sustained by her faith and persuaded that she could transmit the strength of that faith to him across the Atlantic, she remained confident that all would be well. She had cabled her parents the day after the first night:

RECEPTION PLAY MAGNIFICENT ALL HAPPY HAVE WRITTEN FOUR LETTERS RECEIVED ALL YOURS GUY HAVING TREAT-MENT FEEL CERTAIN SPEEDY RECOVERY KEEP IN TOUCH LOVE DARLINGS EDITH

The rest of the story is mostly told in the terse impartial language that people often employ when they cable or telegraph. Sometime at the end of December Guy was taken to a hospital in Guildford. His last letters to Edith make sad reading. There is no means of telling exactly when he wrote them and they are scarcely letters as such, just scraps, disjointed sentences, some in pencil, the words slanting off the page. In one he tried to write of his return to 'sunshine manor' for that was how he had sometimes headed his letters to her from Washenden in happier times. He joked, 'this 'ere bed ain't half devastated my extremis' reverting to the private language he had first employed as a soldier green to the trenches. 'After the Professor's passing' is scrawled across the top of another torn sheet of paper, obviously in reference to a visit from his surgeon. 'Inside I have always burnt with the knowledge that you were the only one . . .' Then the rare face of despair: 'Oh my love my courage has been spent, wasted in breaking myself . . . No matter, I love you and am your man and so it shall be.' Then, possibly as the end approached, he called her 'My lovely love . . . God knows how I want you and to get some sort of focus and purpose into life with your help my beloved . . . it seems to have gone cockeyed and unbelievedly futile at the moment. Will hope to feel better and write you later . . . just hanging on now.' I have no means of telling whether this next note was the last he ever wrote to her, but I put it last for it seems to me to embrace all he ever felt and struggled to say to her. 'I confess at this time of day that in lots of things I feel a shyness with you that does not assail me with others. Love me dear heart and put up your arms just once for me . . . I do so want to kiss you.'

The end came swiftly. On January 8th 1935 Edith again cabled her parents.

PLEASE CABLE PROPER RATE DAILY SPARE NO EXPENSE FOR HIS CARE SEE HIM AND SAY I LOVE HIM ALL MY THANKS EDITH.

While this was being transmitted her poor parents had received a telegram from the hospital:

EVANS EASTBOURNE 1718
REGRET VERY SERIOUSLY ILL SECRETARY
GUILDFORD 2323.

They did not go to the expense of including his name in the telegram, saving that for the second message which was telegraphed the following morning, January 9th.

REGRET BOOTH DIED 9.30 THIS MORNING—SECRETARY.

In death they did at least accord him a surname. The news was cabled to Edith. Sybil Thorndike, who was also in New York at the time, appearing in John van Druten's *The Distaff Side*, went to Edith's hotel the moment she learnt what had happened. McClintic and Katharine Cornell immediately released Edith from her contract. She tried to fly home but New York was fog-bound and all flights had been cancelled. She sent two cables to her parents within hours of each other. The first one read:

TOO STUNNED TO THINK SAILING TONIGHT KEEP STEADY
DARLINGS LOVE EDITH

Edith's character is nowhere better illustrated. Even at the height of her own grief she found words to comfort her parents.

Arrangements were made for her to take the first boat out and her second cable confirmed this.

SAILING ON MAJESTIC JANUARY 9TH
MIDNIGHT ARRIVE SOUTHAMPTON
TUESDAY MORNING LOVE

Many years later when we were both working together on *The Whisperers* she gave an interview to the *Daily Express* in which she said, 'After a while, you know, you can't be hurt by anything else. I have been hurt—all the loves, the falsities, the losing of my husband. The only thing I never felt the loss of was a child, because I never had one. If I had had a child, I probably wouldn't have gone on acting, because I have to cut everything else out when I am acting, and you can't cut out a child. If anything personal goes wrong, it takes me over completely. I am not one of those brave people who can go on. When my husband died I was in New York, and had to wait for a boat to get me home. I eventually got here to find it all over. He was already buried.

'I didn't know where to go. It was like being a little girl again. I had a thought a little while ago; I decided that you have to have been desperately unhappy before you can play comedy, so that nothing can frighten you any more.

'And you can't do tragedy before you know absolute happiness, because having known that, you are safe. I remember saying to my husband once, as we walked in the garden: "I wish I could have my happiness here in my hand". But happiness is an essence, not a chunk. When the sun hits the top of a building, I think: "It must be so marvellous up there."

Life is very precious to me. I must not waste it.'

It was cruel, but consistent, that Guy's funeral had taken place by the time Edith set foot on English soil. Their love story had lasted thirty years. For most of that time they had been apart and even in death fate conspired to separate them yet again.

13

'*A successful artist of any kind has to work so hard that she is justified
in refusing to lay down her sceptre until she is placed on her bier*'

'I nearly lost my reason, during that time. Friends and family tried to
be helpful, but friends can't wipe your mind clean, grief isn't something
you can tidy up like dust on a mantlepiece.'

Her mother and father wrote to her twice a week, their letters a
touching mixture of sympathy and smalltalk, giving me the impression
that they were at a loss to know how to deal with the situation. 'You
must not grieve so much Ede dear, it makes us very unhappy to see you
so broken down . . . You cannot expect to fall in all at once. By the way
Minnie is selling marmalade twopence a pound, wouldn't you like
some?'

Sybil Thorndike wrote to her from Boston; she had been one of the
first to rush to comfort Edith in New York.

> Hotel Touraine,
> Boston.
> February 9, 1935

Darling Edith,

I wrote you last month to 10 Halkin Street!!!! now you'll not get it.
It was just to say how much I'm thinking of you and how wonderful
you were—Honestly you *were* marvellous the way you tried to realize
it all and never just leant on other people. I can say in a letter what
I can't to your face—you're a very courageous *big* person, and you've
got *huge* things to do in the theatre and huge things to give and keep
giving and anything you suffer turns to blessings for others. Even in
that awful time in New York you were *giving* to us all, making us *see*
something. How proud Guy must be that you are starting work
again and fighting for Equity and just holding banners high.
Bless you darling, your Loving Sybil.

Sybil's missing letter eventually turned up. In it she had assured
Edith that 'Guy's going couldn't be just waste—it's unthinkable, and
unreasonable.' A mutual friend of Sybil and Edith, Elizabeth Farrar,

also wrote from New York sending two letters from Guy that had arrived after his death and Edith's departure.

'. . . I opened them hastily thinking there might be something in them Guy had said or some little particular thing that I could radiogram to you. . . . If only these and all the love in them could have come instead of the cold hospital Sister's letters so that you could have had them with you on the voyage. Ever since I have left you the end of one of the sonnets you read that afternoon last October has been going through my head like a time that cannot be stopped . . . 'And death once dead there's no more dying then.' I don't quite know what it means, but I keep hearing you say it.'

If work had once been her hobby, now she tried to make it an obsession. Although in the first shock of her loss she had contemplated selling Washenden, after reflection she decided to live there alone and did so for nine years after Guy's death. She looked for something that would direct her mind away from a grief that was almost insupportable. She missed her 'daily love'—the shorthand Guy had used in telegrams when she was away and he didn't have time to write a letter. 'He was a good man,' she told me when we read through his letters together. 'Always trying to educate people, me included. He gave me courage, you see. After he died, I had to find my own courage and that wasn't always easy.'

Actors have few illusions about their old age, for the scrap heap beckons most of them from the first moment they tread the boards. Success has nothing to do with it, for success is often more lethal than plodding anonymity. There is a theatrical story concerning an actor who achieves a stunning personal triumph. After the first night he received nothing but plaudits. A close friend tells him: 'My dear boy, you were a sensation. It'll run for two years at least.' The actor stares a him. 'That's all very well . . . but what will I do afterwards?'

Help, for Edith, came from an unexpected quarter. She was asked to appear in Rodney Ackland's stage adaptation of Hugh Walpole's *The Old Ladies*. It was a timely piece of casting, for the role of the terrifying, gipsyish Agatha Payne provided Edith with a vehicle in which she could make use of her grief; she was able to sublimate herself and the power of her finished performance, under Gielgud's direction, was described by Charles Morgan as 'a slow nightmare of macabre genius.' 'I've had everything in my life,' she said, 'that's why I know a great deal when I'm up on the stage,' and there is no doubt in my mind that her grief was the clay from which she fashioned Agatha Payne. It was one of her most outstanding creations, still remembered by the discerning, although the play did not enjoy public favour or a long run.

Walpole wrote to congratulate her on her splendid creation; 'no one

166

can know as I do how exactly you have given me my original Agatha—
I lived with her for many years so I know!'

She went back to the New Theatre in October for the historic production of *Romeo and Juliet* in which Gielgud alternatéd the roles of
Romeo and Mercutio with Olivier. Peggy Ashcroft was once again
Juliet and according to Agate Edith knocked the balance of the play
into a cocked hat with her now definitive Nurse—'Agatha Payne meta-
morphosed into good instead of bad angel.'

Peggy Ashcroft has told me that during the run of *Romeo and Juliet*
Edith still wept quite openly whenever Guy's name was mentioned or
something reminded her of those last days in New York when she
was in the Cornell production. Even so, it is obvious that she did not
flaunt her grief to anybody outside the theatre, for Shaw appears not
to have heard of Guy's death until some six months after the event. He
wrote to her from Malvern on 8th August 1935. After putting business
first by discussing the plight of Charles Macdona, he turns to the subject
of Guy's death.

Malvern Hotel,
Malvern.

My Dear Edith

Nobody can appreciate poor Charles's position more keenly than I,
because I am very largely responsible for it. For the same reason I am
anxious to get him out of it if I can. I ruined him by making him try
the experiment of reduced prices at the Winter Garden theatre
(which proved too wintry) where he gave me a very creditable production. If I can shove him into the St. James's, it will be the best
I can do for him, short of writing a play about the modern respectable Mr. Punch, whom he strongly resembles.

He considers me a monster of ingratitude for giving *The Apple Cart* to
Barry Jackson; and Barry's feelings, when I forget all he has done for
me so far as to give plays to Macdona, are beyond expression. I have
not all the managers at my feet as you have. You will find, like me,
that the more famous you become the more precarious your position
will be. Only the secondrate are safe. I heard of the disappearance of
the husband in whose existence I so steadily refused to believe. Well,
that is the end of the avatar in which you met him; but though the
life has left the form that you knew, thrifty Nature has not wasted it:
it has by this time found some other form; it will turn up some day;
so be respectful to flowers and babies: they may have a bit of him or
even the whole of him. Anyhow you will not have to watch him
becoming an old pantaloon like me. But do not let this ridiculous
consolation make you afraid of growing old yourself; for old age, in
spite of all its infirmities and second childishnesses, is the happiest

time of life: something is newly born every day more exquisite than the old things that are dead or on their last legs. So do not be a widow like Queen Victoria: it is the life to come that keeps us young.

Beside, if you were happy with him you are a good chooser, and will be happy with anybody. After the funeral march the wedding march. But perhaps I should not write to you about this; for death never makes me sad.   ever and ever G.B.S.'

Unconventional words of comfort, which will perhaps come as a surprise to some students of St. Shaw. Edith took part of his advice to heart: she did not withdraw from public life like the old Queen, but she remained a widow and Shaw was wide of the mark when he told her she would be happy with anybody. Nor was religion, orthodox or Shaw's variety, a great blessing to her; many friends have related how extreme and prolonged was her anguish. In his reference to babies, Shaw touched upon a lasting regret. 'A doctor once said to me, "Do have a baby, you're *ample*." Lovely word. Ample. But I didn't. You think you've got all the time in the world, but you haven't.' It is difficult to stage-manage motherhood and a career in the theatre; few accomplish it with honours. 'Only the second rate are safe' Shaw wrote, and in this he was on target. Edith scorned the lower levels of achievement, and she never sought safety in her work. Some sacrifices have a selfish origin though they may appear otherwise. I think Edith knew that she would want to play the role of mother to perfection and that, in so doing, she would neglect in her art those standards she pursued with such dedication.

Her correspondence with Shaw had been revived a few days earlier than the letter concerning Guy. Shaw had written on 2nd August 1935 outlying his plans for her to appear in *The Millionairess*.

> Malvern Hotel
> Malvern.

My Dear Edith

The Millionairess is not going into Macdona's repertory, though it will, I hope, go into yours. He has struggled with my plays for so many years, and risked his little all on them so often, that I owe him a play or two to help him plant himself in London at last. But he must make a regular West End production with an ad hoc cast, and not a repertory reach-me-down.

What I contemplate at present is the possibility that his project of reviving my plays at the Cambridge for three weeks apiece may succeed well enough to oblige him to take another theatre for *The Millionairess*. In that case I shall suggest the St. James's on sharing terms with Gilbert Miller, who is keen on the play, perhaps because he has not read it. You are indispensable in this combination, as one of your greatest box office successes has been at this theatre, which is still the most distinguished in London for star work.

It is not really a difficult play. It all depends on your part and not on any great nicety of production: either you can do it or you cannot; and I think you can. The other parts, if played by suitable people, are not at all troublesome. So far I have nobody in mind except Lewis Casson, who is exactly right for the shabby little Mahometan doctor who carries off the prize—or is carried off by her, whichever way you choose to look at it. He is the right size, and has the right voice and the right irascible peremptoriness, also the right intelligence.

If I were not so abominably old I would take on the production myself and protect you from being produced. Anyhow I will do enough to get the right finish on the job. But I am not the man I was: I get tired suddenly.

I will send you a printed copy presently. It is already in type; but owing to a slip I made in correcting the proof (I am always doing foolish things now) I must have a cancel page set up.

Meanwhile there is nothing to worry about. The whole thing is still in my hands and in mine alone.

I have not seen you for ever so long; and my life is desolate in consequence.

G. Bernard Shaw.

Old and foolish or not, he could still produce flashes of the famed gallantry. Macdona, an actor manager, had already written to Edith, telling her of his plans to start a Shaw season at the Cambridge in August, opening with *Man and Superman*. He had invited Edith to recreate her original role in a revival of *The Apple Cart*, and to rehearse *The Millionairess* during the run of *The Apple Cart*. It smacked of repertory, as Shaw suspected, rather than the pukka presentation he was determined to have, Macdona's scheme was to give each play three weeks and by this means hope to raise enough cash to present *The Millionairess* solo at another theatre. But he had reckoned without Shaw, whose grip on his own affairs was that of a Jack Russell terrier.

Shaw's dialogue with Edith continued throughout the summer of 1935 and I suspect that he recruited his wife to the cause. Charlotte wrote to Edith on 13th August 1935.

Malvern Hotel,
Malvern.

Dear Edith (I may, may I not!)

I have just heard you are going to speak here on the 22nd and I want to know may we put you up for the night? This Hotel is a wretched little temperance hole, but we are fond of it, and I think I can make you comfortable, and I know you will like to talk to G.B.S.

So do come,
Yours, C. F. Shaw
(G.B.S's wife)

Edith apparently consented and six days later Shaw wrote a letter full of social and professional advice.

19th August 1935
Malvern Hotel,
Malvern.

My Dear Edith,

The journey here by train to Malvern is intolerably tedious. By far your best plan is to come on Wednesday by the 12-45 from Paddington to Gloucester, arriving (after lunching in the train) at 3-45. Tell the porter to put your bag into a Rolls Royce No BYE 779, which will be waiting for you. You will be here in comfortable time for tea in less than an hour.

You cannot do your lecture and the journey on the same day.

L.H.* would be worse than useless for *The Millionairess*. His business is to take a script that has no quality at all, and make it funny. Epifania is essentially tragic and volcanic: she has no sense of humour. Except the solicitor, who is mildly amused at the follies of the others, everyone in the play is intensely in earnest. The effect may be at times more laughable than L.H's wildest clownings; but the slightest consciousness of this on the part of the players would kill the play.

I must do it myself, no matter who is in the bill as producer.

Let us have a wire to okay the Gloucester arrangement,

thine   G.B.S.

The Rolls Royce seems an admirable ploy to snare a millionairess, and Edith endured the temperance hotel, delivered her lecture and was in turn lectured. The moment she departed from Malvern Shaw went to his typewriter again, and reading between his lines it is all too apparent that they had discussed the play exhaustively and that Edith held to her own point of view.

23rd August 1935

My Dear Edith,

I have just posted a letter to Macdona to break all your suggestions to him. I have impressed on him that the engagements had better be negotiated by G.M.*; and I have been merciless in rubbing in your opinion of himself, myself, and Barry as hopelessly saturated in

* Leslie Henson.   † Gilbert Miller.

provincial amateurism and three pound cheapness. No expense, I have told him, must be spared to make you feel that you are in a first rate production, and incidentally to make the public feel it. Consequently you need have no delicacy whatever in letting Charles see what you think of him.

I have, however, softened these fearful blows by confessing that your state of mind is the just consequence of the fiasco of *Heartbreak House*: a terrible throwaway into which, perhaps, I should not have let any cirstances (*sic*) force me, and after which I do not wonder at your giving me up as a producer and B.J. as a manager. However, you need not change your opinion on that point; for I have told Macdona that I won't produce *The Millionairess* and that he must get Leslie Henson.

'Edith obviously had won several battles during her brief stay at the temperance hotel.'

But *Heartbreak House*, though wounded, is not dead; and another revival is possible if only I can find a Hesione to play against you. this is not easy; and last time it was impossible. But what about Kit?* A London season with you playing Nurse to her Juliet and Ariadne to her Hesione: how would that do?

'I foresee that after a few rehearsals with a real proper expensive west end producer you will implore me to rescue you from his bag of shopsoiled tricks to conceal the emptiness of my dialogue; for after all there is none like unto me; but the truth is I am too old for the drudgery of producing, and am better employed in the sort of work that nobody else can do. I can just look in at the last few rehearsals and upset everything.

We enjoyed your visit extremely; and though you succeeded in convincing me that you are thoroughly ashamed of me professionally, your fun and friendliness and lovableness quite consoled me. I shall just take it out of Macdona, though he, poor soul, is quite innocent of my worst delinquencies.

In haste, but affectionately, yours
G.B.S.

Shaw, the flirt, seems to have been out-flirted on this occasion. It must have been a strange, transitional period for Edith; the public energy contrasted against the private loneliness. She was 'making do', filling in her time as best she could, trying to run Washenden alone (her parents' letters mention that she was purchasing some livestock) but the scar tissue of her grief refused to knit completely.

The year ended with a controversy involving two critics, one her old

* Katharine Cornell.

friend St. John Ervine and the other, Charles Morgan. Morgan had written an article in which he discussed Edith's mannerisms, particularly as they applied to her performance as the Nurse in *Romeo and Juliet*. Edith was hurt by this and wrote to tell him so. St. John Ervine decided to get into the act.

Honey Ditches,
Seaton,
Devon.
11 November 1935.

Edith, darling,

Last week, while I was snatching a mouthful of food between rehearsals, I heard a man say that you had made the Nurse the leading role in *Romeo and Juliet* and that you had run away with the play; to which I replied that you were the leading lady in every piece in which you appeared, and that you would still be the leading lady if your part were no more than that of the noise outside in the second act. If you were to sell programmes in the gallery, every eye would leave the stage to see you doing it! Now, you know what I think of your performance. But, darling, I shall deny with my last breath that Prudence was an old woman, and the letter which was printed in yesterday's *Observer*, in your support, seems to me full of fallacies. I'll answer it on Sunday.

I wrote loosely when I said that Prudence and Lady Capulet are the same age. I meant that they are contemporaneous in the sense that Ivor Brown and Charles Morgan are contemporaneous with me, though both are my juniors, Ivor by seven years, Charles by ten. I give the Nurse forty years at the outside, which makes her about a decade older than her mistress. I suspect that she married a man a lot older than herself, as, indeed, Lady Capulet has obviously done, and that he married her for a consideration, she, saving your presence, being well gone with Susan by a young fellow-me-lad who skipped by the light of the moon when he found her in the family way. The Nurse's reference to her husband are those of a woman who bore him no love, but liked him well enough: a salty old boy, ready to give a girl undone any protection he could, provided his name was paid for. Her widowhood is no indication of her age. You'll find thousands of widows of fifty and less in America who have been widows for at least half a decade. I remember meeting an Englishman in New York who remarked, in a rage, that American women ate their husbands, 'make the poor devils work themselves to death!' 'But, no,' said I, full of that insight which made me what I am, 'these women were married to men about twenty years older than themselves, and their husbands, if they were alive, would be seventy or more. American women want success from the word "go"; they are not willing to fight for it; and as young men can't give them the money they want, they marry old men. Everything about Capulet shows that he is much older than his wife: his impatience with young ambitions and his testiness in general.

Hamlet's mother must have been about the same age as the Nurse, yet Claudius was avid for her to murder his brother to get her; and there was no reluctance on her part to hop into another bed, for she married again in less than two months after the elder Hamlet's death. I take no stock in the young people's references to the Nurse as an ancient—you don't yourself—for I know how venerable I seem to people of thirty-five, though I shall not be fifty-two until the end of December. You don't think I'm exhausted, do you? Lots of these expressions are mere words, often abusive, and have no relation to fact. The Nurse, darling, is as young as you are, as vigorous and alive and game as you are, and nothing like so ancient as I am. Yet I am ready to kick the roof off the world and most unwilling to be treated as if I were fit only for cremation.

My love to you. And Leonora's.

Yours ever,   St. John.

Charles Morgan replied to Edith on 2nd December 1935.

Dear Miss Evans,

I am deeply distressed that my reference to 'mannerisms' should have hurt you. I had hoped that my tribute to the power and wit of the portrait as a whole would have taken the emphasis off the critical phrase.

I do not know how precisely to tell you what I meant by 'mannerisms', and probably you don't want me to, but it may be some indication of what I was driving at if I say that, for example, in the early scene with Juliet and her mother, brilliantly amusing though it was, there seemed to me to be a tendency in the nurse to mouthe and loosen many of her phrases—I mean that one heard the vowels without clearly distinguishing the consonants. It gives a kind of chawing effect which, although I realize much of the fun is derived from it, nevertheless is intensely personal to you in certain passages, and which, for a moment, suggests to me predominantly 'Edith Evans' instead of Juliet's nurse.

If I have said too much please forgive me. Probably now I have said too little; in order to explain fully what I meant by 'mannerisms', I should have to write at a length which would bore you, but I felt that I must make some attempt to particularize my general criticism. With every good wish, and I assure you with deep admiration,

      Yours sincerely,

           Charles Morgan.

There was a strong streak of pedantry in Charles Morgan's writings and in this instance he seems at sea to explain exactly what he did mean, and probably regretted ever writing the offending word in the first place.

As Christmas and the first anniversary of Guy's death approached there was another death in the family to winter the landscape of her grief still further. Her mother died on November 16th 1935, and her father's letters to Edith indicate that the end was merciful for the last illness was accompanied by much pain. So, within the twelve months, Edith had lost two of the people dearest to her. She sat 'quiet and still' as Guy had often urged her, conscious that Christmas at Washenden would be bleak house. Her mother had lived to celebrate her golden wedding, but that was the only consolation. In his letters to her, Edith's father wrote with no self-pity, even though his own bereavement was still raw, and the message he sent on January 8th 1936 showed his concern was mostly for Edith.

> My Dear Edith,
> Tomorrow being the 9th Jan. my thoughts are all concentrated upon you. In this particular instance, I share entirely your sorrow. But we must not look back too far, but in the future wherein lies all that we shall have to contend with.

It was work that healed her. In the spring of '36 she was introduced to the autumn world of Tchehov, seeped as it is in the rediscovery of the past. The occasion was Komisarjevsky's endlessly beautiful production of *The Seagull*. She was acting once again with Gielgud and Peggy Ashcroft and the rest of the cast was equally distinguished—Leon Quartermaine, Frederick Lloyd, Martita Hunt, Clare Harris, Ivor Barnard, George Devine and the young actor Stephen Haggard who was destined to die at a tragically early age. One marvels now at such an assembly on one stage. The revival was well received for Komisarjevsky had conceived it in naturalistic terms, a feast of romantic nostalgia rather than the unrelieved melancholia usually associated with London productions of Tchehov's works. Edith, 'taking the eye like a drawing of Sarah by Toulouse-Lautrec', brought a Parisian elegance to the role of Arcadina. Perhaps the image of what Washenden had been was in her mind's eye when, in the first act, she sat beside Trigorin and recalled happier days. 'Ten or fifteen years ago . . . It was all laughter, and music, and the firing of guns . . . and love-making, love-making without end.' Those who saw her performance remember how exquisitely she delivered this particular speech. The entire production was a landmark of taste, a coming together of so many individual talents under one roof. Agate, in his review, perpetrated a professional pun at the expense of his rival critic, Charles Morgan. Describing Peggy Ashcroft's performance, he concluded, 'she Sparkenbroke all hearts.'

Komisarjevsky felt Edith worked like a Frenchwoman. 'One never knows what they mean. I suppose it was a compliment. Directors say such funny things to me.' Komisarjevsky was an admirer, but not an uncritical one, and voiced a different opinion behind her back. Another member of that *Seagull* cast told me that when Edith had failed to follow his directions exactly during a rehearsal, he once exclaimed: 'How can such a stupid woman be such a great actress?' Edith held equally frank views on many of the directors she had worked with. 'I respected John, but *he* used to say my part for me on the stage. I found that very odd. But I mostly got on all right with directors. You didn't find me difficult, did you?' she asked, turning her lighthouse beam of charm so that it shone full in my face, blinding out any disbelief. In truth, I did not find her difficult to direct, though I must add that I was working with her in a medium that she was not over-familiar with, a medium, moreover, where the director exercises greater moment-to-moment control. Directing in the theatre is a different matter altogether and I never had the privilege of working with her there. Substantial legends have been passed down, as they always are, that she could sometimes be a tartar at rehearsals. I daresay she had good cause; she was a perfectionist. She told me that I 'unlocked her'. 'That's why I must always work with people I love. I don't function if there isn't love.'

Shaw wasn't at all happy with her decision to forsake him for Tchehov; if not in mourning for his life, he was concerned for the lingering fate of *The Millionairess*. He fired off a postcard to Edith, aiming for her heart.

> 4, Whitehall Court,
> s.w.i.
>
> 6 April 1936.

Beautifullest

The situation is that I have extracted the *Millionairess* from all claims by former managers, and find myself almost too late in the season for a production. And here you are apparently tied up with Gielgud, who can make the Seagull fly for months and months even with your positive electricity—fatal to Tchehov—to kill it.

It is like Ellen Terry getting into the clutches of Irving. Must I give you up? Can you escape if I find you the sort of management you want? In haste—ever

> G.B.S.

His mixture of flattery and joking criticism failed to sway Edith and he returned to the task of persuading her on April 25th.

My Dear Edith,

What about *The Millionairess*? I am back on these shores, and am being pressed to settle the Malvern Festival program (*sic*), which

175

may have to include this play and involve me in all sorts of complications. I am writing to Macdona to say that unless he can make me the sort of proposal I want at once I must leave him out and arrange elsewhere.

Are you in any way tied to Gielgud and the New? If not, how soon do you expect to be free?

I write in great haste, as the necessity for settling something about the play has descended on me like an avalanche. Let me have a line to say how you are situated.

Flurried but affectionate   GBS.

Edith continued to resist. Turning aside his entreaties, immune to his charm, she opted for semi-poverty once more at the Vic instead of Shaw's millionairess on a commercial basis. In an attempt to let him down lightly she suggested that he might like to give the play to the Vic, thereby satisfying her art and his commerce. Shaw didn't care for that at all; he had his Rolls Royce to keep up.

4, Whitehall Court,
London, S.W.1.
22nd May 1936

Edith, Edith

You *are* a daisy. You treated poor Charles and all the managers who have ever done anything for me as outcasts, and insisted on an ultra fashionable west end production. I have cleared the ground for that and got rid of them all for you. And now you offer me as a climax of magnificence, what? repertory at the Old Vic! Not even a run at the Elephant and Castle.

Dearest, I can't afford it. I have not written a pot-boiler since *The Apple Cart*; and I must make some money out of *The Millionairess* or drop the theatre. The Old Vic can have the play in repertory as much as it likes when it has been squeezed dry at the west end, but not before. The successes in Vienna, Prague, and now in Milan and Rome are hopeful; and I ought to strike while the iron is lukewarm. The spring season is lost: and if I let the autumn season go after it I shall get badly behindhand with my business. And now you tell me that you have signed on with Lilian for the autumn season! I have a young and beautiful Epifania raging to play the part: it is with the greatest difficulty that I escape, when we meet, without giving her a contract. I keep staving her off with allegations that it is your play. Her name is Leonora Corbett. Can I frighten you with her? Between you I am a most distracted man. Do make up my mind for me. GBS.

It is my belief that the comfort of familiarity influenced Edith's decision. Her sense of loss following Guy's death was still with her, receding perhaps, but nevertheless still keen enough to make her want to hide amongst friends in known territory. She had made the gesture towards Shaw, but since he had declined to let the Vic include the play in its repertory, she would stick to her guns. She returned to Lilian's domain in October 1936. By then Harcourt Williams had been succeeded by Tyrone Guthrie. Guthrie was a man consumed, like Lilian, with a visionary idealism. After some protracted negotiations he obtained the terms and freedom he felt necessary in order to operate and quickly exerted his authority, denouncing the old policy of 'making do' and determined to abolish the general air of tattiness which Lilian scarcely seemed to be aware of. By the time Edith returned to her second home across the river he had transformed the image of the Vic with his own distinctive brand of radicalism, not always to everybody's liking, but at least ensuring that few could ignore it. Curiously, in spite of his overall plans for the reformation of the company, Guthrie greeted Edith with a somewhat conventional role: another Restoration overblown rose—Lady Fidget in Wycherley's *The Country Wife*. He had imported the American actress, Ruth Gordon, the wife of Garson Kanin, to play the role of Margery in partnership with Edith and when rehearsals started Alec Guinness was also in the cast. Guinness failed to impress Miss Gordon who brought to the Vic that particular brand of ruthlessness which so often characterises the Broadway scene. She halted rehearsals one day, came down to the footlights and shouted to Guthrie in the darkened stalls. 'Tony! this man is impossible. Can we have another actor?' Edith recalled the collective shock of the assembled cast. 'We'd never heard of such a thing, and of course we expected Guthrie to defend Alec as his choice. But he didn't. He fired him on the spot. Without a word. I still think it was a dreadful thing. Dreadful of Ruth and dreadful of Guthrie. There it was, it happened and poor Alec had to go.'

What Edith failed to tell me, but I have since had confirmed from three separate sources, is that she waited for Alec to leave the theatre that day and tried to comfort him. He had been to collect the money due to him from Lilian, expecting justice in the form of £12 and receiving only £3, Lilian using the argument that since she had to recast she couldn't afford to pay twice for the same role. 'Don't worry,' Edith told Guinness. 'Everybody has to lose a part some day. Better now than later, and better a small part than a large one.' She could not hide her disgust at Guthrie's behaviour and she was also incensed at Lilian's meanness. I once asked her if she ever got to know Lilian well. 'As well as I wanted to,' she said.

She also told me that she never had any doubt that Alec Guinness would rise from the ashes piled on his head that day. 'He had to succeed, there was never any doubt in my mind.'

The Country Wife also marked the first occasion when she and Michael Redgrave acted together, and he, like Alec Guinness, had reason to remember her kindness to him (for he was fresh from the Liverpool Repertory) and the good advice she gave. Despite Edith's amazement at Ruth Gordon's behaviour, they became very close friends; it was a friendship which endured for some thirty years until jolted by a curious episode brought about by Garson Kanin's controversial book about Katharine Hepburn and Spencer Tracy. By one of those interlaced coincidences I was involved on the perimeter of the drama which affected both Kate and Edith. When the book was first announced Kate was in England and it was from my house that she wrote a letter to Garson Kanin (who, as in Edith's case, had been on the most intimate terms with Kate and Spencer Tracy over many years) begging him to delay publication until after her death. Garson Kanin declined to oblige and the book went ahead, was published and became a best seller on both sides of the Atlantic. Edith was enraged on two counts; firstly because she felt it was an unforgiveable betrayal on the part of Kanin towards Kate, and secondly because of a false reference to her own career concerned, oddly enough, with *The Millionairess*. Kanin's book gave the impression that Edith had never played Epifania, which was untrue. Edith took up the cudgels and wrote with some spirit to Ruth, having searched for and found the box-office returns slips which proved that she had appeared in Shaw's play on a provincial tour. It was a sad conclusion to a three-handed friendship, for from the time of *The Country Wife* until the publication of the offending book, Ruth and Edith had been the closest of friends, finding much joy in the relationship, corresponding frequently and always meeting whenever Ruth was in England or Edith in America. There was a copy of Ruth's play *The Leading Lady* in the bookcase beside Edith's bed at Kilndown, inscribed by the author, 'For Edith, the best actress in the world.' But as Edith had once admitted, she found it very difficult to forgive those who hurt her or hurt her friends, and she set great store by absolute loyalty.

Alec Guinness departed and the rehearsals resumed. The play opened and both Edith and Ruth scored notable personal triumphs. 'Why waste words to describe the images which this great artist conjures up?' asked Agate. He compared her Lady Fidget to a sloop of war—'a Rowlandsonesque cartoon of Britannia turned bawdy! There was no stemming his flood of adoration on this occasion. 'Personally, I do not believe that a committee consisting of Martin Luther, John Calvin, John Knox, William Penn, George Eliot, Mrs. Humphrey Ward, and Mrs. Ormiston Chant would have been able to resist the tremendous fun with which Miss Evans invests Lady Fidget's indiscretions.'

It was just as well that Agate did not include Shaw among his hypothetical committee, for the Malvern Monster was greatly aggrieved.

He was disgruntled about everything and everybody, and wrote Edith from a practically unpronounceable North Wales town called Penrhyndeudraeth, having filled his pen with bile.

14th September 1936

Here I wander distractedly to shake off maddening Malvern before returning home next week. It is raining cats and dogs—real Welsh rain. I have lost all interest in the wretched potboiling *Millionairess*: only a lingering interest in you after all these Leonoras and Wendies still binds me to it. It is rather late in the day for any enthusiasm on the part of Gilbert M. What about C. B. Cochran? he has always declared himself ready at a moment's notice. So had Leon M. Lion, whose resources appear inexhaustible.

I went to the *Seagull*, and disliked it extremely. You kicked it round the stage; and Gg* killed it dead every time he walked on. Tchekov is not in the Terry blood. Komisar has lost his old Russian touch: he filled the last act with pauses of the sort that are bearable only in a first act when there is no hurry and the audience is willing to speculate a little on dumb shows. And anyhow the dumb shows were unintelligible and uninteresting. The passionate bits were ghastly: they reminded me of Granville Barker trying to play a love scene with Mabel Terry Lewis years ago, or Loraine refusing to conceal his hatred of Lillah in *Man and Superman*. You may ask me how I account for the run. I can only explain it by your prodigious draw. And at any rate you *acted*. Gg's nullity was stupendous, considering that the man *can* act when the stuff suits him.

We return home early next week if not sooner.
faithful still   G.B.S.

This letter is full of rare meat from a man who never touched it. In the first place Shaw exaggerated Cochran's willingness to mount a production of *The Millionairess* at the drop of a hat. What Cochran had written to Edith was that he couldn't contemplate it before the autumn of 1937 and asked whether she would be willing to commit herself so far ahead. She wasn't. 'Maddening Malvern' smacks of ingratitude, considering that Barry Jackson had laboured mightily to give Shaw and his works a suitably-gilded frame.

As to Shaw's undisguised dislike of *The Seagull* production it is obvious that his general disenchantment with the whole theatrical scene betrayed him into making sweeping and patently over-stated verdicts. I showed the letter to Sir John Gielgud who was much amused by it, commenting that he was 'fascinated by the Shaw excerpts and find that ill opinions of my acting from long ago do little harm to my

* Sir John Gielgud.

vanity. I had no idea the old boy still took such an interest in the current theatre.'

Even when he came in out of the Welsh rain and returned home Shaw's black mood persisted. After the event, he discovered Edith's involvement with *The Country Wife* and wrote to her again on September 22, 1936, peppering his notepaper with exclamation marks.

Ayot St. Lawrence

What!!!

This thing, with the *Millionairess* at his disposal, offers you an obsolete obscenity like *The Country Wife*!

Enough. He is wiped out of the book of life. He is not fit company for the likes of me. Never mention his name to me again.

This is what comes of playing nurses: you appear as a comic old woman, and, next thing, you are asked to play a pornographic old woman—or is it the Ursula Jeans heroine you are offered?

When the Pioneers produced the C.W., Charlotte rose at the first interval and announced that she was going to her club. I said 'Are you shocked?' 'Not in the least' she replied, with infinite contempt: 'I am *bored*'.

Edith: your cheek is stupendous. Am I a dog, that you should treat me thus? *The Country Wife*!
Well!!!!!!!!!!!   G.B.S.

Contrast Mr. Agate with grumpy Mr. Shaw, as the former quotes, with due alteration of pronouns a contemporary review of Garrick.

'That impartial JUSTICE must pronounce MISS EVANS as the First of her PROFESSION; and that the amazing BLAZE of her EXCELLENCIES greatly obscures, if not totally eclipses her DEFECTS.'

Agate was only slightly less enthusiastic about Ruth Gordon's performance as Margery Pinchwife.

Shaw was not alone in condemning the choice of *The Country Wife*. The old issue of cultural censorship raised its bigoted head in the correspondence columns of the *Daily Telegraph*, with Mr. Sydney Carroll appearing for the prosecution complete with stained credentials (having been responsible for another production of *The Country Wife* in the purely commercial theatre). Mr. Carroll, tucking in his chin over his prejudices, declared that such a play 'containing the grossest improprieties in situations, thought, and language represents a complete abandonment of the Old Vic's standards.' Certainly double-standards were at work here, and doubtless the Editor of the *Telegraph* encouraged the debate in his columns and there is nothing more calculated to sell newspapers in Great Britain than the hint of sexual impropriety in high places. Responses came from Lord Lytton and Agate, the latter quoting Ally Sloper's* maxim that 'a dirty mind is a perpetual feast,' before knocking everybody out of the ring with a masterly defence of Wycherley.

Edith remembered this particular episode as it applied to her. 'I had this improper part, you see, or everybody said it was improper; I suppose it was, and I had to come back having been extremely improper in my investigations off stage and tell somebody on stage what had happened. And who do you think was sitting in one of the boxes? The Charity Commissioners, thank you very much. I was in a fit, because I'd got to do it properly—that is to say, improperly. They'd come down to judge it because of all the fuss and to tell us how to behave. There they were, and I had to go on with the scene. I got through it somehow, got my laughs and afterwards they told me that the Commissioners had been laughing too, and we didn't hear any more.'

Shaw didn't take such a light-hearted view.

6th October 1936

Dearest Edith,

I am much distracted in my mind about this *Millionairess* business. Still more so about this *Country Wife* business. With the censorship now raging in the United States (see my article in the current *London Mercury*) has Gilbert really been able to square Mr. Breen and the American Legion of Decency? Will the Legion face a situation in which *St. Joan* is banned and *The Country Wife* whitewashed? It would be quite like the censorship to get itself into such a situation: indeed it has already been produced by letting Elizabeth Bergner pass as Catherine II, and stopping her as St. Joan; but still there is a risk. Have you considered it?

I have been having a talk with C. B. Cochran who is my selection for *The Millionairess*. He sees without prompting that as to the cast it is a case of E.E. first and the rest nowhere. I explain that though you are bound to me and to the play by every pledge that one human heart can give to another you have thrown me over without a gesture of remorse. But who could believe it? I, the greatest playwright of your time, write a play for you to display all your powers as our most unique actress: one that has succeeded sensationally wherever it has been played. He waits patiently until you have disentangled yourself finally from your engagements. Then you inform him that you have deliberately engaged yourself to return to America, where your future hangs in the balance, in an ancient and infamous play fit for a

* An Edwardian comic strip character.

181

smoking room in a disreputable club only. It is incredible. Posterity will remember you as THE WOMAN WHO WOULDN'T.

However, you know best what is good for you; and you know very well that I am only pretending to quarrel. I write this to remind you of the danger of the American censorship, which you may have overlooked, and which Gilbert Miller is sure to overlook because it is staring him in the face.

Also to take you by the throat and ask you whether you will definitely engage yourself to Cochran to play Epifania for him when this disgraceful Wycherley episode collapses as it deserves.

Remember, you can trifle with me; but I cannot trifle with Cochran. Come! don't funk it.

Yep or Nope.   GBS.

Even this didn't do the trick and one wonders whether Edith invented the possibility of taking *The Country Wife* to America merely in order to give Shaw a face-saver. I say this because we have Michael Redgrave's account of Edith advising him *not* to go to New York. 'It was settled by Edith saying in her most lilting, honeyed and seductive tones: 'You don't want to go to *New York!*'—she managed to imply that only great big babies ever wanted anything so silly—'You'd like to stay and play Orlando with me'. She breathed 'Orlando' more beautifully than any Juliet sighed 'Romeo'. It is a chicken and the egg puzzle. Did Shaw persuade Edith before Edith persuaded Michael Redgrave? Poor GBS! surely no playwright of his standing could have tried longer or harder to persuade a leading lady to accept a role especially written for her. It is also a sad comment on the theatre managements of the day that Shaw was forced to push himself from pillar to post to find a home for his new work. Even now he didn't give up, but wrote again on 29th October 1936.

Edith of Ediths,

You are mistress of the situation; but C.B.C. cannot do anything unless he is sure of you; and neither can I. And it would not be imprudent for you to secure a promising engagement for next autumn. So let's all make our contracts and have done with it. When you are fixed up with him he and I will fix up with one another; and then we can put it all out of our wearied heads until next September. The first production in England is to take place at Bexhill-on-Sea on the 7th with what cast I know not; but Matthew Forsyth, the manager of the Pavilion there, will agitate sufficiently to get the play on the map; and the questions that will be asked as to the London production should be answered with a clear announcement of the Edith-Cochran-GBS contracts.

I shall perhaps run down to a matinee if I can get back in time for dinner. They have raised the question of the pronunciation of Epifania. My Spanish dictionary gives it uncompromisingly as Ai-pee-fah-nee-ya.
G.B.S.

It is astonishing to learn that a new play by the greatest dramatist of his day should more or less have to depend on the charity of a little-known repertory company in a minor seaside resort. What is more, the first night took place out of season. Since most British seaside resorts during the winter resemble Alaska after the gold rush, one hesitates to imagine that sort of audience turned up on November 7th 1936. No wonder even the author felt he could only endure the pilgrimage if he was able to return home in time for dinner. Dinner in Bexhill-on-Sea out of season to an eighty-year-old vegetarian must have been too much to contemplate. However, due tribute should be paid to Matthew Forsyth and his Players who apparently upheld the finest traditions of the profession and earned their modest place in theatrical history.

Despite Shaw's persuasive arguments, Edith did not sign a contract with Cochran and although ultimately a production of *The Millionairess* with Edith playing Epifania was mounted, it never reached London. London eventually got Katharine Hepburn and the cinema screens Sophia Loren and Peter Sellers, but not until long after Bexhill-on-Sea had shown the way.

Following her improper interlude in *The Country Wife* Edith gave her swan-song Rosalind and fell in love again, the cause and the measure being her Orlando, Michael Redgrave, who shared the Watteau-like forest of Arden of Esme Church's production. Nearly forty years later when age had dimmed the poignancy but not the memory of this episode she was in the habit of referring to it as 'my five-minute love'. Perhaps, out of consideration for others, she first coined the phrase to soften the revelation; then, being the actress she was, knowing that it had a telling ring to it, she repeated it publicly many times until, in the end, she convinced herself it was the whole truth. It was poetically true, but forty years of living had washed the poetry white. She would say of Michael, 'I think he fell in love with me for about the same length of time. It was very good for the play, very good indeed.' He did indeed fall in love, as he admitted with infinite tenderness in a filmed foreword which introduced a re-run of my television documentary, broadcast on the eve of the Thanksgiving Service for Edith in December 1976.

His season at the Vic with Edith was the milestone in his long and distinguished career, and their playing together as Rosalind and Orlando was one of those rare marriages of professional talent and private affection that, from time to time, illuminate the lives of those

183

who perform and those who watch. In Rainer Maria Rilke's definition, 'Love consists in this, that two solitudes protect and touch and greet each other.' Edith had begun by protecting her Orlando, but the more a biographer gropingly ponders over the evidence available to him, the more he becomes aware that he must faithfully interpret not only the facts but the emotions concealed within those facts. Whatever secret preparations human beings make to receive love they are invariably surprised by its first appearance. A love pure and unmixed with other passions is that, in La Rochefoucauld's phrase, 'which lies at the bottom of the heart, and of which we ourselves know nothing.' When her stage Orlando made his first tentative real-life declaration—a kiss, given on impulse, on the stairs leading down to the stage at the New Theatre—Edith was shocked. Perhaps she was unprepared for the make-believe to become reality. With disarming honesty, Sir Michael has told me that he was rebuffed, Edith's bewilderment was not feigned, it was not the reaction of a woman so completely an actress that she had forgotten ordinary emotions, but something deeper. For a few days he was crushed, but she consented to have dinner with him at the Café Royal and over the meal questioned him as to his motives. 'Why?' she asked. 'Why did you kiss me?' 'Because I felt like it and because I wanted to.' he replied. Edith's dilemma, given her personality and the way she had always lived her life, was half agony, half hope. She was forty eight, her Orlando twenty years younger who 'clearly adored her.' The perfect dovetailing of their performances on stage was something that she could control, for in this instance, art had come before reality. Now, faced with the physical declaration of a younger man's love for her, I believe she was torn, for the first time in her life, between a woman's need to feel desired and that other side of her nature that had so often turned away affection in others. Much of her life had entailed the ousting of love by duty; the perfect partnership between herself and Guy had involved sacrifices on his part and too late for mending she had discovered that much of the love they shared had gone to waste; the long separations seemed, in retrospect, with the memory of his lonely death unfaded, to have been self-denials without purpose.

In later years she spoke reflectively, tenderly, of her 'five minute love' as though there had always been an hour-glass between her and Michael with the sands running out. Perhaps she felt this at the time, allowing Michael's ardour to persuade her into a more intimate relationship which she had never consciously sought but which, once confronted with, she could not turn away from. They became lovers for a time, and when the parting came and the affair ended, as end they knew it must, there was no bitterness, reproach nor remorse, but an untarnished affection they both carried forward into their later years. With their shared love of the theatre and of poetry perhaps they entered into the affair knowing that, like Herrick's daffodils it must haste away so soon, for many of Michael's letters to her written during this period—which Edith so carefully preserved, some nothing more than scraps of paper, together with every telegram, Christmas card and snapshot he ever sent her—betray an anquish of spirit, that potent mixture of love and guilt, a cement that never completely sets, which binds two people who needs must hide a passion they long to proclaim. They were both strong characters, but perhaps Edith was the stronger of the two and saw the end of the affair before her more youthful lover and found the courage to prepare him for it.

He wrote of her as his 'darling Edieva'—a nickname compounded from Edith and Evans; he called her his 'radiant one' and told her that she was 'the strong one' and must help him to be strong in turn. It would be wrong to assume, however, that Michael did all the pursuing and that Edith remained passive. Once the first shock of recognition had passed, she became as one obsessed and, according to close friends, could think and talk of nothing else. Perhaps, in her heart, she realised that she was keeping a lovers' appointment in Samarra.

After the West End run of *As You Like It* finished, Michael made brief appearances in three minor productions, the last of these being a comedy called *Three Set Out* at the Embassy, Swiss Cottage. When this closed he took a short holiday in the West Country with some friends from his university days—Gervase Smith and Eric O'Dea, both painters, and the novelist and short story writer, G. F. 'Dick' Green. En route to join them he wrote some lines of doggerel for Edith:

RAILWAY LINES (The Ballad of the 9.15.)
It certainly doesn't seem possible
That now at last I'm free,
Just an unemployed actor who's lost his Max Factor
And is off to the West Countree.

No more today to the Finchley Road,
No more to the Embassy,
I'll no more play each week and a day
At the game called OUT SET THREE.

My moustaches litter the dressing room floor
That I wore in Act Two, Scene Three,
My mind is as light as a paper kite
That flies from a cliff by the sea.

The commercial chews at his sandwiches,
The old lady sips at her tea,
My blue rucksack is up on the rack
And we're due in at ten to three.

And there will be Eric and Gerv and Dick
And the beach and the bouncy sea,
And the Chichester Arms with its wild alarms
Of skittles and darts for me.

And Dick will turn into a Channel swimmer,
And Gerv will a Publican be,
And before I know it I'm a Georgian poet,
And Eric's a Spanish grandee.

And the sun will go down and the stars will come out
All over the Tennyson sea,
I'll churn out this metre ten stanzas a litre
If I think some more rhymes in E.

When the curtain fell on the last performance of their memorable *As You Like It*, it was inevitable that their meetings would become less frequent. Edith had entered Michael's life at the vital moment of his career; she 'pumped countless confidence into me' as he put it, and for his part he gave to her the matchless gift of a love that, being unexpected, was all the more to be treasured. In this context, it is worth quoting Agate's wistful, witty Man Friday—Alan 'Jock' Dent. (There were many who felt that Jock was the rightful heir to Agate's throne, but there proved to be no direct line of succession when the king died, and the crown was offered to Sir Harold Hobson. Jock wrote erudite and seldom malicious reviews as dramatic and film critic for the *News Chronicle* and the *Illustrated London News*, nudging with buttoned tip into actors' flesh where Agate had often thrust with naked rapier, but sharing his mentor's passionate rejection of the second-rate.) Writing of Edith's Rosalind, he told his readers that 'she draws and paints a Meredithean lady rich in mind . . . and in the end the audience is made one with Orlando.' It was a description that could not have been bettered, yet he could not have known from his critic's chair that he had gone beyond the evidence into life's truth.

After a visit to Washenden, Michael wrote,

Darling E, it already seems an age since Friday. What an evening you gave us. You were enchanting. Inner radiance indeed! I should think so: Light, Heat, Fire, Air, Water—and the Earth close under your feet all the time. They say you send husbands and wives away more in love with each other, do they? You sent me away more in love with the whole world and if I had never known before that I'd love you all my life I knew it then. How I knew it!

Whatever her astonishing versatility in the theatre, Edith was uneasily cast in the role of a deliberate home-wrecker. There was a deeply moral streak in her and 'all remedies refusing' she saw to it that

186

her own symbolic five minutes was not stretched to become a longer period of happiness bought at the price of others' unhappiness. There could be no room for the truth she valued so desperately in a liaison that could only exist on deception. A choice had to be made and she had to find the courage to make it. She needed romantic love so much, and with Michael she was given a glimpse of the conflict and the intoxication that romantic love demands and extracts. The enduring loneliness of her life, a loneliness that was for the most part self-imposed, had been lifted for a short while. Her eyes had been bandaged, but she had never been blind to the realities and when, on one occasion, she came face to face with the anguish of somebody close to them both, the decision was made for her. It says much for both of them that their friendship survived and their admiration for each other continued undiminished. 'Dearest Edieva,' he wrote, 'Adieu to you, farewell, au revoir. All the sad words I can think of cannot tell you how sad it felt to get your note and to know that you were going to Cornwall and that for once I was the last to know. What could be worse except that I should hear you'd gone. What strangers we are being made to each other!'

Years later Michael gave an interview to Lillian Ross for the *New Yorker* in which he said: 'I was more influenced by Edith Evans than by any other performer. I was very much in awe of her. She asked me, "What kind of actor do you want to be?" I was taken aback by the question. Then she asked, "Do you want to be like Olivier? Do you want to be like Gielgud?" Suddenly I realized that she was suggesting that—if I put thought, passion, and labour into it—I might indeed *be*.

'For me, Edith Evans has the authentic magic. Claptrap word though "magic" may be, it's the only word for the stage. When she comes onstage, the stage lights up. She's a very strict person about her own profession and is without any of the nonsense. She's a real and dedicated artist. Her art is her life. Everything she does on the stage is interpreted through her own morality. It's the way Picasso paints. It's the way Beethoven composed. It's the thing the great artist has that makes him different from other people. I don't mean morality in a pettifogging way. I mean moral values, without which nothing is achieved and nothing is created. Part of it is caring enough about what you do to achieve something beyond the mundane. One reason for the great influence Edith Evans has had on me is that she accepted me in the early phase of my career. Until you act the great parts in theatre literature, you really don't know what acting is. Orlando for me was a great part. I was twenty eight. Edith Evans was forty eight. I had been married about a year, and Rachel and I had just had our first child. But none of that seemed to have anything to do with my special life on the stage as Orlando. We played for something like five weeks in repertory, and then we took the play to the West End and played it for three months, which was pretty good for a Shakespeare run.

'Acting with Edith Evans was heaven. It was like being in your mother's arms, like knowing how to swim, like riding a bicycle. You're safe. The late Michael Chekhov said once that there were three ways to act: for yourself, for the audience, and to your partner. Some of the newer theorists say if it's true for yourself, it's truthful, which is not so. The majority of actors act for themselves or for the audience. I believe that the only way to act is to your partner. As a partner Edith Evans was like a great conductor who allows a soloist as much latitude as is needed but always keeps everything strict. It's strict but free. Never is anything too set, too rigid. The stage relationship always leaves enough room to improvise. For the first time in my life, acting in *As You Like It* I felt completely unself-conscious. Acting with her made me feel, Oh, it's so easy. You don't start acting, she told me, until you stop *trying* to act. It doesn't leave the ground until you don't have to think about it. The play and our stage relationship in it always had the same shape. It was entirely well proportioned, and yet in many respects it was all fluid. In the forest scenes between Orlando and Rosalind, she would encourage me to do almost anything that came into my head. Yet if I had done anything excessive, she would have stopped it by the simplest means. Somehow it didn't occur to my to do anything excessive. For the first time anywhere, onstage or off, I felt completely free.'

Through it all they had led crowded public lives. They had acted together again in *The Witch of Edmonton* in that same Old Vic season, Edith now elevated to the witch herself, and giving a performance which eclipsed her previous suns. When a woman is in love, she blossoms, and when an actress is in love she draws on those extra energies that love bestows and extends herself yet again. Michael played Warbeck in this production, but it was Edith's triumph. She knew the play, of course, having had the role of Ann Ratcliffe in the 1921 production of Dekker's melodrama at the Lyric, Hammersmith. She added layers of horror to her Agatha Payne and once again her Boswell, Mr. Agate, bent his knee to her, doffed his cap, offered his cloak and finally prostrated himself full length. He was second in line to her director, Michel St Denis who paid his homage in a first night speech. 'Miss Evans in a great actress in a great way' (J. C. Trewin added 'which means that she has never reduced shipwreck to a boating accident'.) Of her erstwhile Orlando, St. Denis was less than enthusiastic. 'He decided I was just another young man,' Sir Michael has told us. But Edith's achievement was, by all accounts, a triumph on a scale that surprised all who saw it. 'They did seem to like that one,' Edith remarked to me. 'Yet I don't remember doing anything special. It couldn't have been the way I looked, because I looked a positive fright.'

During this second season at the Vic she received countless letters of praise from close friends and total strangers. Eleanor Farjeon told her 'I hope you will give me the chance, every ten years, to write another letter telling you what a state of joy your Rosalind puts me into . . . When you act youth, you are youth.' In the context of her private life I find this last statement of added interest. It would be patronising and inaccurate to suggest that only those in love can act love, and there is much evidence to substantiate that many a stage and film partnership has flourished on pure mutual hatred, but at the same time there is no doubt in my mind that on this occasion Michael gave her back her youth.

In case the praise of a friend like Eleanor Farjeon should be considered too suspect, we can contrast the adulation of an ordinary fan who wrote to his 'Beloved Rosalind, it was so beautiful that one iota more of beauty would be excruciating . . . Seeing you, one recaptures some of the ecstatic enthusiasm of one's earliest theatregoing . . . I can think of nothing else and while I live the memory of your Rosalind will stand out high above everything.'

But the theatre is a great leveller. This time you scale the heights and next time round you climb again, spurning safety nets, and plunge. In the midst of her private happiness and public acclaim, Edith suffered just such a fall from grace. Her next appearance, as Kate to the Petruchio of Leslie Banks in Claud Gurney's production of *The Taming of The Shrew* was accounted a failure. Perhaps the close proximity to Rosalind was a mistake, but Edith never minded failing. She remembered a remark of Shaw's—'You can be awful, but you can never be worthless.' The worst of her grief was behind her, her love for Michael—whatever sadness it eventually held—had given her a new lease on life and the constant challenge of work was the lasting panacea. Failure or success, it mattered little. She had come alive again.

St. John Ervine also made a reappearance in her life at this time, armed now with a proposal of a different sort.

Honey Ditches, Seaton,
Devon.
February 5th 1937.

My Dear Edith,

As I lay on my silver-grey sofa last night, listening to your voice coming so intimately over the ether, and cursing when, once, the microphone made it fade for a moment or two, I thanked God that someone had at last said what ought to be said about Shakespeare's women, that he had women in his mind when he invented them, and not little boys pretending to be women. Whoo! says I, nearly leaping off the silver-grey sofa, that's a bit of unprofessional sense anyway. Put that in your damned pipes and smoke it, I says to

189

the universities of Oxford and Cambridge. And then when you began to speak the verse—my dear, I rose up and gave three of the heartiest cheers anyone on this earth has ever heard. It was a grand broadcast—gr-gr-grand! and I'll listen like a leech, if a leech can listen, when you broadcast Pope's verse next week, even although you'll have a Bolshy poet by your side, choosing poems for you.

The mere sound of your voice set my mind bubbling over with the play I'm trying to write for you. The first draft of the first act is written and the first draft of half of the second—but they're to be re-written a lot—because you will leap about in the play so disconcertingly that I have to re-write all the previous bits. You're a devil of a woman, Edith Evans, and I can't keep you down, damn you! But I'll tell you this much—you're to be a woman doctor in the play—and a woman doctor I'm determined to keep you. Let you leap about as you may. And you're married to a parson who has a good chance of becoming a dean, only you ruin it. And you have a stepson who is a Cambridge Communist! . . . Oh, my God, it is a household!

However, just you wait and see what happens. I'm coming to see your Rosalind this time. No surgeon won't keep me from seeing it, not if he was ever so. I'll come round and hug you after the performance. I'd have hugged you last night only I don't think it would have looked well on the ether, and I'm sure Sir John Reith would have said something severe about me. This is really to tell you how much I enjoyed your talk and how much I wish you'd talk a lot more. Woman, you've got brains in your skull. And in your tongue!

Yours ever,
St. John.

The play refused to come together as he wanted it and he finally invited Edith to spend a weekend with him and his wife to discuss it (the critic turned playwright is a more modest beast than the critic pure and simple). The play on the stocks was *Robert's Wife*, one of the few modern roles ever written directly for Edith by a major dramatist. 'Not without some misgivings, I finally accepted the invitation. We went to his summer house in the garden and he read the play to me. I was very interested and very moved and that seemed to be all he needed, an audience of that kind, because I certainly didn't contribute anything very helpful—or, if I did, I don't recall it. After that he galloped to the end, finished it straight away, and when we did it, every parson and bank manager in the country came to see it. I used to meet some of them afterwards and they'd say, 'Oh, I brought my wife to see it for our anniversary.'

Robert's Wife was opened at the Globe in November with Owen Nares playing the husband. Nares, a great matinee idol, proved to be an ideal leading man for Edith; they each had a following and although Nares' style of acting differed greatly from Edith's, the combination of talents proved a happy one and the play ran for eighteen months.

'It was an absolutely straight part, if you know what I mean,' Edith told me. 'I didn't have to wear any wigs or padding or anything like that. I just played my own shape, and hair and everything. It was·a lovely part, I adored it.'

She found St. John Ervine easy to work with at rehearsals. 'It's only troublesome if the author isn't sensible, if he expects you to give the finished performance at the first reading, as some of the less experienced ones do. They don't wait for you to *grow into* the part, they get very troubled if the first time you say their lines it isn't quite what they imagined. Well, then, they'd better stay away, and let us get on with it a bit. But I don't remember St. John being difficult at all, except for one tiny tussle we had over a sentence that was always difficult for me to remember. It jarred, just this one sentence. I used to say to him, 'Oh, I do wish you'd alter this and rewrite it.' Authors don't like changing things, and on the first night in Edinburgh I came to that particular bit and dried stone dead. I went over to the corner, got the prompt and continued, and next day he altered it for me, because it was wrong.

'I don't think we got a staggeringly good press in Edinburgh, and I was alone and I remember being so upset and crying and crying and walking about Princes Gardens in the sun. I kept finding a bit where there was sun and walking in it. I thought perhaps the sun would cure me. Then a dear friend, Gwen—Gwen Frangcon-Davies—came to the second performance and said, 'Well, you're there for a year at least.' I said, 'What?' 'Of course you are,' she said. 'No question, it's an enormous success.'

'Just goes to show you, we none of us really know, we're too close, too involved.'

On her first night in London Michael sent her a telegram which said I AM WITH YOU. A few days later he wrote, 'However much they love you as Sanchia, and there was a hell of a lot of love wafting about the Globe that night, they can't love you as I loved you as Edith-Sanchia. Do you wonder I couldn't separate you from Edith-Sanchia? So you know, Sanchia, that you'd be not half the woman you are without Edith? Do you know, Edith, that I wasn't really thinking much about Sanchia most of the time? Do you mind? . . . My dearest dear. Goodnight.'

There was a quotation from Sir Walter Raleigh that Edith often referred to . . . *The graves that hide us from the searching sun, Are like drawn curtains when the play is done* . . . She spoke these words, almost to herself, when last we spoke of Michael and her enduring affection for him a few weeks before her death. By then there were many memories that age had misted; names from the past did not come as easily as they might, but her brief days in Arden were never forgotten.

14

'*It is not in the praise of the critics, nor in the applause at the fall of the curtain that we find an assurance that we are meeting our responsibilities, but during the play itself, in some moment of silence that unites us—author, actor and audience—making the great theatre suddenly become a small and private room where everything is, for a moment, made clear and brilliant as the light of day*'

Ten months after his last pleading, Shaw was still putting the case for a production of *The Millionairess* with Edith. Edith, secure in the success of *Robert's Wife*, was not over-anxious to press Cochran as Shaw wished. John Gielgud has told me that although she was 'a model of behaviour and professionalism . . . she was basically so shy of committing herself— a strange mixture of arrogance and humility. She needed a man behind her as Cornell had McClintic and Sybil, Lewis, to give her the confidence managerially, but I don't think she ever trusted anyone very close to her to advise or manage her.' Having tasted failure as a manager in her own right, I suspect that she was chary of entering into any arrangement whereby she had to share part of the financial risk. Despite all the evidence that Shaw put forward to the contrary *The Millionairess* did not have the scent of success about it. But Shaw kept trying.

7th August 1937
4, Whitehall Court,
London S.W.1.

My Dear Edith,

I am in the same predicament as yourself; I have not had a word from C.B.C. since you came down to Malvern to see us years and years ago.* I felt tempted to stir him up on the subject once or twice to find out whether the Barrie fiasco had given him cold feet; but it seemed better to give him time to get warm again.

* It was barely two years; Shaw deliberately distorted the facts.

The play was a success at Malvern; but nothing fails there because the thing is called a festival, and the audience listen reverently to my works just as they listen to Bach's Mass in B Minor in Worcester Cathedral. Some of the critics were intelligent enough to call for a London performance with E.E. as the one and only possible Epifania. Let me know if you extract a cable from C.B.C. We are just off to the country for a week; but we are spending most of August at home and shall be at hand as usual until the 20th or thereabouts.

Ever and ever   G. Bernard Shaw.

Three weeks later his gloom was positively Ibsen-like in its intensity.

26th August 1937
The Victoria Hotel,
Sidmouth, Devon.

Dearest Edith,

We have been making our wills and packing and trekking hither and forgetting everything. St. John Ervine has just handed me your telegram to remind me.

As I thought, C.B.C's last experience has sickened him of the legitimate. Barry Jackson lies low and says nuffin, you having somehow completely snubbed and intimidated him. What about the Wyndham-Albery combination at the New-Globe-Queens? Hugh Beaumont (I think that's his maiden name) was, as far as I could make out, satisfied with his *Candida* venture and ready for more; but like everyone else he thinks that C.B.C stands in the way. The Ambassadors and Lilian Bayliss are always keen for a try-out; and I would give us a fortnight with enthusiasm.

I am doing nothing about it. I am old, and have lost all appetite for the West End. I live on sums ranging from ninepence to thirty shillings from devoted amateurs in the mining villages. I touch my hat and am grateful.

You must let it be known that a golden opportunity—an Edith Evans play—is going begging. In America Katharine Cornell thinks the part too unamicable for her worshippers even if she could act it; and nobody else shews any consciousness of its existence.

I am now only resurrection pie, it seems. The play went quite satisfactorily at Malvern, just as it did at Bexhill etc etc; *but* Hamlet is not very exciting with an understudy. It is up to you to revive me, bless you!

G.B.S.

The reference to a production at Malvern helps pinpoint the error Garson Kanin made in his book *Tracy and Hepburn* which, as already mentioned, was to enrage Edith in later years. Kanin asserts that Sybil Thorndike played *The Millionairess* at Malvern 'to an indifferent reception'. This is, of course, untrue.

I find the whole episode of *The Millionairess* intriguing and it is one of those rare occasions when Shaw appears an object for pity. Of course he exaggerated his poverty, but despite the delightful, bantering use of the phrase 'resurrection pie' one can detect a layer of real hurt just below the surface.

Nothing came of his efforts for a further three years. At the beginning of 1939 the run of *Robert's Wife* was finally coming to an end: Munich was still in the nostrils, lingering like the stench of fireworks after a celebration nobody enjoyed, and preparations for the inevitable war were all around us. There was an unease in the theatre as in the rest of England: it was difficult to make plans too far ahead; we knew the disease of war was amongst us, that the specialists were meeting and conferring, the common diagnosis had been made and it was only a matter of time before the patients would be told their fate.

Edith's 'great essay in dragonhood' was first unveiled on January 31st 1939, a Tuesday afternoon matinee at the Globe. Gielgud produced and played John Worthing; he was no stranger to the play having acted the same role for Nigel Playfair nine years earlier. On that occasion his mother's sister, Mabel Terry-Lewis made a notable success as Lady Bracknell, but all memories of previous performances were to be effaced by Edith and there are few actors of my generation, male or female, who have not at some time or another, in conversation or on the stage, attempted a parody of Edith's Bracknell voice and delivery. There are some roles which live on to haunt and on occasion almost destroy an actor; Lady Bracknell was to walk Edith's battlements for the rest of her life, and even on the day of her death few commentators could resist mentioning what they [wrongly] regarded as her greatest performance. One radio personality interviewing me a few hours after her death had the tastelessness actually to impersonate her, lapsing into a grotesque version of the famous handbag scene until my cold and unsmiling eye on the other side of the live microphone silenced him. Edith grew to loathe Lady Bracknell. 'I've played her everywhere except on ice and under water,' she once exploded. 'And I daresay Binkie will suggest one of those next. I did play *other* parts, you know!'

Her reference to Hugh 'Binkie' Beaumont contained sorrow as well as affection. Although Edith was in no way Binkie's Norma Shearer, he was certainly her Thalberg, the sibilant mastermind who, in the great tradition of such things, inherited the theatrical empire of H. M. Tennent Ltd at a tender age. A feared legend in his own time, Binkie exercised a profound influence over and an even greater control of so many theatrical careers during the war and the two decades that followed the war. Like God, whom many young actors supposed him to be, Binkie moved in quiet, mysterious ways. One ascended to him when an audience was commanded: ascended by one of the smallest elevators ever constructed, which was sandwiched into the foyer of the Globe theatre just behind the box office, a symbolic choice of location, for the God of Shaftesbury Avenue was never content with mere loaves and fishes. Breathing pure cigarette smoke, he lived at a rarified level and the organisation he had fashioned with so much commercial skill became the premier management to work for. Indeed *not* to have worked for H. M. Tennent was tangible evidence of failure; to have worked only *once* for Tennent's was to reveal to the world that you were lacking in those attributes that made for lasting success. It was sometimes described as 'a benevolent dictatorship within a larger dictatorship': an incestuous empire which fanned out from the Prince Littler Consolidated Trust and which, by the late 1940's directly or indirectly owned or controlled 18 out of the 42 functioning West End theatres and 70% of the No. 1 provincial theatres.

Binkie was good copy for the profession, frequently providing 'interior' jokes for the satirical revues which flourished during this period. He maintained a low profile, seldom gave interviews and employed a publicity woman who reputedly had strict instructions to keep his name out of the papers, with the result that she quickly earned the nickname 'No News Is Good News'. A very self-contained man, who wrote notes to the favoured ones in a slanting schoolgirl hand (official letters from Tennent's were always typed with a blue ribbon) capable of enormous social charm, ruthless when exercising his own judgement and extremely devious when it suited him, he had an uncanny knack for putting together all the right ingredients, moulding them to his own taste (which was good but not infallible) and always demanding total loyalty at his own price. Tennent's did much to advance the prestige of the English classical theatre, but was frequently accused of being too narrow in its outlook. Binkie took this criticism to heart and launched a non-profit-making subsidiary, Tennent Productions Ltd, together with The Company of Four, which he ran with the dedicated assistance of three close aides: John Perry, who was Mr. Mason to Binkie's Mr. Fortnum as a purveyor of quality goods to the carriage trade, Daphne Rye, an inspired casting director, and Kitty Black, an able translator of Sartre and others. These side ventures encouraged and trained new players, directors and playwrights and were rightly applauded, but the fact remained that Tennent's exercised a profound, and many felt unhealthy, influence which narrowed the field of endeavour, as critic Richard Findlater pointed out, for those artists and authors of whom it did not approve. It was a closed society with its own code of behaviour; patronage, once bestowed, could be withdrawn overnight; acts of disloyalty, such as working for a rival management, would be tolerated, but never forgotten; the final seal of acceptance to the inner court circle was an invitation to one of Binkie's private parties at his elegant town house in Lord North Street where, as one exiled wag put it, 'the wall-papers were pasted with actors' blood.' Although Binkie never flinched from spending large sums of money to mount his productions, with the exception of the big star names, salaries were low: the privilege of being employed by Tennent's was accounted sufficient in itself.

Naturally, Edith's status was such that she did not have to concern herself with such intrigues, though Binkie was not above using somebody of Edith's eminence to gain his own ends when it suited him. She acknowledged that she had every reason to feel grateful to him for providing her with settings for her talents, and for surrounding her with an elegance which few, if any, could match. She was dressed by Beaton, acted in sets designed by Oliver Messel and encouraged to believe that she not only had a permanent home with Tennent's, but that they alone recognised her true worth. Edith was never taken in by all this; she knew that Binkie needed her. She never became a true intimate of the inner circle, though remained a welcome distinguished visitor. I always got the impression that she was one of the few star artistes that Binkie was in awe of, and this is born out by his letters to her.

The Importance of Being Earnest moved into the Globe for an extended run when *Robert's Wife* closed, but in the meantime Shaw had returned to his old quest concerning *The Millionairess*. In a letter to Edith dated 4th May 1939 he wrote:

I am bothered by innumerable young ladies who have all made 'an enormous success' as the millionairess in various places from Dublin to Croydon. They want to repeat it in the West End. I do not share their impatience; but being old and muddled I don't know how I stand with you in the matter. *Robert's Wife* seems likely to last until she becomes Robert's Widow; and you are becoming an addict to sympathetic parts. Epifania, though terrifically effective (if all the young ladies' tales be true) is not sympathetic.

May I go ahead with the play as if you didn't exist—as far as my feelings will allow? I think you would be happier in a new play by a comparatively new author of fifty or thereabouts. I am vieux jeu.

Yesterday I finished a play about Charles II. Three whores to cast; but you wouldn't like any of them. And one queen of 42, who must be guiltless of sex appeal.

Edith finally succumbed, her defences penetrated at last. Even so her enthusiasm was qualified. Writing to Gwen Ffrangcon-Davies in Pretoria, South Africa, she confessed 'I would love to stay at home and grow things, but that is not to be . . . we must be very brave and keep going.'

The play went into rehearsal and then embarked on a pre-London tour in August 1940, the intention being that it should be brought to London to open at the Globe on September 11th 1940. This was the evidence that Edith brandished under the nose of Garson Kanin, searching through her papers until she unearthed the weekly returns for the Opera House, Manchester and the Lyceum, which showed that they had taken an average of £840 a week. It was the Blitz which killed the London opening (a curious echo of the prophecy contained in the closing moments of *Heartbreak House*) and the production was abandoned. One can speculate whether, on this occasion, Shaw still wished Hitler 'a comfortable retirement' as he had once stated. He had conducted such a long siege of Edith where this play was concerned, perhaps sensing that it was one of his minor works and needed her presence to make it live as conceived in his mind's eye.

Just previous to the tour of *The Millionairess* Edith had appeared in *Cousin Muriel*, a new play by Clemence Dane, again at the Globe, where she had become almost a permanent fixture. Shaw hadn't seen this production because 'our extreme antiquity makes us afraid to playgo during the blackout.' Edith asked his advice about the character she was playing and even though Shaw was in ignorance of the details he did not hesitate to offer an opinion. 'The public does not like to be asked to love a crude criminal. Barrie's only decisive failure was when he made a murderess of Mrs. Patrick Campbell. Cooking a cheque is all right in Galsworthy's *Justice*; but the cook is not asked to be an enchantress as well. Couldn't we devise something subtler?'

Like most people in England during that time, Edith was leading a double-life: part civilian, part soldier. She was struggling to keep Washenden going, 'doing her bit for the war effort' as she put it by ploughing up the flower beds and planting vegetables. In a letter to Gwen Ffrangcon-Davies she expressed the common hope that 'something lovely must come from all this tearing apart.' So many of her friends had gone to the war. George Devine was in the Artillery, Murray Macdonald, Jack Hawkins and others had also joined up. Edith found the cruelty and heartlessness of the war 'too painful.' 'This is to my mind the real Anti-Christ we are fighting. This ghastly rule of force and force alone, and the complete reversal of any true statement. It is frightening.' She was also up in arms about other aspects of the war-time scene. 'Binkie wouldn't risk *The Millionairess* in London. I'm afraid that it wouldn't have made sufficient money for him. How wrong. How terribly wrong this money first attitude is. Money, yes, in its place, but the good work first and then the money. The money first system drains a country or a profession to the dregs and never really gives anything back. I *know* that it is the root of all evil. Not money, but money first.'

(The Barrie play Shaw referred to was *The Adored One* or *Leonora* as it was called in America. Mrs. Pat had kept him waiting for *Pygmalion* just as Edith had delayed her decision over *The Millionairess*, but in his twilight years Shaw apparently forgot that he had once judged *The Adored One* on a par with *Pygmalion*, advising Mrs. Pat in 1913 that she had 'the two best plays and parts in London in the hollow of your bosom. They will provide for your old age . . . Barrie's play is the surest and most lucrative.' It was not so: Barrie's effort was booed at curtain-fall on the first night, lasting only ten weeks, whilst Shaw's vehicle went on to become the cornerstone of his literary estate.

But Shaw never passed up an opportunity to pursue his own cause, and even found time to rewrite Clemence Dane's last act, sending Edith two typewritten pages of dialogue as an alternative ending. Writing from Whitehall Court on 27th March 1940, he hardly sustained the self-description of 'extreme antiquity'.

My Dear Edith,

I have just written to Hugh Beaumont about the cast. The play does not drop after the first act if the Egyptian is up to the mark. I have suggested Gielgud, Stephen Murray, or (among the elderlies) Arthur Wontner. Blenderbland had better be played by Gabriel Toyne because he knows how to fall, being an athletic expert as well as an actor proclaimed a genius by James Agate. I assume that Miss Ashcroft can be secured for Patricia. The other parts are easy, though Sagamore must be an agreeable comedian and the husband a goodlooking young heavyweight.

But the play is carried by Epifania to the middle of the second act. After that she keeps her lead automatically, leaving the hard work to the doctor and Allah, especially the latter. Hardwicke is in America and wont come back: else I should have named him for the doctor.

I have suggested Irene Hentschel to produce. She will let the play alone and let you alone. Both of these will do the work if they are not interfered with by some crack producer whose speciality is making a worthless script funny or melodramatic. I write for actors, not producers. The producer of *The Millionairess* should be a woman anyhow.

If you like my Muriel ending send it to Clemence: she can work it in in three turns of her pen. But if all is going well let well alone.   GBS.

The amendments to Clemence Dane's play, typed out by Shaw, seem very trite. He would have bitterly resented anybody tampering with his own work, but perhaps expected other writers to feel nothing but gratitude for his interference.

Cousin Muriel came and went (despite the added attraction of the young Alec Guinness), *The Millionairess* was turned back by the Luftwaffe, and for the first time in her career Edith appeared in revue. *Diversion* and *Diversion No. 2*, both written by her faithful admirer Herbert Farjeon, were aptly titled; the theatre in general and Edith in particular were marking time, for few management were willing to risk their money on more ambitious projects when they had no means of telling whether their theatres would be left standing from one day to the next.

(It is interesting to note that Edith still managed her own career at this point, scorning the use of an agent. Her contract for *Diversion* was a simple one-page document drawn up by Bronson Albery on New Theatre notepaper, described by Albery as 'necessarily rather harsh-looking' in that it allowed the Management very wide discretion for the cancellation of individual performances or even the entire production. Edith's salary was £10. 1s per week of six, seven or eight performances, or pro rata for any part thereof, plus twelve and a half per cent of the excess of gross receipts (less Library discounts and Entertainment Tax) over £450 in any week. She was to provide the material and necessary dresses and properties for her 'own turns'.)

One of her 'turns' proved to be an immensely popular monologue, of which Edith was part author, about a Cockney hop-picker. Dorothy Dickson and Walter Crisham were amongst the cast of *Diversion* and the original run of five weeks was extended to nine for the first show. A London starved of entertainment welcomed the new Edith, who was delighted with herself and, as she told North American listeners in a BBC broadcast called 'Democracy Marches', 'I discovered I had quite a reasonable talent for monologues.' The new version, *Diversion No. 2* was equally successful.

Although she had Washenden until 1944, Edith braved the blitz from that most elegant of town addresses—Albany, in Piccadilly. She occupied a set of chambers numbered L4, immediately opposite J. B. Priestley, who like Edith, stayed on in London and made a series of memorable broadcasts which are remembered to this day. She did canteen work after she left the theatre and was often trapped there until the All Clear sounded in the early hours. She enjoyed telling me of the time when, in the blackout, she assured a close friend that the route to the underground cellar in Albany was 'quite flat right through. Wasn't anything of the sort. There were about seven steps and she went headlong. Awful, she never let me forget it. I mean, I did more damage to her than Hitler. I couldn't stick all those people trooping down to the shelter about nine o'clock every night and starting to go to sleep. Nobody *talked*, or told any *jokes*, or anything. It was awfully boring, I thought. Some of them had their coffee brought down by their parlourmaids. That used to make me roar with laughter. I didn't go all that often, only when things got really bad. They dropped a bomb just across the road, on that lovely church in Piccadilly, and that did us all some damage, but most nights I couldn't be bothered.'

In one of her frequent letters to Gwen Frangcon-Davies, this one dated February 5th 1941, she related that 'we are keyed up for this invasion, which I can't help hoping won't come, but there we are. I expect he will have to try. The lighter evenings are bringing more people to the matinees and we are starting two performances on February 8th. . . . I met John* in the street two days ago and he took me to have some coffee and a chat. I like him so much on his own. It's the commercial element that brings out all his 'safety-first' quality that I don't like . . . They are doing *Dear Brutus* at the Globe. Imagine in these times! He could have been so much more adventurous.'

It was to Gwen that she also confessed her chronic loneliness. 'I'm having a birthday in a day or two' (her 53rd) 'and I was lying awake last night wondering what in the world I was good for. Trying to see what I could do to be a bit more the sort of person I'd like to be. I cannot think why I'm destined to live alone when life with a charming man would give just that occupation and companionship that I love . . . However, I don't want one badly enough to go and look for him, so I suppose I'll be alone now for always.'

This letter was written from Albany, and concludes: 'It's about 9.45 p.m. and the guns made me jump just then. I shan't go to bed for a bit. Won't it be lovely when we can all sleep in peace.'

Like so many of her distinguished contemporaries, she made her contribution to the war effort in the only way she knew how: by entertaining the troops. She travelled abroad, first in a revue at Gibraltar, then appearing in *Heartbreak House* at home and overseas, and at the end of the war reviving *The Late Christopher Bean* for E.N.S.A. in India. Her recollections of that continent could hardly be said to be conventional. 'I went everywhere in India looking for a phallic symbol, and I never found one. I was the only person, I think, in the company, who never saw one. Everybody else was always going about saying this and that about them, and I never saw a phallic anything. They must have disappeared when they saw me coming.'

The mental picture of Lady Bracknell searching India for a phallic symbol is a bizarre one, suggesting Wilde rewritten by Tynan, though Edith's views on full frontal nudity when that fad hit the West End hardly coincided with those of the perpetrator of *Oh, Calcutta!* 'I can't think what they're all after, what they're *at*, what they're trying to find out.

* John Gielgud.

What does it mean? One woman's just like another. I see myself every morning in the bath and it doesn't interest me to stay any longer than I have to. Even when I was young and considered to have quite a good figure ... I'm not interested. I can't be bothered with it, really. Mystery, that's what the theatre's all about and there's no mystery in a lot of goose-pimples. All I can say is 'Put your shirts on, stop trying to shock us, start trying to entertain us.'''

In between her patriotic wanderings during the war years she managed to appear in one new play and to revive *The Importance* once more. The new play was John van Druten's bitter-sweet comedy *Old Acquaintance* with Edith playing the role that Bette Davis eventually brought to the screen.

(As it happens, in 1976 I was asked whether I would like to remake the film and by coincidence had tea with Bette at her Westport house the same week that I had re-run the old film to remind myself of the plot. I knew, of course, of the legendary feud that had existed between Bette and Miriam Hopkins, who played the other female star role, during the making of the film. I could not resist stirring the embers of that conflagration. I asked Bette what had finally happened to Miriam Hopkins. She took the inevitable cigarette from her lips, struck a pose familiar to all her admirers and in a voice teeming with Margot Channing said: 'Well, God was very good to the world. He took her from us.' Like Katharine Hepburn, Bette was fascinated by Edith and questioned me closely about her method of working. It was always my ambition, now alas never to be realised, to persuade Edith, Bette and Kate to appear in a film together.)

Binkie had brought *Old Acquaintance* to Edith's notice in June 1941, telling her that it 'has a lightness and gaiety which I think is very much needed in these times.' Edith's acceptance was guarded. She wrote to Binkie that she felt it was too slight for wartime England, but 'if I can be released to play stronger meat should it come, I will do it, as it is a good character study.'

The Miriam Hopkins role was first offered to Marie Löhr who declined firmly, but graciously. The part was eventually played by Marian Spencer and Edith went on to make the role of Kit one of her 'lovelies'. I greatly regret that I did not see this production, for the comparison between Edith's characterisation and Bette's would have been fascinating. Of her own performance, Edith said 'I surprised myself by enjoying it so much. The character of Kit was the sort of woman I always wished I could become. The sort of woman I admire.'

My first sight of Edith as a paying member of the audience was as Lady Bracknell, circa 1942, and I vividly recall that the entire production stunned me. To a Royal Academy of Dramatic Art freshman, as I then was, Edith and Gielgud seemed like two peacocks on Mount

Olympus. The contrast between the stylish, effortless elegance of performance on stage at the Phoenix and the sandbagged drabness of wartime Soho outside almost made me lose my reason. If this seems a remembered exaggeration, I must justify it by explaining that to be a student of acting during that grim period of the war was, in itself, a kind of madness: one unreality superimposed upon another. Edith and Gielgud represented the two pinnacles and they splashed their talents in vivid colours across the backcloth of austerity: one queued for a few ounces of butter and a piece of horsemeat—caviar to the masses—but, as the house lights were lowered in the Phoenix and Wilde's epigrams drifted across the footlights, spoken by two of the most beautiful voices that ever graced the English stage, an artistic All Clear sounded; for a few brief hours one enjoyed a return to the world of style and calm and all thoughts of war and death were mercifully suspended. I went time and time again, sitting in the gods, and my fate was sealed by the experience. We were students privileged to watch a team of master alchemists distil the very essence of comedy and I, for one, became transfixed by the sheer beauty of the perfected experiment. This, I felt— and time has not eroded my opinion— was the quintessence of high comedy and nothing in the contemporary theatre leads me to believe that we shall ever see it repeated.

Behind the scenes Shaw was urging Edith to consider *The Millionairess* in another medium; his tenacity apparently inexhaustible.

20th April 1942

Very Dear Edith,

I believe I suggested a broadcast of *The Millionairess* to the BBC some time ago. I have just had a letter from Val Gielgud which I must answer; and I will seize the opportunity to reopen the subject.

But there must be no nonsense about cutting the play down to the everyday measure of the BBC routine. It must be a big occasion for both of us, or they will rank us for ever after as mere utilities. It must be played in two parts on two nights at full length, just as *Messiah* was given in three parts on three nights at full length last week. It was magnificent: ten times the effect of giving it all in a lump. I will write the announcer's part describing what the audience cannot see, and getting rid of the specifications of doors and windows and right and left which are unvaoidable in prompt books, but silly when read out.

You will be splendid with 24 hours rest instead of 12 minutes, and no changes or journeys to and from your dressing room. And I shall hear it in my slippers at my fireside, without shocking you by the spectacle of a dotard 33 years older than you, whom you can remember when he was young and beautiful. I am no longer even venerable. your decrepit   G. Bernard Shaw.

The broadcast was duly arranged but what went out over the air failed to please the age-obsessed GBS. By July 7th 1942 he was writing again.

My Dear Edith

The Sunday fiasco was not your fault. It was the fault of the production, or rather the absence of any production. For broadcasting, the players, being invisible, must be specially careful not to imitate one another, nor to take their speed and pitch from one another, nor to race or rival one another, nor to pick up a cue and return it as a cricketer fields a ball as smartly and quickly as possible, betraying what should be concealed at all costs: that is, that they knew all along what the previous speaker was going to say and were not for a moment in doubt as to what to reply to it. An actor should always be surprised at what is said—delighted, disgusted, alarmed or what not as the case may be, but always a bit surprised, or taken aback enough to make the audience believe that it is unexpected.

On Sunday the company did all it could to avoid these essentials. It was the business of the solicitor to help you by providing the lightest of light comedy so as to give the utmost contrast to your tragic earnestness: to be amused and astonished at every fresh revelation of your extraordinary character. Instead, he tried to outstrip and outpace you, to play your part instead of his own. When the others came in they joined in the race and set-to to shout one another down, all racing at full pitch. It was worse than ham Sheridan at its very worst, utterly unintelligible, discordant, noisy, until at last Epifania was lost among half a dozen people trying to be more Epifanean than she, and being all mistaken for one another by the distracted listeners. I never heard anything quite so damnable as that first act.

Fortunately the second was an improvement, as it is almost all duet, and the voices cannot be mistaken. The situation too is much simpler; and the two men were quite blameless, and seemed to know what they were talking about.

Monday was all right: quite clear: nothing to complain of. My bombshell evidently had its effect, though Miss B.B.* says she did not show it to anyone. But I doubt whether any of the Sunday listeners listened on Monday. Beaumont didn't. I had written to him to say that the play was killed and we had better cry off a West End production. He heartily agreed.

* Barbara Burnham, a distinguished BBC producer of the times.

I should not have done this if I had not gathered the impression that you did not like the part, and might possibly do yourself more harm than good by playing it. You played it with your farce mannerism and curiously without the music in your speech that came out so beautifully in your Millamant. I believe you were bored by it. You were certainly not in the least tragic; and Epifania is soulless if she is not tragic. And you were dreadfully careless about your key words: you slurred all of them and scored some misses in consequence.

The part, even when treated as farcical, is actress proof; but the play isn't: if Epifania is not interesting as well as funny the play is not quite worth listening to except by an audience of political economists. Anyhow, I concluded that we had better chuck it, for some years at any rate.

What do you think of it yourself, honest Injun? With undiminished admiration, still always yours, GBS.

Although some of Shaw's strictures were lacking in his usual objectivity, his advice to the broadcasting players could well be reprinted and handed to everybody applying for a radio audition. In this instance he was brilliantly accurate in his assessment of what makes for good radio drama.

I saw Edith again when *Heartbreak House* was revived at the Cambridge, with Robert Donat playing Captain Shotover and Deborah Kerr as Ellie Dunn. I must confess that I was not immediately enamoured of the play or the production, and I remember thinking that the Cambridge was too cold and vast for a proper enjoyment of Shaw's intricate verbal fireworks. Edith and Isabel Jeans seemed to me like contenders for a heavy-weight prize, with Miss Jeans pummelling every cushion in sight whenever Edith was in the centre of the ring, and both of them searching for a knock-out punch. Donat, buried beneath a mass of crepe hair resembled nothing more than an animated rug from my distant seat in the back-stalls, and I came away disappointed, for he was one of my screen idols.

For once I can claim to have shared the same opinion as Shaw: 'I saw H.H. on Wednesday afternoon,' he wrote to Edith on 20th August 1943. 'No complaints: the part is too easy for you. But to have to pull the play through against four hopeless miscasts, included a faded maiden aunt as your youthful rival and a Shotover who is obviously a leading juvenile in a stuck-on beard, takes a bit of doing. It should be billed as Half Heart House. I greatly enjoyed all the money in the stalls.'

I feel doubly honoured, having not only matched judgements with the author, but also having contributed my mite towards the upkeep of his Rolls Royce. Shaw was feeling his age at the time, describing himself (on 7th September 1943) as 'a stage effect that reminds people of GBS, an old dotard of 87, all but played out.' On the same postcard he told Edith that Charlotte, his wife, was a crippled invalid and that Edith would find them both greatly changed when next she saw them, if she saw them. Edith was never to see Charlotte alive again, for she died five days later. Shaw was overwhelmed with sorrow, but characteristically concealed it, writing to Edith three days later, the day of the funeral, asking her to visit him. 'Come on Friday with Isabel just as if nothing had happened. I am quite happy. So was she at the last. We finished at Golders Green this morning to Handel's music which she loved, without a word spoken.'

His grief took extraordinary forms and Edith confirmed what St. John Ervine wrote in his biography of Shaw that 'those of his friends who did not fully perceive how he strove to keep his deeper feelings dark, imagined that he was hysterical or callous when, after shedding tears, an act of which he was supposed to be incapable, he would begin to sing almost hilariously.'

It is significant, I feel, that he turned to Edith so soon after the event; he knew that she would understand better than most and, with Charlotte gone, Edith was his remaining female link with the past.

I was happily on leave from the Army when Edith next appeared in a major West End production of a new play. I had missed her appearance in the William Armstrong revival of *The Rivals* at the Criterion which was presented shortly after the war ended. Photographs show her Mrs. Malaprop framed in a magnificent head-dress, and J. C. Trewin tells us that she 'surged along from epitaph to epitaph'.

During the war years Binkie had several times tried to tempt her with major star parts. In 1942 he had offered her Regina in *The Little Foxes* (once again a role that Bette Davis later played on the screen), but Edith declined, judging it wrong for her, and it was Fay Compton who eventually played it with such success. Then in 1944 Binkie wrote and asked Edith to appear in a revival of *St. Joan*. 'Binkie was quite wrong to suggest it,' Edith told me. 'How could I? Nobody could have followed Sybil in that part, least of all me. I was too old for it by then. You can't make a Forest of Arden out of Shaw's France, and Sybil had done it, it was hers and hers alone. But Binkie was like that. Too commercial for his own good sometimes. Of course it would have attracted attention, and probably made money, but it would have been utterly wrong for me to have said yes. Morally wrong.'

In the same letter as he accepted her decision that she could not play St. Joan, Binkie expressed a willingness to assist her in her ambition to produce. He felt that he could devise a scheme which would give Edith all the scope she wanted and where he and Tennent's would shoulder the managerial burden. It was a kind suggestion, but Edith never acted on it.

My return to the post-war London theatre from the culture-less desert of occupied Germany coincided with the run of *Crime and Punishment*, which Binkie presented in the summer of 1946. Rodney Ackland employed his considerable skills to adapt and compress Dostoevsky's epic novel, but the final result lacked dramatic shape, and one feels that novels on this scale can only be translated into multi-episode television series if justice is to be done to the original.

The production was beset with difficulties from the start. Binkie first thought was to have Robert Helpmann play Raskolnikoff with Alec Guinness sharing the production. Olivier had been asked to direct, but was tied up with *The Skin of Our Teeth*; Michael Redgrave could not make up his mind in time to fit in with Binkie's plans, and Guthrie was away in America. Binkie then asked Edith to consider Peter Glenville. A crisis point was reached; of no great consequence, but the theatre is made up of such semi-fabricated emotional scenes; it is the icing on the cake to many, and this was the period in Edith's life when she perhaps enjoyed her eminence to the full. Various other distinguished names were bandied around, but all, for some reason or another, proved unobtainable. It may well be, of course, that people such as Michel St. Denis, George Devine, Glen Byam Shaw, John Burrell and others all read the play and decided that it would not enhance their careers to direct it. In the end Gielgud was persuaded and announced as director. Then Helpmann was taken ill and had to withdraw. Binkie then asked Gielgud to relinquish the role of director and take over as Raskolnikoff. Anthony Quayle replaced Gielgud as director and the rehearsals recommenced. At best it was an uneasy compromise, for Gielgud acknowledged that he was scarcely the popular conception of a poverty-stricken Russian student, and he found it difficult to submerge his personality in the characterisation. Edith, looking remarkably youthful as Katerina, was also not entirely happy, and although any play containing their coupled talents was an event, the combination of the parts proved too much for the whole. My retained memory is of Paul Sherriff's ingenious composite set on many levels and Peter Ustinov's impersonation of Charles Laughton as the sinister Chief of Police.

Perhaps we should all regret that both Edith and Gielgud were absent from the great seasons that Olivier and Richardson gave us at the New Theatre. I am not suggesting that there was any deliberate plot built around their exclusion from the post-war Old Vic company, merely deploring that events did not conspire to bring together under one roof the four greatest talents of that generation.

I have noted that 1946 was the peak of Edith's eminence, and this was officially confirmed for on the 6th December 1945 she had received a letter from the Prime Minister's office informing her that it was the Prime Minister's intention to submit her name to the King 'with a recommendation that he may be graciously pleased to approve that you be appointed a Dame Commander of the Order of the British Empire.'

According to the tradition of such confidential communications, Edith was told that 'the Prime Minister would be glad to be assured that this mark of His Majesty's favour would be agreeable to you.' It was agreeable to her and her name was included in the New Year's Honours list for 1946.

For a woman to be made a Dame is the equivalent of a knighthood for a man. It is a title frequently misunderstood by foreigners to whom the term Dame more commonly suggests a pantomime figure of comedy. (Eric Johns, in his charming book *Dames of The Theatre*, relates how an American fan, meeting Dame Edith Sitwell on a lecture tour, asked 'Why do you call yourself Dame?' 'I don't', replied Dame Edith Sitwell, 'the Queen does.') There is added confusion for the layman in that, once honoured, the theatrical recipients never use their titles on the bill boards or in the programmes: this is considered bad taste. A student of contemporary British history might well remark that the list of women so honoured, in all walks of life, shows greater justification than the list of their male counterparts. There is some tilting of the scales, too, in this touchy age, in favour of the ladies, for whereas when a man is knighted his wife is accorded the courtesy title of Lady, the husband of a Dame remains plain Mister. Perhaps some chauvinistic husband will one day evoke the Equality of Sexes Act and demand equal treatment when his spouse is elevated to the elite.

Edith received her honour at the comparatively youthful age of fifty eight, for most actresses have had to wait until the twilight of their careers before receiving any official recognition. Sybil, another exception, had received hers fifteen years previously and was at that time the youngest actress ever to be singled out. As one can see, the timing is capricious. A further insight into the Establishment mind is provided by the citation which accompanied Edith's D.B.E. She was not given it for thirty years dedication to the theatre, but for services rendered to E.N.S.A. during the war.

As 1946 drew to a close Edith returned to the Nile after an absence of twenty-one years, playing Cleopatra to Godfrey Tearle's Antony in Glen Byam Shaw's production at the Piccadilly. Tynan, still in his teens and flaunting his opinions as blatantly as a green carnation, 'felt anarchy stirring' when Edith's Queen of Egypt took to the stage. Lady Bracknell, he wrote, 'had been involved in a low Alexandrian scandal.' In his collected works, published at the ripe old age of twenty three, despite a preface which apologized in advance for 'a note of smugness, even of insolence which I have observed in some of my judgements,' he sentenced Edith without pity. 'Bereft of fan, lace and sedan chair, Dame Edith is nakedly middle-aged and plain . . . Her

Cleopatra is as hostile as a glacier . . . She remained, even in the last cold moment, a vociferous slut, a barmaid among Barmecides.' The verdict of youth is often without compassion. This is not the place to take up cudgels in defence of subjective opinions, but having witnessed the same performance as Mr. Tynan, I apparently did not witness the same performance. There was no trace of Lady Bracknell in Edith's Cleopatra that I could discern, nor would I employ the adjective plain to describe her appearance (assuming Mr. Tynan to have used the word as meaning ugly). It was not perhaps Edith at her most inspired, but Edith could fire more effectively on four cylinders than most actresses on eight, and I recall the intelligence of her performance, though I also remember thinking that the costumes she wore were strangely at variance with the tragedy.

Following *Cleopatra* Edith was absent from the stage for a period of two years, the first prolonged break in the continuity of her career. Not that she was idle: the film industry finally caught up with her. It is a little known fact that Edith made two silent films when she was scarcely out of Poel's cradle, making her screen debut in 1915 in *A Welsh Singer* for that British pioneer Cecil M. Hepworth at the now-vanished Walton-on-Thames studios. The star and director was Henry Edwards, his female co-star being the 'Vitagraph Girl', Florence Turner. Edith's second film, again for Henry Edwards, *East is East* was made a year later. Edith never referred to these and all mention of them was dropped from her entry in 'Who's Who in The Theatre' and other standard works of reference. It is therefore wrongly assumed that she made her first appearance in *The Queen of Spades* in 1948. This was the Rodney Ackland-Arthur Boys adaptation of Pushkin's story of nineteenth century St. Petersburg in which Edith portrayed the ravaged eighty-year-old Countess Ranevskaya. Ackland himself directed for the first few days and then was removed without ceremony—Thorold Dickinson taking over in an atmosphere which can accurately be described as tense. Edith was a total stranger to the cruel lunacies of the film industry and of course was never consulted on the change of director. Anton Walbrook, then at the height of his romantic screen fame, was her leading man and the production was designed by Oliver Messel and photographed by the superb Otto Heller. Walbrook gave a performance from the 'tank-flail school of Central European acting' and elsewhere there were strong Germanic influences—shades of Fritz Lang in his pre-Hollywood days which many critics remarked upon with varying degrees of enthusiasm. *The Queen of Spades* can therefore be recorded as her first *talking* film.

Edith's performance amazed a new set of critics and with one exception they touched their forelocks at her coming out in celluloid. The dissenting voice came from the *Daily Worker* which doubtless disapproved of anything to do with pre-revolutionary St. Petersburg, accorded the film twenty one lines and dismissed the acting. The *Sunday Chronicle*'s reviewer described Edith in terms which would have sent most leading ladies in search of the nearest nunnery. 'Dame Edith's countess is a figure of unforgettable senility, whose skull one glimpses beneath the skin. The skin itself is not so much wrinkled as *smocked*; and the words, croaked softly from an almost lipless mouth, carry a quality of frog's breath.' (Film critics in those days were disgustingly close to Nature.) Edith was in fact buried beneath so much make-up that it was difficult to discern where artifice ended and art began. Filmgoers had to wait for her second film, *The Last Days of Dolwyn* before they had any idea of her real features. Binkie had written to give his blessing on the venture, saying 'we are lending you to the film industry . . . I am now more determined than ever to have a wonderful play ready for you when you have finished the two pictures.'

The Last Days of Dolwyn was a melodrama centred around the destruction of a Welsh village. It was written and directed by Emlyn Williams who also cast himself in the leading male role. Edith's performance drew curiously mixed responses. She played a humble widow, the leading opponent to Emlyn's scheming villain, and was described by Leonard Mosley, then film critic of the *Daily Express*, as looking 'rather like a shy Cader Idris sheep wearing a bonnet.' There were others who felt that she was not yet at home before the cameras and that there were moments when she looked as 'disproportionate as a life-size Rembrandt in a one-room flatlet.' Paul Dehn, writing scornfully of the 'West End film morons' when *The Last Days of Dolwyn* had been withdrawn from the Empire, Leicester Square, after a single week's run in order to make way for a flashy little musical called *The Kissing Bandit*, bemoaned the fact that idle cinemagoers had missed 'what is almost certainly the loveliest and most moving film performance in British film history,' and went on to quote Agate's 25 year old description of Edith's beauty.

By coincidence, both *Dolwyn* and *The Queen of Spades* were released very close together, becoming, as it were, two bookends between which Edith sandwiched a remarkable series of stage performances on her return to the theatre. It was a period of restlessness for Edith; emotionally and professionally she was disturbed. In April 1947 her beloved father had died. Undoubtedly he had been the dominant male influence in her life. She lived by his truths, was calmed by him, and gave to him the most open of her affections. To the end of his life they corresponded regularly, sometimes two or three times a week. His letters to her were simple and she replied in kind, exchanging items of family gossip and always concerned for his health and well being. She preserved every scrap he ever wrote to her and her letters to him also survived. They are not the stuff of history and scarcely bear the weight of lengthy quotation. He was 'My Darling Dad' for she was Ned's girl to the end and when he responded in kind it was to tell her 'there is never a night in my life but what I have always since you were born, commended you to God's keeping.' A few weeks before he died she wrote to say she intended to have a short holiday in Brussels, but would be back to visit him on the 14th April or thereabouts. Edward Evans died on April 16th, suffering a heart attack while out for a walk. The suddenness of his death, the fact that she had not seen him for the last time, had a profound and lasting effect on Edith. In the last weeks of her own life she referred to the manner of his death many times with that insistence that old age often bestows. She repeatedly asked me to reassure her that she would not die in the same way. 'I don't want to drop dead in the street like dear father. I won't do that, will I?' I did my best to comfort her, promising that the same fate would not be hers. It was a promise I could give with an easy conscience, for by then she seldom ventured far from Kilndown, and then only by car, being driven to the coast for an occasional outing by her faithful chauffeur, William Houghton. In those final weeks it was her father she spoke of most, the 'person I loved best', the quiet gentleman with the beautiful handwriting who had admired the brasses in the theatre and lived his life with a reverence for the truth. His letters to her spoke from a past that was more vivid to her than the twilight of a great career. Sometimes she spoke of him as though he was still in the next room, or writing to her from Eastbourne with words of comfort and wisdom. It was he who had understood her best, taking her through the bad patches, calming her down, proud but not conceited at her success and always there when she failed.

A year after his death she went to Russia. She was then head of the theatrical section of the British-Soviet Society which had blossomed in the days when it was respectable to admire the Russian war effort. The compatibility of Communism and the Christian faith was a subject which concerned Edith. She clipped articles on the subject from the papers and pasted them into her scrapbooks. I know that there was inner conflict between the woman who wanted to embrace the purest concepts of Christian Communism, but who was repelled by any form of totalitarianism. Edith shared her wealth generously but by stealth, as many can testify. I have previously mentioned that she admired Sybil's more flamboyant involvement in social causes, and she envied Sybil her ability to mix. Edith was not at home in a crowd; she served her public, but liked to keep apart. On many occasions I sensed this Jekyll and Hyde aspect and Michael Redgrave added substance when he told me that Edith had once admitted to him that she had to keep herself in check. 'I have to resist the urge to roll in the gutter after a performance', she told him; curiously enough Maugham used almost the same words to describe a facet of his own personal dilemma. Edith's view of politics was a simplistic one, it was not a topic she turned to instinctively and she had few friends who were active in politics. Her celebrated journey to Russia, which she undertook alone, came as a result of a chance meeting with the Russian playwright Simenov. On an impulse she expressed the wish to study the Moscow theatre and an invitation duly followed. She was given a twelve day visit of packaged culture and came home to bubble her enthusiasms in a BBC radio programme. Apparently her method of coping with impossible Russian names was to call everybody Popov: 'Very rude, but they didn't seem to mind.' Armed with a post-war currency allowance of five pounds she returned with the statutory pot of caviar (which she passed on to a friend) and snowdrops from Tolstoy's garden, to be carefully pressed and preserved in her scrapbook. She had nothing but praise for the vitality and enterprise of the Moscow theatre, but the visit did not change her way of life, nor did it affect her political thinking. On the contrary she was distressed by a profile tribute to her in the *Sunday Times* which included a description of her as 'a charming intellectual, apt to be dissatisfied with the world as it is, and to think it can be made better by political action.' She caused a footnote to be inserted in the following week's issue stating that her steadfast belief was that the only remedy for the troubles of the world was the practice and principles of the Christian faith. Party politics, it was stated, seemed to her to compromise the real issues and the second article went on to point out that her association with a society for cultural relations with Soviet Russia had been wrongly assumed to have a political significance; for her it was merely an expression of the Christian precept to love your neighbour, even to love your enemy.

Her return to the theatre was something of a rescue operation, for the 1948 season at the Vic had not begun happily. Edith was glad to be back in familiar haunts, geographically and dramatically, spreading Congreve's wit for John Burrell's revival of *The Way of The World* in such inimitable style that everybody could tell the difference between the margarine and the butter. On this occasion, mindful of the criticism she had received for Cleopatra, she relinquished her dazzling Millamant to the young Faith Brook, to give theatregoers that great ruin of a woman, that 'antidote to desire', Lady Wishfort. One feels sorry for Miss Brook, condemned to efface either the memory of Miss Evans or the 'peeled wall' actuality of Dame Edith. It was an impossible task, for Edith sailed across the Old Vic stage like 'a galleon on the Kensington Pond' broadsiding poor Miss Brook to temporary oblivion. She flamed through the play in a way that threatened to make the rest of the proceedings appear the bungling efforts of a village dramatic society. Only Robert Eddison in the role of Witwould managed to stay afloat in her wake.

(In a letter to me written shortly after Edith's death, Robert Eddison related a typical flash of her humour. 'We once had a rehearsal chez moi, and I prepared a trifle: the custard had curdled slightly, for which I apologised: her eye glinted as she said "I adore making custard . . . it's the element of *danger*." A pity that a Biro can't reproduce her intonation . . . I know that the poet was describing the voice of the Serpent when Ralph Hodgson wrote of it "soft as a bubble sung Out of a linnet's lung" but it never fails to make me think of Edith's. I think her Rosalind the most wonderful performance I've ever seen—run close, in another vein, by *The Whisperers*. I sent her a card from New York when I happened to catch this film: she probably knew anyway that the canopy over the cinema carried the legend "There's nobody like this Dame"!')

In November 1948, Edith gave a performance that many had been waiting for: Madame Ranevsky in *The Cherry Orchard*. Although brand new, it seemed to have been aged in the wood, the blended product of many exceptional years. Such moments in the theatre cannot be adequately described; they are like sunrises or sunsets that one sees when walking alone; you rush back indoors to fetch a companion and share your wonderment, but by the time you have returned to the scene the miracle has passed and you can only stutter your mundane explanation of the unexplainable. Edith's Madame Ranevsky will forever remain the epitome of her art in my memory. To use her own word, she *assumed* a beauty that transcended artifice: I can use my mind like a slide projector and illuminate the screen of past experience with the image of the farewell scene with the axes ringing like some funeral toll outside. It was as if she had never been anybody but Madame Ranevsky; her own personality was obliterated, she had taken Tchehov's imaginary lady and made of her a total living creature. The poignancy of that last scene was unforgettable. I remember returning to my sordid bachelor lodgings, a basement in Bayswater, filled with a mixture of exultation and despair. I was struggling to bring some life to my own minor performance as Gertrude Lawrence's son in *September Tide*, and the wonder of Edith's artistry made me acutely aware of the difference between mere performing and actual genius. I hope this revelation, deliberately personal, does not appear too absurd; but if one is young and ambitious one can live with competence in others, one can just endure the luck and better fortune of contemporary rivals, but total perfection, far from inspiring, slits ambition's throat.

At that time, of course, I was a newcomer to Edith's unique versatility, but collectors who come late to their passions have few equals. Unfortunately, great theatrical performances are not like stamps: there are no duplicates to swop with fellow maniacs. The late arrival in the field must compensate by bidding recklessly for what is to hand, and I did just that, for in the following year, 1949, Edith appeared in James Bridie's *Daphne Laureola* and I auctioned my heart six times.

Bridie's dramatic compost allowed Edith to blossom as never before. Many of the critics were unable to decide whether Bridie had written a play, a whole play and nothing but a play. He had always been a wayward skirmisher from across the border, dancing over his crossed swords of wit and leg-pull, bag-piping his own inimitable tunes of glory in a way that distressed the English, who can never rid themselves of the belief that all comedians really long to play Hamlet. My belief is that Bridie was a Hamlet who insisted that pouring poison into people's ears was a very comic pastime. His enormous virtues as a dramatist of true originality still await full recognition (how often is he revived nowadays?) and although the late Alastair Sim made repeated and valiant attempts to convince the doubters that here was something more than a foreign jester, his true worth was never weighed in critics' gold.

Bridie, whose real name was O. H. Mavor, was chauvinistically disinclined to accord women much credit for anything: Edith was one of the few exceptions he allowed and his devotion to her and admiration of her went back many years. Edith returned his affection and on one occasion, at a civic luncheon in Glasgow when Bridie had torn up his prepared speech and delivered a euology about Edith, she got to her feet to announce that should Mr. Bridie's dear wife ever decide to release him from his present engagement she intended to marry him herself. Bridie's correspondence to her was a mixture of praise and good natured, if firm, scolding, for she turned him down as she turned down Shaw; Edith never let friendship or love interfere with art. There was much of Shaw's temperament in Bridie; I get the feeling that he said and wrote deliberately provocative things in order to maintain the public image of a 'character'. There was little malice in him, though he was too intelligent and too aware of his own gifts to conceal the disappointment he felt that his talents were seldom fully recognised.

Writing from a Military Hospital in Belfast during the war he assured her that she could do no wrong in his eyes: 'They tell me that you are a damned good revue artist, but that went without saying. You would be equally overwhelming as a handcuff queen or an impresario of performing seals. That is not news . . . I have not written a play for you. I doubt if I ever shall. Great actors exist, I think, to breathe the breath of life into dead plays. Anybody could play in my plays (they are alive) and they are, therefore, a waste of great actors—or would be if any great actors were the least bit interested in them. Anyhow there are no great actors except yourself and Spencer Tracy and, perhaps, Harry Baur, Emil Jannings and Gertrude Lawrence. So what the Hell? . . . Nobody loves me and I don't give a damn. But I would still like a letter from you. Ever yours, Great Madam, Jas Bridie.'

After *The Queen of Spades* Edith asked him whether he would like to adapt a novel of Louis Golding's into a screenplay for her, but he declined in characteristic style. 'I don't intend again to adapt another man's novel. If they offered me Rabelais or a job of my own, I might think of it. But not a Louis Golding, even with you in it.'

Just prior to the 1939 war Bridie had written one of the few plays by a contemporary playwright to be produced at the Old Vic. This was *The King of Nowhere* in which Olivier scored a personal triumph in the leading role of Vivaldi, an actor of unbalanced mind. I found an undated letter from Bridie amongst Edith's papers and from it deduced that Bridie had first offered her the female lead.

'I am sad but not surprised at your verdict on *The King of Nowhere*. It is, of course, one of the best plays that has been written in the last fifty years; but there is a little syllogism that applies:

1. No great actress can tell a good play when she sees it in type.

2. Edith Evans is a great actress.

3. Therefore Edith Evans cannot tell a good play when she sees it in type.

No. 1. is a well-known and well-tried axiom, so I am not downcast. It is one of the laws of nature that the Edith Evanses of this world (so unhappily few they are) go down to posterity for their performances in (a) parts written by dead dramatists (b) showy parts in third-rate plays. If you don't believe this read your History of the Theatre; read Shaw's letters to Ellen Terry; read Hazlitt.

Forgive me for answering back! Of course I'd write a play for you if I could; but I am afraid I have strutted my brief hour in the West End of London and must get back to my medicine bottles with an occasional flight on the BBC.

Ever yours, OH.'

He wrote more in the same vein in another undated letter: 'I am not a cowardy custard but a very intrepid person; for I have dared to criticise you and got away with it—more or less.

'Among shoddy plays in which you have appeared are *As You Like It* and *The Taming of the Shrew*. The first a very cynical and anti-social bit of work and the second more suited to Alfred Drayton and Robertson Hare than to one of your Eminence and Sensibility. The Author of both these plays, tho' an Immortal Genius, is, I should point out to you, physically dead. Whereas Mr. Shaw and I are alive and gasping to have the rays of your greatness shed over us. Mr. Shakespeare doesn't give a damn. And, it is all very well to express your affectionate regard for a person and then let a person starve to death and his wife and family!

by not acting in his excellent plays. Yours more in anger than in sorrow, J. Bridie-Chatterton.'

According to Bridie's biographer, Winifred Bannister, Edith had not been his first choice for the role of Lady Pitts, though this statement is difficult to reconcile with the extra evidence at my disposal; having gasped for so long to enjoy the rays of Edith's greatness it hardly seems likely that he would have offered his finest female creation to anybody other than Edith. After the event he pronounced her 'gloriously miscast' and enjoyed his good fortune in securing her. (He particularly enjoyed the 'daily reminder' in the form of the box office return slips with the steady sum of £291+ on them!) The play was presented under Laurence Olivier's banner with Murray Macdonald directing and introduced the late Peter Finch to London audiences in the role of the young Pole, Ernest Piaste, who falls in love with Lady Pitts, echoing Bridie's real-life of 'Goddess!'

Some of the critics professed themselves baffled by Bridie's intent as well as by his execution, but all were united in praise of the finest first act to be seen in London since Barrie's *Shall We Join the Ladies?* This first act framed an Edith that nobody had seen before. She sat isolated, aloofly pensive in Molyneux satin, occasionally downing a double brandy and immediately ordering another. All around the seedy inhabitants of a Soho restaurant called *Le Toit aux Porcs* indulged in desultory snatches of conversation while ordering from the more Anglo than French menu. We knew that a time fuse was burning but had no inkling of what form the eventual explosion would take.

J. C. Trewin has described the historic moment as being like a rocket —Edith soaring 'unheralded into song, Massenet's *Elégie*, in a clear, loud mezzo-soprano: "*Au doux printemps d'autrefois*"'. And after Massenet, Bridie's songs, for when cast and audience had recovered from the shock, Edith gave voice to his prose lyrics, orchestrating them as only she knew how. Nothing I had read about her, nothing I had hitherto seen, had prepared me for this moment. I suddenly realised what all the fuss had been about over the years: the verdicts of Poel, George Moore, Agate, Herbert Farjeon and St. John Ervine were illuminated by the experience of that moment. Here was an actress at her transcendent best in perfect partnership with her material (and perhaps I should add, her *contemporary* material). Whether it was genius pure and simple, or a mixture of genius and observation, I neither knew nor cared. Her technical command of Bridie's invective was a thing of beauty to hear and watch. Of course it was theatrical and if one was foolish enough to push emotion into the background and attempt to analyse the cut and thrust of Bridie's brandy-saddened argument as spoken by Lady Pitts, one could find holes. But what a pointless pursuit! Better by far to surrender to the theatrical tides of emotion and drown in happiness. Bridie wrote superb dialogue for actors to get their teeth into, designing, as it were, the perfect interior for the house of his imagination and then bricking it up any old fashion. His deliberate disregard of the conventions of dramatic form was what antagonised many of his critics. What really mattered on this occasion was that he had written a great female role at a time when there was the perfect actress to play it and his luck held. I would rather have theatricality married to emotion than the play of ideas that is emasculated of all emotion for the sake of those ideas. There were so many individual moments to savour and return to (familiarity, in this case, breeding a hardly-to-be-contained expectation). I recall—hearing it now as though it had been recorded for me on the finest equipment— that brandy-varnished rejoinder Edith hurled like a well-aimed bottle across the stage: 'Keep your blasted trap shut'—a nothing line when lifted from the text in isolation, but, when given the Edith Evans treatment, violent comic poetry.

Bridie was beside himself. He wrote to say he was delighted to be 'living on your earnings . . . I get letters too, of course. The latest was from Mr. Priestley who thought you very effective, though the restaurant scenes pleased him less than the Second Act! The other letters are almost maniacal hoots of delight from start to finish. But what care I for them? I am content that our infant, Daphne, should have your eyes, nose, face and everything else. I am a proud parent.' He had previously written after the first night to tell her that 'If you have read the newspapers you will have seen that even the newspaper boys have realised that you are one of the greatest actresses who ever lived. I say "one of" with what is called characteristic Scots caution, because I do not wish you to know what I really feel about it.'

He sent her a copy of the published play inscribed 'With Love and Gratitude' on the cover of which he had drawn Edith with glass upraised rising, phoenix-like, from a flaming sunset.

The play ran for nearly a year at Wyndham's before going on an extended provincial tour, Cecil Parker replacing Felix Aylmer as the husband when the production went on the road. Edith later spoke of it as 'a very favourite play' and that 'almost all of it was glorious.' She recalled, 'I had to be drinking too much brandy and get very tight, and as I don't drink at all I wasn't sure I was doing it properly and I remember saying to Peter (Finch) "Peter, when I face you, am I really tight?" and he said, "absolutely blotto."' It was quite true that she did not drink; I only ever saw her sip a glass of cider at lunch and she had a horror of real drunks.

It was a time of contentment for her; she said she felt 'refreshed' by the play and London and her peers rose to her. She received some extraordinary tributes from her fellow actors, who knew the real thing when they saw it. Yvonne Arnaud wrote that she had had a few moments in her life when she had experienced great Art, and listed the first time she had heard Beethoven's 9th Symphony, the dancing of Nijinsky and Karsavina, and Edith in *Daphne Laureola*. Anthony Quayle felt that he had never seen Edith '(or any other actor or actress for that matter) give such a relaxed performance. It was as though you brought to the stage a mastery of your art which has now become so habitual with you that you wore it and forgot it, like a perfect garment.' This seems to me the most perceptive description of Edith's magic that I have ever read, and it is fitting that it came from an actor.

When *Daphne Laureola* opened on Broadway in September 1950 the placards proclaimed Edith as *The Greatest Actress of Our Time* ('Flattering, but lacking in taste', was Edith's comment) and the producers Leland Hayward and Herman Shumlin stated that they had 'the honour to present' Edith. It was a red carpet return but, once again, despite personal notices that could not have been bettered, the play itself was savaged. Joe Murgatroyd, one of the imported British cast, gave an interview in which he said 'the notices were so bad I was frightened of opening my dressing-room door on the second night. I expected to find Martin Miller—he shares my room—lying in a pool of blood with a revolver by his side.' The play survived for only fifty six performances. Brooks Atkinson may have stated that 'Miss Evans brings glory to the theatre' but it was not enough for New York audiences and Lady Pitts sang for the last time on November 4th 1950.

Her American producers swallowed their losses with honour and no regrets, Herman Shumlin writing a farewell note which he left in Edith's dressing room.

Dear Dame Edith,
Tonight, riding to the theatre, I was thinking of you, and of the unique experience it has been to watch you on the stage and to listen to you. Most of my life I have heard and read of Duse, and Bernhardt, but I never saw them. I have seen fine actors, many of them, but I never saw in them qualities which deserved the sort of wonder the name of Duse evoked. I know now there is another level, the level of greatness. Now I know what people must have known when they saw Duse. I have seen you.

Ten days after *Daphne* closed on Broadway Edith was speaking Christopher Hassall's commissioned Prologue for the gala reopening of the restored Old Vic in the Waterloo Road. It had been dark for nine years. Lilian Baylis, dead since 1937, would have enjoyed the irony of the occasion. It had taken one of Hitler's bombs to provide the fillip for building the theatre of her dreams. 'This is Lilian's day,' Edith declaimed. 'London, be glad! Your Shakespeare's home again . . .'

She came home not only to honour, but to be honoured, receiving the first of three degrees *honoris causa*. The Senate of the University of London had written to her in May 1950 asking if she would accept a Doctorate of Literature and the ceremony of the conferment was performed on the Celebration of Foundation Day, November 24th 1950. It was a year for awards, for 1950 had commenced with her being voted Actress of the Year by the *Daily Express* Film Tribunal for her performance in *The Last Days of Dolwyn*. Arthur Christiansen, the Editor, wrote telling her that the award carried with it a gift up to the value of £100, and asked her to name her choice. Edith replied by saying she would like the £100 sent to the Equity Benevolent Fund. She was always uneasy about acting awards. I think they offended her sense of propriety. 'I don't really agree with it,' she once told me. 'In my young days, if they liked you, people gave you a dinner or something, but all this voting . . . what a business it is. I'm not very fond of voting. When they say, One Man One Vote . . . I don't think so. You should have to justify yourself, we all ought to qualify for our right to vote . . . I'm not at all sure I'd qualify. And acting awards, no, I don't think so, thank you very much. I wish they'd do away with them.'

1950 brought sorrow, too—grief for the death of Shaw who died two days before *Daphne Laureola* closed in New York. 'That's something else I never understood. Why was I never close when those nearest to me, those I loved, died? It's as if God arranged it that way—but did he arrange it for good or bad, I wonder?'

At the end of January 1951 the Shaw of Scotland died; thus within three months the two greatest contemporary dramatists were gone; two close friends, so much alike. Bridie had been ill for some time, anticipating his end with his own brand of the macabre. 'Death looked me in the face,' he quipped, 'and cut me Dead.' Edith wrote a tender obituary for him and consented to serve on the newly-formed committee to establish a memorial Trust for Shaw at his bleak Ayot St. Lawrence home. She was fast becoming a pillar of the theatrical establishment. At 62 she still had a zest for living and gave the outward appearance of enjoying her every moment, but admitted to me that this was a period of intense personal loneliness. So many of her old friends had died and each new death reminded her of Guy and her parents. She had never been more successful in the public eye—Cambridge University followed London in honouring her with a Doctorate of Letters—yet never more conscious of her private isolation. Years before Sickert had captured the darker side of her moon in a portrait painted at Thanet which to the end of her life hung in the sitting room of her home in Kilndown: the shyness that disarmed close friends but kept casual acquaintances at a distance; the lazy eye she tried to hide with her long tresses as a young girl; the slightly petulant mouth in repose—an unconventional portrait dictated as much by the subject as by the style of the artist. She didn't feel any older, she didn't look any older than she had done twenty years before. 'Marking ages is a sign of deterioration,' she used to say and before long was writing to the Editors of *The Times* and the *Daily Telegraph* requesting that henceforth her birthdays should not be noted in their social columns. She became more fashion conscious and her visits to Hardy Amies salon became more frequent. She was asked to serve on numerous committees and was very active working for her less fortunate colleagues. This was the period when the annual Theatrical Garden Party in aid of the combined theatrical charities was a great social event and Edith could be found dispensing tea and taking part in side-shows, though she drew the line at selling kisses for 6p a time ('It's always a mistake to sell affection,' she said in one of those rare moments when she lapsed into her Lady Bracknell voice).

It was at such a garden party, I believe, that she first made the acquaintance of a middle-aged admirer, Judith E. Wilson. Miss Wilson had followed Edith's career for many years and had formed the habit of sending small but regular donations with the requests that Edith make use of them as she thought fit. Nothing in Edith's life ever followed conventional patterns and her eventual close friendship with Judith Wilson began in improbable fashion. Edith did not like coming in contact with her audiences, and although she was always gracious to fans and would reply to their letters, she never cultivated them or allowed them to intrude into her private life.

In the beginning Judith Wilson wrote most formally, starting her letters 'Dear Dame Edith' and signing them 'Yours most sincerely.' There was an element of schoolgirl crush about them, and a kind of humbleness which, taken to excess, could have become embarrassing. Miss Wilson was a woman of some means, much travelled, well read and a devotee of the arts. Now, in her middle years, she concentrated her admiration on Edith, tentatively at first, apologising for 'having trespassed so audaciously into your leisure' and indeed her early letters are touching in their simplicity, revealing, I suspect, that she was basically a very lonely person. At all events she touched a chord in Edith, who at one point asked what it was that had prompted such interest. Back came the reply in the round, schoolgirl handwriting, 'The answer is simple—just "Gratitude"—Gratitude because I love all the arts and the theatre in particular. And to you not only because you possess qualities which only the very greatest artists down the ages have possessed and have acquired the skill which enables you (and them) to show us the beauty of intangible things in their simplest form . . . I suppose at the back of all my gratitude is a love of life, which is what art represents.'

They eventually met, Edith having sent Judith a ticket to attend the conferring of one of her honorary degrees. Judith responded by sending her a gift of an antique coffee pot which, rather surprisingly I think, Edith accepted. Other gifts followed, including a diamond butterfly brooch which, Judith wrote, 'seems to belong to you so I hope you will accept it with my love in memory of one of your loveliest parts and of our friendship which I value more than this butterfly or any words of mine can ever express.' Edith kept the butterfly all her life and it is mentioned in her Will, her Trustees being instructed to 'sell the same and apply the proceeds thereof to buy guide dogs for the blind.'

Perhaps the friendship blossomed because of a shared loneliness. Edith was increasingly solitary after the death of her father and the companionship which Judith provided may have stemmed from hero-worship in the first instance, but over the years it matured, like some late-flowering plant, to lighten a dark patch in Edith's life.

Daphne Laureola was a hard play to follow, and with Bridie's untimely death all chances of a sequel from the same pen had vanished. Edith was sick and tired of revivals, bored with being asked to rework previous performances. Bridie had given her a taste for experiment, but the younger playwrights—possibly awed by her reputation and, in ignorance, assuming her to be only a *grand dame*—failed to pick up the thrown glove and write for her in contemporary terms. Equally, nobody in the film world accepted the challenge (though in fairness I must add that Herbert Wilcox toyed with the idea of filming the Lilian Baylis story with Edith in the title role). Eventually she narrowed her choice of what was available to her and selected a Tchehovian pastiche by N. C. Hunter called *Waters of the Moon*. Frith Banbury, an ex-actor turned director, justifiably praised for his quiet, unflamboyant inter-pretations of Wynyard Browne's plays, and a man who has never received proper recognition for his significant contribution to the post-war theatre, used Edith as the lynchpin of his cast. He then achieved a notable double by securing the services of Dame Sybil to play opposite her and surrounded them both with players of the calibre of Wendy Hiller, Kathleen Harrison, Cyril Raymond, Nan Munro, Owen Holder, Patricia McCarron and Harold Scott.

The advance reports in the press made much of the fact that this was the first time in the history of the theatre that two Dames had appeared in the same play, and soon the tattle was that they were feuding at rehearsals: give the gossips gold and they will turn it into dross. Dame Sybil made a characteristic, bring-them-down-to-earth observation: 'I'm one up on Edith,' she said. 'I've been closer to a pantomime dame' referring to the time she had played the White Queen in a Christmas production of *Alice In Wonderland*. She also sent Edith a postcard photograph of herself inscribed 'The other old Dame Doctor!' (Lewis Casson and her family had been against her accepting a lesser role than Edith's, but such considerations had never bothered Sybil. She liked the play, she liked and admired Edith and there was the added bonus that her role called for her to perform some of Schumann's piano music on stage, which she thought would be fun. Like Edith she was never so happy as when she was working, and if there was an extra challenge, so much the better.) At the weigh-in the spectators were disappointed that both contenders observed the Queensbury Rules, and rehearsals proceeded without undue incident. Critics sharpened their pencils and studied their Roget's Thesaurus' in expectation.

It was Festival of Britain year, and London powdered its bomb sites, opened a Fun Fair at Battersea in the park and a new concert hall on the derelict South Bank, eventual home, twenty five years later, of the long-awaited National Theatre. There was an element of desperate improvisation about certain aspects of the Festival (some of the exhibits on the South Bank looked as though they had been constructed from a child's Meccano set) but there was a conscious, national desire to throw off the war-time austerity and don some glad rags for a change. The gaiety was somewhat forced at first and the British indulged their capacity for self-mockery to the full, but gradually, reluctantly in places, tongue in cheek perhaps, we started to wave the flag and enjoy ourselves for the first time since the hysteria of VE Day. (VJ Day, as I recall, was a curious anti-climax).

Waters of The Moon may not have satisfied those pedants who were demanding only works of pure genius to grace the Festival, but it did provide a play of quality, mood and elegance worthy of Edith and Sybil. The audiences certainly got their money's worth. Edith, like a brilliant bird in perpetual migration, alighted on the seedy Dartmoor guest-house which was the setting for the piece, and proceeded to dazzle the humdrum inhabitants. Sybil, a cardiganed owl, burning primly in ferocious silence, sat perched and watchful. One critic, Gerard Fay, remarked that 'anybody intent on getting the full flavour of the acting would need to see the comedy twice, concentrating on a different dame each time—for how can a person with two eyes watch simultaneously the extravagant antics of Dame Edith and the glacial repose with which Dame Sybil tries to smother them?' Honours were evenly divided, but audiences and the profession remained fiercely partisan and it was all good for business.

Doubtless enjoying their new double-act, both ladies gave performances of another sort at the annual Equity meeting that year. The issue on which they both spoke so passionately was concerned with regulated entry into the profession. Sybil, wearing 'a startling green hat and beating the air' was violently opposed to the motion. 'We must have freedom!' she declared. 'The great bother about the whole profession is that we have become too darned respectable and everybody wants to get into it.' Ignoring the heckling from certain sections of the meeting, she swept on, 'People ask, why don't I get jobs? Probably because they bore the audience and they bore the managers. We don't want bores in the theatre. We don't want standardised acting, standard actors with standard-shaped legs. Acting needs everybody, cripples, dwarfs and people with noses so long. Give us something that is different. You have to get through the rabble to get to the top—there's tons of room at the top.' It was stirring stuff, delivered with gusto and obviously enjoyment. When Edith's turn came she gave another of those delightful examples of platform-acting which, mercifully in our union, do much to relieve the tedium of routine business at the annual meetings. Like Sybil, she did not mince her words. 'We should all shut up telling people acting is so glamorous. Tell people about the boredom and hard work they must survive to get anywhere on the stage. I know that if I'd had to go and take an exam for acting, I wouldn't have got anywhere. You don't take exams for acting, you take your courage.'

Despite their combined efforts, the motion was carried on the day but never, thank goodness, put into practical effect, though the same motion in one form or another still comes up with depressing regularity every year. As Edith once remarked: 'I can't bear people who, having got inside themselves, want to exclude everybody else. Such arrogance.'

The friendship between Edith and Sybil although firmly based on mutual respect was not without its occasional volatile moments. John Casson's memoir of his parents includes a wonderful story built around an incident when Sybil indulged in a little overacting for the benefit of two of her grandchildren who happened to be in front for a Saturday matinee. Such a lapse from discipline reduced Edith to tears and the stage manager felt compelled to ring Frith Banbury. He dealt with this 'border incident' with a diplomacy that should have earned him a Civil List pension from the Foreign Office (although his actual letter to Edith is somewhat more explicit than his memory of it as related to John Casson). It was a passing peccadillo, but graphically illustrated the difference in temperament between the two distinguished Dames. Sybil's ebullience and *joie de vivre* could never be suppressed, while Edith was made genuinely ill by what she considered unprofessional behaviour. The spat did not last for long. When the play had been running for a year, Binkie, who was presenting it, felt that Edith's Balmain costumes should be replaced with new ones. Edith was graciously pleased, but would not be favoured alone. 'Sybil,' she insisted to Binkie, 'must have a new cardigan.'

During the run of the play she found time to chair the committee formed to present a special matinee performance at the Old Vic to mark the centenary of the birth of William Poel. Edith took part, speaking with Lewis Casson of Poel's work and methods. She also made an addition to her Will, expressing a wish to be cremated and her ashes placed in St. Paul's, Covent Garden (known as the Actors' Church). St. Paul's is also the final resting place of Ellen Terry's ashes, though to the best of my recollection Edith never made any mention of this.

By now Edith had acquired an agent to conduct her business affairs, selecting Olive Harding who worked for the London office of Myron Selznick (brother of David and the first of the really high-powered Hollywood hustlers who revolutionized the terms actors obtained during the long-gone era of studio contracts). Olive also happened to be my agent, and indeed mothered a whole roster of clients, Claire Bloom, Paul Scofield, Michael Gough, Dorothy Tutin and Virginia McKenna amongst them, concealing a Churchillian tenacity behind the most feminine facade. It was Olive who first introduced me to Edith, in 1952, when I was fortunate enough to be sharing a set of chambers in Albany with an old friend. Our chambers were directly across the Ropewalk from Edith's and when, in February 1952, King George VI died, Olive asked me if I would squire Edith to the agency's premises in St. James' Street. A selected number of clients had been invited to watch the funeral procession from the balcony of the building which afforded a splendid vantage point. I accepted the commission with some trepidation, being frankly in some awe of Edith, having been guilty of accepting all the stories about her at face value. At the appointed early hour I presented myself at her door, soberly attired and feeling somewhat like an actor auditioning for the role of John Worthing. Edith was instantly charming and before we had gained the outer courtyard of Albany I had been put at ease. We walked together through the damp and silent streets; the combination of that solemn hour and my sudden intimacy with a living legend loosened my tongue and although I doubt whether she was impressed by my conversation, she gave no indication. She looked magnificent, and I noticed that our progress across Piccadilly and through the back streets to St. James' was the object of much attention from other passers-by. It was a heady moment for me, though when, in later years I recounted my emotions to Edith and professed how much I had been in awe of her, she seemed genuinely astounded. 'That's something I've never been able to understand. Why anybody should ever be in awe of me, I'm such an *ordinary person.*'

I remember that we stood side by side at the open windows that looked down into St. James' Street. The sounds of military orders being given in the courtyard of St. James' Palace where part of the funeral procession was being formed up seemed amplified in the dank, still air. From far away a military band began a funeral march; orders passed along the ranks and, like cards in a slowly falling pack, the Guardsmen lining the route reversed arms and dipped their busbied heads. Edith reached for my hand and gripped it as the lone officer leading the cortege came into view. That morning had the very stuff of history all about it and whereas there are many things that the British botch, we are unsurpassed at staging our public entrances and exits. I applaud the theatricality of our pomp and circumstances, and to witness such an example by the side of someone like Edith heightened all my perceptions and the memory is still deep-etched. Edith, too, was deeply moved and I cried with her. She was a Londoner and London was saying farewell to a beloved king, its inhabitants coming together in their hundreds of thousands in unrehearsed but perfect homage, bearing silent witness to a faultless piece of pageantry.

That was the sombre beginning of our friendship and although I often entertained hopes that I would be asked to join the cast of one of her plays, I had no idea that I would one day direct her, for my debut behind the camera was a decade away. I cannot boast of immediate intimacy, for to tell the truth I doubt whether Edith was aware of me other than as 'that nice young man who brought me to the funeral' as from time to time she enquired of Olive Harding. We stopped and exchanged pleasantries whenever our paths crossed in Albany's Ropewalk, but the eagerly awaited and always regretted opportunity to act with Edith never came my way.

I followed her career more avidly than before and doubtless exaggerated my friendship with her to anybody who would listen, actors being prone to exaggerate everything from their notices to their love affairs, and mine was a love affair. Such an admission is sure to offend those who take the narrow view that no biographer should declare his hand. I cannot help it. There is no such thing as a totally impartial opinion.

While *Waters of The Moon* continued to employ the House Full placards at the Haymarket, Edith found that she could not escape Lady Bracknell. She took part in an all-star radio broadcast, reunited with Gielgud and Gwen Ffrangcon-Davies, and then was persuaded to carry her celebrated handbag to Pinewood Studios and commit it to celluloid for Anthony 'Puffin' Asquith's film version of *The Importance*. Michael Redgrave, by now firmly established as a film star of international status, replaced Gielgud as John Worthing, for in those days Sir John was considered too mannered and uneasy before the cameras, a typical illustration of the idiocy that has always bedevilled the British film industry. Asquith's film, though lavishly mounted, was not, alas, spectacular cinema but had the supreme merit of preserving Edith's matchless characterisation for posterity. Alan Dent's verdict was 'a farce of much importance' and long may it so remain.

Waters of The Moon achieved 834 performances and when the run ended on May 2nd 1953 all previous records for the Haymarket had been broken. Edith and Sybil had never missed a performance. The arguments for and against mammoth runs such as this continue unabated. Edith's view, which I share, was that they are bad for the living theatre. They restrict inspiration and stifle spontaneity, for it is impossible to ensure that every artist in a long-running play will be able to play at peak form month after month, or indeed, in some cases, year after year. The commercial theatre is not geared for regular rehearsals of the main cast during the course of the run, managements and directors are lazy, content to watch only the box office returns and not the general level of performance. The average West End play, if it settles down to a long run, usually becomes a pale imitation of its original self. There will be nights when everything comes together and the adrenalin is shared, but more often than not unsuspecting audiences are cheated of the vitality necessary to sustain true interest on both sides of the footlights. I am not pointing a finger at any particular play, but over the years I have observed many instances where the boredom of constant repetition has reduced a once vibrant production to the level of a Ford assembly line. A repertory system such as enjoyed by the Royal Shakespeare and National Theatre companies is a revelation by comparison.

Edith confessed that she felt buried and sometimes disorientated by long runs. Naturally it is not so critical for a major star to be tied to one play over a long period: they have the greater responsibility and the disciplined talents they have acquired to merit billing above the title carries them through. For lesser-known actors an extended run can become a prison sentence; the money is regular, but they have been taken out of circulation to occupy a luxury cell, release from which pushes them out into a world that has often forgotten their existence.

During the last year of *Waters of The Moon* there had been much talk of a new play from Christopher Fry, then heralded as the New Elizabethan dramatist—for as the Coronation of the young Queen approached comparisons with the reign of Elizabeth I abounded. Everest was climbed at a propitious moment and we were assured that the post-war tiredness would finally give way to a new age of adventure. There was much speculation about the renaissance of the poetic drama and the laurel wreath passed from T. S. Eliot, to the younger and immensely more attractive figure of Christopher Fry. He at least *looked* the part and in the space of six years had become the brightest hope of the British theatre, bringing some dazzling verbal invention to the otherwise fairly impoverished post-war scene. He was not a man who wrote at white heat ('How I wish I could write plays faster,' he wrote to Edith) and his promised offering to her was a long time on the drawing board. It finally went into rehearsal, under Peter Brook's direction, at the beginning of 1954, and the author's advance description of it was 'a winter comedy'. It had the Hungarian revolt of the 1840's as its setting and bore the enigmatic title *The Dark is Light Enough* (which Noël Coward perversely insisted on referring to as The Light is Dark Enough), taken, as Mr. Trewin informs us, from Fabre on the butterfly that moved without hestitation to the end of its pilgrimage in storm and profound darkness. Like that other lover of butterflies, Nabokov, Christopher Fry has always been intoxicated with the sound and mystery of words, and in Edith he found a perfect practitioner of his art. Using her unique voice to net Fry's choicest specimens she made of his Countess Rosmarin Ostenburg an enchantress of infinite variety. Although most of the critics allowed that it was a pleasure to be exposed to the quality of Mr. Fry's mind, there was much argument as to what exactly was the meaning of the play. Mollie Panter-Downes, the London correspondent of *The New Yorker*, expressed the collective doubts with some elegance: 'The net result . . . is curiously like looking at figures through a sheet of glass traced with the frosty ferns and diamonds of Fry's verse.' Edith's Hungarian butterfly became another collector's item.

Trailing Cambridge as in a number of recent Boat Races, Oxford gave Edith her third Honorary Degree in June 1954, the ceremony taking place in the Sheldonian Theatre. 'Lo and behold a most welcome guest, whose countless curtain calls and tributes of flowers have become a familiar sight to us,' declaimed the Public Orator as Edith was led to his side. 'If many of her qualities spring from nature and not from art, if the rest have come to her from the very best of teachers, if she has fulfilled three old ambitions—to bring out in her speech the full beauty of English, to match finely written plays with fine performance, and in peace and war alike to spirit away the cares of mankind by her acting— she has never taken the credit to herself, but has counted these things as blessings bestowed by fortune and has striven to be worthy of such gifts. She is the jewel of our stage.'

An entry in her near-neighbour's Diary for September 22nd 1954, sheds lights on another aspect of Edith's character which is sufficiently rare in the theatre to be worth noting. Sir Harold Nicolson was not only a fellow resident of Albany, but his country home at Sissinghurst Castle, Kent, was close to the house Edith moved to the following year. Having taken his wife, Vita, and Rose Macaulay to see *The Dark is Light Enough*, Sir Harold invited Edith back to Albany for supper with pink champagne. He found the play 'a silly pretentious' piece 'redeemed only by the excellence of Edith's acting' but in the same entry also recorded that he was becoming very deaf and could scarcely hear a word, which hardly gave him the right to judge Mr. Fry of all people so harshly. Speaking of Edith, he wrote: 'Like all the older generation, she regrets that younger people are not trained sufficiently. She says her own training was rigorous and at times almost unendurable. Unlike most actresses, she says nothing unkind about other actresses, speaking with real warmth of admiration about Peggy Ashcroft.'

I am glad to have this confirmed by another writer, for in my experience it was rare indeed for Edith criticise other people's work. The most she would volunteer, if pressed for an opinion, would be to say, 'I didn't care for it much' but the usual elaborations, so fondly indulged by the majority of actors of my acquaintance who like nothing better than to score points at their best friends' expense, were entirely alien to her. She could express intense irritation if she was subjected to slovenly diction or unprofessionalism, but her diatribes never descended to the level of character assassination.

Sir Harold and Vita Sackville-West were responsible for discovering the Gatehouse at Kilndown in Kent where Edith made her final home. They both wrote to Edith, sending particulars of the property which was of considerable historical and architectural interest, being a superb example of a late 15th century Kent weald hall house which had once belonged to the Sabbes, clothiers of nearby Goudhurst. The house had been the subject of a long article in *Country Life* in 1937 when the then owner, a Mr. Grinling, had carried out extensive renovations to restore it. The outstanding feature of the house was a Great Hall supported by massive arched trusses cut out of the solid oak in the time of Henry VII.

After disposing of Washenden Edith had tried to convince herself that she had no need to put down roots in the country again, that the elegance of Albany was sufficient, but once persuaded to view Gate-house, fell in love with it. Her enthusiasm did not blind her to the fact that it was far too big for one woman of simple social ambition, and she also felt that the asking price (by today's standards a modest £8,000) was beyond her means. Again it is worth noting that Edith had no head for figures and in the years that I enjoyed her confidence would periodic-ally become convinced that she was poised on the brink of penury. She could be very generous to those in need, but was curiously ashamed of indulging her own whims. The solution to Gatehouse was provided by Judith Wilson, by now a close and most valued friend. Judith suggested that she purchase the house and that they share the running costs and after some deliberation Edith fell in with the scheme.

'Darling Coz,' Judith wrote when the contract was finally signed, 'I do feel rich not only in money, but in qualities far more precious. I have been given such a lot in life, but what I have valued most is the trust people have put in me and though the responsiblilty (because it is a great responsibility to have in your hands the trust of great people) sometimes frightens me I shall do my best to be worthy of the honour and with God's help I hope I shall never fail in that respect.

'On the way home I bought such a lot of things! in the shop windows!!

'Thank you darling for all your love, ever your devoted Judy.'

The element of innocent hero worship persisted despite their changed relationship, but there were sceptics amongst Edith's circle who doubted whether Judith would survive under the same roof. Perhaps some of their doubts were not devoid of envy and malice, since those who claim the closest bonds are often quickest to resent any newcomer to the fold. Judith was an outsider, but from her formal introduction to Edith's way of life she went on to become one of Edith's dearest friends, and she provides yet another example of the way in which the pattern of Edith's life refused to conform. Edith could not have been the easiest of people to live with. When working and especially in rehearsal nothing and nobody was allowed to interfere with the creative process. Although in later years she claimed with unquestioned sincerity to be ordinary, she patently was not ordinary to other people. She could be demanding of attention, had lived most of her life alone, even a greater proportion of her married life had been spent parted from Guy, and such solitary habits are not easily disposed of. Whatever the problems, Judith surmounted them and the setting up of their shared home proved a success. Judith provided material as well as financial comforts, furniture and paintings, including some superb Augustus Johns. She was extremely well read and many of her books in the library which Edith eventually inherited show that she had always been a student of the theatre. Thus her scholarship complemented Edith's instincts and the marriage of minds was a source of endless pleasure to them both. She gave Edith what I think she always secretly craved: an intimate friendship without sexual bonds.

1955 brought other upheavals beside that of settling in a new home. In May of that year Edith signed a new contract with Binkie to appear in André Roussin's *Nina*, translated from the French by Arthur Macrae and to be directed by Rex Harrison. The announcement was greeted with some surprise, for it was Edith's first attempt at a contemporary farce and the Broadway production with Gloria Swanson in the same role had been abortive. From the outset the project was beset with problems. Indeed few productions have been more dogged by disaster. That admirable actor Charles Goldner had originally been cast as the male lead, but was taken ill after the first reading and died ten days later. The play was a three-hander and naturally Edith had cast approval; Binkie and Rex Harrison had to strike a delicate balance when suggesting a replacement for Goldner, but eventually everybody agreed on David Hutcheson, who joined James Hayter to make up the trio. Rehearsals commenced but soon became bogged down with differences of opinion between Edith and her two leading men as to the style of acting that should be adopted. Rex Harrison has described how whenever he went up on stage to personally demonstrate a scene with Edith she would sigh with relief and openly state how much happier she would be if only Rex was playing opposite her. Naturally I was not present at these rehearsals, but I have ample personal experience of how flirtatiously persuasive Edith could be whenever she wanted to get her own way. Rex Harrison had the perfect escape route for such ploys, since he was then appearing in *Bell, Book and Candle,* and the rehearsals staggered on in a growing atmosphere of discontent. In his own autobiography Rex has described how things got to such a pitch that he was even able to set aside Edith's aversion to any form of drug and persuade her to swallow a phenobarbitone time bomb, which she took out of sheer desperation. Although the rehearsals proceeded to a dress rehearsal that Rex termed 'an absolute glory' Edith's emotional volcano was still building to the final eruption. I have no doubt that she willed herself into a state of panic, sensing that she was not giving and could never give of her best. Her personality was such that could not have admitted to a mistake, but had to find a solution that, to herself at any rate, she could justify. It was something she had never previously experienced: a sense of failure *before* the event, the classic nightmare that lurks beneath the surface of every actor's subconscious.

The play was due to open out of London, in Liverpool. Rex arrived at the Adelphi Hotel there, lulled into a feeling of complacency by the smoothness of the final rehearsal in London, only to be told by Binkie that Edith had undergone some form of nervous breakdown and was unlikely to appear. The unfortunate understudy was inadequately prepared for such an emergency, being some light years away from word-perfect. A further dress rehearsal was held in Liverpool with the understudy reading from the prompt script and everybody else beseeching that a miracle should happen. An atmosphere of profound despondency settled over the theatre while they awaited the medical opinion as to whether Edith would recover in time for the opening night. She did not recover and the first night was, to those most closely concerned, an unparalleled disaster. It is difficult to imagine a more ghastly theatrical situation than the opening night of a three-handed French farce in which the star attraction fails to appear and her marathon role is taken over by an unrehearsed deputy who 'wings' the dialogue from an ill-concealed script. Adding his personal element of farce to the proceedings, the distinguished and all-too-unsuspecting author arrived from Paris in the fond expectation of witnessing England's greatest actress score a triumph and was greeted with a shambles. Rex very sensibly retired to a pub across the road until the dispirited audience had dispersed.

That good old standby 'influenza' was used as the reason for Edith's non-appearance in the press statement, while behind the scenes Binkie and Rex retired to lick their wounds and decide what, if anything, could be retrieved from the debacle. Coral Browne was brought in to replace Edith for London and Michael Hordern took over the David Hutcheson role. *Nina* finally opened at the Haymarket in July 1955 and there is irony contained in Alan Dent's *News Chronicle* review which began 'We come away from André Roussin's play, not so much regretting that

Dame Edith Evan's indisposition has prevented her appearing in it, as wondering why she ever had the notion that it would suit her.'

Edith deliberately blotted out this sad episode in her mind and could never be persuaded to discuss it in after years. I am sure she was deeply ashamed of her inability to uphold those standards of personal and professional behaviour by which she had always set such store. Unable to excuse herself, she took the only other course open to her and by a conscious act of will persuaded herself that it had never taken place. If this seems conjecture, I can only state that Edith always sought to give me this impression; it was not an act of dishonesty but an act of self-deception. The heart of the matter was that, at some point early in the rehearsals, she had come to the conclusion that she was miscast. Her professional pride refused to allow her to admit of such horror and she therefore worked herself into such a mental state that she produced the physical symptoms of ill health. It was, I suppose, acting of a high order on another plane.

By an accident of timing, although the live audiences were denied seeing her on the West End stage, the newly-launched commercial television channel (which Edith had once lobbied against in the House of Commons, rightly fearing that it would lead to an invasion of canned American reruns to the detriment of the British film industry and British actors) brought her into numerous homes during the Fall of 1955. Inevitably she was asked to parade her Lady Bracknell again like some prize specimen from a theatrical Cruft's dog-show; her Agatha Payne from *The Old Ladies* was also displayed for the wider audience of television, and here some viewers and critics found Edith's characterisation too overwhelming for the small screen. During the filming of *The Old Ladies* she met Dr. Billy Graham. He remarked: 'We in the ministry could learn a good deal from you how to put our message over.' 'Yes, but you ministers have an advantage over us,' Edith replied. 'You have long-term contracts.'

She was mobbed by 500 theatre fans, most of them women, when attending a dinner given in her honour by the Gallery First Nighters' Club, an organisation which, in its heyday, could strike terror into the hearts of managements and actors. A certain clique within the club always fancied themselves as budding Agates and showed their disapproval by what is euphemistically known as 'the bird'. On this occasion, when she rose to reply to the toast in her honour, she commented on the 'lack of unity and corporate craftsmanship in the theatre. We shall get people back into the theatre again when we are able to enchant them.' The advent of the commercial television stations had hastened the demise of many theatres and cinemas. The actors, unable to lick them, joined them, and Edith was amongst those who joined. She appeared for a third time in twelve months gracing the small screen in a truncated version of Wynyard Browne's *A Question of Fact*. She took the role first created in the stage version by Gladys Cooper, and was required to smoke a cigarette, something she accomplished with style, albeit without pleasure.

Her professional path crossed that of Gladys Cooper again when she agreed to appear in Enid Bagnold's *The Chalk Garden*. Miss Cooper had played the same role in the smash-hit Broadway production that had flirted with failure before achieving success. During rehearsals Miss Cooper had shown a certain reluctance to speak Miss Bagnold's exact words, stating at one point, 'I'll approximate them'—a suggestion that brought the redoubtable Miss Bagnold out of her corner ready to send gum-shields flying. 'Nobody approximates me,' she said, determined that a play that had taken four years to write would not be paraphrased by Miss Cooper or anybody else. Miss Cooper took a count of eight, recovered and went on to learn the lines and give a performance that delighted author, audiences and critics.

Anxious to have a London production, Miss Bagnold (in private life Lady Jones, the wife of the late Sir Roderick Jones, former head of Reuters) sent the play to Binkie. 'He took the script home with him to the country on a Friday and on Tuesday I got a letter in his curiously childish writing turning it down in which he said that he couldn't stand allegorical things. I wondered what on earth he meant. The only thing I could think of is that chalk is dry and the heart is dry, but that seemed very tiresome.' I immediately told Harold Freedman, my agent, who said "never mind" and showed it to Irene Selznick. She refused it at first but couldn't get it out of her head. She came back to Harold and said, "I can't forget it, but I think it wants altering, titivating." She was frightfully good at that. I'm not a plot woman, I'm very bad at plots. When I've made a mountain I make a valley which undermines the mountain. Irene pulled out the valleys and threw them away and she was at it with me for about two years, and then she took it. Harold then paid one of his yearly visits to England and Binkie asked him whether he had any new plays that might interest him. Harold said, "I don't think so. There is one that Irene Selznick has taken." "Oh," Binkie said, "what's that?" "It's called the Chalk Garden." Harold told me, "Binkie never moved a muscle." Binkie's great thing was choosing the right actors and actresses at the right moment. He was not really much for choosing the right words.' At this point Miss Bagnold had not shown the play to Edith, but now, on October 13, 1953, she wrote to Edith. (I must apologise to the reader for now slipping back two years, but it is important to tell the whole story, and the history of Edith's involvement with *The Chalk Garden* was spread over three years).

Dear Dame Edith,
Years ago I was to have tried to write a play for you. I admire you
more than any living actress and I have always been teased by the
longing to do something you would want to act. I have now been
nearly two years on a play called *The Chalk Garden*, in which,
alternately, you seemed to me to be Miss Madrigal or Mrs. St.
Maugham. . . . I had already sent it to Binkie who turns it down
categorically as being obscure, symbolistic, confusing, mad, and
altogether too full of cross sections of character. I don't ask you to
plead my cause. *That* is not why I am sending it to you. If he doesn't
like it he won't do it.

But do *you* like it? It is not meant to be symbolistic for a moment. It is
maniéré, written in an odd language (as my Serena was), and is a
comedy, if that's the word. It has a bearing on life . . . quite obviously
seen in the last act—that the murderess has had fifteen years *think*—
and is a grown-up person.

I know you are rehearsing. But if you have time to read this play I
shall be deeply grateful. You have never been out of my thoughts for
these last 22 months . . . as I saw you move about the stage of my
mind. Yours Enid (Jones or Bagnold)

The previous play referred to had proved stillborn, but an interesting
letter exists, dated November 23, 1942, which throws much light to the
darkness that surrounds a playwright in the throes of creation.

My Dear Edith,
I am horribly in need of help, and don't know where to look for it. It
is an old need, never properly attended to. I will tell you about it.

At the beginning of each book I have written (certainly *Serena
Blandish* and *The Squire*) I have spent several *years* groping about and
making half-blind gestures towards a kind of inner gleaming shape,
very dimly and uncertainly lit at first, but clearing and becoming
definite gradually. Several years. *The Squire* certainly ten years.
Serena several years.

Now no one can write plays like that. It would be agonising; and bad
for the *movement*. But here I am . . . doing it again. It makes me quite
sick.

There are two things you can do (one of which you mustn't do). You
mustn't talk to me *spiritually*; or suggest I make the play of any
mixture—love, tenderness, or anything like that. Either I can or I
can't or I don't want to. I mean if you suggest the *inner shine* you will
be pulling the kernel out of my nut. Try to remember that because it
has a terrible effect on me. I am powerless to forget what has been

suggested and also powerless to try and do it.

But if we could have a practical talk it might mean all the world; and I might get off on my race instead of this dreadful hanging about at the starting post. I have, I am sure, all sorts of qualities to write a play. I am very observant; my dialogue is nearly what I want it to be; I am capable of making talk carry two meanings; I have a sense of the theatre; and when I am lucky I can make people live. I have even a sense of construction, when there is something to construct. But, oh, that's the crux. I can't often say to myself 'Look at Shakespeare, he had the same trouble'. But then he didn't bother. Any old story and he hung it like a Christmas tree with his great baskets of golden words. But still—he *had* the same trouble.

You said 'Write the story of a day', when you were in the kitchen. And I felt too it would be something that I could do, and do well. But where is our conflict? And must we have it? Don't write to me about this. Much better talk about it.

I suggest that you come down here this coming Sunday in time for lunch (no clothes, just a little attache case and a tooth brush and the bus); that we don't talk about it *at all* that day (that's very important, because it's Timothy's leave from his Brigade and Laurian will be here and I am three quarters of a mother on Sundays and it bothers me, in front of them, to have them reminded of the writing part and I answer, half-ashamed and preoccupied and feel at my worst about writing and even when Roderick is there I don't like talking about it. It isn't that it isn't important to him and valued by him but I just keep it very much apart until it's finished) . . . Well, to continue after that large bracket—stay the night, and that next morning we come over into my writing room and spend the two hours that I should ordinarily be in front of my typewriter (and staring at white paper) talking very practically, as though we were two hack playwrights intent on screwing out a plot to please the public, good sturdy professional plot-hunters about the play, its construction, the meat there is to be served up in the first act, the second and the third. We'll talk as though it just had to be done for an exam, or for our living. I'll hold my spider's web tendrils up, my little airy nothings, and my little tiresome, un-joined exquisitenesses and you'll say, 'Heavens, but that's not enough to make one act! Let alone a play!' And then I shall believe you and know we must get some stuff into it. I believe I could get over a great difficulty like this. I do hope I shall hear from you that you can. Desperately   Enid.

It was a fairly formidable request, but Edith accepted the challenge and twelve years later Miss Bagnold still remembered with gratitude. Despite their combined efforts the collaboration did not, apparently, produce the required results. Now, jumping forward once again to 1953, Miss Bagnold was eagerly awaiting Edith's reaction to *The Chalk Garden*. The verdict, when it came, was thumbs down.

29, Hyde Park Gate,
London, SW7
November 11.53

Dear Edith,
My head, bloody under misfortune, is still unbowed. But it is a bit bent.
Bad notice of my trifling play at Q last night . . . and much worse is that you don't want to play in the other play . . . which to me isn't trifling. Oh dear, oh dear—and how I saw you walk about in my mind. Never mind—at the moment I don't believe in age and will find the ability to write something you do like—in the next twenty years. Thank you for saying the things you did. They weren't easy. I know the whole letter wasn't easy. . . . Yours Enid.

Those who pursued Edith seemed cast from the same mould. Like Shaw before her, Enid Bagnold refused to take the first 'no' as being the end of the affair. She worked at the play again and following its successful opening in America it was resubmitted. Just to jog Edith's memory she wrote in July 1955 a week or so before sailing to New York to begin rehearsals there with Gladys Cooper. '. . . It's always been my longing that you should act in a play of mine. Never mind that it isn't this one. Perhaps it will be the next. Or even perhaps—if this *were* a success in New York—you would do it in London? Anyway—you are the greatest actress speaking English and I pray for you one day . . . I do hope you are better . . . I sail on August 11. Pray a second for me. I am a grandmother. How can a grandmother iron her old clothes and sail off to face Broadway . . . Yours Enid.

As a postscript she added 'from Enid Bagnold (in case—humbly—you don't know).'

News of the play's success travelled back to London, to Binkie and to Edith and the case of Lady Jones *v.* Tennent's and Evans was reopened. Both Binkie and Edith had a change of heart. Edith hedged a little and at first expressed the wish to take the part of Miss Madrigal, the role eventually played so brilliantly by Peggy Ashcroft.

'I told her, You are a goose and a genius both,' Miss Bagnold related to me, recalling all at age 87. (At the time she was enjoying yet another success: Katharine Hepburn was packing them in with a post-Broadway tour of *A Matter of Gravity*.) Edith took the compliment and the rebuke. 'I think it's true', she answered. 'That's why I don't like parties. The goose talks always.' Finally, it was agreed: she would do *The Chalk Garden* and she would play Mrs. St. Maugham. Or would she?

235

                                            Rottingdean,
                                            Sussex.
                                            Dec. 9.55
Dear Edith,
I am taking it as true—that you really said you would play Mrs. St.
Maugham. I am covered with a film of happiness which makes me
immune to any doubt that you might not have said so.
I kept hearing that note in your voice that I heard in America when I
was longing to have you, longing to hear everything I wrote said by
you. A sort of silvery caress on a word here and there—the sort of
caress that the writer gives her own words when she whispers them to
herself . . .
Did you ever know Catherine d'Erlanger? There are things in Mrs.
St. Maugham that I learnt from her—from Ottoline* and from Lady
Sackville . . .† and finally a little from Margot.‡ The extraordinary
authority that power gives to a woman who can provide a platform
for the world. Such women who, by their wit attract, by their wealth
can provide, by their position have never to seek . . . develop something which queens should have—a facility in words, a rapid appraisal,
a power to defend, a power for accolades . . . an unfair power often,
but a power that gives them magic. They cannot escape arrogance,
they are often extremely selfish, they are spoilt—but nevertheless they
are *rare* (and fast disappearing). My Mrs. St. Maugham is an aristo-
crat, overbearing, wilful, ageless, defiant of age, able to tip out words
like a jet plane, while thinking of something else, but she has something of the 18th Century about her—a Whig pride, a Regency carelessness. The situation of the daughter is so well known—the daughter
who will not conform, who has not the same standards or the same
ideal and drives her mother mad. But all the same, beneath the
exasperation, Mrs. St. Maugham deeply loves—though she hides it . . .
and 'she did not know she would one day so need a daughter.'
For me there is no one like you on any stage.
For fifteen years I have been wanting to write something that you
would play. This part will suit you, Edith, I swear it. And as for
'fretting' you, you won't hear a word from your breathless and happy
author . . . Enid.

I find this an extraordinary document: moving, humble, but not
falsely so, shot through with acute observations on the nature of female
power and, finally, exuding that rare form of happiness which attacks
authors when they sense that what they have so painfully and for so long

* Lady Ottoline Morrell.
† Mother of Vita Sackville West.
‡ Margot Asquith.

236

struggled to convey has found recognition. In parts, Enid Bagnold could have been describing Edith, in parts she was describing aspects of herself.

She wrote again in December, asking how Edith was settling in at Gatehouse and inviting her to come and have lunch in London to discuss the play and the character of Mrs. St. Maugham. She felt 'so proud that you are going to do it and so full of curiosity at what you will give to it.' But Edith had grown into the habit of keeping authors at a respectable distance during the gestation periods. Safe in the knowledge that her perfect Mrs. St. Maugham had been netted, Enid Bagnold could take Edith's aloofness without panic.

'I know what you mean about not talking to me about Mrs. St. Maugham,' she wrote on January 10, 1956. 'I would feel the same (and always do) when I am writing. There is a far and infinite horizon, and if anyone discusses—it limits it. Don't be afraid I shall—unless you ever want me to. But all the same there is the whole world to talk about besides the part! Come and lunch with me soon, either alone or with the whole family (I'd so love them to know you before it all begins) and we'll breathe no word of play. I am tremendously excited and oh so tremendously lucky. I shall never forget (I never do) the talk you and I had about playwriting one day in the Courtyard at Rottingdean . . . No hurry, but let us meet. We are so important to each other that it's wisdom on your part to stipulate that our main subject lies still as a pool between us. Love, Enid.'

Enid and her family watched Edith play Agatha Payne on television on January 14th 1956, which Enid pronounced '*absolutely* wonderful . . . I couldn't recognise you, except for the extraordinary acting I would never have thought it was you. I kept thinking of what miracles you will eventually do with *The Chalk Garden*. Don't bother to answer this— and don't think I shall ever exclaim 'Oh, it's not like that!'

By the end of February the play was in rehearsal. A cast befitting the occasion had been assembled around Edith and Peggy. Felix Aylmer, George Rose, Rachel Gurney and Judith Stott were amongst those who came together under Gielgud's direction. From Enid came 'my little prayer of faith . . . My love, and *never let me bother you by a breath*. You'll find me no trouble.'

During rehearsals Edith asked Enid to lunch with her 'on condition that you don't mention my way of acting or anything about it at all until I say you may.' Enid agreed and described to me what happened after that. 'We began and we lunched and we talked, rather drearily, of all sorts of other things. The lunches went on every day, and it was a big order to lunch with one person. Well then one day came when she said, "Now I will tell you. Trying to get hold of a character like I am trying to get hold of Mrs. St. Maugham is like trying to put on a dress. You keep taking them off and putting on another dress. If you are disturbed during all that you get a feeling that you will accept second best, you put on any old dress because you are so sick of changing, and you are perhaps rather sick of boring the author by changing the dresses so often. But I have got the dress now, the script, and you may say something if you like. One thing only, you may say." "Alright," I said, "I have got a very small thing—it's a dash, if you like, a pause in the middle of a certain sentence which you don't make and you should make." I showed her the sentence I meant. "Now you've ruined it," she said, "you've ruined the whole thing and I don't know whether I can go on. I shall dry up every time I get near it." That went on. Of course she didn't, she forgot all about it, but that was the sort of thing that happened.'

The play opened at Birmingham's Alexandra Theatre on 21st March 1956, the opening night being delayed until the Wednesday—an unheard-of-day for a Midlands premiere—because extra rehearsals were required. It came to the Theatre Royal, Haymarket the following month, on April 11th. Edith's devoted author had seen it on tour and wrote her a pre-London letter of comfort.

> North End House,
> Rottingdean,
> Sussex.
> April 1. Easter Sunday morning 1956.

My Dear Edith,
I slept badly last night and thought a great deal, and of you . . . It must be so easy for an actress to *disbelieve*. Praise is a sort of need—to cover the wounds of creation. Our relationship, yours and mine, is delicate. I have to pass what I value most dearly over to you; and you, in receiving it, are in deadly earnest to do it as I would wish it—and yet must find your own way.

Having pointed out that the relationship must be delicate (like Solomon's two women over the one baby) I want you truly to believe that this time the thing has worked, for me. Whatever else happens to my play this strange and satisfying thing has happened—that your outer voice has used the same terms and song as my inner voice when I wrote it. *Please* believe that. Sometimes you look at me so doubtingly. But perhaps it is that humble half-doubt of yourself? You are so little confident.

For me when I am in that state (of little confidence) it is when I am writing. And then I am hidden. But you, when you are in the act of creation are on show (even if it's only the author in the stalls of an empty theatre—and I can see that matters almost most of all) and you have to conquer your humility and find your way to the heart of the character and listen to your inner voice—all at once and in the open. That is the big difference.

238

Mrs. St. Maugham in Enid
Bagnold's *The Chalk Garden*,
Haymarket, 1956.

The Countess of Rousillon in the
modern-dress production of
All's Well That Ends Well,
Stratford-upon-Avon, 1959.

Judith Bliss in Coward's *Hay
Fever* with Louise Purnell,
National Theatre at the Old Vic,
1964.

Right: Being directed by Fred
Zinnermann in *The Nun's Story*,
with Audrey Hepburn.

Above: Taken at Gatehouse during the making of my television documentary of her life, just after her first heart attack.

Right: Leading Edith on to the set at Pinewood for *The Slipper and The Rose*, 1975.

The last photograph of Edith –
taken in the garden at Gatehouse
on 5th October, 1976.

But I'm rambling on. What I want to do, before the play comes under the eyes of the critics, is to say that *me* you have satisfied! More than satisfied. Delighted. It was the Evans voice I heard, as I wrote and it's that voice I hear again, with a curl like a silver branch in it, a branch across the moon.

I'm dying to see all the points and delicacies that will have crept in under your hands. I do so love to listen to you in the play. This is to thank you—so truly, so sincerely—from my heart . . . With my love, Enid.

Enid Bagnold described herself to me as a poet, 'a poet who's no good at plots', and the letter I have just quoted at length reveals, I think, not only the poet, but a remarkable lady. Her patience with Edith, her understanding of Edith, but above all her ability to write in perfect harmony with Edith's genius is something that the theatregoers of 1956 will always have cause to remember with undiluted pleasure. What an evening in the theatre it was! A play of complex, compelling interest, exquisitely staged by Gielgud and played to perfection by the entire cast. London rose to it, and Tynan, finding his authentic voice, opened his *Observer* notice with the pronouncement: 'On Wednesday night a wonder happened: the West End theatre justified its existence . . . The occasion of its triumph was Enid Bagnold's *The Chalk Garden*, which may well be the finest artificial comedy to have flowed from an English (as opposed to an Irish) pen since the death of Congreve . . . London gives her the actors she needs. Dame Edith Evans . . . suggests a crested wave of Edwardian eccentricity vainly dashing itself on the rocks of contemporary life . . . In this production we see English actors doing perfectly what few actors on earth can do at all: reproduce in the theatre the spirited elegance of a Mozart quintet.'

The play nobody wanted became the play that everybody rushed to praise. Edith and Peggy were headlined as a 'Parnership of Glory' and for Enid Bagnold it was an unqualified vindication of her unwavering convictions. She had bided her time, knowing exactly what she had mined during the long years it had taken her to write what is, I think, her masterpiece, and her patience had outlived everybody's doubts, and in the end, seeing all with her poet's eye, she lived to enjoy her 'silver branch across the moon.'

15

'What I want to give in the theatre is beauty, that's what I want to give'

Edith's life at Gatehouse with Judith during the all too short time they enjoyed together was different from anything she had previously experienced. The home they made together was warm and comfortable rather than elegant. Edith had no hobbies and few real pleasures outside the theatre, but she encouraged herself to potter around the sloping garden that enclosed the house on three sides. The fourth, and blind side, of the house butted against a farmyard, the boundary being a cattle shed which caused offence in a hot summer. The garden was shapeless as most English gardens go, and Edith was no Vita Sackville-West, but she liked to walk between the broad herbaceous borders that led from the double-windows in the sitting room, a walk on grass that was always damp and spongy, and which descended to a circular pool where fat carp swam lazily in water made perpetually bottle green by the overhanging trees. One entered the house through the kitchen, for the main door leading directly into the great hall was never opened to my knowledge. White doves fluttered from the side of the tithe barn, a section of which had been converted into a series of dormitories for hop-pickers in the days when Cockneys made the annual pilgrimage. The other half of the barn housed great quantities of hewn oak to be burnt on the superb open fire-place in the hall. It was the sort of fire that once you sat in front of it of a winter's afternoon you were doomed to a nap; sleep engulfed you like a warm sea. It was one of those perfectly constructed fireplaces where the fire, once lit, never goes out. William, Edith's chauffeur-handyman-caretaker, would bank it with a dozen or more logs some three feet long and they would slow-burn their way to fine ash. In the mornings it needed but a few smaller logs to crackle into life so that by the time the guests had come down from their rooms the heat would have risen to warm even the vastness of that hall.

Even though she still retained her chambers in Albany, Edith spent more time at Gatehouse than she had at Washenden. She and Judith entertained modestly, for Edith was no gourmet, preferring simple dishes —good, farmhouse cooking, as it were. She was very proud of the fact

240

that she had helped design and build a brick fireplace in the sitting room, a smaller and cosier room where afternoon tea was taken and where the Sickert portrait stared down at the photographs of Guy in his army uniform. Despite the fact that Judith brought a considerable library with her, Edith was never an avid reader, spurning most fiction, but increasingly drawn to biographies and poetry. Her great friend, the poet Richard Church, sent her inscribed volumes which she treasured, but her love of poetry was catholic and to hear her read Ogden Nash or Betjeman was sheer delight.

Her bedroom was spartan and her dressing table held few cosmetic aids. She was not a great one for perfume and once amazed my two daughters by suddenly giving them half a dozen unopened bottles of expensive Chanel and the like. 'They were given to me, but I shall never use them' she said as they made off with their prizes, quickly drenching themselves with such a variety of fragrances that they smelt like two old Gerrard Street whores. All unbeknowing of her exalted position in the theatre, my children, when small, treated her as they would a slightly eccentric aunt and this, I think, pleased Edith. Although she had many godchildren and religiously observed their birthdays until age 14, she was never completely at ease with the younger generation and lacked any real comprehension of the patterns of child behaviour. My wife, Nanette, had cause to observe this when she and Edith were playing together in my film *The Whisperers*. My script called for Nanette to launch a violent verbal attack on Edith, and the continuity was such that Nanette had to act with a black child in her arms. We 'borrowed' a suitable baby for the occasion and Nanette felt it expedient to warn Edith before the scene was shot that babies are very unpredictable. 'Don't worry, Edith dear,' she said, 'if he starts to squawk during the scene. I'll just plough on.' 'No, that won't happen,' Edith replied. '*All* babies sleep after lunch.' Nanette didn't think it worth exploring the matter further and, after lunch, we duly began shooting the scene. Under the lights and with Nanette in full swing the baby set up an almighty howl and pushed the soggy remains of a rusk into Edith's face. I think it was the one and only time I ever saw Edith completely at a loss as to how to react. I invented some technical fault and cut the take. 'That child,' Edith said, 'is an exception.'

Like so many childless women she thought that the only method of dealing with children was to spoil them and she took great pleasure in ordering a particularly delicious chocolate cake, which she had specially made in a Soho patisserie for the many birthdays she faithfully remembered. She kept the letters and drawings that her godchildren sent her, and there is an element of sadness in her keepsake books, for they reveal a sentimental streak she was careful to hide from most people.

Her diaries, in contrast, were sparse of comment, recording only the minimum of detail. For twenty years, almost without exception, she used a pictorial calendar and diary published by the Norway Travel Association; a study of them reveals nothing more than a series of appointments, mostly written in pencil in her large and, to many people, indecipherable handwriting. (Sadly, quite a number of her friends have confessed to me that the reason they did not keep her letters was that they could seldom understand them.) Likewise her scripts are mostly devoid of any personal comments; her role would be underlined and occasionally she would jot down a stage direction to remind herself of a move, but they bear no resemblance to the usual run of dog-eared documents that the majority of actors end up with. In many ways, the state of Edith's scripts bear out her whole approach to the art of acting. She was not an intellectual and she did not intellectualise her studies of a role. Everything had to come from within. Enid Bagnold has told me how, during rehearsal of *The Chalk Garden*, Edith suddenly stopped at a certain line and stood motionless on the stage. The rest of the cast and director waited. Finally Edith said, 'I don't think I can play this part.' Gielgud asked what was troubling her. 'This line . . . "and by some extraordinary carelessness she was violated in Hyde Park at the age of twelve." I can't say that.' There was a whispered consultation in the stalls and then Enid Bagnold ventured an explanation that the line was not meant to be taken literally, but was merely another example of Mrs. St. Maugham's eccentricity. Edith thought about this. 'I daresay I'm just a silly old woman,' she said and went on with the rehearsal.

Her success in *The Chalk Garden* was so total that again it proved a difficult play to follow. Everything that was submitted to her seemed an anti-climax. She was to wait another eight years before Enid Bagnold, a painstakingly slow worker as we have noted, produced another play for her. Failing to find any contemporary vehicle that attracted her, she returned to the Old Vic in 1958 to join Gielgud in a production of *Henry VIII* with Sir John as Wolsey and herself as Katharine of Aragon. The late Robert Speaight described Edith as having 'authority still intact in the face of death and humiliation' and I recall the performance for its quality of stillness. Few actors could listen as well as Edith did and there were moments in this performance that once again made me regret that Edith and Gielgud had never established a more permanent company together. Their partnerships were always made in heaven, whether Edith was acting alongside John or being directed by him. So different in temperament—John gregarious and volatile, working with a sentimental intensity of emotion to gain his ends; Edith withdrawn, feeling her way by instinct—they were yet ideally suited and on those occasions when they found the right vehicle for them both they complemented each other superbly.

This production of *Henry VIII* visited Paris in July 1958, the first time in 14 years that an Old Vic Company had been seen in the city. The play was presented in the Sarah Bernhardt Theatre as part of the British contribution to the International Theatre Festival. Somewhat crossly the London *Times* commented on the choice of 'this tedious piece of Tudor propaganda' being selected to open the British season. Surprisingly, it was Gielgud's first appearance as an actor in Paris; both he and Edith impressed the French critics, Tudor propaganda or no.

She stayed with Shakespeare the following year, this time at Stratford for the 100th season at the Memorial Theatre, appearing as the Countess of Rousillon in a modern-dress version of *All's Well That Ends Well* that Guthrie directed. Again there is a certain curiosity value in the fact that —apart from her two special performances as Cressida as far back as 1913—Edith had never appeared at Stratford. 1959 saw the end of her friend, Glen Byam Shaw's regime at Stratford, Peter Hall taking over at the start of the following year. She followed *All's Well That Ends Well* with *Coriolanus*, playing Volumnia, with Olivier in the title role. It was a production that aroused fierce, partisan feelings. I remain firmly in the camp of those who applauded, for Hall's production generated a tearing intensity, not unlike the atmosphere that pervades a boxing arena when two great heavyweights—in this case Olivier and Shakespeare—come together to settle a grudge. A portrait of Edith as Volumnia by Robert Buhler, R.A. was included in the 1960 Royal Academy Summer Exhibition and attracted some attention, for unlike some of her contemporaries Edith did not sit for many artists. (The Sickert portrait was painted from a newspaper photograph, much to Edith's annoyance at the time.)

During the run of *Coriolanus* she was involved in a car crash; she was thrown out of the front passenger seat and broke her wrist, cracked some ribs and was very badly bruised. She was out of the company for three weeks as a result, returning before she had completely recovered with her arm in plaster. It so happened that on the matinee of the day she resumed her role the young Albert Finney, understudying Sir Laurence, was called upon to deputise for him. They had a rehearsal for Finney on the morning of the matinee. 'The set had a lot of steps in it,' Finney recalled. 'We all had to do a lot of going up and down, I remember, and there were a couple of occasions with Dame Edith where, as her son, I had to hold her and guide her and go up the stairs with her. When we broke at the end of the rehearsal, I said 'Dame Edith, is there anything I'm not doing right, anything that worries you or throws you?' She said, 'Just be careful when you hold me because my ribs are a little bruised. So don't hold me, because it'll make me want to wince. I'll become aware that I'm bruised. Just put your arm within an inch or so, so that I'll know it's there if I need it, but don't grip me.' I said, 'Okay, yes, but is there anything, any move I'm making that's not the way Larry does it, that's sort of, you know, wrong?' 'Albert,' she said, 'move where you like, dear.

I'll get my face in somewhere.'

Early in 1960 Edith journeyed to Canada. She had changed her image. Her hair was shorn in a very unbecoming bob which aged her (she looked curiously like the novelist G. B. Stern) and almost for the first time in her life she had put on weight. She had been persuaded to take a solo 'turn', as she put it, to Toronto, to coincide with a CBC television production of *The Importance*. 'I even *exported* Lady Bracknell, they should have given me a Queen's Award or something for helping the blasted balance of payments.' Her live solo performance at the Crest Theatre in Toronto was the forerunner to her much-loved poetry readings that she gave a decade later. Choosing from a wide range of favourite poets, she proved to a packed and unfamiliar house that her mastery of comedy was not confined to purely theatrical roles. She could take a poem like Belloc's *Lord Lundy* and give it such light and shade as to make one believe that she alone had discovered the poet's meaning.

It was a period in her life when, slightly fretful, she was flitting between the different mediums. Like every other actor she grew depressed and withdrawn whenever she was between engagements and despite her unquestioned position in the theatre could easily convince herself that she would never work again. In the latter half of 1959 she had been persuaded to return to the cinema, playing Ma Tanner to Burton's Jimmy Porter in the film version of *Look Back in Anger* which Tony Richardson directed. It was not a role that demanded much of her, yet it seems to have surprised many of the critics. Here was the great Dame Edith Evans playing a common old woman and what is more playing her to the manner born. 'Doesn't it make you sick!' Edith exclaimed. 'I'm an *actor*, for goodness sake! The way they go on you'd think I can only play ladies of quality. I know more about the Ma Tanners of this world than I do about the so-called gentry. She's *real*, she's a *person*, isn't she? Well, what's all the fuss about then?'

She followed this with a small, but telling role, in her first truly international film, Zinnerman's *The Nun's Story*. She confessed she was astounded by the amount of fuss lavished on her by studio, director and crew; not that she was unaware of her 'exalted status' as she jokingly referred to it, but because it was an entirely new experience for her. The inclusion of a superstar like Audrey Hepburn, plus Zinnerman's own reputation, ensured that Edith was 'given the works.' The studio publicity machine went into top gear and she was given a glimpse of a world that she did not wish to inhabit to the exclusion of all else, but which, for a short period, fascinated her. There is no doubt that, had she so wished, she could, in the parlance of the movie industry, have written her own ticket to Hollywood at this period, becoming, in due course, the natural successor to Dame May Whitty and claiming every dotty, titled or eccentric old lady that Hollywood produced. But that wasn't Edith's scene. She enjoyed the cosseting she received, she certainly enjoyed the inflated salary, but she was not to be seduced away from England or the theatre on any permanent basis.

She became part of the film world and was invited to film premieres. One such occasion was the first night of *La Dolce Vita* and she took as her guest her Albany neighbour, novelist Margery Sharp. According to Miss Sharp Edith gave the film 'courteous attention until there appeared on the screen the bacchanalian orgy which was to demonstrate not only how *dolce* could *vita* be, but how terribly, truly shocking. At its climax, which as I recall involved young women, naked, riding upon the backs of young men on all fours, the unmistakeable tones rose loud and clear: 'I don't call *that* much of an orgy,' proclaimed Dame Edith disappointedly . . .'

Miss Sharp also took the trouble to relate an anecdote of a different sort. 'Late after supper at Albany one night she suddenly decided to demonstrate the art of playing Restoration Comedy. 'You must never *move*, my dear,' she instructed. 'Take the centre of the stage, then stand still and let your petticoats do the work. Swing them to the right, look over your shoulder' (here one saw the killing glance at Mirabell) 'or to the left (here Witwould was put down) but never be *busy* . . .' Miss Sharp concluded: 'All very well, I thought, if the petticoats had Dame Edith inside them . . .'

The remainder of 1960 was a lost year, a year of tragedy once again, plunging Edith into a despair blacker than any she had experienced since the death of her father and Guy. Judith died on April 11th 1960 after a painful illness. Death was always inexplicable to Edith; she felt she was being singled out and her religion did not provide the answers. She had felt that, in Judith, she had found a true friend with whom she could share the remainder of her years. They had made such plans together and, confounding those who had believed that such a chance liaison could not succeed, their friendship had matured into something rare during the five years that they shared Gatehouse. In her will, Judith left the house in trust for Edith for the rest of her life. As with Washenden, and in spite of her grief and loneliness, Edith stayed on alone, but it was the last time she gave her heart so completely to anybody.

Her public saw little of her during 1960. She appeared twice on television, once for the BBC in *The Country Wife* playing Lady Fidget again opposite Joan Plowright's Margery Pinchwife, and a few weeks later as Judith in Coward's *Hay Fever* for the rival commercial channel. She did not come out of her shell until the following year and even then her appearances were muted. Peter Hall persuaded her to return to Stratford-on-Avon for two plays the first being William Gaskill's production of *Richard III* with Christopher Plummer in the title role. Edith played Margaret, the widowed queen of Henry VI. Unfortunately I was unable to get to Stratford for any of the performances that season and therefore

245

cannot express any personal opinion. Some critics were disappointed with Edith, and indeed the entire production got a very mixed reception. Edith followed Margaret with what was to be her last appearance as the Nurse in *Romeo and Juliet*. The young lovers on this occasion in a complicated production by Hall himself that was described as 'anti-Zeffirelli' were played by Dorothy Tutin and Brian Murray. Over the years Edith had refined her performance, narrowing the angles of light and shade, 'tearing away', as she used to put it, like a painter, until she had reduced everything to the simplicity of a Matisse line drawing: only the essentials remained.

There were no stage appearances during 1962 and indeed, at age 74 even her redoubtable energies were beginning to wilt. One can truthfully say that you were never aware of age with Edith: she made no reference to it and it was generally known that the subject was taboo. Nevertheless she was to find the committing of a new role to memory increasingly painful. Her life, which alternated between weekdays in Albany and the weekends at Gatehouse, as had been the pattern with Washenden during the time Guy was alive, was tranquil, though, I suspect, empty. She had many friends who were pleased to visit her in the country, notably Masie Knox Shaw, who came most years from her home in South Africa to spend a long holiday with her. As always, Edith was concerned with the financial burden of maintaining two homes; she felt that it was too self-indulgent but perhaps sensed that a complete break with London might herald the end, and she was certainly not ready for that.

In 1963 she agreed to appear in a new play by Robert Bolt, called *Gentle Jack*. Enid Bagnold had sent her new play (*The Chinese Prime Minister*) the year before, but as with *The Chalk Garden* Edith's first reaction had been negative. Miss Bagnold, justly confident in view of their past association, had sent the script in November 1962.

Rottingdean, Sussex.
November 14, 1962.

Darling Edith,
Several things occur to me.
Don't show the script around (I meant to say this at the time). Also if you take advice (I know one does however certain or uncertain one is) don't take Binkie's or John's! John is in a 'Wesker state', I think. Dying to be new! And the 'new' becomes old before you can turn round. One of the charms of life is to see the rebellious angry young men becoming on the verge of fifty! Like Cyril Connolly.
I'll tell you this. Worsley* and Terence Rattigan and Trewin have seen the play and all three say it is better than *The Chalk Garden*. It is a

* The late T. C. Worsley, dramatic critic.

woman's play and that is why, though Lynn would have played it if there had been a part for Alfred, I couldn't in the end write a part for him, try as I would, because the integrity of the play wouldn't let me. It would have destroyed the whole point, which is, that one must take stock before Eternity. I mean—a *woman* must. Because women are not completely themselves most of their lives.

There! Bless you. And I await what you say with a longing heart. No one in the world like you for what I want to say. Love, Enid.'

She did not have to wait long, for Edith's reply must have reached her the same day as she wrote that letter.

> Rottingdean, Sussex.
> November 15.62.

Darling Edith,

I bore your blow this morning with grief and fortitude. You won't play it. But then you have a reason. And I want tremendously to know the clear reason. There is a most peculiar jinx about this play. Either people like it very much and madly defend it or they reject it, but without saying why. I *must* know why. It will be the very greatest help to me if you can look inside yourself and put your finger on the sort of instant distaste you must have felt. Is it something in the *hard* spirit of the play? That She rejects everyone, children and grand-children and husband, in order to get herself into spiritual shape? Is it that? Or is it what appears to be a 'trivial' approach? An approach which is intended and part of my own kind of irony. Dear Edith, please try and tell me. I know about the dentist and I do hope you aren't going to have a beastly time. I think it's only four more, you said. But what you won't like doing is to talk to me in the toothless interval . . . unless he jams new ones in on top? Sometimes they do (nothing about this distressful subject I'm not conversant with!) I must say—if I'd asked you to do the *Chalk Garden*—I mean now—you would either have relished (or not relished) the line 'Are my teeth on the writing table?'

Couldn't you dictate to me a letter soon, as soon as you can, saying frankly (I shan't mind) . . . 'I hate this play because there is some-thing hard and cruel about it' or 'I don't hate the play but I think the End takes a tumble.' Or—'I couldn't play that woman. She is a trivial, self-seeking woman.' Or 'It's just a bad play.' You see I can take it all. But for goodness sake let's have a reason. It's fair to me and oh so helpful. *Your inner immediate re-action.* That's what I want. I don't want an effort to criticise like a critic. Nothing that will take you trouble. Just the sort of instinctive thing you would exclaim to a friend in the room—when you lay the play on your lap, having read it.

Try. Soon. Not long. Just a few lines.

(then follow two lines, over-typed and obliterated)

All my love, Enid.

What I'd scratched out is . . . I hadn't read properly the last two lines of your letter before I flew to the typewriter, and now (brave Edith) I see you probably *can* come and dine on Wednesday night. Oh *hurrah*. Shall I have something very soft to eat? (for you) without mentioning it? Or will you toy with gravy and potato while delicately arranging meat round edge of plate? I'm so *delighted*. I had read 'dentist's chair' but was so put about—about your not doing the play—that I got to the typewriter, as I said, without taking in that you were probably going to be gallant and come. 8 pm. Wed. 21st. 29 Hyde Park Gate. Just Lynn, Alfred, Diana, Richard and me. And just possibly one other man. Doesn't put my table wrong in the least. Nothing ever does, and surely not *you!*

As is self-evident from this last letter, Edith was bravely facing up to what is, to most of us, an unwelcome decision. For an actress, especially an actress like Edith who had relied so much on her voice, to have to succumb to dentures is both mentally and physically painful. It meant, of course, that she had to learn to master a new technique, for although modern dentistry has overcome the old-fashioned disadvantages of false teeth, the fact remains that they are alien and in the beginning at any rate produce a psychological barrier. Poor Enid Bagnold had inadvertently chosen the very worst time to submit a new play. Edith was in a state of turmoil, about herself, her career, the state of the world. She telephoned Enid and told her: 'How can I be interested in a group of selfish people when there's Cuba, the bomb to worry about?' She also delivered herself of the opinion—always the reddest of cloaks to an author—that the play had no plot.

Back came Enid's spirited response.

Rottingdean, Sussex.
November 23.62

Dearest Edith,

If you want to send the play back here is an envelope.

But I am going to say first how wrong I think you are . . . You said on the telephone it had no plot. But we learn every day that to want a plot is old hat! . . . It's not the size of the subject that matters. It's the quality of the thought that is bent on the human heart. And the heart *makes* Cuba, *makes* the state of the world, makes everything tick.

In this play I write of a woman who, having experienced all womanhood, love, passion, birth, marriage, motherhood, grand-motherhood, exclaims

'I have never conquered the Me in me and don't intend to! Without it nothing has importance!'

She is seventy. She intends to be done with her loves, her time-table, her domestic harness, and stand up like a rock alone and look out with her eyes over the last sea. She sheds 'woman'—as a snake casts its fine silver skin. Who else but I could have written it? Because this is how I feel. This is an honest play that is written out of an honest heart. This woman isn't 'playing grandmother—playing cosy—playing abdication'. If I am not to live for myself *now*—she says—after three score years and ten—then when can I do it? She says in a speech, every word of which I could hear you say as I wrote it—

'I don't know what I am doing here, past seventy, being a mother!

—The *sheep* knows better than that and the *tigress* knows it!'

And because I have wound in—in my own manner—the great with the little—the passionate with the ironic—you think they are 'a group of selfish people.'

Listen to this—as an example.

Act Three

Bent

Didn't it do?

She

No, it didn't. Human love and human quarrels and reconciliations . . . and neither of us has time for it. We have each agreed we should be better concentrating alone—For after death I shall never know him again.—And I may have to know myself.

Bent

I am glad you are back. You were born to be a single woman. Women of individuality, are so uncomfortable for men!

You see that I purposefully counteract the deep truth of what She says with Bent's trivial and spiced irony? This is my way of writing. This is my way of presenting truth.

And you. You have two sides to you. One side is blinkered and hampered with want of judgement. One side depends on advice—and my God, who is there to advise who hasn't got an axe to grind among managers and their petty cohorts! One side reads with some curious difficulty so that she can't see the wood for the trees. One side is too afraid of where the other side is to take a stand!

Then there is (waiting) the grand Edith—who starts blind—not knowing what she's about. Then with nerves, terror, humility and greatness (I ought to know! I've watched her at it!)—breathes up the meaning through her hair, her arms, her feet—till the whole thing that is Edith is inhabited by what one has written. I don't wonder you're nervous at setting this incalculable and magnificent woman into action. About *committing* her. And perhaps committing her wrongly. But there is no one to tell you that *my* play is the ground on which you should stand—except *me*. And I tell you it hotly. Not because I am the wooing author, but because you and I together could make something understood that can only be said by a woman —and that perhaps hasn't been said before.

With all my love, Enid.

There, for the moment, the matter rested. It was to be another three years before Edith was convinced, persuaded, or perhaps the right word is flattered, into playing *The Chinese Prime Minister*. Enid Bagnold, a remarkable lady, who has written one of the best volumes of auto-biography of the past thirty years and who deserves to be judged along-side the other female giants of literature that England produces so regularly—understood Edith very well. Understood her, admired her extravagantly, but perhaps did not wholly like her. She worshipped the genius, but was irritated by the goose. Even so, she never allowed her irritation to divert her from her true purpose; she knew that Edith was the supreme interpreter of her words, and she never took the first no as the end of the story. Twice, and commendably, her tenacity was rewarded.

In spite of the well-argued pleas that Enid Bagnold put to Edith during 1962, *Gentle Jack* was the play Edith chose to do next. I think there was a streak of stubbornness in Edith which, as the years advanced, became more pronounced. *Gentle Jack* could not be counted amongst her major successes. She seemed, at times, curiously ill at ease in it, as though part of her—perhaps what Enid Bagnold referred to as 'the grand Edith' —never overcame the difficulties she always experienced with a new role. The play did not enjoy a long run and when next she appeared in the theatre she joined, for the one and only time in her career, the National which was then still occupying temporary quarters.

The choice of play showed belated imagination, and perhaps owed something to her television appearance four years previously. It was a choice that prompted intense and somewhat carping criticism in certain quarters when first announced. The idea of the National Theatre doing Noël Coward's forty year-old comedy *Hay Fever* offended some purists, but Kenneth Tynan, who first suggested it to Sir Laurence, stuck to his guns, and Sir Laurence supported him. I have mentioned earlier that I always felt it cause for regret that Noël never wrote directly for Edith, and there was a certain irony in the fact that, when they were both nearing the ends of their careers they should be united in this revival.

Noël's biographer, Cole Lesley, has described the genesis of Noël's play *Waiting in the Wings* which examined the lives of a group of retired actresses. Noël originally intended Edith to play one of the leading roles, sent the play to Binkie in the first instance (who refused to have anything to do with its presentation) and was subsequently informed by Binkie that Edith loathed the very idea. Binkie's perfidy on this occasion eventually came to light, and I can support Noël's own contention that Edith was never shown the play by Binkie. Edith kept every letter, every scrap of paper and yet I have failed to discover any correspondence from Binkie to Edith, or Edith to Binkie or her agent concerning *Waiting in the Wings*. We have seen that although Edith often turned down plays from distinguished authors, she was never so ill-mannered as to ignore them and I am quite certain that she was never given a chance to consider Noël's offer. Although not a close friend, she respected Noël and he was fond of her. It is inconceivable that Edith would have deliberately set out to offend somebody of Noël's standing by rejecting the offer of a role in a new play by him without so much as a word. Binkie appears to have played the same game with Gladys Cooper and the leading roles were eventually played by Sybil Thorndike, Nora Nicolson, Una Venning and Mary Clare, the play being presented by Michael Redgrave in association with Fred Sadoff.

Edith went to stay with Noël and Cole Lesley at Les Avants, Noël's Swiss residence high above the Lake of Geneva, before rehearsals for *Hay Fever* began. It was a great and unaccustomed adventure for her and Cole told me how she blossomed. One evening Noël suggested that they cross the French border to visit a casino for a spot of gambling. Edith didn't sit at the tables herself, instead she gave Cole some money to gamble for her at roulette while she watched Noël's prowess at *Chemin de Fer*. Cole won a modest amount, which thrilled Edith and the following morning they went for coffee in the village and bought each other gifts Edith gave Cole some eau de Cologne and he gave her some bath oil. That night as she went upstairs to bed, Cole shouted out, 'Don't forget to use your bath oil in the morning, Edith.' 'What will it do for me?' Edith asked.

'It will give you a skin you love to touch.'

'Oh,' said Edith. 'Then I must get some "touchers" mustn't I?' And she swept out of sight in the best tradition of Judith Bliss, leaving the Master and Cole well pleased.

Thus, *Hay Fever* was a bonus from afar and the role of Judith Bliss ideally suited to Edith's mannerisms and sense of theatricality when the occasion demanded. The sadness is that she played it too late in life. After a somewhat shaky first night, she settled down to give a stunning display which delighted the author. Noël went on record as saying that he felt Edith had more stature than Marie Tempest, who had created the role. 'Edith's comedy, when she is sure of what she is doing, is perfection.' There had been occasions, during the rehearsals when the Master had expressed doubts as to whether Edith knew what she was doing with his lines, but once her performance had been set he expressed nothing but gratitude and love. The main reason for their slight differences of opinion during the rehearsals stemmed from their totally different working methods. Noël usually insisted that all his actors came word perfect to the first reading, but Edith had never been able to work this way and she was too old to change. There is a much quoted story from these rehearsals which perhaps bears repeating once more. Edith continually varied the rhythm of one line by inserting an extra word not in the text. The line was 'On a clear day you can see Marlow' which Edith changed to 'On a very clear day you can see Marlow.' The Master's patience finally snapped and he delivered one of his crisp, finger-wagging instructions from the darkened stalls. 'Edith, dear,' he called out. 'The line is, "On a clear day you can see Marlow." On a *very* clear day you can see Marlowe *and* Beaumont and Fletcher.'

They had both come such a long way from Ebury Street and *Polly With a Past*, but they both shared to a remarkable degree a love of professionalism and a respect for the disciplines of the theatre. I do not think it was by chance that on the night of the special Midnight Matinee staged to commemorate Noël's seventieth birthday, the whole theatre rose to applaud Edith's appearance on stage, a prolonged burst of spontaneous affection that almost equalled that given to Noël. The profession as a whole may have many defects in the public eye and is often guilty of absurdities, but it has never been lacking in heart or in perception for those of its members who have never betrayed their calling. It is a curious and telling coincidence that two of the greatest names the British theatre have ever produced should, at the beginning of their careers, have walked hand in hand down the same street; their lives did not cross very often beyond that early point, but they both refused to stray from the chosen path and in the end both arrived at the same destination.

Although her stage appearances were becoming more and more spaced out she embarked, in 1963, when she was well into her seventies, on a full-blown film career and, once launched, found that she was in great demand. I think there were two reasons for this, the most important being that she could more easily assimilate the shorter scenes that are part and parcel of most films. Her memory, understandably, was not as good as it had been. I also think that she was quite keen to earn the sums of money that film companies offered, for she became increasingly worried about the time when she would no longer be able to act at all. She could not contemplate going into the actors' home; this was something that filled her with dread, not, I think, from any snobbish reason but because she hated the idea of being cooped up with lots of people. Her financial worries had no basis in fact, but were nevertheless very real to her.

In 1963 she worked for Tony Richardson again in what was to become one of the most phenomenally successful films that decade, *Tom Jones*. Her performance in this film proved memorable, for she brought her impeccable timing and sense of period to a cast that was largely allowed to indulge in a riot of over-acting. This was followed with a film version of *The Chalk Garden*, produced by Ross Hunter who had made a considerable reputation and fortune with a series of Doris Day movies. It was not a happy adaptation, for there are few purely theatrical experiences which lend themselves to the medium of film. Something was lost in the transfer; perhaps Miss Bagnold's language (like Giraudoux's, as I was later to discover) does not survive the journey into celluloid. It is perhaps too rich, too literary for the screen. Edith brought all her expertise to the filmed version of her Mrs. St. Maugham and one should be grateful to Ross Hunter in that he preserved the ghost of her stage performance for future audiences, but it was not the electrifying experience that some of us remembered from the Haymarket. Mr. Hunter, writing to Edith in shock, described the London reviews as 'sordid'. He had never imagined that his film would be given such a public execution without mercy. He tried to convey some comfort to his star from the fact that he had secured the famed Radio City Music Hall for the American opening, but in the event, although the New York critics wrote with a weakened solution of vitriol in their pens, the final result could only be counted a disappointment.

Her energy continued to astound all who came in contact with it. She was immensely popular with film crews who always respect the real thing, and she proclaimed she was in love with the camera. It was like discovering a new toy. 'They make such a fuss of you,' she said. 'I suppose it's rather shameful in a way, but at the same time very enjoyable.' Since recovering from Judith's death she had been free of all emotional ties. 'Life,' she said, 'is very precious to me. I must not waste it.'

I think she had known moments of absolute happiness, but happiness for Edith was something she leased; she never owned it outright. And despite her brave, wise words I am not convinced that she ever felt completely safe. She disciplined herself out of loneliness and self-pity, but loneliness was often waiting in the wings and only somebody of her iron determination could have survived the bleak periods. 'It seems as though I was meant to be solitary,' she told an interviewer, but within the bald statement, with its hint of defiance, lurked the contradiction that some of her closest friends had learnt to detect. To an extent, she isolated herself; the solitary woman, distinguished, revered, became, over the years, yet another character role in her gallery of portraits. It was, in Graham Greene's memorable title, a sort of life.

There had always been a patchwork quality to the pattern of her career; one of those unique articles, now much valued, which the daughter of a family would commence in early age and add to through-out her life—sewing into it the colours and design, often haphazard, that life forced on her. The theatrical patches of Edith's career became rarer: she had only three more to add.

The first of these was her final acceptance of *The Chinese Prime Minister* which went into rehearsal in 1965. As with *The Chalk Garden* there had been a prior production in New York, with the incomparable Margaret Leighton in the same role of Mrs. Forest. Alan Webb, that superb portrayer of octogenerians, was the common denominator between the Broadway and London casts, playing the part of Bent in both cases. Edith's leading man was Brian Aherne and she commenced rehearsals in high spirits. *The Chinese Prime Minister* is a play rich in thought and language and the role of Mrs. Forest is a complex and demanding one. Enid Bagnold had, as we have seen, been at great pains to explain Edith's suitability for the role, and indeed re-reading the text I was immediately struck by the number of echoes of Edith's own personality contained in the character of Mrs. Forest. By that, I have no wish to denigrate Miss Bagnold's artistry, but she admitted to seeing Edith walk across her mental stage all the time she was writing it and Edith's personality is ingrained into the fabric of the text. I bring no pleasure to the task of recording that the hopes of all concerned were quickly dashed. The facility for memorising a long role was receding all the time, and Edith encountered great difficulty during rehearsals. It was not a question of taking against the author's words, as had been the case with Gladys Cooper in the American production of *The Chalk Garden*, but simply that time had eroded the powers of memory. Author, director and management were in despair and during the pre-London tour a crisis point was reached. On one occasion, during a performance at Brighton, Edith cut five pages at one go, thus making nonsense of the play to the utter bewilderment of the audience. Knowing something of this—the worst nightmare that can befall an actor—I can more readily under-stand the tragedy of the situation. Without Edith, the play could not succeed; with Edith lost and floundering the play could only fail. She fought with all her old tenacity, but the years were against her and the reserves of energy, those vital reserves without which all was lost, were just not there any longer. It became a vicious circle: the more Edith struggled to regain lost ground, the more her energies were depleted. It is easy for outsiders to criticise, but one must look beyond the evidence of failure and consider the human dilemma: Agate's 'superb creature' still able to act brilliantly, wanting to act brilliantly, but defeated, as in time we are all defeated (though privately in most cases) by the inevitable toll of old age. An actor cannot hide his failures, but must perforce parade them: I could quote many examples of actors forced to die in harness. Until recently a once distinguished household name who had been admitted to the actors' Denville Home would get up every morning firmly convinced that he was on a film location. He would shave and dress and go down to examine the Notice Board. 'What scenes are we doing today?' he would invariably enquire. A fellow resident, compassionately aware of his fantasy, would then tell him: 'We're not on call today, dear. They've given us the day off.' The actor accepted this daily explanation quite happily, but the following morning the routine would start all over again. But often there is not even this grain of comedy, merely the unrelieved sadness of once-noted performers eking out their remaining days in a fruitless search for a paradise never to be regained.

At the very start of her career Edith had been witness to the decline of Ellen Terry, and now she faced the identical situation. It made her physically ill, for her personality was such that she had to give herself an explanation. She could not admit to the real reason for the failure of *The Chinese Prime Minister*. Pride played an important role, of course—foolish pride, perhaps, to those who could only appreciate the exterior evidence. But to those of us who can look back over the entire career, unaffected by the emotions of the particular moment, an understandable pride.

Having rationalised it to herself, she picked herself up off the floor and went back to work. She played in another film, *Young Cassidy*, with a leading man who, at their first meeting, professed a total ignorance of her career. It was a less than auspicious introduction, but Edith could manage such situations and long before the film had finished shooting, the actor was eating out of her hand.

It was at this point, knowing something of the crisis she was passing through, that I seized an opportunity to create a major screen role for her. I had been approached out of the blue by two young Americans, Ronald Shedlo and Michael Laughlan, would-be film producers at that time, who asked me if I would adapt and direct a short novel called *The Whisperers* by Robert Nicolson. When I read the novel I could conceive of no actress other than Edith to play the central role of Mrs. Ross. I quickly entered into partnership with Ronald and Michael, put a blank sheet of paper in my typewriter and finished the screenplay in under two weeks. I will not put forward the claim that speed necessarily equates with quality, but there are occasions when everything falls into place without effort, and this was one of them. Robert Nicolson's novel was beautifully constructed, sparsely written and a rare pleasure to adapt for the screen. I took the unusual step of adding a dedication page, inscribing the script to Edith, and posted it off to her. She read it in a matter of forty eight hours and rang me to say that she would be delighted to play Mrs. Ross. I next contacted David Picker, who was then the executive in charge of United Artists, told him of my plans and asked if his company would finance the film to the tune of $400,000 (in Hollywood terms, a modest amount.) He agreed with an alacrity hitherto unknown; I had never met with less resistance. With Edith cast and the finance obtained we were quickly into production. That fine actor Eric Portman was engaged to play the recalcitrant husband, and my wife Nanette, Leonard Rossiter, Avis Bunnage and Gerald Sim took the other leading roles.

Nicolson's novel had been set in Glasgow, and the only stipulation David Picker made to me was that I avoid Scottish accents because he felt that this would work to the film's disadvantage in the United States. (Whereas British film audiences are compelled to endure a variety of American accents, some of which are virtually unintelligible to our ears, their American counterparts will apparently never make the effort, and many a British film has foundered because of this.) I therefore set the film in the Midlands and Edith agreed to assume a flat accent.

I elected to shoot the film in the Moss Side area of Manchester; in 1966 this was in the process of becoming a planners' Hiroshima; whole areas had been flattened by the bulldozers in preparation for a petrified concrete forest of high-rise tenements. It was a waste land, the only buildings left standing being the pubs and the churches; they too were condemned, but had been granted a stay of execution—perhaps in order that the displaced inhabitants could drown their sorrows or else pray for deliverance until the eleventh hour. It provided me with the requisite desolation I needed for my story and I moved my film unit into the area.

It was the first time I had actually worked with Edith. As I recall we only had one meeting prior to shooting when we discussed the script. Edith asked if I would insert one additional line of dialogue for her. Although she greatly admired Eric Portman as an actor she was not, I think, enamoured of his private personality. 'Do you think,' she said, 'you could add a line to indicate that she married slightly beneath her?' I promised to consider it. A few days later I met with Eric to discuss his reactions to the script. He admired Edith as an actress without qualification, but confessed, with more bluntness than Edith, that there were aspects of her off-stage personality that grated on him. 'Do you think, dear boy,' he said, 'you could somehow insert an extra line which would indicate she married a much younger man?' I kept both confidences to myself, duly made the amendments and neither of them ever referred to it again.

I had no pre-conceived idea of how I would direct Edith. Obviously her reputation preceded her. She was then in her 78th year and common sense dictated that I make every allowance for her age, for filming on location is an exhausting process for all concerned, especially in England where the weather is invariably unpredictable and usually the exact opposite of what a director desires. On the day one is scheduled to shoot an elegant garden party, the heavens open; when one wants grey skies there isn't a cloud on the horizon. I have never enjoyed the luxury of being able to wait for ideal conditions in the manner of David Lean and

Stanley Kubrick. On my shoestring budget of $400,000 I knew in advance that I had to shoot come what may. Edith was seldom off the screen and was scheduled to work every day but two during the eight-week shooting period, and we had to make provision for several night locations.

When the film was finally shown and was enjoying a considerable artistic success, I was interviewed in New York by a gentleman who knew all there was to know about acting. 'Obviously, Mr. Forbes, you and Dame Edith spent many months preparing her for her role as Mrs. Ross.' 'No,' I said, 'we scarcely discussed the characterisation at all.' He couldn't accept that answer. 'But, surely, she lived amongst these people and studied them?' I shook my head. 'Well, what's her method then? She must have a method.'

'Her method is that she is simply a great actress.' I then proceeded to outline what had taken place before the first day's shooting. Edith and I drove up to Manchester from London on the Sunday afternoon and checked into the Piccadilly Hotel. After a quiet dinner we were joined by my costume designer, Julie Harris, who had brought with her a motley selection of old hats, coats and shoes purchased from second-hand stalls in the Portabello Road. We retired to Edith's suite where she tried on various garments, selected those she felt were right for the character and which she could wear comfortably, and then announced that she felt tired and would get an early night.

The following morning I had my camera in position for the first set-up when she arrived on the location. She wore no make-up other than a little powder, she was dressed in the old clothes and was the Mrs. Ross of my imagination come to life. 'What do you want me to do, dear?' she asked. I explained the mechanics of the scene, which involved her coming out of her house, walking along an alleyway, fishing some rubbish out of a dustbin and descending some stairs to the derelict area below. 'Do you want to rehearse?' I asked. 'Not unless you do,' she said. She took up her position, the clapper-board went in and marked the first take, I said 'Action' and Edith became Mrs. Ross. She walked differently, her ankles slopped over in the second-hand shoes, she clutched her button-less shabby coat as though terrified it was going to be snatched from her, stared past camera with suddenly-rheumy eyes and did everything to perfection. 'First-take, Evans,' I said when the camera had been cut. 'Was it all right?' she asked. 'Did I get her?'

I can't claim to have directed Edith in the way that I have directed other artists; I positioned my cameras carefully to catch every nuance of her extraordinary performance and from time to time I was able to guide her, but for the most part I was content to be led by her. Yet she asked my help constantly. 'What d'you think, dear?' she would say. 'Would she do that?' always talking in terms of Mrs. Ross, never in terms of Dame Edith Evans. She conserved her energy between takes and frequently dozed off in her chair whenever we had to wait for the light. But she was always word perfect and seldom needed a second-take. I think the entire crew felt it a privilege to watch her at work, to observe how she became the character so completely without any artificial aids. There was only one moment when she was totally at a loss. It happened when we were filming the scene where Mrs. Ross discovers a brown-paper parcel left by her criminal son. When she cut the string the parcel fell open to reveal a mass of one pound notes. I shot the scene to my satisfaction on the day, but when I viewed the results the following morning I felt that I had not been close enough with my camera for the moment when the money was uncovered, and that audiences might be confused, which is always fatal. I therefore decided to shoot that section of the action with a close-up lens, showing only Edith's hands and the parcel. This meant that Edith had to recreate the previous day's action exactly. My continuity girl, Penny Daniels, carefully instructed Edith as to the position of her hands, how she held the knife that cut the string, and so on. Edith tried to follow everything precisely. We shot the insert twelve times without success and on the thirteenth take she burst into tears. 'Why can't I do it?' she cried. 'I ought to be able to do it, it's my *job* to do it.' It was distressing to watch her and we were all greatly concerned.

I explained to her that it was nothing to do with acting as such, that it was merely a piece of boring film mechanics and of no lasting importance. She refused to be convinced. 'Look,' I said finally, 'let me show you how unimportant it is. Give me your cardigan and your wedding ring.' I put on the cardigan and slipped the wedding ring on my left hand. Because it was purely a technical exercise, and because I knew that the image would only be on the screen for a few seconds, certainly not long enough for anybody in the audience to detect the sleight of hand, I was able to accomplish the shot with ease. 'There,' I said, 'that's all there is to is. Finished.' 'How d'you mean, finished?' Edith said. 'Don't I have to try again?' 'No,' I said, 'nobody will ever know the difference unless we tell them.' And until now nobody outside the actual crew has known. But, for those few seconds, they are my hands and not Edith's on the screen.

When it came to the real business of acting, she had no peer. I remember the big emotional scenes in the film, scenes which the majority of actors would approach with genuine apprehension, not to say fear; Edith sailed through them. I suppose she trusted me implicitly in matters of cinematic taste, and because she trusted me she could work freely. She never wanted to see work in progress. 'That's your business,' she said. 'If you're satisfied, then I don't want to be bothered.' We employed a great number of old-age pensioners in one sequence and she mingled with them and was lost amongst them, anonymous and nondescript. After the first hour or so they seemed scarcely conscious of her as Edith Evans and engaged her in conversations about their personal lives which she entered into, slipping, like an undercover agent, into a world she had never known, and being accepted there. She never asked favours, never demanded special privileges, worked all hours in atrocious weather sometimes, and would never leave the set without first asking my permission. By the end of the first week there wasn't anybody in the crew who wouldn't have laid down their life for her. It was, beyond any doubt, a performance, on and off screen, of the highest order and I doubt whether I shall ever see it surpassed.

When the film was shown the truth of her portrayal was universally applauded. *The Whisperers* became the official British entry for the Berlin Festival of 1967 and Edith received the Golden Bear for the Best Actress. Although she did not really approve of awards, there was no escaping them. The British Film Academy bestowed its accolade, the New York Film Critics followed suit and in due course she received a nomination for an Oscar. By the time the Oscar ceremonies came round in the Spring of 1968 I found myself in a curious situation. By then I was working at the Studios de la Victorine in Nice, directing *The Madwoman of Chaillot* with Katharine Hepburn as La Folle. I had replaced John Huston a few weeks before shooting commenced—he having left the project as a result of artistic differences with the producer—and I inherited most of his all-star cast. In addition to Kate Hepburn my viewfinder was aimed at Yul Brynner, Danny Kaye, Charles Boyer, Margaret Leighton, Giulietta Masina, Irene Papas, Nanette Newman, Richard Chamberlain, Oscar Homolka, Donald Pleasance, Fernand Gravet, John Gavin and Paul Henreid. After I had been shooting for some weeks and during the height of the 1968 'French Revolution', Miss Papas, who I think had been unhappy in her role from the beginning, asked to be released. I was faced with the daunting task of replacing her and reshooting all those scenes in which she had already appeared.

That evening I phoned Edith in London. I somewhat hesitantly explained the dilemma and pointed out that it was hardly the most attractive offer she had ever received. All I could promise her was a holiday in the sun and a lot of hard work. 'Dear boy, of course I'll come,' she said. 'I'll leave tomorrow.'

By that time the French crisis was at explosion point. Only military planes were flying in or out of Nice, food supplies were short, petrol was unobtainable except from a black market which had sprung up overnight and communications to anywhere outside France were extremely difficult. True to her word Edith caught a plane to Milan and then drove back to the Italian-French border, arriving unruffled and telling everybody how thrilling the journey had been. 'Such a nice pilot,' she told us.

'He flew very low so that we could get a good view of the coastline.' She was dressed in a pale lemon Hardy Amies suit, wore a splendid hat and white gloves and might well have stepped from the pages of *Vogue*. After she had settled herself in her hotel I enquired whether she would like to meet Kate Hepburn. Yes, that would be very pleasant. So I drove her, with Nanette, to Kate's rented villa overlooking the bay at Cap Ferrat. Kate's elegance was of a different variety. Off screen she always sported a highly individual costume, which owed something to the Afrika Corps (a battered desert cap), something to her beloved Spencer Tracy (an old cardigan) and a once elegant silk shirt: the combination, on her, was the ultimate in bizarre chic. Kate had confessed that Edith was an actress she admired above all others and when I had told her that Edith had accepted the role she said, 'Well, that's the end of me, then. If your girl friend's on her way, well, shoot, I'd better give up.'

Their first meeting was, by any standards, historic. Phyllis Wilbourn, Kate's devoted companion, served tea out on the terrace and we all admired the view and engaged in small talk for the first quarter of an hour. Both ladies, I observed, were somewhat amazed by the appearance of the other. Kate was impressed that Edith could have survived the horrendous journey and appear as though dressed for a Royal Garden Party, and Edith was wondering whether Kate was still in her Mad-woman costume (for at that point Edith had no idea of the style of the film, who was in it, or what her role consisted of. She had taken the whole thing on trust). They had many mutual friends and gradually relaxed with each other. Kate was distressed that Edith was in a hotel—some-thing which didn't bother Edith at all—and generously offered to share her villa. This was politely declined by Edith, who as we know did not like to have her daily routine organised for her. 'Well, even if you don't move in,' Kate said, 'just treat the place as your own. Come and go as you wish, because I know how boring hotels can become. If you want Phyllis to go over your lines with you, just ask, and please don't hesitate to make use of this place. Come and have your meals with us, we're very free and easy. The only thing is I get up early and so I go to bed early. We're usually in bed by half past seven, but otherwise the place is yours.'

There was a pause. In retrospect it seems a long pause. Edith tilted her head and looked out across the bay. 'How very kind of you, dear,' she said. 'Very kind . . . But . . . what do people do who *don't* go to bed at half past seven?'

In the event they became great friends and Edith lifted the scenes they played together: the challenge she presented to Kate spurred Kate, for when two extraordinary personalities act together they invariably fillip each other onto a higher plane. It couldn't have been easy for either of them, I realise. The sudden introduction of an actress of the calibre of Edith, plus the fact that Kate and the other members of the cast had to repeat with fresh energy numerous scenes they had already done once before must have been irksome. There wasn't time to get fresh costumes for Edith, so those designed for Irene Papas were quickly adapted for her. Phyllis Wilbourn helped her with learning the lines and forty eight hours after she arrived we commenced shooting again. Edith's first scene took place in the enormous cellar set which spread over two stages. She had to make an entrance at the top of a long flight of stairs, talking all the while, join Kate, Margaret, Giuletta, Danny and a host of extras who were waiting below and deliver a long and complicated piece of Giraudoux as revamped by Mr. Edward Anhalt. It was a difficult baptism. Nanette who was playing the maid, Irma, had to announce her. The camera turned and I said 'Action.' Nothing happened. I looked at my cameraman, Bernie Guffey, and whispered, 'D'you think she heard me?' He shrugged. 'Action, Edith, darling,' I repeated. Nothing. Could she have fainted, I wondered? But if she had fainted, Nanette would have stepped into the scene and told me. Film was still running through the camera. 'Whenever you like, darling,' I shouted. And at this point Edith's unmistakeable voice rang out on the silent set. 'Is this a real cellar?' she asked Nanette, 'or did dear Bryan build it?' 'Bryan built it,' Nanette said, 'and I think he's waiting for us.' 'Well, I'm ready,' Edith replied, 'so let's get on with it.' With that she made an impressive entrance, marched down the stairs, delivered her dialogue with aplomb, hit all her marks and before I could recover enough to say 'Cut' turned to me and ended with: 'It's very dark down here, I hope they can see me.' The entire cast and crew collapsed at that point and gave her a round of applause, led by Kate.

I think she really enjoyed herself in the South of France during those strange, turbulent weeks. We survived a typically French strike; our crew had been instructed by their Paris office to stop work, but out of loyalty to me, ignored the order. The Paris office dispatched two officials who arrived and remonstrated with their members. When they had departed the union spokesman came to me and explained that they had no alternative but to obey their instructions. 'We have to join the strike, cher maître,' he said. 'But we have decided that we will only strike during our lunch hours.'

Despite the many extra difficulties and the daily struggle with the obliterating sound of aircraft (the studio is built so close to the runway of Nice airport that we could actually see the pilots from our exterior set) it was a happy film, and I believe that it gave Edith one of the few real holidays she could enjoy without a conscience. Most of her life she had fretted to get back to work, but her time on the *Madwoman* contained no such pressures. She struck up an immediate friendship with Yul Brynner, accepting that he called her 'the old broad' from affection and she was

261

amongst a whole host of people she admired and who, in turn, worshipped her.

I faced a curious dilemma which had nothing to do with the film I was shooting. It was this: both my leading ladies were nominated for that year's Academy Award; Kate for *Guess Who's Coming To Dinner?* and Edith for *The Whisperers*. My loyalties were divided, but I suppose, in my heart, I wanted Edith to win whilst not wanting either of them to lose. Because of the time difference we didn't get the news until the morning following the Hollywood ceremony. I arrived on the set at my usual hour, just after seven and as I stepped from my car, my French First Assistant, Louis, ran up and shouted 'She's won!' For about ten seconds I was convinced that he meant Edith and had started towards the make-up rooms to congratulate her when I suddenly paused. 'Who? Which one?' 'Miss Hepburn,' he said.

Immediately she heard, Kate went to Edith's dressing room. 'It should have been yours, Edith,' she said. 'They only gave to me out of sympathy.' That is what makes Kate a great lady.

We had a farewell dinner at La Résidence du Cap, sitting on the terrace with the sea just beyond the cricket-infested garden, all of us sensing that, whatever the outcome of the finished film, there would never again come a time quite like it. It was as though we had all survived a war and because so many of the faces around that table were legends, in the midst of the laughter and that special feeling that always infects a film company when the unit and the cast disperse, the gaiety was mixed with sadness. We exchanged presents, but what we could never exchange was the experience of a lifetime that had been crammed into twenty two weeks.

Naturally there is no justice in the film industry and when the film appeared the majority of the critics derided my all-star cast simply because they were stars. The film, I was told, was 'top heavy' with them, 'swamped' by them, they were 'too much of a good thing.'

When we were all back in England and I was editing the film, Edith rang me one day and said she would like to ask a favour. She had in mind to give a one-man poetry reading, but before facing a paying audience she wanted to have a try-out. Could I possibly invite a few friends to the house and ask them to be guinea-pigs? Nanette and I told her we would be delighted and honoured. 'It won't be anything much, you know,' Edith said. 'But it would be awfully useful. You see, I've no idea how it'll go. And be sure and invite some young people. I think young people understand me better than some of the others.'

We gave great thought to the choice of guests and the final assembly was as mixed as we could make it. Her Royal Highness Princess Margaret consented to come, Yul Brynner and his wife, Jacqueline, flew from Normandy in a private jet, and they were joined by Dudley Moore, Suzy

Kendall, Hugh Johnson, then editor of *Queen*, and his wife, pop star Dave Clark and Cathy McGowan, Dickie and Sheila Attenborough, Julie Harris and Edith's wig-maker Stanley Hall, artist Bryan Organ and his wife Elizabeth, Georgia Brown and Gareth Wigan, Frank Muir and his wife Polly, Noël Coward's biographer Charles Castle and my ex-commanding officer from my war-time army days, Noel MacGregor. After dinner they all sat around on the floor in our living room while Edith occupied an old admiral's chair. I had the presence of mind to switch on my tape-recorder, then the lights were turned out except for a reading lamp behind Edith, and she commenced her programme. I doubt whether I can ever recapture in words the particular magic of what followed. Edith had selected a wide variety of poems, ranging through Shakespeare to Belloc and including many old favourites by Virginia Graham, Ogden Nash and, of course, Betjeman; a very personal choice which she read from typed pages that were constantly shuffled and dropped, for she began nervously. Gradually, as her small audience responded (we were nervous with her at first) her confidence grew and grew into a perfection of timing which, allied to that voice which could play so many tunes, gave those present a glimpse of something divine. We laughed and we cried; roaring approval when she gave her own light and shade to Betjeman and Belloc, made silent and moved by Virginia Graham's *Patterns*—a poem I shall forever associate with Edith. The recording I made was a ragged technical effort, unbalanced, and at times Edith's voice was partially obscured by the enthusiasm of her audience, but, with all its imperfections, still a memento to be treasured and one, I hope, I shall play to my grandchildren for their fresh delight.

Edith performed for an hour and a half and although we clamoured for more, declined any encores and departed into the night. She had exhausted herself and one of the tests of a true professional is to know when to quit the stage. From this intimate rehearsal she developed her stage show which she gave to audiences all over the country under the title *Edith Evans . . . and friends*. It was produced and directed for the stage by Roger Clifford. I saw her stage presentation three times, the last occasion being at the Phoenix Theatre, which marked her last appearance in the West End. It was simply done, the perfect farewell, for she had always been a loner and there she was, centre stage, with no props, no artifice, just her talent, still in love with words and giving her audience their money's worth.

She appeared in other films—*Prudence and The Pill*, *Fitzwilly*, *Crooks and Coronets* and the musical version of *A Christmas Carol* called *Scrooge* with a score by Leslie Bricusse. With the exception of *Scrooge* none of these gave her much opportunity to display her unique qualities. Once again we can turn to Albert Finney who described what happend to her during the shooting of this film. 'She was playing one of the ghosts and in the story the description said she was growing out of a candle, which is impossible. So they dressed Edith in a Grecian robe and gave her a frond. On the first day we worked together there was a technical hold-up, because we had to have a magical effect and it didn't work for some reason. And during all the endless retakes Edith kept forgetting her lines and this worried the production company. She was then 81, and between takes I'd been talking to her, and she'd said to me, 'How do you play a ghost? I don't know anybody who's a ghost. Where's the ghost from, what this Grecian costume, where is it all from? I don't understand who she is, who I am when I'm the ghost.'

'I told this to the director and to Leslie Bricusse, and I think they thought, well, you know, Dame Edith Evans, 81 you know, maybe her memory is suffering. Then Leslie said, 'I don't think we're helping her with that Grecian thing. In the story she takes Scrooge back to scenes of his childhood, so why don't we dress her in costumes of the period Scrooge's Grandmother would have worn?' They talked to her about it, and Edith thought it was a wonderful idea. We came to do the scene again, two weeks later, and she had this new costume, this new idea. The light was shining from her eyes and she said, 'I know exactly who I am now. When I was young I had an Auntie who treated me like I treat you in this, and that's who I'm going to play.' On the retake she had no problem with her lines. It wasn't her memory going, it wasn't age, it was that she, as an artist, couldn't humanise the character that had been given to her initially—but giving her this costume enabled her to liberate her imagination, and she just took off. That was a great lesson for some of us. A great lesson for me. There was Edith at 81, and as great as she was, and as marvellous as she was, still looking at problems of acting that intensely. Still able to say, I'm afraid I'm stumbling here. Still willing to admit that. I adored her.'

So many of her colleagues hoard stories about Edith and as with any great personality many of them have been embroidered over the years. When this book was announced a great number of people wrote to me; some had known Edith intimately, some had met her but once, and others were total strangers to her but had followed her career and wished to convey the effect she had had on their lives. I was particularly grateful to Patrick Garland who took the trouble to write at length and give me his impressions of Edith. Patrick had directed her in a filmed version of *A Doll's House* with Ralph Richardson and Claire Bloom during the winter of 1973. He described how on several occasions he and Claire took her to lunch during rehearsals. 'While she talked about Rosalind the years seemed to slide away from her, and she was a young, vivacious girl of twenty or so . . . She constantly complained about the loneliness of her life outside the theatre. Both Claire and myself often thought she resembled Chaucer's Prioress, cultivated, refined, a little vain about her appearance, and profoundly devoted. Sometimes, when talking of her personal loneliness, and the absence of her theatrical life, she would cry . . . However, once we began shooting the scene between Nora and her old nurse, as in so many former performances, her miraculous transformation from an elegant, refined artist to a primitive, inarticulate peasant woman, took place. . . . It is extraordinary, of all our actors and actresses, she alone had no sense of 'class', only of rank . . . Looking at her watching herself in the mirror, eyes screwed up critically, she looked to me exactly like a great Rembrandt painting of a peasant woman . . .'

She was lonely, but she was also determined to go on working until the last moment. The patchwork was almost finished. I will loosely stitch the last square of stage acting, an appearance in Anouilh's *Dear Antoine* during one of the Chichester Festivals, but here again she had to relinquish the role after a short while. I think she realised that she would never learn a major stage role again, but she did not give in easily and from time to time the burnished steel of her old resolve would flash and catch a ray of past suns. She acted in another television film of *David Copperfield*, playing Miss Betsey. Legend has it, and I believe legend to be partially true, that during one scene she was required to have a cat in a basket she was carrying. The cat had been sedated by the prop man, but under the studio lights the effects of the drug wore off. During a take and while Edith was in the middle of delivering a long speech, the soporific animal attempted to struggle out of the basket. Without pausing, Edith pushed it back with the muttered aside, 'Don't be such an ambitious pussy. You're not in Dick Whittington.' I once attempted to verify this story with her. 'I don't remember,' she said. 'Perhaps I did. They tell me I'm quite funny from time to time, but I never remember. I'm always being told I say funny things, but they never seem funny to me.'

She was funny, she had a way of describing things that coloured them differently from anybody else. Perhaps this is nowhere better illustrated than in my own experience shortly after she had just suffered a massive heart attack. It was late on a Saturday evening, August 7th, 1971, when the news was phoned to me. By one of those coincidences which seem part and parcel of my own life, I happened to be spending the evening with Bette Davis. Masie Knox Shaw, Edith's South African friend, rang me from Kilndown to say that she had been told Edith had but a few hours to live. Before lapsing into unconsciousness she had apparently asked for me. I had a chauffeur in those days, Reg Howell, who had often driven Edith, and we immediately journeyed through the night to Kilndown. There I was told that the attack had happened three weeks previously, but Edith, clinging to her Christian Science beliefs, had refused all orthodox medical aid. Her condition had gradually worsened and in the end those closest to her had taken it upon themselves to call in the local doctor. By then she was in a coma. The doctor felt it imperative that she be removed to a cottage hospital near Tenterden, and it was only then that I was informed, for until the final crisis she had insisted that nobody was to be told.

Reg and I arrived at the hospital at first light. I explained my mission to the Matron, but she was under orders to allow nobody into Edith's room. I argued with her for a few minutes, but she was adamant and, in fairness, acting under instructions from her medical superiors. Equally firmly I gave her to understand that I could not accept her ruling as final and that I would certainly return after breakfast. Reg and I drove away in search of a small wayside cafe, where we nibbled without appetite. We went back to the hospital an hour or so later and as we parked the car I distinctly heard Edith's voice. The hospital had once been a private dwelling and Edith's room was at one corner to the front of the building. When I went inside the stern Matron was nowhere to be seen. I listened and once again heard Edith speak, though I could not distinguish any words. A young nurse came out of her room and naturally asked who I was and what I wanted. I again explained my mission. 'She's dying,' the nurse said. 'We can't let you see her.'

'But, if she's dying, what possible harm could it do?' I said. I could hardly contain my mounting anger. It wasn't the young nurse's fault; she was low down in the chain of authority and doubtless fearful of her own position. 'Do you know *who* she is?' I continued. 'The person in that room is Dame Edith Evans, and it's unthinkable that if she's dying, she should die alone. She's asked for me and she has every right to see me, doctors or no doctors.'

At that moment, doubtless hearing the by now heated exchange outside her door, Edith called out my name. I needed no further prompting. Ignoring the young nurse, I opened the door and went inside.

Edith was propped on pillows and looked closer to death than anybody I have ever seen. Her fine hair, usually so carefully attended to, was unkempt; they had taken her teeth away, making her face seem like a doll from which some of the stuffing has been extracted; her skin was stretched tight over the bone and seemed almost transparent. She started to cry when she saw me, making no sound, but the tears misted her eyes and ran down her cheeks to fall on the starched envelope of sheets that kept her imprisoned. I felt for her hand. As with her face the skin had tightened over the bones and it was like holding a bunch of clothes pegs. 'I knew you'd come,' she said. 'I knew you'd come.'

I know it sounds far-fetched, but some of my energy seemed to flow into her as I stood there and it could only have been a matter of ten minutes or so (during which time I was ever fearful that the nursing staff would return and order me out) before a faint semblance of colour appeared in her cheeks. Minus her teeth, she found it difficult to arti-

266

culate, but with a determination that amazed she framed the words, 'Give me a mirror, Bryan dear.' There was a small hand-mirror on the dressing table and I brought it to her. She slowly raised it and considered her changed appearance. 'They all think I'm going to go, you know,' she said. 'But I'm not going to go looking like that.' She let the mirror fall and felt for my hand again. 'They won't let me have any food, you see. And I want . . . I want lamb chops for lunch.'

'Well, I'll see about that,' I said, though I confess I did not anticipate being able to convince the Matron.

'I knew you would. I knew if you got here you'd put things right.'

I left the room to do battle with the authorities. It was a tall order, but for once I was determined to be equal to the occasion, girding myself to give a performance of such righteous indignation that, to my astonishment, it succeeded. Perhaps the outrageousness of Edith's demand took them off guard, but in the event her request was granted. That day she sat up in bed and ate lamb chops, and from that moment onwards began the slow climb to recovery.

During the long months when she was finding her feet again, she had to come to terms with herself, pushing the demon of energy into the background. Reluctantly, she allowed herself to be convinced that she should give up her chambers in Albany, for they were on the first floor and had to be reached by a long flight of treacherous stone stairs. Even so, she would never totally acknowledge what had happened. 'They say there was some little thing wrong with my heart, but it's all right now, and I'm sailing along beautifully. The doctor's awfully pleased with me.' The doctor was more than pleased, he was dumbfounded.

There remained the question of what she would do with her life. It was obvious to me during my weekly visits that her total recovery was being impeded for want of something to do. She couldn't bear being so idle. Life without any more expectations was unendurable to her. Then one day I casually mentioned putting her poetry reading on film, with a view to having it shown on television. The idea delighted her and she could think and talk of nothing else. In the first instance I had made the suggestion without any prior thought, but once she had embraced it with such touching enthusiasm there was no turning back. So in May of the following year I took a film crew down to Gatehouse and began shooting. I had no pre-conceived plan, no script, just a general idea which I thought might occupy her but could well peter out. I financed the project myself and chose my crew very carefully; they were briefed as to her condition and immediately grasped what was required. I had no previous experience of being a television interviewer, so I merely set up a camera, sat with my back to it, and talked to her. The first day went remarkably well. She blossomed, enjoying the chaos that the film crew brought to her house, insisted that they stay for lunch, and once started, her flow of reminiscences was only halted when we ran out of film. It was only then that the shape of the programme came to me. I saw that with patience I could go beyond a filmed performance of her poetry reading and perhaps trap on celluloid some part of the cause and the measure of her life.

In the early days she could work for only a few hours at a time. After lunch she invariably fell asleep and if, after her nap, we attempted to shoot again the results disappointed. At that time she could only walk with difficulty (a lift had been installed in the house to take her to her bedroom). I therefore established an easy routine. I would bring my crew to the house every two weeks, visiting her alone between times to discuss what we would shoot on the next occasion. During the course of these discussions I gained a more intimate insight into her early life and, at Edith's urging, commenced the task of sorting through all her private papers. Thus it was that, late one afternoon, searching in a cupboard, I chanced upon an old hat box. Inside were bundles of letters tied with faded ribbon. I took them downstairs to Edith and asked if she could identify them. She peered at them. 'They're from Guy,' she said. At that point I knew little or nothing about her marriage and had no idea whatsoever of Guy's background or personality. 'Read them to me,' she said. So, in front of the great fire, with the light fading beyond the Tudor windows, I read his love letters to her. She cried at certain passages, silent tears such as elderly people try to keep to themselves. There was the hatbox, the symbol of Mr. Blackaller's young milliner who had once fallen through the glass roof of the workroom, and there were the love letters with the Venezuelan postmarks. She was silent for a while when I had finished.

'I never realised,' she said, 'how much he loved me. Such beautiful letters. I suppose . . . I suppose I was always too busy. Such beautiful letters and you found them for me. You found him.'

16

'*Every day is Sunday now*'

The finished film was not shown on television until March of the following year, 1973, under the title *Dame Edith Evans*—'*I caught acting like the measles*', a somewhat ponderous mouthful which was pressed on me by the company presenting it. Edith had seen nothing of work in progress and confessed she had no recollection of what she had talked about during the six months or more we had been shooting. There was a hint of anxiety in her voice, a suggestion of second-thoughts and I was naturally perturbed at this, because obviously the film could not be shown without her consent. In the final editing stages I arranged a special screening for her. She drove up from Gatehouse with the faithful William at the wheel of the stately Rolls, bringing with her two people who were very close to her during the last years: her nephew by marriage, John Booth, and her companion Mrs. Avis Merton. John Booth handled her business affairs and attended to her still considerable correspondence; Mrs. Merton looked after her social needs; both were devoted to her. Together with my editor, Philip Shaw, we sat in a dismal basement viewing theatre littered with plastic coffee cups and full ash-trays, characteristics of the trade, and screened the cutting copy. To my relief she watched my celluloid tracing of her life with every evidence of enjoyment and when the lights went up at the end of my anxious hour, she turned to the young projectionist (who I suspect knew little of her career or reputation) and said: 'Did you like her? She's quite funny, isn't she? The way she moves her hands! I've never seen her before, you know. Not like that. Not being herself.'

The final version, with incidental music by the young British composer Robert Frost, had an overwhelming response: between us, Edith and I received well over seven hundred letters from total strangers. This tangible evidence that her life's work had touched a common chord did more than anything to restore Edith's faith that she could, and would, work again.

She had failed to realise, as many of us do, that the vast television audiences are birds of a different breed from those who pay for admission to theatres and cinemas. A few months previously she had been a guest

269

on the Michael Parkinson Show, a reluctant guest at first but on the night proving that she could tame and charm any interviewer and studio audience. It was a quite stunning debut into the specialised world of the television talk-show, and she gave a totally different performance from the one I had obtained in my more leisurely film. It was the audience that made the difference. Although she was frequently very funny in my film, she never *heard* her laughs; whereas on the Parkinson Show the moment she brought the house down, which was a few seconds after her entrance, she was away. She conquered television just as she had conquered the theatre and films, and proved so popular that she was in constant demand on both the BBC and the rival channel's Russell Harty Show. I am amazed they didn't give her a show of her own.

She needed those excursions from the solitude of Gatehouse, for although she returned physically tired, her enthusiasm for life was always stimulated. There were too many reminders of death. I made every effort to visit her once a week, usually going for lunch on a Wednesday, because John Booth's day was normally Thursday and thus between us we were able to break the monotony of her life on two separate occasions. Seldom a week went by without word of another old friend's death. Binkie and Noël died within days of each other, shortly after the transmission of our documentary film and I recall how this double blow depressed her for weeks afterwards.

Apart from the occasional film crew coming to solicit an interview, there were very few other visitors to Gatehouse during the final years. Her great friend Masie Knox Shaw spent regular holidays with her, but she saw few people from the world of the theatre. To the end she maintained a correspondence with colleagues from the past, writing her replies in her bold and increasingly sprawled handwriting, for she distrusted the telephone. She indulged herself by buying two reclining armchairs which were positioned in front of the great fireplace and which ensured that she and I fell asleep with even greater speed and comfort after the excellent lunches she always provided. She never lost her interest in the quality of everyday life and was constantly irritated by what she considered the lowering of standards. Arriving one Wednesday I was greeted with the announcement that she had just written to the Prime Minister (then Sir Harold Wilson) complaining bitterly at the high postal charges and the declining service. 'My father would never have tolerated it,' she said. She was Ned's girl to the end.

On sunny days her favourite spot was the garden room and there she dozed beneath the Topolski portrait, the floor around her chair a litter of old letters, poetry pamphlets, and books with the pages marked. She liked nothing better than to have me read letters from the past. It was during one of these afternoon sessions that she surprised me by suddenly announcing she had instructed her solicitor to make me her Literary

Executor. 'I want you to write the book,' she said. 'I shall never do it, and I suppose it ought to be written. All these lovely letters. All the things that have happened to me. I once thought I didn't want it told, but I've changed my mind. You do it, dear. We'll work on it together.'

The legal document was duly produced and knowing of the multitude of treasures from Shaw, George Moore, Michael Redgrave and others I installed a Xerox machine and began the task of photocopying the mass of documents for safety's sake. The eventual contract with my publisher led to an amusing story against myself. Knowing little or nothing about the true state of Edith's finances, I felt it only proper that she should share in the advance against royalties that I received. After consultation with Edith's solicitor I suggested the sum of £2,000. He felt that this was more than generous and made the counter-suggestion that a figure of £1,500 would be sufficient. During a visit to Gatehouse he put both suggestions to Edith. 'Well, if it makes Bryan happy, we should accept £2,000', was Edith's verdict, and £2,000 it was.

Once I commenced work on the book it became my habit to take the manuscript with me on my weekly visits and read her work in progress. 'Tell it truthfully,' she would say 'If it's not worth telling truthfully, it's not worth telling at all.' Incidents I recorded from her childhood were always her favourites and I would often be made to repeat them. She was the most understanding of collaborators, not always reliable when it came to checking dates and names, but with a keen eye for the shape of the book. Where there were notable gaps in the documented evidence, I would sit beside her with a tape-recorder running and gently nudge her into a monologue. She had the gift of talking about her life without false modesty and the resulting hours of tape contain many original 'Edith-isms' which I have included in this work. Of course the printed word cannot give the flavour of her voice, or conjure for the the reader the picture of this ever-regal figure pushed deep into an armchair, staring past me to the garden that was now seldom walked in, the afternoon light fading but falling to soften further a face that was wrinkled but never old.

She not only talked of working again, she did work again. She made long journeys to fulfil engagements for her poetry reading and when I announced that I had been asked to direct a musical based on the Cinderella legend, she immediately said 'I hope you can find a part for me. Nothing much, but something.' I introduced the character of the Dowager Queen into my script, though naturally I had to bear in mind the ever-present possibility that her health would give out. Despite every precaution taken by the watchful Mrs. Merton, Edith frequently took a tumble. She cut her head open on at least two occasions, cracked ribs and bruised most of her limbs. 'I've learnt the trick, though,' she told Michael Parkinson during one of her return visits to his show.

271

'When you fall down at my age, the great secret is not to try and get up too quickly. Just lie there. Have a look at the world from a different angle.' She always made light of her injuries, though it was often obvious that she was in considerable pain and discomfort. 'You have to push pain to one side,' she would say.

When plans for *The Slipper and The Rose* were well advanced she complained to me that she wasn't being asked to sing or dance. I hastily consulted the composers, Robert and Richard Sherman and together with the musical director, Angela Morley, we devised a way of giving Edith one verse of the song *What Has Love Got To Do With Getting Married?* The technique usually employed with film musicals is to make the actual singing recording before one shoots the song, the actors being then required to mime the words to a playback of their recorded voices. It is not an easy technique to master. Edith duly paid a visit to the Anvil studios at Denham, spurned the use of headphones ('They get in the way and they mess up your hair.') and within two or three hilarious takes had recorded her verse. When later we shot the complete sequence at Pinewood studios she sailed through it.

All the interior sequences were filmed during the endless heat of the summer of 1975 and conditions on the sound stages at Pinewood were frequently unbearable. They were not air-conditioned and when you have some three hundred bewigged and costumed actors and dancers confined on a set that requires lighting which generates as much heat as several hundred electric fires, it can be readily appreciated that the art of acting naturally is no easy task. Some days the temperature on the set hovered only one degree below the optimum point when the fire sprinklers would have come into operation. Electricians on the overhead gantries working the scores of arc lamps passed out from the heat and had to be relieved at frequent and short intervals. Edith wore very heavy costumes and although the high temperatures bothered her, she was determined to give of her best. 'Tell them to sit still and conserve their energies,' she would say to me. Again, as had been the way on *The Whisperers*, she would never leave the set unless I pleaded with her. She took to the floor and danced a stately minuet with Christopher Gable, accepted the ready homage that the young dancers gave her, joked with Kenneth More (who, like Yul Brynner, made no concessions to her age and flirted outrageously, much to her enjoyment) and completed her role without giving us a moment's hindrance. When the finished film was selected for the Royal Film Performance of 1976, she was presented to Her Majesty Queen Elizabeth, the Queen Mother, and gave a television interview in which she announced that she would like to make more film musicals. During the actual premiere performance she got an enormous laugh with her very first line and in a voice which sailed across the Royal Circle enquired: 'What did she say? Is she being funny? I can't hear a word.'

Her deafness was becoming an increasing problem, but much to my amazement she readily agreed to have a hearing aid fitted when her nephew John suggested it. John and I had expected a spirited resistance, but it was always a mistake to anticipate Edith's reaction to any given situation.

She was to make three further professional appearances: once on television with Edward Heath, reading Shakespeare's 'Fear no more the heat of the sun' while he accompanied her on the clavichord with William Byrd's *Victoria*; a small role with Glenda Jackson in the film of Muriel Spark's *The Abbess of Crewe* (the title being subsequently changed to *Dirty Habits*, which Edith would undoubtedly have denounced as inexpressibly vulgar); and lastly a BBC sound broadcast on the 15th August 1976 before an invited audience. She was in poor health by then, having suffered a stroke in April 1976 which, for a period, caused her to lose the power of speech. She fought this as she fought everything else. The true nature of her condition was carefully kept from her and she convinced herself that it had come about as a result of food poisoning. She was irritated because Mrs. Merton had eaten the same meal the night before it happened and had, inexplicably to Edith, suffered no such ill effects. When I went down to Gatehouse two days after the incident her speech was virtually unintelligible. There was no self-pity, merely fury, and she immediately commenced to give herself voice-production lessons, and within a month, although a few words remained slurred, she was talking articulately and with all her old vigour. It was an astonishing example of her will power.

The farewell broadcast on August 15th was beautifully stage-managed. She told me she had agreed to do it, but said little else. She spent several days going over all her favourite poems and the producer of the programme, Hallam Tennyson, has told us that when she arrived at the studio she informed him 'Of course you know this is going to be my last appearance and I hope I'm going to be all right.' Her mind was made up, and she had arranged the order of her departure. No fuss, no histrionics. The last words she ever spoke in public came from a poem written by her great friend, Richard Church.

Some are afraid of Death.
They run from him, and cry
Aloud, shrinking with fear
When he draws near.
Others take their last breath
as though it were a sigh
Of sheer content, or bliss
Beneath a lover's kiss.
Perhaps it is not much,

After life's labour,
That summoning touch
Of Death, our neighbour.

The final summons was but two months away. I had continued to
visit her nearly every week during that second blazing summer in
succession and once I had persuaded her to come and take lunch with
us at our home in Virginia Water, but she wasn't at ease away from
Gatehouse. On one of my visits I had been driven by my own nephew
by marriage, Richard Brown. He is totally divorced from the world of
entertainment and I had warned him that Edith was sometimes
guarded in front of strangers. She took to him immediately, and thereafter always insisted that he accompany me, and to Richard went the
distinction of being her last new friend. While I sorted through dusty
files in the summer room he would sit with her and indulge in conversations about gardening and the countryside, which she liked and
which relaxed her. She had always been able to communicate with
young people.

With me her conversations became increasingly preoccupied with
death. John Booth and Mrs. Merton told the same story. Late in
August Nanette and I drove to the Ellen Terry Museum at Smallhythe
before arriving at Gatehouse in time for tea. We found Edith 'looking
like a buttercup' in Nanette's words, for she had obviously made a
special effort and was dressed in one of her favourites, a bright yellow
affair with white organdie sleeves. She immediately complained to us
that she couldn't help sleeping all the time, and blamed this on the pills
she was having to take. We had cucumber sandwiches for tea—it was
like the setting for a typically English play—and said that she hoped
for rain. 'Every day is Sunday now', she said, and obviously the endless
fine weather must have added to that sameness. We tried our best to
divert her, telling her of our visit to Smallhythe and what we had found
there. The Curator of the Museum had told us that Ellen Terry had
'coached' Edith those many years ago and I mentioned this in passing.
Edith seized upon it with a sudden flash of her old spirit. 'She certainly
didn't coach me. I didn't need it.' In the next sentence she had returned
to the topic that now constantly occupied her. Taking Nanette's hand
she related how her father had lived to be 88, the same age as herself,
and that he had dropped dead in the street. 'I don't want that to happen
to me,' she said. 'I shan't go like that, shall I?' We both reassured her,
knowing all too well that she was unlikely ever again to venture far from
Gatehouse.

I saw her three more times after that, the last occasion being a few
days before her death. Physically, she seemed stronger, but her thoughts
were turning inwards more and more. On that final visit, a day in early

274

October when the leaves were just turning, she talked of only one thing. 'I'm going to have the vicar to tea,' she said, 'because he's got to tell me a few things.'

'What sort of things?' I enquired.

'I want to know what to expect, what's on the other side. I want to see Mother and Father and Guy and Judith and all my other friends, but I don't want to meet a lot of unpleasant people.'

'What sort of unpleasant people?'

'People like Queen Elizabeth.'

'Do you think she was unpleasant?' I said, at a loss to know how to direct the conversation.

'I'm quite sure she was, and I don't want to meet her. That's what he's got to tell me. I mean, is there anything there, or is it all nothing?'

'I don't know, darling,' I said. 'I wish I did.'

'Well, he's the vicar and he ought to know, and that's what I'm going to ask him.'

In the event the vicar was spared this Bracknell-like interrogation, for the date was never kept. Two days after my visit, Mrs. Merton rang me to say that Edith had caught a chill and was taking things very gently. There was no immediate cause for alarm in her opinion, but Edith had asked that I be told. I was editing a short commercial film during that week, but promised I would drive down to see her on Friday 15th October.

Arriving at my cutting rooms shortly after lunch on the Thursday, I began work unaware that anything had happened. My editor, Philip Shaw, suddenly turned to me and said, 'You obviously don't know, do you?'

'Know what?'

'Edith has died. They announced it on the one o'clock news bulletin.'

For the rest of that day I went through the motions of attending to those things which, today, the media demand whenever a great public figure dies. Because of my known close friendship nearly every daily newspaper, and many radio and television stations wanted me to speak of Edith. The art of the immediate obituary is not something one perfects in advance, and I found it difficult to say what I felt and do her justice.

Early the following morning Richard and I drove to Gatehouse once more, a house completely without Edith, for the body had already been removed. She had died peacefully in her own bed at 12.20 p.m. on Thursday October 14th, 1976, in her 89th year. Her devoted Mrs. Merton had been with her at the end and told me that her last words were to enquire whether I was coming to lunch.

Tributes were already beginning to pour in, and the official obituaries that morning had been long and generous, *The Times* according her three columns under the heading 'An actress of genius and dedication.' Sir John Gielgud was appearing in Washington, D.C. but wrote, with his usual elegance, a moving tribute for the American papers which ended: '. . . the name of Edith Evans must surely rank with the greatest of her sisters in the history of our theatre—the Abingdons and Brace-girdles, Madge Kendal, Marie Tempest and Ellen Terry.'

The funeral took place on October 20th in the small village church at Kilndown. The electricity failed on the morning of the service and consequently there was no heating and no organ. The family mourners were drawn from Guy's relatives, the small congregation being mostly people from the village of Kilndown. Edith had expressed the wish that the service be short and simple. My eldest daughter, Sarah, and Richard accompanied me and there were a few old friends from her professional life: Olive Harding, her one-time agent, Julie Harris and Michael Laughlan, who had co-produced *The Whisperers*.

When the church service was over we drove to the crematorium just outside Tunbridge Wells, where the same vicar conducted a second short service. As is the custom with cremations the floral tributes were laid in the covered way outside the chapel of remembrance. I noticed that the undertakers had assembled them around a card which read: Edith Mary Booth. I remember thinking, but that isn't who we have said goodbye to; we have just said goodbye to Edith Evans. It seemed that we had taken part in a ceremony for a stranger and the only thing about it that Edith would have enjoyed was the drive through the autumn lanes in the pale, misty sunlight.

When her Will was published it revealed that she had left an Estate totalling £126,000, a figure strangely at variance with her fears of penury. After bequests to John Booth and his family, her faithful William and his wife, Mrs. Merton and other close friends, she divided the bulk of her Estate four ways, donating sums of money to the First Church of Christ Scientist in Sloane Square, London, The National Trust, and King George's Pension Fund for Actors, with the remaining and largest sum going to the Actors' Charitable Trust 'to use the same primarily in connection with Denville Hall.' I was touched to see that she had included the gift of 'the framed fan on the wall of my bedroom at Gatehouse' to George Watts, my focus-puller on the documentary film who had repaired the article for her during the shooting of the film. She named me as her literary trustee and asked that I be given the awards she had received for *The Whisperers*.

She had requested that her ashes be placed in an urn and deposited in St. Paul's Church, Covent Garden, traditionally known as 'the Actors' Church', and it was there on December 9th 1976 that a Thanksgiving Service to her memory was held.

We chose for her a simple service with no pomp or circumstance. Sir Michael Redgrave said farewell to his Rosalind by reading one of her favourite sonnets, *Upon Westminster Bridge*, by Wordsworth. A packed church then sang the hymn *To Be a Pilgrim* and this was followed by Dame Peggy Ashcroft and Gwen Ffrangcon-Davies speaking Shakespeare's *Fidele*—'Fear no more the heat of the sun'. Afterwards the resident organist, Ralph Elston played 'Nimrod' from Elgar's *Enigma Variations* on a piano that had been specially placed in front of the congregation. To me was given the honour of speaking the Address. I tried to give a glimpse of the whole spectrum of her achievement, and to remind those present of her humour and greatness of spirit. I could in no way approach the beauty and dignity of her own public farewell when she had quoted those telling lines of Richard Church's poem, but I recalled an incident within my own family, speaking of how, when it had become obvious to me that Edith had but a little time left, I had felt that I ought to prepare our youngest daughter, Emma. I did not want Edith's death—the first that would touch her young life—to shock her. So I said to her, 'You know, one of these days, dear Dame Edith will have to die. She's very old and very tired, and I expect she'll just go to sleep and never wake up.' Emma pondered this for a few moments, and then she said, 'No, I don't think she'll die. She's not the type.'

Perhaps Emma gave the verdict of us all. Perhaps all that happened was that Edith was given her last cue and walked off stage, into immortality.

Career of Edith Evans

Born London February 8th, 1888—Died Kilndown, Kent October 14th, 1976.

1910 October	Viola in *Twelfth Night* produced by Roderick L. Eagle for Miss E. C. Massey's Streatham Shakespeare Players.
1912 April 20th	Beatrice in *Much Ado About Nothing* directed by Miss E. C. Massey for the Streatham Shakespeare Players.
1912 August	Gautami in Kálidása's *Sakuntala* directed by William Poel at the Cambridge University Examination Hall
1912 December	Cressida in *Troilus and Cressida* directed by William Poel for the Elizabethan Stage Society at King's Hall, Covent Garden.
1913 April 12th	The Duchess of York in *Richard II* directed by Miss E. C. Massey for the Streatham Shakespeare Players.
1913 May 12th	Cressida in *Troilus and Cressida* directed by William Poel at the Shakespeare Memorial Theatre, Stratford-upon-Avon.
June	Martin in *Elizabeth Cooper* by George Moore, Haymarket Theatre.
1913 July	Knowledge in *Everyman*, directed by William Poel at the Crosby Hall, Chelsea.
1914 January	The Queen in *Hamlet*, directed by William Poel at the Little Theatre.
February	Isota in *The Ladies' Comedy* by Maurice Hewlett, Little Theatre.
	Mrs. Taylor in *Acid Drops* by Gertrude Jennings, Royalty Theatre.
April	Moeder Kaatje and Miss Sylvia in *My Lady's Dress* by Edward Knoblock at the Royalty Theatre.
October	Mrs. Rhead in *Milestones* by Arnold Bennett and Edward Knoblock at the Royalty Theatre (revival).
1915	First screen appearance in *A Welsh Singer* directed by Henry Edwards (who also starred in it) made at Walton-on-Thames studios for Cecil M. Hepworth.
1916 February	Lady Frances Ponsonby in *The Conference* by Delphine Gray, Royal Court Theatre (Pioneer Players).
July	Miss Myrtle in *The Man Who Stayed At Home* by Lechmere Worrall and J. E. Harold Terry, Royalty Theatre (revival).
	Film: *East is East*, directed by Henry Edwards for Cecil M. Hepworth.
1917 November	Mistress Ford in scenes from *The Merry Wives of Windsor*, with Ellen Terry, at the London Coliseum.
1918 February	Nerissa in the Trial Scene from *The Merchant of Venice*, with Ellen Terry, at the London Coliseum.
	The Nurse in *The Dead City* by Gabriele d'Annunzio at the Royal Court Theatre for the Stage Society.

May	Toured variety theatres with Ellen Terry, again as Mistress Ford in Basket Scene from *The Merry Wives of Windsor* and Nerissa in the Trial Scene from *The Merchant of Venice*.
July	The Witch of the Alps and Destiny in *Manfred* by Lord Byron at Drury Lane for the Stage Society.
August	Ann Rutherford in *Rutherford and Son* by Githa Sowerby presented in the Y.M.C.A. Le Havre by The Havre Repertory Company, produced by Herbert Lomas for the Lena Ashwell Players.
1919 May	Nona in *The Player Queen* by W. B. Yeats at the King's Hall, Covent Garden for the Stage Society.
June	Sir Randell in *The Return from Parnassus* (as acted in St. John's College, Cambridge, 1598–1602) directed by William Poel at the Apothecaries' Hall.
October	Nerissa in *The Merchant of Venice* at the Royal Court Theatre, produced by J. B. Fagan.
1920 March	The Wife and Salvation Officer in *From Morn to Midnight* by Georg Kaiser, translated by Ashley Dukes at the Lyric Theatre, Hammersmith, for the Stage Society.
May	Captain Dumain in *All's Well that Ends Well* directed by William Poel at the Ethical Church, Bayswater.
June	Moeder Kaatje and Lady Appleby in *My Lady's Dress* by Edward Knoblock at the Royalty Theatre (revival).
August	Mrs. Hunter in *Wedding Bells* by Salisbury Field, at the Playhouse.
November	Aquilina in *Venice Preserv'd* by Thomas Otway, at the Lyric Theatre, Hammersmith, for the Phoenix Society.
1921 January	Madame Girard in *Daniel* by Louis Verneuil, adapted by Sybil Harris, at the St. James's Theatre.
March	Mrs. Van Zile in *Polly With a Past* by George Middleton and Guy Bolton at the St. James's Theatre.
April	Ann Ratcliffe in *The Witch of Edmonton* by Thomas Dekker, John Ford and William Rowley at the Lyric Theatre, Hammersmith, for the Stage Society.
April	Mrs. Chester in *Mother Eve* by C. F. Montagu at the Ambassadors Theatre, for the Playwrights' Theatre.
June	Mrs. Barraclough in *Out to Win* by Roland Pertwee and Dion Clayton Calthrop, at the Shaftesbury Theatre.
October	Lady Utterword in *Heartbreak House* by Bernard Shaw at the Royal Court Theatre (first production).
1922 February	Mrs. Faraker in *The Wheel* by James Bernard Fagan at the Apollo Theatre.
March	Cleopatra in *All for Love* by John Dryden for the Phoenix Society.
September	Kate Harding in *I Serve* by Roland Pertwee at the Kingsway Theatre.
November	Cynthia Dell in *The Laughing Lady* by Alfred Sutro at the Globe Theatre.
December	Ruby in *The Rumour* by C. K. Munro at the Globe Theatre for the Stage Society.
1923 February	Marged in *Taffy* by Caradoc Evans at the Prince of Wales' Theatre (one performance only).
October	The Serpent in *In The Beginning*, Part One of *Back to Methuselah* by Bernard Shaw, at the Birmingham Repertory Theatre.
	The Oracle in *The Tragedy of an Elderly Gentleman*, Part Four of *Back To Methuselah* by Bernard Shaw, at the Birmingham Repertory Theatre.

The She-Ancient and the Ghost of the Serpent in *As Far As Thought Can Reach*, Part Five of *Back to Methuselah* by Bernard Shaw, at the Birmingham Repertory Theatre.

December   Mistress Page in *The Merry Wives of Windsor* at the Lyric Theatre, Hammersmith.

1924 February   Mrs. Millamant in *The Way of the World* by William Congreve, at the Lyric Theatre, Hammersmith.

March   Daisy in *The Adding Machine* by Elmer Rice, at the Strand Theatre, for the Stage Society.

June   Suzanne in *Tiger Cats*, adapted from *Les Félines* of Mme. Karen Bramson by 'Michael Orme', at the Savoy Theatre.

July   Mrs. George Collins in *Getting Married* by Bernard Shaw, at the Everyman Theatre, Hampstead.

September The Serpent She-Ancient and the Ghost of the Serpent (but not the Oracle) in *Back to Methuselah* at the Royal Court Theatre. (Edith did not appear in the first London production (at the Court Theatre) during February 1924, but only in the special matinee revivals of Parts One and Five during September).

December Helena in *A Midsummer Night's Dream*, Basil Dean's production at Drury Lane.

1925 March   Ann in *The Painted Swan* by Elizabeth Bibesco, at the Everyman Theatre, Hampstead.

May   Evadne in *The Maid's Tragedy* by Beaumont and Fletcher at the Scala (Renaissance Theatre).

September
to
1926 May   First season at the Old Vic during Andrew Leigh's regime.

Portia in *The Merchant of Venice*.
Queen Margaret in *Richard III*.
Katharina in *The Taming of The Shrew*.
Mariana in *Measure for Measure*.
Cleopatra in *Antony and Cleopatra*.
The Angel in *The Child in Flanders* by Cecily Hamilton.
Mistress Page in *The Merry Wives of Windsor*.
Kate Hardcastle in *She Stoops to Conquer* by Oliver Goldsmith.
Portia in *Julius Caesar*.
Rosalind in *As You Like It*.
Dame Margery Eyre in *The Shoemaker's Holiday* by Thomas Dekker.
The Nurse in *Romeo and Juliet*.
Beatrice in *Much Ado About Nothing*.

June   Maude Fulton in *Caroline* by W. Somerset Maugham, at the Playhouse Theatre (revival).

September Rebecca West in R. Farquharson Sharp's translation of Ibsen's *Rosmersholm*, at the Kingsway Theatre.

November Katharina in scene from *The Taming of The Shrew* at Drury Lane matinee in aid of the Shakespeare Memorial Theatre, Stratford-upon-Avon.

1927 January   Mrs. Sullen in *The Beaux' Stratagem* by George Farquhar, at the Lyric Theatre, Hammersmith.

September Maitre Bolbec in *The Lady in Law*, by George Berr and Louis Verneuil; English version by Bertha Murrey, at Wyndham's Theatre. (Own management with Leon M. Lion).

November Mrs. Millamant in *The Way of the World* by William Congreve, at

Wyndham's Theatre. (Own management with Leon M. Lion).

1928 March   The Serpent, the She-Ancient and the Ghost of the Serpent, in Bernard Shaw's *Back to Methuselah*, at the Royal Court Theatre.

July   Miriam Rooth in *The Tragic Muse* by Hubert Griffith (adapted from the novel of the same name by Henry James), at the Arts Theatre.

September   Josephine in *Napoleon's Josephine* by Conal O'Riordan, at the Fortune Theatre.

1929 January   Florence Nightingale in *The Lady With a Lamp* by Reginald Berkeley, first at the Arts Theatre and subsequently transferred to the Garrick Theatre.

August   Orinthia in *The Apple Cart* by Bernard Shaw at Sir Barry Jackson's Malvern Festival (first English production).

Lady Utterword in *Heartbreak House* by Bernard Shaw, again at the Malvern Festival. (revival).

September   Orinthia in *The Apple Cart* when it was reproduced at the Queen's Theatre.

December   Constance Harker in Halcott Glover's *Wills and Ways*, at the Arts Theatre.

1930 January   Diana in *The Humours of the Court* by Robert Bridges, at the Art Theatre.

June   Mrs. Sullen in *The Beaux' Stratagem* by George Farquhar, at the Royalty Theatre (revival).

In *Plus ça Change*, one-act thriller by John Hastings Turner (special performance in aid of Oxford Preservation Trust.

September   Delilah in *Delilah* by H. R. Barbor, at the Prince of Wales Theatre (Edith produced, having once again entered into management).

1931 March   Mrs. Carruthers in *O.H.M.S.* by Reginald Berkeley, at the Arts Theatre and subsequently transferred to the New Theatre.

May   Suzanne in a revival of *Tiger Cats* at the Royalty Theatre.

September   Laetitia in *The Old Bachelor* by William Congreve, at the Lyric Theatre, Hammersmith.

November   Florence Nightingale in *The Lady With a Lamp*, by Reginald Berkeley, at the Maxine Elliot Theatre, New York.

1932 February   The Nurse in *Romeo and Juliet*, at the New Theatre, Oxford; John Gielgud's production for the Oxford University Dramatic Society (O.U.D.S.)

March   Returned to the Old Vic and played Emilia in *Othello* and Viola in *Twelfth Night*.

April   Lady Utterword in further revival of *Heartbreak House*, at the Queen's Theatre.

June   Irela in *Evensong*, adapted by Edward Knoblock and Beverley Nichols from the novel by Beverley Nichols, at the Queen's Theatre.

November   Irma Petersen in *Bull-dog Drummond* by 'Sapper', a special performance at the Adelphi Theatre in aid of the King George Pension Fund.

1933 January   Irela in *Evensong*, at the Selwyn Theatre, New York.

April   Took over the role of May Daniels in *Once in a Lifetime* by Moss Hart and George S. Kaufman, at the Queen's Theatre.

May   Gwenny in *The Late Christopher Bean* adapted by Emlyn Williams from *Prenez garde à la peinture* by René Fauchois, at the St. James's Theatre (John van Druten had previously adapted an American version).

1934 May   The Duchess of Marlborough in *Viceroy Sarah* by Norman Ginsbury,

	at the Arts Theatre.
December	The Nurse in *Romeo and Juliet*, at the Martin Beck Theatre, New York. (The Katharine Cornell-Guthrie McClintic production).
1935 April	Agatha Payne in *The Old Ladies*, adapted by Rodney Ackland from the novel by Hugh Walpole, at the New Theatre.
October	The Nurse in *Romeo and Juliet*, at the New Theatre (John Gielgud's production with Gielgud and Olivier alternating the roles of Romeo and Mercutio).
1936 May	Irina Arcadina in *The Seagull* by Tchehov, at the New Theatre.
October to December	Returned once more to the Old Vic and played:
	Lady Fidget in *The Country Wife* by William Wycherley, production by Tyrone Guthrie.
	Rosalind in *As You Like It*, production by Esme Church.
	Mother Sawyer in *The Witch of Edmonton* by Dekker, Ford and Rowley, production by Michel Saint-Denis.
1937 February	Rosalind in *As You Like It*, revived at the New Theatre.
March	Katharina in *The Taming of the Shrew*, at the New Theatre, production by Claude Gurney.
	Sanchia Carson in *Robert's Wife* by St. John Ervine, at the Globe Theatre.
1939 January	Lady Bracknell in *The Importance of Being Earnest* by Oscar Wilde, at the Globe Theatre. (Special matinees during the continuing run of *Robert's Wife*.)
August	Lady Bracknell again, at the Globe Theatre, for a normal run.
1940 March	Muriel Meilhac in *Cousin Muriel* by Clemence Dane, at the Globe Theatre.
August	Provincial tour of *The Millionairess* by Bernard Shaw playing Epifania Fitzfassenden, in a production intended to open at the Globe Theatre, 11th September 1940. Unfortunately the London opening had to be abandoned because, by September, the 'blitz' was at its height.
October	Appeared for the first time in revue: *Diversion* by Herbert Farjeon, in which Edith created the role of the Hop-picker, at Wyndham's Theatre.
1941 January	Second edition of the revue: *Diversion No. 2*. again by Herbert Farjeon, at Wyndham's Theatre.
December	Katharine Markham in *Old Acquaintance* by John van Druten, at the Apollo Theatre.
1942 October	Lady Bracknell once more in a revival at the Phoenix Theatre.
1942 December	Travelled to Gibraltar to appear in revue for H.M. Forces.
1943 March	Hesione Hushabye in *Heartbreak House* by Bernard Shaw, at the Cambridge Theatre.
	During remainder of 1943 and part of 1944 she toured widely, both at home and overseas, entertaining the troops in *Heartbreak House* under the auspices of E.N.S.A.
1944	When she returned from her overseas tour she joined Murray Macdonald at the Garrison Theatre, Salisbury (a major area of troop concentration) where she produced and appeared in a number of plays.
1945	She took a production of *The Late Christopher Bean* to the troops in India, under the E.N.S.A. banner.

	September	Returning home, she appeared as Mrs. Malaprop in *The Rivals* by Richard Brinsley Sheridan, co-directing with William Armstrong, at the Criterion Theatre.
1946	June	Katerina Ivanovna in *Crime and Punishment*, adapted by Rodney Ackland from the novel by Dostoevsky, directed by Anthony Quayle, at the New Theatre.
	December	Cleopatra in *Antony and Cleopatra*, directed by Glen Byam Shaw, at the Piccadilly Theatre.
1948		Film: Countess Ranevskaya in *The Queen of Spades*, Screenplay by Rodney Ackland and Arthur Boys from the story by Pushkin, directed by Thorold Dickinson.
		Film: Merri in *The Last Days of Dolwyn*, screenplay and directed by Emlyn Williams.
	October	Rejoined the Old Vic and appeared as Lady Wishfort in *The Way of The World* by William Congreve, at the New Theatre.
	November	Madame Ranevsky in *The Cherry Orchard* by Tchehov, again at the New Theatre.
1949	March	Lady Pitts in *Daphne Laureola* by James Bridie, at Wyndham's Theatre.
1950	September	Lady Pitts in *Daphne Laureola* at the Music Box, New York.
	November 14th	Spoke the Prologue before *Twelfth Night* at the re-opening of the Old Vic Theatre.
1951	April	Helen Lancaster in *Waters of the Moon* by N. C. Hunter, directed by Frith Banbury, at the Theatre Royal, Haymarket. (This play ran for over two years).
		Film: *The Importance of Being Earnest*, recreating her definitive Lady Bracknell under the direction of Anthony Asquith.
1954	April	Countess Rosmarin Ostenburg in *The Dark is Light Enough* by Christopher Fry, directed by Peter Brook, at the Aldwych Theatre.
1955	May– June	Rehearsed leading role in André Roussin's farce, *Nina*, translated from the French by Arthur Macrae and directed by Rex Harrison. The play opened in Liverpool but Edith was taken ill before the first night and never gave a public performance in the role.
	September 22nd	Television: Lady Bracknell yet again. Scenes from *The Importance* were televised on the opening night of commercial television.
	November 12th	Television: Mrs. Smith in *A Question of Fact* by Wynyard Browne, adapted by Rodney Ackland.
1956	January	Television: Agatha Payne in *The Old Ladies*, adapted by Rodney Ackland, produced and directed by Quentin Lawrence in association with Frith Banbury.
	March 21st	Mrs. St. Maugham in *The Chalk Garden*, by Enid Bagnold, directed by John Gielgud. First performance at the Alexandra Theatre, Birmingham and subsequently opened in London at the Theatre Royal, Haymarket on April 11th.
1958		Old Vic: Katharine of Aragon in Henry VIII, with John Gielgud as Wolsey.
	July	(This same production of Henry VIII had a special limited seasons in Paris, Antwerp and Brussels).
1959		Royal Shakespeare Company, Stratford-upon-Avon. Countess Rousillon in *All's Well That Ends Well*, directed by Tyrone Guthrie. Volumnia in *Coriolanus*, directed by Peter Hall.

	Film: Ma Tanner in *Look Back in Anger*, directed by Tony Richardson
	Film: The Mother Superior in *The Nun's Story*, directed by Fred Zinnermann.
1960	Went to Canada to give a poetry reading at the Crest Theatre, Toronto.
	Television: Lady Bracknell once more in the CBS production of *The Importance*.
	Television: Lady Fidget in BBC production of *The Country Wife*.
	Television: Judith in *Hay Fever* by Noël Coward for ITV.
1961	Royal Shakespeare Company, Stratford-upon-Avon. Played Margaret, the widowed Queen of Henry VI in *Richard III*, directed by William Gaskill. Last appearance as the Nurse in *Romeo and Juliet*, directed by Peter Hall.
	Television: *Time Remembered* for American television and subsequently for the BBC.
1962	Film: *Tom Jones*, screenplay by John Osborne, and directed by Tony Richardson.
December	Recital with Christopher Hassall, Marlowe Theatre, Canterbury.
1963 November	Violet in *Gentle Jack* by Robert Bolt, at the Queen's Theatre.
	Film: recreated her original stage role of Mrs. St. Maugham in *The Chalk Garden* in the Ross Hunter production, directed by Ronald Neame.
1964 October	National Theatre: Judith Bliss in *Hay Fever*, by Noël Coward, directed by the author.
1965 May	Mrs. Forest in *The Chinese Prime Minister* by Enid Bagnold.
	Film: *Young Cassidy*.
1966	Film: Mrs. Ross in *The Whisperers*, adapted from the novel by Robert Nicolson by Bryan Forbes. Produced by Michael S. Laughlin and Ronald Sedlo and directed by Bryan Forbes. (For her performance as Mrs. Ross, Edith received the Golden Bear for the Best Actress at the Berlin Film Festival, the British Academy Award, The New York Film Critics Award and was nominated for an Oscar.)
1967	Film: *Garden of Cucumbers (Fitzwilly)* .
	Film: *Prudence and the Pill*.
1968 February	Female Narrator in *The Adventures of The Black Girl in Search of God*, Mermaid Theatre.
	Film: *The Madwoman of Chaillot*, directed by Bryan Forbes.
1969	Appeared in *Reading for Pleasure*, a programme of poetry and extracts from some of her noted classical roles, Edinburgh.
	Film: *Crooks and Coronets*.
	Film for Television: *David Copperfield*, playing Miss Betsy.
1970	Film: *Scrooge*, a musical based on *A Christmas Carol* by Dickens, with screenplay and score by Leslie Bricusse, directed by Ronald Neame, in which Edith played the Spirit of Christmas Past.
	Appeared in *Red Peppers* by Noël Coward, during a BBC television tribute to celebrate Coward's 70th birthday. The cast included Bruce Forsyth, Dora Bryan, Anthony Quayle and Cyril Cusack.
1971 May	Carlotta in *Dear Antoine* by Jean Anouilh, at the Chichester Festival.
1973	Television: appeared in a documentary of her life and career for Yorkshire Television entitled *I Caught acting like the Measles*, produced and directed by Bryan Forbes, with executive producer Tony Essex.
	Television: frequent appearances on the Michael Parkinson and Russell Harty talk shows.
	Film: *The Doll's House*, directed by Patrick Garland.

October 8th	Stage: *Edith Evans . . . and friends*, an entertainment devised by Roger Clifford with Anthony Lindsey and Simon Young at two pianos, Theatre Royal Brighton, and subsequently at the Richmond theatre (November 1973).
1974 April 15–27th	*Edith Evans . . . and friends*, revived at the Theatre Royal, Haymarket and subsequently (July 22–27) at the Oxford Playhouse, and then again at the Phoenix Theatre, Charing Cross Road from September 19th to October 5th. This was her last appearance on any West End stage.
1975	Film: *The Slipper and The Rose*, a musical version of the Cinderella legend in which she played the Dowager Queen. Music by Richard M. Sherman and Robert B. Sherman, produced by Stuart Lyons, co-authored and directed by Bryan Forbes.
1976	Film: brief appearance in *Nasty Habits*.
August 15th	Radio: Final Broadcast on BBC, giving a selection from her favourite poems.

286

Index